The Bolsheviks and the Russian Empire

This comparative historical sociology of the Bolshevik revolutionaries offers a reinterpretation of political radicalization in the last years of the Russian Empire. Finding that two-thirds of the Bolshevik leadership were ethnic minorities – Ukrainians, Latvians, Georgians, Jews, and others – this book examines the shared experiences of assimilation and socioethnic exclusion that underlay their class universalism. It suggests that imperial policies toward the Empire's diversity radicalized class and ethnicity as intersectional experiences, creating an assimilated but excluded elite: lower-class Russians and middle-class minorities universalized particular exclusions as they disproportionately sustained the economic and political burdens of maintaining the multiethnic Russian Empire. Political exclusions and quasi-assimilated social worlds enabled reinventions, as the Bolsheviks' social identities and routes to revolutionary radicalism show especially how a class-universalist politics was appealing to those seeking secularism in response to religious tensions, a universalist politics in which ethnic and geopolitical insecurities were exclusionary, and a tolerant "imperial" imaginary where Russification and illiberal repressions were most keenly felt.

Liliana Riga is a Lecturer at the University of Edinburgh. She holds a BA in political science from the University of California, Berkeley, an MA in political science from Columbia University, and a PhD in sociology from McGill University. She is an Honorary Fellow at the University of Glasgow, Scotland, and has taught sociology at McGill University, the University of Strathclyde, and the University of Edinburgh. Her work has appeared in, among other publications, the *American Journal of Sociology, Sociology, Nations and Nationalism*, and *Comparative Studies in Society and History*. An article drawn from material in this book appeared in the *American Journal of Sociology* and was awarded Honorable Mention in 2009 for Best Article in Comparative Historical Sociology by the American Sociological Association.

The Bolsheviks and the Russian Empire

LILIANA RIGA
University of Edinburgh

CAMBRIDGE
UNIVERSITY PRESS

CAMBRIDGE UNIVERSITY PRESS
Cambridge, New York, Melbourne, Madrid, Cape Town,
Singapore, São Paulo, Delhi, Mexico City

Cambridge University Press
32 Avenue of the Americas, New York, NY 10013-2473, USA

www.cambridge.org
Information on this title: www.cambridge.org/9781107014220

First published 2012

Printed in the United States of America

A catalog record for this publication is available from the British Library.

Library of Congress Cataloging in Publication data
Riga, Liliana, 1962–
   The Bolsheviks and the Russian Empire / Liliana Riga.
      pages   cm
   Includes bibliographical references and index.
   ISBN 978-1-107-01422-0
   1. Soviet Union – Politics and government – 1917–1936.   2. Communism – Soviet
Union – History.   3. Revolutionaries – Soviet Union – History.   4. Radicals – Soviet
Union – History.   5. Minorities – Political activity – Soviet Union – History.
6. Ethnicity – Political aspects – Soviet Union – History.   7. Assimilation
(Sociology) – Political aspects – Soviet Union – History.   8. Marginality,
Social – Political aspects – Soviet Union – History.   9. Social classes – Soviet
Union – History.   10. Soviet Union – Social conditions – 1917–1945.   I. Title.
DK266.5.R54   2012
324.247′0750922–dc23   2012017767

ISBN 978-1-107-01422-0 Hardback

*To my mother Carla, my father Giorgio, and my sister Roberta
and to Piccola, Devs, and Emma for love throughout*

Contents

List of Tables   *page* viii

Preface   ix

Note on Transliterations and Names   xiii

PART I. IDENTITY AND EMPIRE   1

1. Reconceptualizing Bolshevism   3

2. Social Identities and Imperial Rule   24

PART II. IMPERIAL STRATEGIES AND ROUTES TO RADICALISM
    IN CONTEXTS   55

3. The Jewish Bolsheviks   58

4. The Polish and Lithuanian Bolsheviks   90

5. The Ukrainian Bolsheviks   123

6. The Latvian Bolsheviks   155

7. The South Caucasian Bolsheviks   186

8. The Russian Bolsheviks   227

    Conclusion   265

Appendix A   277

Appendix B   280

Bibliography   283

Index of Names   303

Subject Index   307

Tables

1.1. Ethnic Composition of the Bolshevik Leadership and
the Russian Empire   *page* 16

2.1. Imperial Strategies of Exclusion and Integration, 1861–1914   41

2.2. Socioethnic Composition of the Main Political Parties Near
the End of the Russian Empire   50

A1. Social Origins (Father's Class or Estate) of the Bolsheviks, by
Nationality/Ethnicity   278

A2. Occupation (Class or Estate) of the Bolsheviks, by Nationality/
Ethnicity   279

Preface

This book is the work not of a historian, but of a comparative historical and political sociologist. So I note at the outset that there is no claim to have exhausted – or even extensively mined – the primary archival data on ninety-three Bolsheviks, or, to be sure, on the Russian Empire as a whole. Rather, this book is intended as a comparative historical sociology of a revolutionary elite, a collective biography of the emergence of "charisma" in the form of an excluded, but empire-oriented and multiethnic, intelligentsia. So I have made use of primary biographical sources as well as numerous political and historical studies of the Russian Empire and its many diverse constituent parts. I have drawn on these latter works quite shamelessly, in fact. But I have read both primary and secondary sources simply with a view to trying to understand lives and experiences, so my hope is that although there may be disagreement with an interpretation here or there, and although there may be errors or omissions here *and* there, in its totality I might have done justice to the cause of interpretive comparative historical sociology by getting right the essence of Bolshevism.

Guided by a broadly Weberian search for "elective affinities," much of my thinking in this book has been inspired by Barrington Moore's *Social Origins of Dictatorship and Democracy: Lord and Peasant in the Making of the Modern World* (1967) and Ernest Gellner's *Language and Solitude: Wittgenstein, Malinowski and the Habsburg Dilemma* (1998). Although there is little substantive or direct engagement with these two very different works, they suggested ways of organizing the material, and, taken together, they offered a way to combine very particular social worlds with a more general comparative social explanation – mindful that although there are no straight causal lines, it is still worth trying to discern those political alignments and social patterns that do seem sociologically powerful. More specifically, they prompted me to think about how to interpret individual internal landscapes against those external landscapes that can shape the contours of social thought as much as they can the possibilities of its political expression; that is, I thought to combine an account of the larger forces that impact individual radicalizations with a deeper and richer elaboration of the diverse ways in which smaller and more intimate contexts might themselves seek to valorize those larger forces – especially in lives experienced along boundaries of assimilation and exclusion. I also came to appreciate that, in addition to the class dislocations inherent in the "making of the modern world," living in complex diversity could also produce relevant social experiences; so I took the idea that as important as its class analyses no doubt were, socialism's *political* implications might also be crucial to defining both internal and external landscapes.

In short, my aim has been to offer a substantive social explanation, and to extend a tradition of comparative historical sociology of revolutions by contextualizing – and indeed by re-embedding – revolutionary Bolshevism into the imperial context from which it emerged. Accordingly, I prefigure a methodological point made in Chapter 1: the biographical reconstructions that comprise this book are interpretive accounts, pieced together from autobiographies, biographies (official and non-official), census data, Tsarist police records, studies of specific political mobilizations, area studies, studies of nationality policies or specific ethnic groups, urban and rural studies of specific locations, studies of working classes, and the like. I have attempted as carefully and as plausibly as possible to reconstruct the intricate variety of social worlds that produced the Bolshevik revolutionary elite. My aim has been to ensure that the macro explanations offered are also sociologically true, in their most intimate and relevant implications, at the individual level. So while contextual biographical details obviously differed across the many individuals, to the extent that there was a universally shared dimension of experience in the particulars, that is where I began, and I built outward from there.

In doing so, it seemed to me that a particular sociology of political marginality – one often inflected by the failed promises of assimilation – constituted a very potent and defining social experience with considerable political implications. As individuals negotiated social worlds characterized by quasi-integration, ambiguous social statuses and dislocations, socioethnic marginalities, and political exclusions, they also marked out new boundaries around both cultural and class assimilations. And this, it seemed to me, produced its own quite distinctive kind of alienation and political aspiration. Or, to put it another way, the dislocations, exclusions, and rootlessness that paid the costs of empire also enabled considerable reinvention, assisted by underlying social and political crises that helped define the qualities of a generation.

More practically, some biographical reconstructions involve greater detail than others – partly because of the unevenness of the sources and partly because of the dictates of the data set itself: there were too many Russians, for instance, to treat each in detail even if the sources had allowed it; and some of the ninety-three Bolsheviks are treated briefly, or not discussed at all, if sources were too limited. So the chapters that comprise Part II are purposely uneven: Chapter 4 considers three Bolsheviks in some detail to provide a more textured and nuanced sense of distinct, but overlapping, individual worlds; Chapter 8, on the other hand, offers only brief, illustrative summaries of individuals to allow the presentation of a more general finding. The remaining chapters are arrayed somewhere in between. Taken in their totality, however, my hope is that a sense of collective biography emerges through the accumulation of these variations in the presentation of the data.

Nevertheless, it may be that if for some readers there is too much biographical detail, for others there may not be enough. For the former reader, it is possible to simply ignore the "local detail" of the various biographical reconstructions and to extract the central claims of each chapter from its introduction and conclusion, and from the setup pages to Part II, mindful of their place in the wider claims of the book. The concerns of the latter reader are more difficult to satisfy, other than simply referring to the more extensive primary and secondary sources.

And finally, a comment on the *matryoshka* organization of the chapters in Part II and their relation to the wider argument: although this is a single case study – that is, a study of a single elite – there are six comparative ethnicity/ nationality case studies within it, and within them still further nested comparisons. But the six chapters are each differently organized. For instance, Chapter 3 on the Jewish Bolsheviks is organized "ethnically," to examine comparatively Lithuanian Jewry, Ukrainian Jewry, and Russian Jewry; Chapter 9 contrasts three nationalities – Georgians, Azerbaijani Turks, and Armenians – but it does so against a view of the South Caucasus as a single imperial borderland; and whereas Chapters 6 (the Latvians) and 8 (the ethnic Russians) divide the Bolsheviks by their respective class compositions, Chapter 5 explores the diversity within Ukrainian Bolshevism geographically or regionally. In other words, different elective affinities within Bolshevism's constituent groups dictated the chapters' internal organizations – mirroring the general argument. Table 2.1 (Chapter 2) seeks to capture these analytical pieces, tying the politics of the empire's intricate socioethnic mosaic to the socioethnic composition of both leftist and rightist politics in revolutionary Russia; and the four strategies of empire, also outlined in Chapter 2, provide the frame on which the subsequent empirical material hangs. The chapters in Part I, then, present the broad context and the main contours of the argument, whereas those in Part II deconstruct it in case studies.

Several acknowledgments are due. Most immediately, I owe an enormous debt to John A. Hall. His early intellectual guidance, incredible knowledge, and consistent encouragement have meant everything. As importantly, John's own scholarly work – elegant and important sociology, articulated with clarity and substance – has been a North Star, an intellectual vision that has influenced me immensely.

I am also extremely grateful to Michael Mann for carefully and generously reading the manuscript. His critical comments greatly helped sharpen and clarify the argument, while the methodological influence of his *Sources of Social Power* will be evident throughout. Jack Goldstone and Dingxin Zhao read an earlier version of the general argument and offered incisive and very useful suggestions for improving it, and I am very appreciative. For early comments or suggestions on pieces of the manuscript, I thank Dominic Lieven and John Klier. I thank Terry Cox for the very kind support of an Honorary Fellowship at the University of Glasgow's Centre for Russian, Central and East European Studies, and Norman Naimark for allowing me to conduct research at a key moment with a Visiting Scholarship at Stanford University's Center for Russian, East European, and Eurasian Studies. The University of Edinburgh has provided a wonderful academic home for the past several years, in large part attributable to the sustained support of Donald MacKenzie, for which I am very appreciative. I am grateful to Svetlana Klimova for mixing critical conversation with warm friendship. But I am especially grateful to James Kennedy, a fellow political sociologist, for innumerable helpful discussions on almost every part of this project, each one making it better.

At Cambridge University Press in New York, I am indebted to Lewis Bateman, Anne Lovering Rounds, and Shaun T. Vigil for their expert guidance in bringing this book to press, and to Cambridge's anonymous reviewers for very useful criticisms and suggestions. Parts of some chapters are drawn from the following articles: "The Ethnic Roots of Class Universalism: Rethinking the 'Russian' Revolution," *American Journal of Sociology* (2008/9): 114 (3): 649–705; "Reconciling Nation and Class in Imperial Borderlands: The Making of Bolshevik Internationalists Karl Radek and Feliks Dzierżyński in East Central Europe," *Journal of Historical Sociology* (2006): 19(4): 447–472; and "Ethnonationalism, Assimilation, and the Social Worlds of the Jewish Bolsheviks in fin de siècle Tsarist Russia," *Comparative Studies in Society and History* (2006): 48(4): 762–797.

This book is dedicated my parents, Carla and Giorgio, and to my sister Roberta. I also owe so very much to Catterina Paschetta Larese. And for love and friendship, I thank Valerie Collette, Scott Rezendes, Francesca Benevento, Sheila and Graham Kennedy, Janice Lindsay, and Kirsty, David, Emma, and Rachel Wylie. My deepest debt is to James Kennedy, however, for love, patience, intellectual advice, belief, and bloody-minded constancy – and especially for knowing when, and in what doses, each has been needed most.

Note on Transliterations and Names

I have generally followed the Library of Congress system for transliteration, except where sources themselves differ substantially, or where the most common usage is otherwise. For the Bolsheviks' names, I adopt the form that is most commonly used in the general secondary literature: so I use Trotsky, not Trotskii. For some, the Russified form (Dzerzhinskii) is now less commonly used than their "ethnic" form (Dzierżyński), so in those cases I use the latter. But at the place where the Bolshevik is first introduced, and if I adopt a more common usage, I note both Jan Danishevskii (Julijs Daniševskis).

For cities and provinces in the Russian Empire, I generally follow the typical or most common usage in the primary sources or, if more common, in the secondary literature. So I refer to Tiflis, not Tiblisi, and Vilna, not Vilnius or Wilno.

PART I

IDENTITY AND EMPIRE

I

Reconceptualizing Bolshevism

Feliks Dzierżyński, the Bolshevik revolutionary father of the Soviet Cheka (forerunner to the KGB), once wrote to his sister about the fact that one-quarter of his life had been spent in Tsarist prisons, forced exile, or hard labor: "I can assure you that I am happier than those who live an aimless life in freedom… and if I were faced with the choice: prison or a life of liberty without purpose I would chose the former, otherwise life would simply not be worth living" (Dzerzhinskii 2002: 129). This is what we would perhaps normally associate with political radicalism, and especially with revolutionary Bolshevism: committed, disciplined, ideologically monochromatic individuals. And indeed this book was originally conceived as an exploration of the emergence of Bolshevism as such a Weberian, heroic-charismatic elite, one that responded to a moment of acute social and political crisis with a revolutionary vision of a new social order.

No doubt elements of this Weberian conceptualization have still left their mark in the chapters that follow. But careful and systematic reconstruction of the Bolsheviks' biographies suggested that an entirely different dimension of their radicalizations and political mobilization needed elaboration: Dzierżyńsi also remarked that he would not have been able to introduce a certain "Bernstein" to his most committed Christian workers because even the best of them had not yet "mastered their anti-Semitism," so "to succeed in … mass agitation, we have to avoid certain questions" (quoted in Tobias 1972: 102–3). Of course the irony was that Dzierżyński – soon to become one of the most famous leaders of the Russian Revolution – was ethnically Polish, something of sufficient influence on his politics that Lenin bemoaned that he and the Georgian Grigorii Ordzhonikidze had become "too Russian" in compensation for their non-Russianness (Service 2000: 468). Georgianness, however, was not a problem for Stalin in the early years – he proudly published polemics and poetry in his native tongue. And yet, the Jewish Trotsky had to famously defend himself as "an internationalist and not a Jew," the russified (Ukrainian) Mykola Skrypnyk could vigorously promote a Ukrainianized Bolshevism, and the Old Believer Alexandr Shliapnikov openly identified as a sectarian. In other

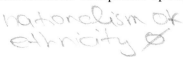

words, the subtle calibration of ethnic origins in revolutionary socialism was not idiosyncratic. It was striking because of its ubiquity.

These ethnic dynamics within the socialist class-revolutionary movement went beyond questions of organizational tactics or strategy; they were constitutively built into the core of the movement through the identities and experiences of its social carriers. Put differently, the ideological framing of this revolutionary struggle did not fully reflect the powerful underlying social dynamics that gave it rise, shape, and momentum. So while there are traces of how a charismatic-heroic movement organized itself, this book centrally offers an account of how a revolutionary class-universalist ideology was materially organized around – and indeed was itself constituted by – socioethnic particularism.

More concretely, most of the scholarly work on the Russian Revolution has assumed that its leadership drew from the Russian intelligentsia and that its socialist ideology was a response to the class conflicts and exclusions generated by an autocratic, industrializing Russian state. Substantively, this book challenges both the Russianness and the class basis of Bolshevism's political mobilization. It takes as its point of departure the empirical finding that the Bolsheviks were largely ethnic minorities. Ethnic Russians were a significant minority, but Jews, Latvians, Ukrainians, Georgians, Armenians, Poles, and others comprised nearly two-thirds of the revolutionary elite. And, in a highly distinctive social composition, ethnicity was strongly aligned with class, suggesting that class and ethnicity were intersectional experiences of varying significance in the political radicalism of the Bolshevik revolutionaries.

The central analytical claim is that Bolshevism may represent an interesting case in the construction of a universalist, class ideological movement based on socioethnic identities, networks, and experiences. Whether socialist or liberal, universalist ideologies are usually not products of "citizens of the world," but of very specific material and social conditions (Calhoun 2003). Yet if the social and political conditions that give rise to, and sustain, universalist ideas are kept analytically distinct from the ideological content of the universalist projects themselves, then a universalist ideology about classes and class conflict may not necessarily be a response to class conflict alone. Indeed the evidence shows that Bolshevism's Russian-inflected class universalism was especially appealing in those social locations across the Russian Empire most affected by socioethnic or imperial exclusions. It particularly appealed to those seeking secularism in response to religious tensions, a universalist politics where ethnic violence and sectarianism were exclusionary, and an ethnically neutral and tolerant imperial imaginary where geopolitics or Russification were especially dangerous, or where imperial cultural frameworks predominated in the case of the ethnic Russians. But because Bolshevism emerged out of particular imperial networks and experiences of socioethnic exclusion, it necessarily embedded ethnicity into its socialist class universalism. The political mobilization was framed around class, and socialist class conflict was its master narrative, but the most important segment of the movement's social carriers were radicalized

largely around socioethnic experiences and exclusions, giving its revolutionary
class ideology a significant ethnic inflection.

Of course it has long been acknowledged that the early Soviet elite comprised a significant number of non-Russians. Yet most scholars focused on
their class origins and paid little attention to how ethnic backgrounds might
have interacted with class and influenced Bolshevism. Early accounts of the
Bolsheviks viewed them as part of the Russian intelligentsia; rootless, alienated intellectuals drawn to radical ideologies and to the eschatological aspects
of Russian revolutionary socialism, their moral and messianic politics were
seen as responses to an exclusionary state or to disengagement from a weak
civil society; they were ideologically motivated political actors who seized
power in a moment of social unrest and political collapse by leading disaffected social groups (Pipes 1964; Seton-Watson 1967; Schapiro 1968; Raeff
1984). In response to these political accounts, and prompted in part by E.P.
Thompson's (1963) classic work, attention shifted away from elites and intellectuals to popular social movements (Haimson 1964, 1965; Koenker 1981;
Bonnell 1983; Mandel 1983; Smith 1983; Suny 1983, 1994). The pivotal role
of the Bolsheviks was to lead revolutionary action, create and articulate the
political discourse, and generally provide ideological orientation and focus
for more general social unrest. Others specifically conceived of the Bolsheviks
as modernizers, or functional revolutionary elites, who emerged for develop-
mental purposes in a "backward" state to organize the process of catching up
(Moore 1966; Janos 1991; Jowitt 1992).

Despite these accounts' considerable differences, however, class remained
the dominant framing narrative for understanding both elite and popular revolutionary politics – a framing borrowed from the revolutionaries' own discourse – and "Russian" remained the implicit or explicit contextual reality.
Skocpol's (1979) account of the effects of geopolitical fiscal crises on state
finances and agrarian reform, for instance, neglected the Russian state's considerable imperial anxieties over the loyalty of its non-Russian minority populations on its borders. Although consistently referring to the Russian state as
"Imperial Russia," Skocpol omitted the consequences of its imperial qualities
from the analyses that were then joined. Similarly, McDaniel's (1988) account
of Russia's autocratic-capitalist development neglected the fact that much of
the regime's anticapitalism derived from its anti-Semitism and Jews' historical association with the commercial professions and with peasant "capitalist
exploitation" (Witte 1921; Löwe 1993: 111–22, 139). And no distinction was
made to account for the fact that there were several national intelligentsias and
working classes in play.

Tsarist Russia, then, was not only a modernizing autocratic state, but also a
nationalizing, multiethnic empire whose key geopolitical threat was conceived
by elites as laying in internal sedition, irredentism or separatism, and ethnic
disloyalty, and whose autocratic capitalist development was actually highly
ethnically differentiated across the empire. Bolshevism not only emerged out
of both of these tensions, but it instantiated both into its contentious politics.

There was, in short, an exceedingly thin distinction between foreign and nationality policies in the minds of imperial elites and administrators (Starr 1978; von Hagen 1998; Lieven 1999; Weeks 2001; Lohr 2003: ch. 4; Rieber 2004; Baron and Gatrell 2004). And the Russian state's most socially consequential domestic policies resulted precisely from the entwining of geopolitics and multiethnicity, and from the securitization of ethnicity (Seton-Watson 1967; Kappeler 1982; Lieven 2000; on the concept of securitization of ethnicity, Kymlicka 2004). The key objective was to maintain the territorial empire, something that would be replicated in the platforms of all the major political mobilizations in revolutionary Russia, on both the left and the right, albeit under different rationales.

Indeed in 1917, Tsarist Russia was only 44 percent ethnically Russian, with more than 130 recognized nationalities (Bauer et al. 1991; Kappeler 1992).[1] This was not yet a modern class society, but an intricate, multiethnic empire: socioeconomic class positions were cross-cut by traditional status categories of estate, confession, occupation, region, culture, ethnicity, and emergent nationalities. In fact, the field has recently seen excellent empirical research on the Russian Empire's nationalities and on the sociological workings of the imperial realm, adding the very imperial qualities that were omitted from previous work (for general discussions see inter alia Lieven 2000; Suny and Martin 2001; Lohr 2003; Brown 2004; Miller and Rieber 2004; Miller 2004b; Gerasimov, Glebov, Kaplunovski, Mogilner, and Semyonov 2005; Petrovsky-Shtern 2009b). More specifically, we know that nonclass identities predominated both official categorization and self-ascription as state practices in the documentation of identities shifted from organizing diversity around estate and religion to ethnicity, nationality, and even race across various regions of the empire (see inter alia Reshetar 1952; Freeze 1986; Haimson 1988; Wirtschafter 1992, 1994; Fitzpatrick 1993; Slocum 1998; Pomeranz 1999; Holquist 2001; Steinwedel 2001; Steinberg 2002; Werth 2002; Crews 2003; Sanborn 2003; Cadoit 2005, 2007). Increasingly, the emphasis has been on identities and analyses of culture and power (Suny 2000: 487; Wortman 2000); on Russian nationalism and on the role of religions (Orthodoxy, Judaism, Islam); on the complex hybridity of the imperial borderlands in the Tsarist period and beyond (Martin 1998; Brown 2004; Hirsch 2005; Badcock 2007); and on the ways in which Russianness was constantly rearticulated in connection with colonization, encounters with the non-Russian indigenous – and often Muslim – populations, and in Russian settlements in frontier areas (Brower and Lazzarini 1997; Geraci 2001a, 2001b; Jersild 2002; Khodarkovsky 2002; Sunderland 2004; Mamedov 2008). These new bodies of research should be folded into any account of Bolshevism's revolutionary mobilization – if only to properly reconstruct and contextualize the

[1] I use Bauer, Kappeler, and Roth (1991) throughout for statistics assembled from the 1897 All-Russian Imperial Census. For the data in the original, see *Pervaia vseobshchaia perepis' naseleniia Rossiiskoi imperii 1897g.* (St. Petersburg: Tsentral'nyi statisticheskii komitet, 1897–1905).

social worlds, experiences, identities, and routes to racialization of its social carriers.

We should not, therefore, accept uncritically the class narrative or political framing of Bolshevism's revolutionary mobilization. Given the Bolsheviks' socioethnic composition, it may not have been solely class conflict to which they were responding, but also to regional-nationalist, ethnic conflicts, interests, and ideas. A good part of socialism's appeal lay in its secularist and universalist theory of an implied *Rossiiskii* or imperial state, in its ecumenicalism, and in its seeming indifference to ethnicity – its antinationalist value. Socialism may have been an antidote to the disintegrating effects of a multinational empire as much as, or indeed more than, to the alienating effects of an industrializing state.

Methodological Approach, the Data, and the Sources

Goldstone (2001) noted that comparative historical sociology's fourth generation of revolutionary theory entwines work on social movements with that on revolutions. It explores identities, leaderships, ideologies, and social networks, and in particular draws attention to neighborhoods, communities, occupations, and schools as important sites of identity formation and radical mobilization (Gould 1995; Zhao 1998, 2001). In the Russian case, revolutionary elites' class origins are usually examined (Haimson 1955; Koenker 1981; Bonnell 1983; Mandel 1983), but little attention is paid to the influence of ethnocultural networks, ethnic neighborhoods and communities, and to the intersection of ethnicity and places of employment (key exceptions are Brym 1978; Frankel 1981; Suny 1993a: 11–18; Rieber 2001).

But examining this dimension of their radicalism entails an analytical reorientation. It moves us away from conceptualizing radical politics in revolutionary Russia as either working-class formations or as the alienation of privileged elites and intellectuals, and toward an analysis of key social (ethnic) groups in civil society, and the positions of professionals and middling-class groups in particular (e.g., Zhao 1998, 2001; Goldstone 2001; Mann 2004; Clemens 2007: 24.11). If marginalized groups, in articulating alternative social orders, can be critical to the spread of transformative ideologies (Skocpol 1979; Goldstone 1991: 425), then a set of otherwise diverse social groups can share a common dimension of experience or social location that funnels them into revolutionary politics. In method, then, I follow Michael Mann's general sociology. Groups defined by common experience can carry with them shared practices and orientations that facilitate coordinated action in a social movement, so in Mann's account shared experiences and occupational identities created the path to fascism (see also discussion in Clemens 2007). Mann (1993: ch. 6, 2004, 2005) emphasizes how particular social locations (e.g., refugee status or state employments) entailed distinct but limited opportunities for action that, in turn, both accommodated a variety of motives (e.g., opportunism, anti-Semitism) and sustained group interactions to generate the early commitment of individuals to fascism. By examining the social locations of the mobilization or group emergence, we can see how Bolshevisms' political narrative was framed around class, but actually organized largely around socioethnic networks of schooling and employment, or communal solidarities. Class and ethnicity were contested and intertwined identities as they meshed both grievances and loyalties in intricate ways, and these were in turn reflected in Bolshevism's composition and in the Bolsheviks' political mobilization.

I therefore explore the specific social locations of the Bolsheviks' radical mobilization in the imperial matrix and trace their individual routes to radicalism. In places where social inequalities had ethnic markers, revolutionary challenge was more potent because it could manipulate conflicting loyalties and mobilize more than one dimension of identity and more than one set of grievances. I highlight, for instance, the empire's borderlands, multiethnic urbanism, and quasi- or problematic assimilationism as such shared dimensions of experience, drawing attention to the distinctive associational lives of the empire's ethnic minorities, as well as to social groups other than the economic bourgeoisies: culture, identity, education, and urbanization were as important to their forms of social organization as were capital, income, or class (Bradley 2002; Steinberg 2002; Meir 2006). Class was increasingly becoming a viable identity alternative to *sosloviia* (or estates, similar to *états* or *Stände*). But while *sosloviia* by themselves could not provide an index of patterns of shared experiences or collective behavior, especially among the urban classes, when combined with education, occupation, ethnicity, religion, and social location, they can begin to define the social worlds of key socioethnic groups (Haimson 1988: 2).

And yet transformative socialist ideologies also require a sense of "totality and alternative" (Mann 1993). When the politics of class is confined to workplaces and does not involve ethnic spaces, totalizing ideologies are undermined (Katznelson 1981). Yet ethnic ties can provide the necessary shared experiences and social trust to form the basis of certain workplaces radicalisms. Gould's (1995: 27–9, 154, 181, 197–201) work on revolutionary France showed that in 1871 in Paris, insurgents' identities were rooted in neighborhoods, networks, and urban communities that also served as mobilizing structures for the emergence of a unified class-conscious movement. Ethnic networks can factionalize political movements, they can sectionalize class movements, or they can appropriate their own ideology (nationalism). In late Imperial Russia, both class (economy) and status (politics) were autocratically organized around ethnicity, so imagined class communities were most often built around ethnic, religious, or cultural solidarities. Bolshevism drew from ethnic communities, socioethnic professional networks, and networks of sectional and local-regional identities, mobilizing them into a political movement based on class. This, and the fact that social inequalities were combined with ethnic or cultural markers, made totalizing challenges to the larger social order easier: political repression first incorporated, and then suppressed, ethnic divisions, and so it helped shape the emergence of a class-universalist ideology constituted by ethnic and imperial marginality.

The Data Set

The choice of a data set – or the choice of the Bolshevik leadership – itself implies certain judgments. Focusing on Lenin and the small pre-1917 Bolshevik Party renders the data set exceedingly small and limits its theoretical scope to the ideological influence and social significance of a handful of revolutionaries (e.g., Haimson 1955; Lane 1975). Recent work using the 1917 Central Committee and Military Revolutionary Council similarly limits theorization only to those elites that seized power at a particular moment in 1917.[2] And yet a data set comprising the leadership from 1917 (or earlier) through the 1930s, with the close of the longer revolutionary period, would count more than 700 individuals and require theorization of revolutionary Bolshevism as well as "high Stalinism." It would also virtually preclude a meaningful collective biography, much less detailed biographical reconstruction.

Therefore this study follows Mawdsley (1995) and uses the ninety-three members (full or candidate) of the RSDRP(b)/RKP[3] Central Committees (CC) in the key revolutionary years from 1917 to 1923, inclusively. These CCs included members of the Politburo, the Orgburo, and the Secretariat, or the key organs of power in the new Soviet state. The CC membership of 1917–23 provides a useful historical, analytical, and practical demarcation. Analytically, these elites were the social carriers of Bolshevik ideology in its insurgent, revolutionary, or transformative phase: this leadership took power in a key moment of (geo)political collapse, dismantled the existing order, and designed a new social order with Lenin largely in control of the revolutionary effort. It was this early elite that provided the ideological and institutional frameworks that mapped the transition from an empire problematized by ethnicity to a "nation-state" problematized by class.

This data set also offers a useful historical demarcation. Whereas there was little biographical variation within the 1917–23 elite, significant qualitative and quantitative changes took place in the CCs from 1924 with Lenin's death: Stalin's consolidation hugely expanded subsequent CCs and proletarianized and russified the Soviet elite. So 1924 marks off the heterogeneity of revolutionary Bolshevism – a product of the empire – from the homogeneity of the Stalin years, a product of the revolution.

An additional issue is raised in this connection: there may have been lots of ethnic minorities in the leadership because they were recruited that way – to solve strategic and political problems in the peripheries (hence explaining the presence of many South Caucasians, but not why there were so few Ukrainians and so many Jews); or because of Lenin's well-known fondness for Jews and Latvians; or because of Bolshevism's popularity (or lack of) in a given region; or indeed any combination of these. However, first, we know too little about the inner workings of the early Bolshevik party to fully assess its mechanisms

---

[2] See the forthcoming work by Michael Mann, *Sources of Social Power*, Vol. III (Cambridge University Press).

[3] The Russian Social Democratic Worker's Party (Bolshevik)/Russian Communist Party.

for recruitment. There is, for instance, evidence that the ethnic minorities were themselves instrumental in recruiting coethnics, in the border regions especially, thereby shifting the question from one of recruitment into the leadership to one of ethnic mobilization (in the case of the Caucasus, for example, see Rieber 2001: 1682). Moreover, as I suggest in Chapter 8, it was similarly true that ethnic Russian workers were also recruited for "narrative" purposes. Second, while certain patterns of recruitment were no doubt operating, these individuals would have had to have been available for recruitment in the first instance, still leaving open the question of the appeal of Bolshevism to various minorities. But most significantly, and as I show in Chapter 2, other radical parties of the center-left (Constitutional Democrats [Kadets], Socialist Revolutionaries [SRs], and Mensheviks) were remarkably similar in socioethnic profile to the Bolsheviks. So unless they all had the same recruitment mechanisms and rationales, something contextual also had to be operating: if other radical organizations had similar ethnic compositions, then ethnic diversity was more likely related to wider strategies of empire and nation-building processes than to the specific nature of Bolshevik recruitment per se.

Measuring Class
The second key methodological issue concerns the measurement of class. Measurement of two key classes in revolutionary Russia – the intelligentsia and the working class – is particularly difficult because they were relatively new socioeconomic realities. As late as 1917, official categories for socioeconomic position were still represented by the *sosloviia* or estates. *Sosloviia* were ascriptive and usually hereditary, and they defined individuals' rights and obligations toward the state. But official classification bore little resemblance to economic realities: the *sosloviia* became poor social indicators as increased education, urbanization, migration, and the geographic penetration of industrial capitalism created new socioeconomic positions. Shifts in wealth could result in downward mobility to lower guilds or out of the *sosloviia* entirely, and with that came a concomitant loss of rights (Rieber 2006: 600). Moreover, the intelligentsia and urban working classes did not fit easily into these *sosloviia*. A growing number of industrial workers still ascribed to the peasantry even if they lost most of their ties to the countryside, whereas many in the free professions ascribed to the *meshchanstvo*, in effect the petty townspeople estate (Haimson 1988: 2). In practice, *sosloviia* were ceding to professional and occupational social ascriptions, particularly among the urban and middle strata, both Russian and non-Russian. So any meaningful measurement of class in imperial Russia has to incorporate this modernizing tension between *sosloviia* and *sostoianiia*, respectively, the legal status assigned by the state and the occupation in which one actually engaged (Haimson 1988: 1; Cadoit 2005).

I therefore situate the class origins of the Bolsheviks using a combination of *soslovie*, profession, and class because together they capture the complex reality of social identities in the last decades of the empire, and because these ascriptions are variously – if unevenly – found in (auto)biographies, census data, and Okhrana or Tsarist police records (Appendixes A and B).[4] This, then, necessarily combines Marxist and Weberian criteria such as landholding, relations to the state, occupational/employment positions, relational positions to capital, and educational market positions (for an example on the mixing of these criteria, see Mann 1993: 546–71). For instance, the (lower and upper) middle class or, more commonly in Russia, the intelligentsia (urban and rural, petty and upper) in effect drew from several *sosloviia* to include the classic petite bourgeoisie, or well-off independent artisans and small shopkeepers at one end (the *meshchanstvo*), and professionals, intellectuals, and cultural elites, through to high-level civil bureaucrats (in Russia usually "service nobility") at the other. I also distinguish between the educated middle classes and the commercial or capitalist bourgeoisies, both urban and rural. Similarly, references to working and peasant classes (and the corresponding *sosloviia*) include urban and rural positions relative to occupation, education, and capital. Given high levels of migration in Russia's industrialization, most urban workers were from the rural areas, but officially considered peasants (hence the common use of "peasant/worker"). This working-class category includes skilled, artisan, and unskilled factory labor of peasant origin, whereas "peasant" is reserved for skilled and unskilled rural labor only.

Appendix Tables A1 (parents' occupation) and A2 (Bolsheviks' occupation) offer both class and *soslovie* classifications for the ninety-three Bolsheviks, broken down by ethnicity/nationality; these are followed by a more detailed discussion of the intersectional measurement of class and *soslovie*. For example, in official documentation, Lenin was from the noble estate because his father had risen up the Educational Ministry to formally attain noble rank; but in practice, Lenin was in effect second-generation professional middle class, because the Educational Ministry was the least "noble" of all the ministries, and because the noble *sosloviie* had anyway lost much of its earlier potency and coherence, especially among the lower strata in government service. Put differently, most of the bureaucratic nobility was in reality a professional or careerist middle class by the last decades of the empire, despite official *sosloviia* classifications. So I locate Lenin in the noble (service) estate because he was officially classified this way, but I render Lenin's social origins "(upper) middle class."

Finally, in practice there was also a blurred zone between professional and official occupational status. So while almost two-thirds of medical doctors in the empire worked for the government, armed services, or the state in some capacity, they did not consider themselves government officials or educated civil servants, but rather members of the intelligentsia. Yet *gimnaziia* and *Realschule* teachers were not considered a professional class, but rather petty officials of the state bureaucracy well through the 1880s (Alston 1969: 99–100). The *advokatura* or legal profession, too, was referred to as both an estate and as a

---

[4] I use the term *Okhrana* as a common designation for the more formal Ministry of Internal Affairs at the highest level and the security divisions at the lower levels.

profession and reflected elements of both; indeed, as a social category it had largely overtaken the estate system (Pomeranz 1999: 251, 265).

Measuring Ethnicity and Using Census Data

The terms "ethnicity" and "nationality" are both used here throughout. I follow the generally accepted distinction (Weber 1968; Gellner 1983; Eriksen 1993): ethnicity (in the Russian context, variously *narodnost, narod,* or *plemia*) is the more inclusive term (*narodnost'* from the root *narod* or people), which includes culture, nationhood, language, and so on; nationality (*natsional'nost*) invokes a political principle and specific forms of community claims to political autonomy or independence. Russian nationalists used *plemia* (literally: tribe) to argue for a unity of Russians, Ukrainians, and Belarusians, whereas nationalist groups more often used *natsional'nost,* from the root "nation." In Imperial Russia, both existed in practice and in official classification, and both *narodnost'*and *natsional'nost* were used interchangeably by the regime and by the educated classes. Although ethnicity may be the more accurate description of most of the empire's diversity until 1914, the state often referred to its interventions as "nationality policies."

In the chapters that follow I rely on ethnic/*soslovie* data from the 1897 Imperial Census. Although extremely useful in providing comparative data on the socioethnic structure of the empire's constituent ethnicities, the 1897 Census warrants caution. Not all of the material collected in the Census was published, the language of some of the questions was poorly conceived, the categories used were often problematic, and there were concerns about the manner in which data was collected (see, inter alia, Cadoit 2005, 2007). In addition to the tendency to count "Little Russians," or Ukrainians, as Russian, classification by ethnicity/nationality was further compounded by the tendency of official ethnic counting to exaggerate the number of Russians in the border areas (Velychenko 1995: 191; Weeks 1996: 83). Moreover, census data regarding sectors of the economy and occupation often did not distinguish between wealthy owners of industrial plants, for example, and the factory worker, as it categorized both as "manufacturing." And it typically tracked only primary occupation, a particular problem for many in this elite, who were teachers or doctors *and* published literary works, or even changed careers (as did the Azerbaijani Nariman Narimanov).

So in part because of issues raised by Tsarist statisticians, ethnographers, and geographers' searches for objective measurements, using the 1897 Census inevitably runs into methodological problems because of the various ambiguities embedded in its categories. While no official all-imperial census between 1811 and 1897 had categorized nationality or ethnicity, the 1897 Census captured the ethnographic composition of the empire with a question on native language (*rodnoi iazyk*), designed to measure nationality.[5] Language stood for

---

[5] In response to a request by the local authorities, a question on nationality was included for the Caucasus in addition to that on language (Cadoit 2005: 442). Here *rodnoi iazyk* (native language: Mingrelian, Imeretian) or religion (Muslim, Orthodox) were used for Georgian nationality, with

nationality or ethnicity, but it was often controlled for by *soslovie* – to the point where ethnicity was indicative of a particular social status within the imperial social hierarchy (Cadoit 2005: 442). The relationship between *soslovie* and ethnicity was often elided. In Siberia, for instance, many responded "peasant" to the question on language to distinguish themselves from the surrounding populations, whereas Russian colonists relied on their estate status to affirm their Russianness in a context of cohabitation and otherwise blurred cultural boundaries. Religious conversion and social mobility could also alter ethnicity: a move from *inorodets* (non-Russian, or "of different descent") status to peasant status was equated with assimilation into the Russian population (Cadoit 2005: 442–4); for Bashkirs and German colonists, ethnicity was equated with estate; for the state, however, a change in status was not recognized as assimilation, but religious conversion was, because being Russian was equated with being Orthodox. And inconsistencies between language/ethnicity and *soslovie* were reflected in the Census results: 73.07 percent of those of Ukrainian "nationality" considered themselves peasant by occupation, while the figure for those of Ukrainian "native tongue" who considered themselves peasant by occupation was 90.9 percent (Bauer et al. 1991: 156, 227). Indeed, the category of *inorodtsy* itself changed in terms of the underlying empirical reality that it was trying to capture as the empire expanded (and as Russian changed meaning) and new "alien" groups were placed under this rubric, Jews most notably (Slocum 1998).Difficulties also arose in measuring assimilation or the success or failure of Russification, thereby prompting a question on knowledge of Russian, which created complex elisions, for instance, among Jews as a language-based ethnicity, their levels of assimilation, and the possibility of bilingual or dual identities.

Sources and Biographical Reconstructions
The final methodological issue concerns the use and analysis of biographical sources (also included in Appendix A). I explore how socioethnic experiences influenced routes to socialist radicalism through an interpretive use of historically situated or embedded biographies. Mann's brief work on the social background of revolutionary Bolshevik elite used biographical data: he found that they were radicalized very young, at approximately seventeen years of age, so their careers were "substantially contaminated by their adolescent

---

some categorized of Georgian language but of Muslim faith. Of the Caucasian language groups only the Armenians and southern Georgians were religiously Christian Orthodox; the remainder were linguistically related but religiously Sunni Muslim (Abkhazians, Chechens, Cherkassians, Ingush, Dagestanis). There was also a passive bilingualism between the Chechens and the Ingush. Tadjiks and Ossetians were in the Iranian language group, but the former were Sunni Muslim and the latter were Christian Orthodox. The Turko-Tataric linguistic group comprised mostly Sunni Muslims (Uzbeks, Bashkirs, Kazakhs, Kirghiz), but the ethnolinguistically related Chuvash were religiously Christian Orthodox (see Bauer et al. 1991: 210). And whereas "Caucasian Tatars" (Azerbaijanis) were ethnolinguistically Turko-Tataric and most were Shi'a, a substantial segment of Azerbaijanis were Sunni.

activities and by police harassment"; so he concluded that we should look at "high schools, at apprenticeships, and at other juvenalia for a better understanding of Bolshevism" (Mann 1994: 44–5). This is a fair characterization, and I build on this and expand the sources. I draw mostly on pre-sovietized (auto)biographical accounts written before the late 1920s,[6] supplemented by Tsarist Okhrana (police) arrest records to identify socioethnic backgrounds and early politics often omitted from other accounts. But the biographical data has certain limitations. First, it is of uneven quality, quantity, and reliability across individuals: for some, sources abound, whereas for others, there is scant reliable evidence. Second, because of the repressiveness and fear surrounding social identities in Tsarist Russia, and because of the subsequent sovietization of the revolutionary movement, unambiguous and non-sovietized self-ascriptive motivations are rare, particularly where ethnicity was concerned. Ethnicity had become entwined with Russia's repressive system of social control and surveillance (Steinwedel 2001), so through constant migration, name changes, and falsified passports or identity documents individuals could (re)create identities to evade authorities, for self-protection, for advancement or social mobility, to claim rights, to conduct radical politics, or to obscure stigmatizing backgrounds (Shearer 2004: 881). Matters hardly changed during the revolutionary period when stigmatized identities merely shifted from ethnicity to class (Torpey 1997: 849–50). So first as socialist revolutionaries, and then as soviets, the subjects of (auto)biographies struggle with the need to erase problematic social/ethnic identities and political affiliations – and this has to be taken into consideration. The Bolsheviks' Marxist language of class – and ethnicity – is not taken at face value; I do not read these identities as biographical background, but as intersecting dimensions of class/ethnic experiences, specific to certain social locations and important to reconstructing social worlds.

The claim is made that for some individuals in certain social locations – particularly those with problematic ethnic biographies – a Russianized socialist universalism had powerful appeal: class universalism was a product of specific socioethnic conditions. However, this is not intended as reductionist or socially determinative: not all individuals in these locations became Bolsheviks. Individual temperaments, psychologies, and access, among other things, mattered, and indeed two brothers could embrace opposing political orientations. Individuals from similar backgrounds could – and did – gravitate to different groupings. But if not everyone in these social locations became Bolsheviks,

[6] Especially useful is *Granat*, a collection of pre-sovietized autobiographical and authorized biographical accounts that are often remarkably candid about social origins. *Granat* was prepared between 1921 and 1926 to coincide with the tenth anniversary of the revolution, and for most of its 246 contributors, *Granat* entries were their only efforts at autobiographical accounts of their revolutionary careers. Written before the "heroes of October" archetype became standard, they contain numerous details of the revolutionaries' pre-1917 lives, which were then buried in subsequent historiography. Although there is unevenness in the accounts of the most contentious protagonists (Stalin, Lenin, Zinoviev, Rykov, or Trotsky), there remains much detail about ethnic and religious origins and memberships in nationalist politics that has been relatively unmined (Haupt and Marie 1969).

all the Bolsheviks *did* come from these social locations, and this requires explanation.

Class, Ethnicity, and the Bolshevik Elite

So what was the Bolsheviks' precise class and ethnic composition?[7] Jews were in fact the most significant minority contingent after the Russians, but

[7] Older, synthetic works on the social and/or ethnic composition of Bolshevism are relatively few, albeit of high quality. Rigby's (1968: 85–7) class analysis of the Party, based on 24,000 members in 1917, found 60.2% of working-class origin, 7.5% peasant, and 32.2% white collar or "other." But this referred to occupation on the eve of the Revolution, not to social origin. Rigby found that despite an increase in the number of proletarian workers and the withdrawal of the intelligentsia, the white-collar and educated strata continued to be overrepresented vis-à-vis their numbers in the population as a whole. Lane's cluster sampling technique of 986 SDs for an earlier period (1898–1907) was based on class as an economic position. He concluded that the RSDLP was primarily a working-class party and not a party of middle-class intellectuals (Lane 1975: 17–27). Based on regional studies of the RSDLP in St. Petersburg, Moscow, Ivanono-Voznesensk, Tver, Ekaterinoslav, Baku, and Omsk, Lane found that while the Bolsheviks remained tightly connected to the working class and tended to be more downwardly mobile than the Mensheviks, their strength lay in the Russian-speaking areas of the empire (Central Russia and the Urals), whereas the Mensheviks received greater support in the south and in the Caucasus among national minorities. Accordingly, Lane found that Bolshevism was more Russian, and that Menshevism had greater national divisions, but that whereas Menshevism had more townsmen (*meshchane*), Bolshevism had more members of gentry origin. And in his analysis of the composition of the party between 1917 and 1922, Schapiro focused on the youth of the party (in 1919, one-half of the party was under thirty). He found that that they had little political experience, and that based on a Soviet study in 1920, only 8% had secondary school education and 5% had received higher education (Schapiro 1960: 233). Schapiro found, and other scholars have generally concurred, that Jews abounded in the lower levels of the party machinery, especially in the Cheka and the GPU/OGPU (All-State Political Administration or Directorate) and NKVD (secret police) of 1937 in which more than 11% of the 407 officials were of Jewish origin (Schapiro 1968: 286). Finally, Schapiro found that in 1923, 45% of the party membership (not just the leadership) were workers, 26% were peasants, and 29% were "others," which, if taken together with the party census of 1922, defined two-thirds of the party as "proletarian" (or those with only elementary education). In terms of ethnic composition, and based on the same 1922 Party Census, Schapiro quoted Pipes' figures: 72% of the Party was Russian, 5.88% Ukrainian, and 5.2% Jewish. He viewed the predominance of Russians and assimilated non-Russians as a result of the party's centralization and its urban population base (Schapiro 1960: 223–7).

Differing figures for ethnic composition reflect data sets from different years. So, of his sample of 246 revolutionaries, Mosse (1968: 147–8) found 45% to be non-Russian, but he counted Ukrainians and Belarusians as Russian. Mawdsley (1995: 204) found the 1917–23 CC elite (seventy-eight, including candidate members) was only one-half (thirty-eight) Great Russian. Rigby's study of CPSU elites covered the period from the Revolution to 1967; Lane's work concerns early Bolshevism and SDs in the years between 1898 and 1907; and Mann's work-in-progress is concerned with the revolutionary seizure of power (Mosse 1968; Rigby 1968; Lane 1975; Mawdsley 1995). Moreover, discrepancies in class or social origins and occupation stem not only from different data sets, but also from difficulties in finding commensurate measures for class or status. A problem in accurately determining social origin was the Bolsheviks' deliberate concealment of non-proletarian origin. Also problematic is the use of occupation as an indicator of class origin (Mawdsley) or the use of class as an economic position, with *soslovie* membership marking off both social origin and occupation (Lane).

TABLE 1.1: *Ethnic Composition of the Bolshevik Leadership and the Russian Empire*

Ethnicity	N	% of Bolshevik Leadership	% of Empire's Population
Russian	39	42	44
Jewish	14	15	4
South Caucasian	9	10	2
Ukrainian	8	9	19
Latvian	6	6	1
Polish	3	3	6
Lithuanian	1	1	1
Belorussian	1	1	1
German	2	2	1
Other	10	11	...

Note: N = 93. The "other" percentage of the empire's population is left blank because those remaining nationalities in the Bolshevik leadership do not correspond to the far larger number of nationalities across the Russian Empire not enumerated here.

Bolshevism's ethnic profile was on the whole much more complex. Their ethnic composition and corresponding representation in the empire are shown in Table 1.1. The birthplaces of the Bolsheviks – and for most the place of first or early radicalization – were in the empire's southern and western peripheries and the Volga-Urals. Only one in four came from the historic Russian core; the rest came from the empire's geopolitically sensitive or multiethnic frontiers, highlighting the borderland factor in Bolshevism's revolutionary politics.

Only thirty-nine (or 42 percent) of the Bolsheviks were ethnic Russians. This is a conservative figure, because the number of non-Russians was likely in the range of 66 percent to 70 percent. This is because I have defaulted as Russian those Bolsheviks for whom I was not able to obtain sufficiently reliable data on ethnic background, or where the sources were conflicting. A second source of skepticism derives from the fact that sources often reflect name Russifications; in all likelihood several were Jewish, Belarusian, German, or Ukrainian, the "invisible" nationalities. Non-Russians were overrepresented in the Bolshevik leadership as against their overall 56 percent representation in the empire, within statistical odds by conservative counting but, as noted, likely much higher. Interestingly, however, there were significant variations across nationalities, and this requires explanation: Jews, Georgians, and Armenians were each overrepresented by a ratio of 4:1 and Latvians by 7:1, whereas Poles and Ukrainians were underrepresented, and absent were Estonians and Poles and Jews from Russian Poland.

Data on social background (parents' occupation) are notoriously difficult to determine precisely, not only because of the unevenness of the source material, but also, as noted, because of the complexity of overlapping estate and class ascriptions. Across the entire elite, 43 percent of the Bolsheviks were of peasant-worker origin, 44 percent were from the middling classes, and 13 percent were from noble or military families (see Appendix A). These figures are consistent with key works on wider data sets of revolutionaries (Mosse 1968; Haupt 1969; Lane 1975), particularly with Lane's (1975) finding of a disproportionately high noble element inside Bolshevism, but they depart substantially from Mawdsley's (1995) study of the Bolsheviks, which found a higher proportion (60 percent) of workers.[8] Putative estate membership confirms this class stratification: twenty-five of the nine-three Bolsheviks originated from the most privileged and exclusive *sosloviia*: the noble, distinguished citizen, clerical, and merchant estates. This places one-third of this revolutionary leadership in the most privileged 2.4 percent of imperial society; if the *meshchanstvo* is also taken into consideration, two-thirds of the Bolshevik revolutionaries had their social origins in the top 13 percent of the empire's population.

In this most general sense, then, the Bolsheviks were typical in social profile to most historical revolutionary elites, such as the Jacobins or the Chinese Communist elite. However, distinctive patterns emerge when (1) occupation is taken into consideration to assess patterns of social mobility, and (2) social origin and occupation are broken down by ethnicity. Comparing the Bolsheviks' fathers' occupations with those of the Bolsheviks themselves suggests something about social mobility. Most immediately, those whose fathers were in the middling classes were nearly evenly divided between commercial pursuits (*Besitzbürgertum*) and educated or professional careerists (*Bildungsbürgertum*). Yet none of these Bolsheviks were occupationally in the commercial or petty capitalist arenas. In addition, nine of the eleven sons of rural/urban noble-gentry and clergy families, and three of the four sons and daughters of military fathers, found employment in the urban liberal professions. Comparing fathers with sons (social origin with occupation), there was marked occupational movement from rural/urban commercial or capitalist enterprises to the educated, urban professions. Within these there was considerable occupational diversity: six lawyers, five doctors/assistants, five teachers, five economists, and four professional journalists, distinguishing this from other revolutionary elites in which the legal profession is usually overrepresented.

Occupationally, then, the Bolshevik leadership was comprised of three main socioeconomic groups: urban liberal professions, rural déclassé but propertied nobility/service gentry, and urban laborers of rural origin. In an important sense, traditional scholarship had much of this right: these revolutionaries largely came from new migrant labor and from the new, educated, (semi) professional intelligentsia, as the first generation to slip out of the traditional *sosloviia*. But it also reveals that blocked social mobility in a strictly economic sense was a factor of varying significance to their social experiences.

---

[8] Variations are also a result of different data sets and/or different criteria for social categorization.

However, when social origin is considered in terms of ethnicity, strong class-ethnic alignments emerge. Of the thirty-five Bolsheviks of peasant/worker origin, twenty-two were ethnic Russians; the Russian Bolsheviks had proportionately greater working-class compositions (nearly two-thirds were classic "proletarians"). By contrast, of the thirty-nine Bolsheviks in the middling classes, only eleven were ethnic Russians, the remainder mostly Jewish, Caucasian, or Ukrainian. Of the nine Bolsheviks of (impoverished or service) gentry/noble origin, four were Russian and five were non-Russian, mostly Georgian. Drawn from the most privileged social strata of the empire's national minorities, occupationally one-half of the Jewish Bolsheviks would have been among the top 3 percent of Jewish society; three of the four Georgians were within the only 0.5 percent of Georgians in the free professions; five of the eight Ukrainians fell within the 0.46 percent of Ukrainians in the free professions; and four of eight from the three most elite estates in the empire.

In other words, class representation was relatively homogenous within ethnic group but heterogeneous across them. Additionally, class and occupation were closely aligned with ethnicity. The Bolsheviks were comprised of (1) an urban middle class of non-Russian nationalities, (2) a predominantly ethnic Russian working class of rural origins, and (3) a small (often impoverished) service gentry or propertied rural bourgeoisie, including both ethnic Russians and minorities. So with the exception of a small number of upper intelligentsia or service gentry Russians, Bolsheviks of the lower classes were Russian and those of the middle-higher classes were ethnic minorities. Importantly, however, the ethnic minority Bolsheviks experienced socially insecure status ascriptions more acutely than those of Russian origin because of the former's overrepresentation in the liberal professions and because of imperial strategies of ethnic exclusion.

This turns attention to the relationship between assimilation or Russification via education and ethnic exclusion, something I explore in detail in subsequent chapters. Levels of education and activism in groups other than Bolshevism are suggestive of their assimilation and of the appeal of Bolshevik ideology. My findings on educational attainment are broadly consistent with those of occupation and class background. Using this statistic alone, they reflect broad opportunity for educational advancement, with the crucial qualification of the Jews because of ethnic quotas and other severe anti-Jewish restrictions. As a group, twenty-three (or 34 percent) Bolsheviks received only elementary level education, thirty-two (or 48 percent) attended universities, and another thirteen (or 18 percent) attended postsecondary vocational schools, technical schools, or teachers' institutes. But the ethnic minority Bolsheviks were better educated. Of the thirty-two with university/higher education, two-thirds were ethnic minorities (among them six Jews, five Ukrainians, five Caucasians, and three Latvians). The majority of Bolsheviks with only elementary education were Russian (fifteen of twenty-three).

Most of the Bolsheviks attended the empire's elite *gimnazii*, whose Russian language and classical curricula were successful social locations for Russification.

This is significant because it holds across ethnicities, although there was some diversity within groups. Of those Bolsheviks who attended secondary schools, twenty-five attended *gimnaziia*, nine attended parish schools and *Realschulen*, two attended *zemstvo* schools, and one attended a Protestant school. Eight out of the ten Jews attended *gimnaziia*. A more differentiated analysis shows that *gimnazii* and parish schools were most common among Caucasians, and *gimnazii* and *Realschulen* were most common among the Ukrainians. Many were the first in their families to attend Russified educational institutions, so they were in important respects ambiguously assimilated, still able to bridge ethnocultural boundaries. These experiences are also elaborated in the chapters that follow.

Related to secondary school experiences was pre-Bolshevik political activity. Most were radicalized in their adolescent years, usually while in *gimnaziia*, or for the Russians, while working in factories and ateliers in their teen years. Of the twenty-six Bolsheviks in this elite who attended universities or advanced institutes, twenty-one had been politically active before age seventeen, or prior to attending university. This highlights the need to focus attention on the classical *gimnaziia* and so to correct the traditional view of the empire's universities as the primary source of youth radicalism (Mann 1994). Most of the Bolsheviks' first encounters with Tsarist authorities occurred very shortly *after* their first political activities. Before age nineteen they were already targets of state repressions and Tsarist Okhrana surveillance. Political activism in groups other than Russian Social Democracy was particularly common among the non-Russians. This is a highly neglected dimension of revolutionary Bolshevism, and one I explore systematically for each group. While only seven of the thirty-eight Russians had been active in other radical groups, typically *Narodnaia Volia* (People's Will) or the SRs, thirty-one of the non-Russians were active in mostly nationalist groupings prior to Bolshevism.

Class-Universalism, Assimilation, and Imperial Marginality

There were many roads to Bolshevik radical politics: a Russian peasant-worker in Saratov, an Armenian intellectual in Tiflis, a déclassé Polish gentry in Vilna, a middle-class Jew in Kiev, and a Russified Ukrainian worker in Kharkov all became Bolsheviks. Each was characterized by a different route to radicalism, and therefore by a precise elective affinity between class, ethnicity, and the appeal of a Russian-inflected politics. But if each socioethnic location entailed specific experiences, together they offered distinctive – though in their totality, ultimately coherent – intersections of opportunity and motive that made a class-universalist politics attractive. Class and ethnicity were not parallel experiences, but rather articulated each other in complex ways: in some cases ethnic and class conflicts infused each other, in other cases they were competing political alternatives, but in most cases socialist class politics was shaped by intricately calibrated ethnic, imperial, and socioethnic experiences.

As the biographical chapters will show, many Bolsheviks were involved in nationalist groups before Bolshevism; many more had "imperial" or *rossiiskii* experiences in education, employment, or radicalism; many more still had ambivalent experiences with assimilation, Russification, and ethnocultural belonging; and in places like Ukraine, the South Caucasus, and Polish-Lithuania, the Bolsheviks were members of highly multiethnic socialist party leaderships, while the rank and file were more ethnically homogenous. In some places, interethnic cooperation came from a sense of ethnic insecurity or social fragility (as in Vilna); in other places, it derived from a similar imperial-minded Russification (as in Riga or Kharkov); and in other places still, it was a result of geopolitical necessities or numerical weakness (as in Tiflis). In short, as a *rossiiskii*-oriented intelligentsia that was the product of a multiethnic empire, the Bolsheviks were experientially sensitized to the political benefits of cultural recognition (or its absence) given the strategies of a Russianizing multiethnic empire. The argument, then, is that Bolshevism's class-universalism was a product of socioethnic particularism. It was a movement of assimilating – but socioethnically marginalized – outsiders seeking belonging, identity, and position in a less autocratic and exclusionary, universalist political imaginary. As a result, socioethnic marginality was embedded into the universalist class movement – but it did not disappear. Bolshevism was a story of the social dislocations and political exclusions that enabled reinvention, and a quasi-assimilated way of existence in the empire that generated a distinctive kind of alienation.

So this book offers a reconceptualization of Bolshevism by situating its political emergence in its original imperial context. It moves beyond class alienation theories of the revolutionary intelligentsia by sociologically embedding the early Soviet elite within the "fourth time zone" of nationalism (this concept is Gellner's 1994: 113–18; 1997: 50–8). This was an imperial realm of complex ethnic stratifications and ethnopolitics, where Russian rule entailed socioethnically differentiated access to elite, professional, and bureaucratic hierarchies. Crucially, the burdens and benefits of empire were inequitably distributed across both classes/*sosloviia* and ethnicities. Class and ethnicity became intersectional social experiences for both ethnic Russians and minorities, and social inequalities became most visible by their ethnic markers. The social and political costs paid by those in particularly vulnerable locations in the imperial matrix were often substantial. In other words, if distinctive patterns of social mobility precede revolutions (Goldstone 1991), then attention should be paid to those groups that disproportionately paid the costs or burdens of empire to better understand their routes to a revolutionary political mobilization.

So I offer five related claims. First, and most generally, revolutionary ideologies can effectively frame movements in ways that do not fully reflect the underlying social dynamics that give them force, shape, or momentum. In an industrializing, multiethnic empire, class and ethnicity offered subtle intersectional experiences, but ethnocultural background was generally the more salient dimension in understanding the marginalizations of the Bolshevik leadership. In a significant number of cases, class exclusions mattered more to political radicalism. But while class and ethnicity converged in complex ethnic rankings or stratifications, class was usually experienced through ethnic or imperial location, and exclusion – with certain exceptions – tended to be ethnically inflected in an illiberal multiethnic empire. So the disconnect between the universalist class narrative of the movement on the one hand and the identities, experiences, and marginalizations of its social carriers on the other perhaps requires a more sustained analysis.

This suggests the second claim: instead of concentrating on the ideological or discursive narrative of revolutionary Bolshevism, careful reconstructions of the Bolsheviks' biographies and social experiences offer a way of excavating how a revolutionary narrative takes root, embeds itself in particular social locations, social networks, or experiences, and then organizationally moves across them. This is, in short, a Weberian exercise in understanding elective affinities. But this forces a shift in empirical focus away from narratives and discourses toward social relationships and to the social locatedness of revolutionary ideologies. In the case of Bolshevism's mobilization, a class narrative appealed to a particular combination of minorities who were both culturally assimilating and suffering illiberal socioethnic exclusions or repressions. As the six biographical chapters show, class mobilizations could draw on political, cultural, and organizational resources of ethnic communities and solidarities, with workplaces and communities tightly bound together. Bolshevik revolutionary politics rendered experiences of socioethnic particularism into a commitment to universalist revolutionary politics. In effect, Bolshevism's revolutionary movement became an institutional and mobilizational product of ethnopolitical marginality and organizational isolation.

Third, as Chapter 2 and some of the biographical chapters also show, other radical political mobilizations (the Socialist Revolutionaries, Mensheviks, and Kadets) were in significant ways similar in composition to Bolshevism. This is important because it should prompt us to rethink more generally the class and ethnic basis of politics in the last years of the Russian Empire. As I noted earlier, class backgrounds were strongly aligned with ethnicity or nationality: with significant exceptions, the Bolsheviks of lower class, peasant/worker origin were ethnically Russian, whereas most of those of (upper) middle or professional/intellectual origin were ethnic minorities. But this was also broadly true of other leftist/centrist political mobilizations, crucially distinguishing them from the empire's rightist or nationalist movements. So in Chapter 2 I try to relate the radical organizations' ethnic diversity to wider imperial strategies and to nationalist and nation-building processes. I argue that lower-class Russians and (upper) middle-class ethnic minorities universalized particular imperial exclusions because they disproportionately sustained the social and political burdens of empire in the half-century before the Revolution. A socioethnically marginalized intelligentsia was in large measure a product of complex – if unintended – strategies of imperial rule

Fourth, Russia's imperial experience had embedded within it an incomplete Russian nationalism or nation-building process, creating partially assimilated non-Russian intelligentsias as well as a lower class of Russians with weakly articulated Russian identities but stronger imperial identifications. In a multiethnic mobilization this new imperial-minded elite was able to reimagine diverse ethnocultural frameworks into a homogenous, Russian-inflected class-universalist politics. Bolshevism's core mobilizational identity, one premised on class-universalism, managed to submerge substantial socioethnic and ideological heterogeneity, or complex and subtle class-ethnic alignments, into a coherent multiethnic, *rossiiskii* movement. Put differently, it effectively organized a socially wide and diverse recruitment and resource base under revolutionary conditions because it could culturally homogenize its membership both vertically (in cross-class coalitions) and horizontally (in ethnocultural networks). This functional requirement of the social movement also functionally served as "nationalist" homogeneity in a key nation-state-building moment under conditions of imperial collapse.

And fifth, in an important sense, Bolshevism represented a better version of "the good imperial ideal" where Tsarism was faltering. By this I intend the following: the Bolsheviks' experiences oriented them toward a *rossiiskii* politics, or a multiethnic *rossiiskii* vision that mirrored the empire itself – something that developed both in confrontation with and in conjunction with the Tsarist Imperial state. Their multiethnic, *rossiiskii* political mobilizations generally espoused a universalist, but Russian-inflected, inclusiveness because of their levels of assimilation. This is not to equate class-universalism with imperialism; the Bolsheviks were not "imperialists" as such. But depending on ethnic group and regional context, most did tend to imagine a better *Rossiia* as a better *imperiia*: as we will see in the chapters that follow, some sought to maintain the empire's territorial integrity or its imperial borders for geostrategic reasons, others for reasons of adoption and identification with Russia's imperial culture, yet others for status/position worries, and still others, who were perhaps more geographically dispersed, for the protections a universalist empire (not a simply a multinational state) could accord to those most threatened by violent ethnopolitics and exclusionary nationalisms. If protest groups can sometimes gain commitment by embodying those qualities that are expected from the state (Goldstone 2001), Bolshevism's *rossiiskii* political expression sought a universalist, socialist, and inclusivist imperial imaginary, as against the Russianizing, autocratic, and exclusionary imperial qualities of late Tsarism.

Put differently, Bolshevism's political imaginary offered certain marginalized, albeit assimilating, elites an ideology that would sustain certain imperial structures and protect belonging, identity, and position. The elective affinity between the revolutionary narrative and its social carriers suggests that commitments to a Russian-inflected revolutionary politics were very context dependent. Social location, assimilation, ethnopolitics, socioethnic positioning, imperial policies, and the group's relationship to the Russian state all mattered. In other words, revolutionary Bolshevism was paradoxically ideologically conservative in this respect: it offered an ideological underwriting of the sociopolitical organization of the empire for those borderland and middle-class minorities, as well as lower-class Russians, most threatened by its collapse, most displaced by its imperial strategies and politics, or most socioethnically marginalized by the political, geopolitical, and economic burdens of empire.

So the chapters that follow explore the socioethnic coordinates or social locations of radicalism in connection with the Bolsheviks' political mobilization. The argument is presented in two parts. The first (Chapter 2) analyzes the imperial context and the architecture of Tsarist policies, paying particular attention to the ways in which imperial policies of inclusion and exclusion disproportionately targeted those in particular social locations. It is an attempt to understand the coordinates in the imperial matrix that produced those whose common or shared dimensions of experience brought them into Bolshevik radical mobilization. Then the next six biographical chapters situate individual Bolsheviks across the imperial mosaic to examine the precise appeal, or elective affinity, between Bolshevism's political ideology or class-universalism and its constituent ethnic adherents. For each ethnic group that constituted revolutionary Bolshevism, I try to show how a particular ideological (class) narrative or political framing both struck roots and emerged out of specific socioethnic relationships, identities, experiences, and communities, and how, in turn, this ethnic inflection became inscribed in the revolutionary mobilization itself. In their totality, then, the six biographical chapters elaborate the processes by which socioethnic and imperial identities and experiences were transformed into a revolutionary, class-universalist ideology.

Social Identities and Imperial Rule

How did an ethnically diverse group of minorities and Russians successfully create a Russian-inflected political mobilization framed around class politics? What was the context, and what were the mechanisms, that gave the revolutionary mobilization its force and that shaped its commitments? How did strategies of imperial rule create a marginalized, multiethnic intelligentsia committed to a class-universalist but Russian-inflected, or *rossiiskii*, politics? This chapter outlines key features of the imperial context and the social locations that produced Bolshevisms' revolutionary politics. It highlights two basic dynamics and pays particular attention to the empire's ethnic minority elites and lower-class ethnic Russians – the two socioethnic groups disproportionately represented in the Bolshevik elite. The first briefly explores the ethnic and class effects of economic development, broadly understood, on a traditional, ethnically stratified, status-based society as it became socially mobile. The second examines the state's imperial strategies for maintaining stability, control, and cohesion over its diverse subjects, and how state policies affected particular social groups in particular social locations in the imperial matrix, ultimately funneling recruits into political radicalism. Taken together, these dynamics meant that social identities were in flux and open to redefinition by state elites and by political actors; new self-ascriptions often came into conflict with traditional official categories, creating social identities that formed the bases of new social conflicts, new solidarities, and ultimately new revolutionary political alignments. This chapter closes with an account of how the burdens or costs of maintaining the empire inequitably affected certain socioethnic groups, thereby paving routes to radical and mobilizational politics – and distinguishing the Russian Empire's politics of the left from those of the right.

Class, Ethnicity, and Radicalization in the "Fourth Time Zone"

Ernest Gellner (1994, 1997) famously referred to the lands of the Russian Empire in the late nineteenth century as the "fourth time zone" of nationalism because, following the first (Britain and France), the second (Italy and

Germany), and the third (Central Europe), it was characterized by late emerging nationalisms within an imperial context. This multiethnic "fourth time zone" was socially organized around a complex and intricate ethnically ranked society in which status and ethnicity overlapped, cross-cut, and reinforced each other in myriad ways. Late Russian imperial society was characterized by complex socioethnic stratifications: *soslovie*, *Berufstande*, professional, and occupational categories, both urban and rural, were cleaved by – and organized around – ethnicity/nationality and religion as the most significant social markers (Iukhneva 1984, 1987; Haimson 1988; Kappeler 1992; Cadiot 2005). This ethnic ranking had an enormous effect on revolutionary and mobilizational politics in the decades before 1917. As noted, two dynamics were at play: the various processes associated with the transition from a traditional society organized around estates to a modern society organized around class, and the Russian state's policies over its heterogeneous subjects. I discuss the second dynamic in the next section.

Modernizing dynamics of urbanization and migration altered traditional socioethnic niches, *sosloviia*, and occupational-corporative identities. Russian rural peasants famously became the new industrial proletariat as they migrated to cities and provincial towns in the Russian core, the Urals, and the Volga regions; Georgians migrating to Tiflis in significant numbers after midcentury not only challenged Armenian demographic and political dominance, but the substantial influx of Georgian peasants and Russian officials, army officers, and craftsmen into the southern peripheries also changed ethnic economic structures and regional ethnopolitics; Estonians and Latvians from the countryside migrated to the cities in the Baltics and became workers or small shopkeepers as the more prosperous middle classes remained German, and officials and state employees, Russian. Across the Pale and western borderlands, and in the Russian interior, Jewish migration caused many to perceive Jews as challenging their status, livelihood, and social power. Russian migrants from the interior to Novorossia competed with new, "alien" rivals in employment, trade, and livelihood: "The discontents which had made them walk or ride great distances for a better livelihood were worsened rather than assuaged in raw industrial settlements or urban slums and their awareness of being Russian or Ukrainian was heightened in a multi-ethnic environment" (Rogger 1992: 336–7). And the colonizations of the Caucasus and the Steppe by Russian settlers – peasants and farmers, administrators, workers, and Orthodox missionaries – also altered traditional frontier identities and ethnic balances organized around religion or particularistic socioethnic niches.

As this complex, ethnically stratified imperial society became socially mobile, new sources of social conflict developed, and with them the possibilities for new social and political realignments amenable to mobilizational politics. Three specific dynamics are worth highlighting. First, ethnic groups were becoming increasingly internally socially stratified because of educational opportunities, greater social mobility, and urbanization and professionalization. The Jewish lower classes, for instance, entered middle-class urban

[handwritten: educt + social mob = assimilation = detachment from ethnic communities]

professions thanks to midcentury openings in *gimnazii* and universities (Halevy 1976); social boundaries redrew new cultural markers and status distinctions from lower-class *shtetl* Jews. Education and social mobility meant assimilation into Russian society and therefore detachment from ethnic communities (Brym 1978; Nathans 2002). Similarly, rapid industrialization in the Latvian provinces – together with Russification – resulted in sharper class distinctions within Latvian society, with a rural middle class and a multiethnic working class. So greater social differentiation *within* ethnic groups undermined stable ethnopolitical patterns, often excluded and radicalized the newly assimilated or quasi-Russified, and created openings for new political configurations. This characterized the experiences of the ethnic minority Bolsheviks.

Second, changes in patterns of social mobility created multiethnic, urban middle classes, which in turn shaped the character of civic associations and political mobilizations, often creating new ethnic and interethnic identities based on occupation, profession, craft, or culture. Because of the combined effects of midcentury liberalizations and capitalist industrialization, traditional ethnically ranked social statuses in the empire's peripheries were compressing: the relative decline of (impoverishing) nobilities (Russian and Polish) into a new professional urban intelligentsia of noble origin, the increasing numbers of middling peasants and lower-middling urban groups of various ethnicities (Ukrainians, Lithuanians, Poles, and Belarusians), and the already highly urbanized Jewish lower-middle classes all combined to form highly multiethnic urban middling classes. The upward mobility of lower-class ethnics into urban middle classes challenged professional hierarchies (e.g., Jewish and Latvian Bolsheviks); at the same time, rural landed bourgeoisies and landed nobilities, confronted with socioeconomic decline and political repression, experienced downward mobility into the same urban intelligentsia milieux (e.g., Polish and Georgian Bolsheviks).

In short, by the last decades of the nineteenth century, the sons and daughters of previously privileged Russian, Polish, and Georgian elites descended into urban middle-class professions, while upwardly mobile Jews, Ukrainians, and Armenians rose into them. The arrival of these impoverished but educated children of rural nobilities and landed bourgeoisies brought particular social identities into urban milieux. Noble cultural values fused with the ethos of the urban intelligentsia, and together they stood in opposition to the civil imperial bureaucracy, constituting a key ideological split among the middle strata. In a manner that would have impressed Tocqueville – and just like pre-Revolutionary France – these new multiethnic, urban middling classes were becoming similar or homogenous in terms of social status and position, but differentiated in terms of political access.

And third, ethnic neighborhoods retained their importance in large cities and provincial towns across the empire and in the borderlands. But increased social mobility meant that cities had ethnic pockets that were internally class stratified as employment opportunities continued to close around ethnic, religious,

[handwritten: up- and downward social mobility]

or cultural associations and communities (Iukhneva 1984, 1987; Nathans 1996; Plassarand and Minczeles 1996: 67–79). New class identities were gradually organizing around ethnicity. To the extent that socioeconomic position was experienced, it was through these more immediate ethnic associations, communities, and residential neighborhoods. Moreover, localism and regional or community economic interests not only dominated the lives of the lower classes, as studies of various regions of the empire have shown, but also patterned the responses of the rural intelligentsia to directives from political elites, and strongly shaped local associational life more generally (see, for instance, Meir 2006 for Kiev; Badcock 2007 for Nizhegorod and Kazan). Revolutionary associational life under Tsarist illiberalism showed remarkable resilience in terms of sociability (Burbank 2004; Gaudin 2007); professional, entrepreneurial, artistic, and other associational forms of civil society were often anchored around ethnic communities (Bradley 2002). And as we will see, localities and regional and ethnic associations and communities were social locations that significantly shaped the content and momentum of radical politics on both the left and the right. In certain parts of the empire, ethnic and religious ties actually facilitated or strengthened class mobilizations, while in others, multiethnic, cross-class alignments required specific, compensatory mobilizational strategies.

Taken together, then, these patterns shifted traditional socioeconomic niches and *soslovie* or corporative identities, but traditional frames of reference persisted underneath as new boundaries and distinctions continued to be blurred by occupation and ethnicity (Wirtschafter 1997; see, more generally, Lederhendler 2008). As Gellner (1998: 141) noted, in preindustrial societies, estates were often social strata "who knew their place," but with increasing mobility and occupational differentiation, this social rigidity ceded. Although in practice most of the *soslovie* categories endured until the Revolution (Freeze 1986: 13, 20, 25), and although they were still used in Tsarist Okhrana records to indicate social backgrounds of arrested revolutionaries and participants in social movements, most educated society viewed the *sosloviia* as an anachronistic and embarrassing relic of backwardness and stressed the need for alternative, Western-style class representations (Haimson 1988). The 1897 Imperial Census for the first time included more than one hundred nationalities of the empire, but even with this addition to traditional estate and confessional categories, officially ascribed identities no longer fully captured the ethnic diversity and class/status differentiation of imperial society (Cadiot 2007).Social identities were caught in tension between the ascriptions imposed by state authority and the subjective self-definitions that emerged as a result of migration, urbanization, education, assimilation, and social mobility (Werth 2000: 494). So in a moment of social crisis, with identities in flux and individuals creating their own social definitions, revolutionary politics could – and did – enable new social identities, distinctive cross-class solidarities, and political realignments.

Imperial Strategies and Socioethnic Exclusions

Industrialization, urbanization, and secularization contributed to the collapse of traditional hierarchies and identities of estate and confession, but so too did the state's centralizing, homogenizing, and divide-and-rule strategies. This was particularly true in the multiethnic imperial borderlands where ethnic tensions and ethnically ranked stratifications created challenging policy environments (for examples, see Beauvois 1993; Slezkine 1994; Klier 1995; Kuromiya 2003; Lohr 2003; Brown 2004; Hirsch 2005; Staliunas 2007; Avrutin 2010). Generally, Tsarist policies oscillated between those seeking an imperial stability based on divide and rule and those seeking social cohesion based on cultural homogenization, although often divide and rule *was* integration policy. This oscillation was reinforced by the ethnosocial geography of the empire, which made uniform rule difficult to implement and old regime particularistic rule comparatively more straightforward. Tsarist elites struggled with elements of both, but because of persistent cultural and linguistic differences marking off elites from peasants, divide and rule was often more readily applied within ethnic groups than between them. The need to prevent any kind of cross-class or intraethnic association drove a lot of policy, as did the need for bureaucratic centralization for purposes of social control.

In important ways, the sociology of the empire's nationalities policies was intimately connected to the logic of empire itself. Policies were repressive or exclusionary for fear of cultural influence or for fear of local, non-Russian rule at the provincial level where local elites were disloyal or "exploitative" (Poles, Ukrainians, Jews, and Muslim peasants); but the state tread lighter where local elites and nobles were loyally inside the imperial bureaucracy or aristocracy supporting the imperial state (Baltic Germans, Georgian nobles in Kutais and Tiflis, Tatar nobles in the Caucasus, Crimea, and the Volga). Similarly, policies were more conciliatory and integrationist toward those social groups that relied on the imperial state for licensing, or estate membership and civil service, and toward the non-Russian peasantries who were viewed as traditionally loyal to the Tsar as a social bulwark against provincial non-Russian landed elites.

More specifically, however, there were significant differences in the way different status groups within ethnicities or nationalities were treated. Four specific social and political dynamics characterized how various socioethnic niches or social locations across the empire produced revolutionaries and funneled them into particular leftist (or rightist) mobilizations: (1) the ways in which minority elites were incorporated or excluded from imperial civil or military bureaucracies or political hierarchies; (2) their access to – or exclusion from – education or cultural, *assimilatory Russification*; (3) the identity regimes and social ascriptions created by various state systems of social surveillance, policing, measurement, and control; and (4) more general nationality policies shaping patterns of social mobility and ethnic exclusion in the form of *dissimilatory Russification*. Together these broadly defined the experiential contexts, social relationships, and social locations that produced not only

Bolshevik revolutionary politics but also most leftist, antistate radical mobilizations. I elaborate on each in order to analytically anchor the contextual chapters that follow.

Minority Elites and the Empire's Bureaucracies

Historically, minority elites – and particularly those in the higher estates – could make careers in imperial civil service. The nineteenth-century expansion of the imperial civil and military bureaucracies provided new administrative roles for sons of landed nobilities especially. As estates were sold, young *dvorianstvo* (nobility) went to towns to find employment in the expanding bureaucracy or in the new professions. Economically they became urban upper-middle class, but in functional terms most became the empire's bureaucrats. The empire's non-Russian provinces were typically governed either by these non-Russian bureaucrats with considerable local administrative experience or by military men, particularly in the south and the steppes. The borderlands were governed by those with imperial experiences cultivated through local administrative posts, requiring not knowledge of the region but simply a commitment to empire (for example, Hargrave 2004: ch. 1 on Count Witte).

Yet minority elites were differentially incorporated. While Ukrainian and Tatar nobles easily dissolved into the Russian *dvorianstvo*, German nobles retained distinctive privileges and identities (Suny 2001: 41; Hargrave 2004: 3–5). In the southwest, Poles were precluded from imperial administrative posts, and Baltic Germans and Caucasians were assigned to Polish-Ukrainian provinces because sending Russian officials from the interior was deemed too expensive (Velychenko 1995: 205). By contrast – and counter to other Ukrainian repressions under Tsarism – the number of Ukrainians serving in their native provinces actually *rose* through 1900. Similarly in the Estonian *gubernii* in 1908, even after the Russification of the Baltic civil service, considerable numbers of Estonians continued to be present in the middle and lower ranks of the civil service (six of twelve were Russian, five were Estonian, and one was Polish), and in Courland *guberniia* (Latvia) in the same year, 88 of the state's servitors were Russian and German and nearly as many (83) were Latvian (although the Latvian numbers had decreased from 110 in 1906 to 83 in 1908) (Hagen 1978: 58). High-level civil service Germans, Poles, and Tatar elites, then, served the imperial state in large numbers but not in their native provinces, while educated Estonians, Latvians, Ukrainians, Jews, and some Poles made careers in middling and lower-level civil service in the imperial bureaucracies. In short, for many educated minority elites state service provided access to careers that local civil and political society did not, particularly for Jews, Poles, and Ukrainians.

This changed, however, in the later years of the empire. The growing Russification and militarization of the imperial civil service had its social effects (see Reisner 1999 for its application in Georgia). Policies began to privilege ethnic Russians in the borderlands to strengthen the processes of assimilation, if not so much to assimilate individuals as to nationalize larger abstractions such as the economy or the land or populations (Lohr 2003 makes this argument; see also Miller 2003: ch. 7). When *zemstva* were introduced in six western provinces, property qualifications for suffrage were lowered to favor the small, ethnic Russian population. This elevated the relatively weak social position of ethnic Russians in the peripheries. Similarly, the Baltic civil service was Russified as the state lowered entrance and educational qualifications for posts in the ministries in order to privilege ethnic Russians (Hagen 1978: 59–60), opening up careers for certain educated lower-class and lower-middle-class Russians. There were inconsistencies, however: the War Ministry had a greater degree of pragmatism and awareness of the empire's diversity, often overriding even the anti-Semitism on the right in the search of a more civic sense within the army (Petrovsky-Shtern 2002, 2009b; Sanborn 2003).

Generally, however, the blocking of minority elites' access to social mobility via imperial service mirrored their political exclusion from provincial or regional civil and political society. The political foundation of provincial society was the *zemstvo*, and access for ethnic minority elites was restricted. In 1864, when local provincial assemblies were granted to the Russian provinces, *zemstva* were not introduced in the Baltic, Polish, and western provinces (the six Lithuanian provinces, the Belarusian provinces, the three provinces of southwestern Ukraine, Archangelsk, Siberia, the Don region, the Caucasus, and Central Asia) primarily because these regions lacked strong Russian landed nobilities. Chernigov, Ekaterinoslav, Kherson, and Poltava were all considered sufficiently Russian, but in 1864 in the nine western provinces, property owning (the backbone of the *zemstvo* mandate) was overwhelmingly Polish and therefore they were not permitted self-government (Weeks 1996: 131–7). When the Tsarist state revisited *zemstvo* laws in 1903, 1905, and again in 1910–11, six Belarusian and Ukrainian provinces were granted *zemstva* with an eye to safeguarding the local Russian population, but they were still not granted to the three Lithuanian provinces (Vilna, Grodno [Hrodna], and Kovno [Kaunas]) for fears of local Polish influence.

Imperial rationales for withholding them varied depending on regional ethnopolitical context. *Zemstva* were withheld in Polish-dominated provinces for fear of flaming Polish separatism and influence; in the Baltic provinces they were withheld to avoid unduly undermining the socially conservative Baltic German *Ritterschaften*; whereas in the eastern empire considerations were religious: Tsarist elites feared Muslim aristocratic and intelligentsia participation in *zemstva* and school boards, prompting an 1888 edict that barred all non-Christians (Muslims and Jews) from participating. Here the religious basis of the *zemstvo* exclusion was clear, although the fear was not conservative Islam but reformist, progressive Islamic movements (Kreindler 1977: 106–10). The Jewish question played out more ambiguously. Jews were barred from participating in *zemstva* elections as of 1890 because *zemstva* were now considered matters of state, of no concern to Jews (Löwe 1993: 72). Yet after 1905, when municipal government reforms were considered to give townsmen (i.e., Jews) representation in Russian Poland, it was not Tsarist intransigence but Polish anti-Semitism that prevented Jewish municipal government participation; that is, Russian policy was driven by Polish fears of increasing Jewish urban influence in city government because of their overwhelmingly townsmen status and the fact that they were perceived as a Russifying social force (Weeks 1996: 151–3, 166–9).

Moreover, while the imperial civil bureaucracy expanded to make education more important than wealth or noble status by slowly eliminating landed interests (Pinter and Rowney 1980: 377–8), in the *zemstva* and in some municipal government reforms, landowning, wealth, and property were becoming increasingly important: by 1890, they were almost entirely predicated on estates as the franchise was extended to increase the number of noble landowners. So by 1905, electoral laws privileged (1) landowning as a criterion in certain areas, (2) urban landowners, and (3) peasants on tax lists, pointedly excluding workers, lower-urban middle classes (craftsmen and lower-level civil servants), and intelligentsia (Weber 1989 [1905]). This pattern held even regionally. After the Tiflis uprising in 1865, St. Petersburg restructured municipal government, shifting power away from the Armenian merchant guilds to the Georgian nobility. But between 1870 and 1874, municipal reforms began to distinguish the population by wealth and property, not by estates, establishing a property qualification for political participation. Consequently the Armenian middle classes reemerged as the leading political force in Tiflis, to the new exclusion of the Georgian nobility (Suny 1994: 120–1).

Overall the net effects of these exclusions were substantial for the empire's middle-class minorities, from which the Bolsheviks (and leftist radicalism) generally derived. Most immediately, the development of a local civil and political society capable of integration into imperial society was stunted. As noted, the bulwark of provincial civil society in the Russian regions came from within the noncommercial elements of the *meshchanstvo*, which included lower-level government officials, professionals, and *zemstvo* officials and clerks. Those most active in the *zemstva* were landowners, small agricultural entrepreneurs, and active local farmers. Given the increasing importance of education and ability in the professionalization of the civil and military service, the crisis of the landowning gentry had caused many to turn away from imperial service and become involved in provincial public life, agriculture, *zemstvo*, and noble assemblies. But because *zemstva* were not introduced in many of the borderland western provinces, in Congress Poland, in the Pale, and in the Muslim and Caucasian provinces, non-Russian ethnic minorities were not permitted this venue into provincial civil society. So in the chapters that follow, an important argument is that Russification meant membership in imperial society, usually because of exclusion, marginalization, or escape from provincial civil and political society. And the appeal of *rossiiskii* political mobilizations mirrored these bureaucratic exclusions. Notably, no *zemstva* were set up in those locations that produced most of the Bolsheviks – and indeed those locations that funneled leftist, anti-state political mobilizations more generally.

In sum, then, certain counterpressures were in evidence. As the civil service professionalized and opened to educated minority elites – thereby shifting estate as the determinative social stratifier – the state also privileged wealth, property, and economic status in its provincial and municipal local government. This differentially affected certain ethnicities and certain status groups within them, and it shaped opportunities and motives for radicalism: Tatar merchants remained tied to local concerns whereas the Tatar intelligentsia was provincially excluded; Armenian merchants remained tied to local concerns whereas (Russified and non-Russified) Armenian cultural elites radicalized; a similar dynamic occurred between wealthy Georgian magnates compared to déclassé Georgian petty nobles seeking careers in the educated middle classes. More generally, as the imperial state increasingly found its Russian identity, midcentury co-optation and inclusion of educated ethnic minority elites ceded to exclusion and blockages of venues for social mobility, at both the provincial and the imperial levels. Socioethnic marginality and radical politics were propelled by exclusions in these particular social locations or imperial coordinates.

Education and Assimilatory Russification

The Russificatory effects of education were the second broad social dynamic that contributed to the shape and character of political radicalism. After the mid-nineteenth century, the key instrument for imperial integration and social control shifted from militarist to educational policies, to attempts at cultural homogenization. Russification policies have been variously characterized as administrative-bureaucratic, linguistic, religious, restrictions on marriage, assimilatory, imperial/national, voluntary/forced, as another word for development or enlightenment, and via the democratization of the civil service. And indeed there is a large, detailed, and largely unsystematic literature on this (see, inter alia, Kreindler 1970; Raeff 1971, 1984; Hagen 1978; Thaden 1981; Kappeler 1982, 1992; Weber 1989 [1905]: 109–28; Slezkine 1994; Anfimov and Korelin 1995; Klier 1995; Weeks 1996; Rodkiewicz 1998: ch. 4; Miller 2002; Lohr 2003; Werth 2004; Staliunas 2007). The qualifications for entry or assimilation varied over time, by region, and at overlapping points on a continuum, depending on the terminology used and its context: *assimiliatsiia* (assimilation), *obrusenie* (Russification), *sliiane* (fusion), and *sblizhenie* (rapprochement).

Importantly, however, education policies overlapped considerably with policies aimed at social integration, giving the leftist radicalism of the empire's minorities a very distinctive imperial-minded or *rossiiskii* quality. The key locations for cultural Russification and assimilation were the state's secondary schools and universities. After a significant midcentury expansion of the secondary and university school system of *Realschulen* and *gimnazii*, in the late 1880s the state instituted restrictions. The most significant were the 1887 "contraction" policy restricting the lower classes or townspeople (*meshchane*) – Russian and non-Russian – and the anti-Jewish *numerous clausus*.

The contraction policy had the effect of shrinking the academic population in *gimnazii* by 17 percent between 1887 and 1889, whereas the *numerous clausus* placed severe quotas on Jewish enrollment in both *gimnazii* and universities. The intent was to decrease the number of urban, non-privileged commoners and raise the proportion of privileged in the empire's schools. By 1894, the policy was abandoned everywhere, but most of the Bolsheviks in this elite had attended *gimnaziia* in the years of contraction and exclusion – a testament to the social privileges of some and a source of bitterness for others.

Though heavy-handed and ultimately effecting mixed results, it was a sign that the state was targeting educational institutions for the twin purposes of social control and cultural homogenization. State elites believed that Russian-language education was a way of absorbing minorities toward a unity of state and society (Katz 1966: 150). Language policies operated at three levels: the elite institutions such as the non-Russian universities, the empire's secondary schools or *gimnazii* and *Realschulen*, and state primary education in the ethnic peripheries. Over the course of the nineteenth century, the universities (and many of the seminaries) in the multiethnic frontiers were closed or Russianized. Yet in the elite non-Russian universities and institutions – Vilna, Warsaw, Kiev, Dorpat, or Armenian seminaries – linguistic Russification was intended primarily to prevent the influence of ethnic revolutionary intelligentsias more than it was to assimilate them. State elites considered these institutions hotbeds of social unrest – hardly different from their view of the Russian universities in St. Petersburg and Moscow. University contexts were less important in radicalizing youth (Russian or non-Russian) than is usually assumed, because most students were politicized before they attended university (as in the case of the Bolsheviks), but exclusion from university was nevertheless keenly felt.

If the universities were Russified in order to curb the cultural influence of revolutionaries and to maintain social order, the empire's *gimnazii* were used as the most important imperial instruments and social locations for Russification and assimilation, both linguistic and cultural. This was where Russian-imperial culture was reproduced. For political reasons, the Tsarist state located most of its schools at state expense in the ethnic borderlands. In 1908, of the sixty-eight *gimnazii* and *Realschulen* supported only with state funds, twenty-seven were located in Poland alone as instruments of Russification (Alston 1969: 205). As institutional settings for acculturation to imperial state's culture and language, *gimnaziia* educational experiences were in important respects cultural experiences. The materials studied in *gimnaziia* reflected the high culture of the imperial state and classical humanism, and the attraction of ethnic minorities to the Russified *gimnazii* was powerful. Parents sent their children to the empire's elite *gimnazii* in large numbers and often at a substantial financial sacrifice, and indeed the non-Russian Bolsheviks were overwhelmingly a product of these Russified elite institutions.

By contrast, Russian-language primary schools were virtually nonexistent in the ethnic peripheries. This is unsurprising given the absence of mandatory,

state-sponsored primary education in the Russian interior. The Russian provinces had parish schools for peasants and the lower urban strata, while the
ethnic borderlands continued with their regional and local schools; in the east
there were local confessional schools for Muslims and Buddhists. The Il'minskii
educational system sought to turn native languages into tools for Russification,
among the Tatars most especially. And although designed as Russificatory, its
effects were actually mixed and more ambiguous. Denied *zemstva*, the western
borderlands had no state assistance in primary rural education, and neither was
the Russification of primary education ever attempted – not even for Jews. So
because primary education was generally everywhere ignored, the lower classes
of the empire's minorities tended to be less linguistically Russified. These linguistic constraints led socialist political movements to adopt national appeals.
In the end, one of the most important practical consequences of the failure
of the Russian state to promote a centralized Russian *primary* education was
that by the 1880s and 1890s, most national peasantries were not linguistically
Russified and therefore available for nationalist mobilizations (Rodkiewicz
1998: ch. 5).

Russification of the educational institutions in the less developed regions
of the empire, then, had the effect not of preventing, but of stimulating the
emergence of ethnic intelligentsias and mobilizational politics. Among the
more "advanced" Poles, educational Russification backfired within already
developed intelligentsias; among the "moderately advanced" Ukrainians,
Russification's effects were mixed; among the more "backward" and, curiously,
among Jews (albeit for a different reason), Russification educational policies
had educated intelligentsias among people with only weakly articulated literary cultures. Il'minskii schools – tied to missionary objectives and intended to
prevent the Islamicization and Tatarization of the East – saw linguistic diversity in primary schools (or the promotion of particularist Turkic languages)
as a social bulwark against Tatar universalism (Dowler 1995: 518; Geraci
2001a: ch. 2; Werth 2002: 184–9 on Kazan's famous Ecclesiastical Academy).
By the 1880s–90s, Russianized education had provided the basic cultural tools,
and educated national intelligentsias capable of using them, for progressive
and oppositional politics (Alston 1969: 112; Kreindler 1977: 10, 206–10).
In fact, the radicalization of these Russified intellectuals may have been one
of the immediate causes of the reform movement and the revival of Islam in
late-nineteenth-century Russia. At the center of these movements were teachers, especially in the Volga-Urals region, among Tatars, Kalmyks, Bashkirs,
Chuvash, Udmurts, Mordvidians, Cheremis (Mari), and Buriats. The state first
educated Kazakh Tatar elites and then barred the religious leaders and teachers
from working in the Russian-Kazakh schools, with the consequence that they
could work only as a distinct intelligentsia promoting, in this case, a progressive form of Islam (Kreindler 1977: 176–202; see also Tuna 2011).

In sum, through educational and linguistic Russification administrators tried
to create educated, Russified minority elites loyal to the imperial state. But it practice they (1) politicized certain educated elites (particularly Poles and Germans)

both in universities and in *gimnazii*; (2) created educated and Russified ethnic intelligentsias that, by virtue of their new education and Russified middle-class status, found themselves in (generally progressive) opposition to an illiberal state; and (3) left the vast majority of national rural peasantries without primary education, linguistically unassimilated, and so available for later nationalist mobilizations. As we will see, the non-Russian Bolsheviks were radicalized in each of these scenarios, most especially in the second, in which acculturation or Russification (linguistic and cultural) occurred against a backdrop of civic and political rightlessness, radicalizing *rossiiskii*-oriented non-Russians and providing them institutional venues for networking and mobilization. The radicalizing political dynamic here was classically Tocquevillian: the non-Russian Bolsheviks' radicalism was characterized by the promise of social mobility and access upon assimilation or Russification, but by the reality of ethnopolitical exclusion. As we will see in subsequent chapters, the ambiguities of a culturally (quasi-)Russified, yet politically marginalized, existence had the effect of excluding them from certain nationalist politics or ethnic mobilizations while making empire-wide, *rossiiskii* political movements more attractive.

Identity Regimes and Social Control
A third dynamic also contributed to the empire's radical political mobilizations' shape and content: the state's policing, surveillance, and social control regimes powerfully ascribed and inscribed new social identities and new individual relationships to a Russianizing empire. For instance, policies in the last decades of the empire that sought to "nationalize the land" in various expropriation decrees shifted ownership to Russian landowners, and even though this often ran counter to the demands of local non-Russian peasants, one important effect of these expropriations was to increase the salience of ethnic markers (Lohr 2003: 103–10); documentation practices regarding Jews ascribed their legal status, but in trying to make Jews "legible," they had difficulties finding a stable category for Jewishness (Avrutin 2010: chs. 1, 2); and Tsarist census "nationality specialists"– later transformed into early Soviet nation-building experts – sought to manage the empire's diversity, often by privileging language-as-ethnicity over traditional ascriptions (Cadiot 2007). In fact, in the last decades of the empire, ethnicity and nationality superseded *soslovie* as the basis of, among other things, the control of elections and representation to the Duma, police surveillance and the social control of revolutionaries by the Okhrana, assessments of the strength of the Russian presence in the borderlands, appraisals of foreign policies, forced migrations during World War I, qualifications for provincial assemblies and legal statuses, ways of identifying involvement in political parties, social movements or efforts to locate particular interests, the political repression of civil society and associational life, residency restrictions and migration, measurements of the imperial population, judgments about levels of agricultural development, the collection of data on schooling and education, the control of religious education and the influence of non-Orthodox clergy, and local administrative allocation of resources.

As Tsarist elites sought to realize a certain social control or "grasp" over the empire's diversity, the imposition of bureaucratic and administrative practices gave the empire's subjects mechanisms for participating in these state practices, and thereby changed their self-ascriptions vis-à-vis the state. In simply administering the realm through taxation, and with the culmination of the personal income tax, for instance, imperial practices constructed a system whereby there was an unmediated relationship between the individual and the state (Kotsonis 2004). While land assessment and taxation in Turkestan handed the allocation process to local elites' native administration, it withheld full property rights for Russian settlers in the region (Penati 2011). Tensions between Tsarist institutions and peasant administrative structures and customs in Russia's central regions resulted in redefinitions of local practices and strategies and new modes of peasant self-organization (Gaudin 2007). Similarly, the penetration of imperial legal structures and institutions in the form of township courts, for instance, prompted substantial rural litigation in civil matters, over land, labor, property, and inheritance, as peasants participated in their own social transformation (Burbank 2004). The conflicting and burdensome identity regimes and administrative procedures that sought to define and ascribe Jewish legal status were used by Jews as new identity documents in which to try to subvert or maneuver documentation practices and participate in imperial society (Avrutin 2010). Finally, in the last years of the empire, even the Okhrana could not prop up a faltering, illegitimate regime, so it began to treat everyone, in effect, as potential revolutionaries (Zuckerman 1996). In all these cases, the empire's subjects were not simply passive recipients or victims; rather, they adopted local strategies for accommodating the empire's identity practices or attempts to grasp the diversity of the realm and reduce administrative anxiety, but in so doing they altered their own social self-ascriptions.

More generally, both imperial policies and political associations increasingly organized around ethnicity because of worries of domestic social radicalism and separatism in the borderlands. This resulted in a greater centralization and militarization of the realm, in the Russianization of imperial bureaucracies, and in "autocratic techniques to fix, measure and control the population" (Steinwedel 2001: 68). This was most evident in debates around the 1897 census categories and in their implementation, because the Census was itself partly designed as a system of social control. While language, *soslovie*, and religion were taken together to ascribe identities and assess the imperial population, native language (*rodnoi iazyk*) effectively became the basis of ethnicity (*narodnost'*) or nationality (*natsional'nost*) (Cadiot 2004, 2005). Importantly, Tsarist officials did not want individuals to decide their own nationality, which was deemed to require specialized knowledge or expertise. But this had the effect of giving the Census a policing or homogenizing character, which was deeply resented in the non-Russian rural regions of the empire especially (Lohr 2003; Cadiot 2005: 454). In the imperial provinces resistance grew, and this was experienced as assimilatory and coercive pressure for uniformity. In Kazan, for instance, false rumors abounded of forced conversions of Muslim and Uniates (who did not want to be counted as Orthodox), or the forced baptism of non-Orthodox populations; as a result, Russian military and police forces intervened in order to implement the Census (Cadiot 2004: 449–55). Resistance to the Census became, in effect, resistance to a form of forced assimilation, something that minority elites easily politicized for purposes of social mobilization.

For their part, imperial elites worried as much about what the Census was measuring in terms of assimilation. What, for instance, did the language question – designed to assess origins – say about the effectiveness of Russification policies (Cadiot 2004: 460)? How could invisible ethnic roots be uncovered for those who had converted? Was instrumentally motivated assimilation (e.g., to achieve social mobility) unstable because it lacked conviction? In the past, imperial elites had been surprised to discover, for instance, that ethnic Russians were disappearing as they assimilated into Siberian cultures (Slezkine 1997), or that Russian administrators and military officers "went native" in the Caucasus (Mamedov 2008). These developments prompted concerns about the empire's ability to reproduce its ruling class of ethnic Russians, and more general worries about the size of its Orthodox populations in relation to rest of empire (Darrow 2002). As a result, the 1897 Census encoded new ascriptive identities around ethnicity, and it legitimized and reinscribed traditional status categories of the vertical and ethnically ranked *sosloviia*. At the same time, however, it elided newly emerging class ascriptions. So the politicization of census categories was an inevitable but consequential outcome of efforts at social policing and control. Ethnicity and racialized identities became more stabilized determinants of political identity markers, used by both the Russian state and by the revolutionary political mobilizations themselves (Ascher 2001: ch. 7; Steinwedel 2001; Shearer 2004; Avrutin 2007; Cadiot 2007).

Nevertheless, there were counterpressures, as the imperial state spoke with more than one voice. In addition to the Census, metrical books (parish registers of births, marriages, and deaths) and internal passports (noting estate, religion, marital status, military service, residency, and physical descriptions) were central to the state's growing identity and surveillance regimes. Internal passports were crucially important identifiers in Tsarist Okhrana records, often including very specific references to ethnic origins. Historically this kind of documentation was used to measure and control the population according to *soslovie* and confession – and these remained important ascribed identities until 1917. But the state began to erode some of these distinctions in new identity regimes: the importance of religious categories declined because of a 1905 Edict on Religious Toleration (Steinwedel 2001), which had the effect of privatizing confessional beliefs; residence restrictions on the lower classes (particularly artisans and lower urban groups) were removed in 1905, so the relevance of estate similarly declined and ethnicity came to the fore; and with the creation of the "enemy alien" categories during the war, ethnicity was securitized and a new militarized approach to ethnicity was introduced (on the latter, see Lohr 2003: 110–11, ch. 5, 170). Ethnicity was reinscribed as a function of wartime conditions. With the militarization of social surveillance and the general increase in emergency measures designed to address growing social radicalism, imperial elites sought to draw the lower social classes into a more direct and controlled relationship with the state – something that also had the effect of reducing the hold of the very confessional and estate categories that were rein-scribed in the Census (Steinwedel 2001). In fact, these practices of documen-tation and administration of identities were instruments of imposing a certain unified social order on very great diversity (Cadiot 2007; Avrutin 2010).

Taken together, then, imperial impositions of social categories and assump-tions around assimilation increasingly used ethnicity and nationality as the bases of the individual's relationship with the repressive state, with a concom-itant decrease in religious categories (see, for instance, Geraci 2001a: ch.1 on the Volga peoples). Ethnicity and nationality were used to situate individuals in terms of political loyalty, political parties, to identify groups and social move-ments, and as the foundational cultural marker for the Duma. Tsarism rein-forced ethnicity in its various policies and identity regimes of social control, and in certain cases imperial policies even made certain nationalities possible: when imperial elites wanted nomadic Bashkirs to identify with a particular territory, changes in their status and landholding fixed them to the land and to a nationality as they went from being categorized as nomads to having their own Bashkir *soslovie*, equating the poorer Bashkirs with peasants and Bashkir elites with nobles. In this way, for Bashkirs, nationality and estate were eventually merged (Steinwedel 2001). Similarly, in the Volga-Urals region, a (pagan-animist) Chuvash or Votiak (Udmurt) who converted to Islam was ren-dered into a self-ascribed "Tatar" (Geraci 2001a: 30).

Moreover, the development of the term *inorodtsy* (variously, "those of other stock," "other birth," "alien," or "of other descent") as an empirical refer-ent accompanied broader trends in nationality policies and marked a basic shift from a form of social classification predicated on ethnicity defined reli-giously to one defined linguistically (Slocum 1998: 176). This was bound up with changing conceptions of Russianness, the Russian nation, nationality, and "otherness." Indeed "otherness" and "alien" were key features of this social classification: as Russian ethnicized, *inorodtsy* shifted, and it became harder to become Russian (Slocum 1998: 181). Therefore, the term was latterly used derogatorily by rightist Russian nationalists to mark off the unassimilable *inorodtsy* based on language: Poles, Lithuanians, Latvians, Estonians, Tatars, Finnic tribes, Baltic Germans, Armenians, Jews, and so on. But this usage point-edly excluded Ukrainians and Belarusians based on the same linguistic criteria, so that the apposition came to rest on the Eastern Slavs (*russkie*) and everyone else (*viz.* unassimilable, politically active non-Russians) (Slocum 1998: 186–7, 190). Not only were alien, "otherness," or *inorodtsy* defined in opposition to evolving conceptions of Russianness, but the very evolution of Russianness was itself changed by these shifting categorizations.

In short, the imperial state started to politically detach ethnicity from *soslovie* in consequential ways. Traditional distinctions within the imperial hierarchy based on *soslovie*/status and religious confession began to erode, and they were increasingly replaced by ethnic forms of classification, expressed as *nardonost'* or *natsional'nost*. Ethnic ascriptions were now regarded as more durable than estate or religion, because both of these could be changed by social mobility or conversion. As a form of political identification and self-ascription, then, ethnic awareness was becoming politically and socially encoded; a political entwining of one's ethnic identity with the state's emergency measures, systems of surveillance, and social control politicized ethnicity. This was as true for Siberian Buriats (Hundley 2010) as it was for the Volga Tatars (Campbell 2007) or the empire's Jews (Avrutin 2010). In a tendency toward ethnic essentialism, then, ethnicity became *the* basis of bureaucratic systems of social surveillance and the most consequential way of policing social and political radicalism. Indeed the Russian state increasingly constructed the social threat in ethnic or nationalist terms (Steinwedel 2001: 79; Shearer 2004: 842, nt. 13, 845). So emerging revolutionary movements – socialist, nationalist, leftist, and rightist – similarly folded these newly politicized identities into their mobilizations, tactics, and memberships.

Social Mobility, Ethnic Exclusion, and Dissimilatory Russification

The fourth and final social dynamic that contextualizes political radicalism in revolutionary Russia is more macro and structural, and it brings together the three dynamics just discussed: imperial strategies that combined social mobility with Russificatory ethnic exclusions disproportionately and inequitably affected certain socioethnic niches or coordinates across the empire. Russian rule entailed specifically imperialist policies that inequitably distributed the imperial and political costs of maintaining both social cohesion and geopolitical stability. As we saw, liberalizing reforms from the 1860s through the 1880s admitted most ethnicities into elite and professional hierarchies and opened access to education and geographical mobility. This had the intention – and the effect – of creating Russified minority elites loyal to the imperial state through the offer of social advancement and an attractive high culture into which to assimilate (something particularly appealing to culturally marginalized elites in the peripheries). These policies opened possibilities for the Bolsheviks' parents.

But from the 1880s, and especially after 1905, the empire found its Russianness and entered an illiberal and nationalizing phase characterized by repressive policies of socioethnic exclusion and Russification. Midcentury reforms gave way to bureaucratic ethnic closures, minority elite co-optation ceded to political exclusion, and Russification consisted alternatively of assimilatory homogenizing policies and ethnically exclusionary ones. In short, Russification policies were now as much – if not more – dissimilatory than assimilatory, as a kind of Russification as dissimilation (using Brubaker's [1996] definition). Either because of geopolitical sensitivities in the borderlands, or because of worries of a growing and undesirable "cosmopolitan" civil society, the Tsarist state was as concerned with vertical associations between social strata as it was with horizontal associations within them. It was as necessary to divide cultural elites

from coethnic peasantries as it was to repress within-class radicalism. This in
turn made certain groups especially vulnerable to ethnic exclusion. So in the
half-century before the Revolution, Russian imperial rule resembled a feature
of Tocqueville's France: midcentury ethnic openings (affecting the Bolsheviks'
parents) had set in motion rising expectations, which were followed by ethnic
exclusion and illiberal repressions (affecting the Bolsheviks) – with maximum
radicalizing effect (Tocqueville 1955 [1856]: ch.12).[1]

But Tocqueville's analysis of the French middle classes before 1789 also helps
better understand these ethnic exclusions, particularly among those segments
of the multiethnic intelligentsias that produced many leftist political mobilizations, including Bolshevism. For Tocqueville, the creation of the French urban
middle classes was characterized by groups of differing social origin becoming
similar socioeconomically but remaining divided from each other by unequal
access to political rights and preferments because of the state's divide-and-rule
politics (Tocqueville 1955 [1856]: chs. 8–10; see esp. Hall 1995: 8–10). As
socioeconomic leveling made them more class homogeneous, competition for
political privileges kept them in politically isolated competition with each other.
A similar dynamic was at work in imperial Russia: by the late nineteenth century, emergent middle classes were socioeconomically homogeneous but ethnically differentiated (for examples, Iukhneva 1987; Nathans 1996). So while
there was general opportunity for social advancement, ethnicity remained a
key criterion for incorporation into the state (Kappeler 1992; Weeks 1996:
70; 2001). In the illiberal Russian Empire, the new multiethnic middle classes
competed for the same sources of social mobility and for the state's inequita-
ble distribution of political resources, generating new ethnic exclusions. Social
class inequalities were signposted by ethnocultural differences.

So while the Tsarist state never had anything like an organizing theory of
empire, its combined imperial strategies of access and exclusion did have certain organizing features, as outlined in Table 2.1. These were broadly four:
(1) policies reinscribed status particularism, because inclusion/exclusion was
based on specific socio-status groups, not entire classes, ethnicities, or religions;
(2) policies had a distinctive urban–rural dimension; (3) policies split different
segments of the emergent middle strata and declining nobilities; and (4) policies toward the empire's religious diversity were calibrated to increase social
control over the lower classes as their primary aim. I briefly discuss each in
order to better understand which social locations tended to produce which
forms of political radicalism.

First, because incorporation and exclusion involved granting or withholding
corporate or status-type eighteenth-century privileges, not nineteenth-century
citizenship rights, status particularism persisted, with the consequence that,
despite a few crucial exceptions between 1905 and 1914, *neither* classes *nor*
ethnicities were incorporated or excluded wholesale; rights and exclusions were
particularistically given to specific social groups or through differentiated legal

---

[1] I thank John A. Hall for guidance here.

TABLE 2.1: *Imperial Strategies of Exclusion and Integration, 1861–1914*

Exclusionary Repressive		Integrationist Conciliatory	
Group	Constituents	Group	Constituents
Urban Groups			
Intellectuals	All Russians, Jews, Armenians, Poles, Tatars (Azerbajani), Ukrainians	Urban estates	
Liberal professions	Jews, Poles, Armenians, Ukrainians, Tatars (Azerbajani), Georgians, Russians	Licensed urban professionals	
Urban lower classes	Jews, peasant-workers of all ethnicities including Russian	Imperial civil service nobles	
		Nationalities in civil service	Baltic Germans, Armenians, Tatars, wealthy Georgian and Polish magnates and service nobles, court Jews, lower and mid-level Ukrainian, Russian, Estonian and Latvian civil service
		Urban large capital	Jewish haute bourgeoisie, Russian, Armenian and Tatar merchants, Baltic German capital, Greeks
Rural Groups			
Landed nobles/elites	Polish, some Lithuanian, Georgian small/middle, some Russian, all Jewish	Peasants	Polish, Ukrainian, Lithuanian, Belarusian, Estonian, Latvian
Rural clerics	Polish and Lithuanian	German colonists (despite their being Lutheran or other Protestant)	
Rural non-Russian capital	Polish and Jewish	Rural clerics	Russian Orthodox

practices (Burbank 2006; Rieber 2006: 600). Imperial policies were aimed at particular social strata within ethnic groups in attempts to Russify, to control social rebellion, to prevent separatism, or to limit the cultural influence of elites over peasantries and lower classes (Alston 1969; Kappeler 1992; Klier 1995; Weeks 1996; Rodkiewicz 1998; Elyashevich 1999). For instance, the Polish landed elite was sometimes Polish as part of a nationality and sometimes Catholic as a confessional group. Most policies did not conceive of Poles in strictly ethnic terms, but as an upper-class status minority, alternately geopolitically threatening (sedition) and culturally threatening (influence over Slavic peasantries). This was similarly true of Armenians, Jews, Tatars, Ukrainians, and Germans. In fact, in entrepreneurial and corporate networks in the last decades of the empire, restrictive policies on minority capitalists – particularly Jews – substantially reduced the ethnic diversity of the networks and rendered them more ethnically homogenous (from 44 percent coethnic Russian in 1893 to 68 percent coethnic Russian in 1900) (Hillmann and Aven 2011). So the imperial state had neither the desire nor the ability to impose cultural homogeneity or universalist privileges on the realm, and the accommodation of substantial diversity was achieved through differentiated, ad hoc, and flexible strategies.

Imperial policies ambiguously sustained particularistic boundaries and redefined them in order to control civil society's growing politicization. The ennoblement of commoners through the system of the Table of Ranks, the recognition of peasant commercial rights, and the gradual erosion of the Orthodox clergy's corporative structure all had the effect of reducing differences between *sosloviia*. But after the 1870s, the Russian state rigidly refused to recognize new ones – urban workers, doctors, lawyers, and other professionals remained ascriptively suspended between *soslovie* categories. Moreover, corporative and traditional estates were often sustained as much by civil society as by the state itself: those social groups within civil society that had legal or economic privileges (landed nobles, high-level bureaucrats, Cossacks, Russian merchants, and the Orthodox clergy) sought to reinforce and maintain their particularistic privileges and social positions (Freeze 1986: 26–7; Lohr 2003: 27–9; Rieber 2006: 601).

Especially important to the emergence of the empire's revolutionary mobilization in this connection was the fate of the *advokatura*. As a unique social group in the empire governed by an ethos of public rather than state service, the *advokatura* was not a hereditary profession-estate: membership was based on knowledge and open to qualified applicants regardless of social, religious, or ethnic origin (Baberowski 1995; Pomeranz 1999: 246). So it became an ethnically open venue for social mobility. Unlike the civil service, it had no direct links to the state, and it was unlike the medical profession, which was governed by traditional estate principles and remained state controlled. In the last third of the nineteenth century, however, the Russianization of the *advokatura* blocked this venue for social mobility. Three bar associations had existed – in St. Petersburg, Moscow, and Kharkov – but between 1874 and 1904, the state prohibited the formation of state-licensed bar associations in other cities for fear that minority elites in non-Russian regions would come to control them (Pomeranz 1999: 253, 256). At the heart of this fear lay anti-Semitism. By the 1880s, Jews had turned to the *advokatura* in large numbers because it was the only institution that admitted them to practice law – indeed by 1889, 22 percent of all St. Petersburg sworn attorneys and 42 percent of all attorneys-in-training were Jewish, and between 1890 and 1895, 89 percent of all applicants to the *pomoshchniki* (assistants or attorneys-in-training) were Jewish (Pomeranz 1999: 251–2). This contributed to the decision to block the introduction of a bar association in Odessa. Just as worrisome was the potential for a Polish-dominated Warsaw bar. So Russianization blocked the considerable social mobility that the *advokatura* had represented for the empire's most educated minorities, funneling many into revolutionary politics – and indeed they show up in large numbers in all the leftist and center-left political mobilizations.

Second, there was a rural-urban dimension to imperial strategies. The Tsarist state had historically co-opted elites in a constant and flexible renegotiation of *dvorianstvo* membership, caring very little about the peasant masses of any nationality (Kappeler 1992: 94–5; Rieber 2006: 600). Sometimes this took the form of land redistribution or nationalization policies (for instance, see Breyfogle 2003; Lohr 2003 on "colonization by contract" in the Caucasus). But midcentury this shifted, and rural elites and landed nobles were systematically targeted. The non-Russian rural western borderland areas were of particular concern because of the cultural, political, and economic influence of certain elites (e.g., Polish *szlachta*, Ukrainian intellectuals, and Jewish rural capitalists) where Russian social and administrative presence along geopolitical frontiers was weak. So in a reversal of traditional imperial policies of co-opting borderland minority elites and nobilities, repressive policies toward rural landed and cultural elites affected Poles, Jews, Lithuanians, Ukrainians, Germans, and, in some cases, Georgians. To protect Polish and other Slavic peasantries, for instance, the 1882 May Laws, or temporary Jewish regulations, were designed to restrict Jewish rural "exploitation" and the influence of Ukrainian intellectuals and Polish *szlachta*.

More generally, the peasantries of the empire's constituent ethnicities were emancipated at different historical junctures, under different social conditions, and with varied emancipation settlements depending on the state's assessments of provincial ethnopolitics. The degree to which peasant or landed elite bore the cost of the settlement varied considerably across ethnic groups, particularly in European Russia. For instance, on emancipation, the Lithuanian peasantry received generous settlements that directly contributed to the emergence of a landed, privileged, quasi-aristocratic Lithuanian rural elite – which in turn became the backbone of the nationalist movement. The Latvian peasantry's emancipation settlements in the early nineteenth century similarly set the course for rural socioeconomic differentiation among Latvians by the 1870s. Polish peasants received comparatively generous emancipation settlements at the expense of the Polish *szlachta*, in part explaining both the Polish peasantry's relative social quiescence in moments of social unrest and the *szlachta*'s presence in radical groups. Georgian middling and petty landed nobles were harshly treated in land reforms in the South Caucasus, while Georgian greater magnates and peasants were not, thereby sending many of the former into radical nationalist-socialist movements (on Georgia, see Jones 2005: ch. 1).

In the urban areas, by contrast, the state was conciliatory toward ethnic elites in those higher urban commercial and service sectors that were firmly within traditionally recognized *sosloviia*, but repressed the newer, urban lower classes of peasant-workers, Jewish *meshchane*, lower intelligentsia, and liberal professions. This was especially notable with the merchant estate, where proportionately more ethnic minorities were in the more recently created urban estates of distinguished citizens and merchants than were ethnic Russians.[2] Indeed a significant portion of imperial commercial society in these estates was non-Russian – Jewish, Greek, Armenian, Tatar, Central Asian, and Baltic German. These latter groups remained relatively privileged, because imperial elites were generally supportive of the social usefulness of non-Russian commerce (Starr 1978: 25), and therefore they do not show up in revolutionary movements. The urban distinguished citizens and merchant estates comprised elements of both the educated middle classes (which often required state licensing) and the capitalist middle classes; the former was typically repressed, the latter was not. But because these categories were in flux, there was a blurring between those professionals and government service bureaucrats who entered the "personal nobility" and those who remained "distinguished citizens"; the nucleus of the intelligentsia and the free professions drew from both the noble estates and the distinguished citizens of the upper-educated middle classes, and they were well represented in both nationalist and socialist revolutionary movements.

Third, imperial policies split emergent middle strata and noble estates. While the imperial bureaucracy did provide venues for certain educated minority elites, they were pointedly excluded from the liberal professions. Cultural elites and those in the liberal professions were the primary targets of oppressive nationality policies. They therefore had the highest rates of political radicalization and show up disproportionately in revolutionary mobilizations. As noted, policies were typically repressive or exclusionary either for fear of cultural influence or for fear of local, non-Russian rule at the provincial level, where local elites could be disloyal or "exploitative," or where the assimilatory appeal of non-Russian cultures could be strong (this affected, for instance, Poles, Ukrainians, Jews, and Volga Tatars). But the state tread lighter where

---

[2] According to the 1897 Census, 1.12% of the empire's Moldavians were "distinguished citizens," 0.83% of Germans, 0.82% of Armenians, and 0.44% of Russians. Of the empire's Jews, 1.42% were members of the merchant estate, 0.86% of Armenians, 0.66% of Germans, and only 0.29% of Russians. Combined, these two categories of the upper-middle educated and commercial classes were 1.68% of Armenians, 1.54% of Jews, 1.49% of Germans, and 0.73% of Russians (Bauer et al. 1991: 198; Kappeler 1992: 328).

local elites were firmly ensconced inside the imperial state (Baltic Germans, Georgian nobles in Kutais and Tiflis, or Tatar nobles in the Caucasus and Crimea). Policies were integrationist toward those upper-middle classes inside the imperial state by virtue of licensing, estate membership, or civil service, or those of urban, non-Russian substantial capital. Although this is not well researched, the urban intelligentsia with its newly arrived déclassé sons of rural elites generally stood in political opposition to the civil imperial bureaucracy (Lieven 1989: ch. 3). But this constituted a key ideological split within the middle strata. Imperial divide-and-rule strategies may be part of the explanation behind the political opposition between educated elites in the imperial bureaucracies (from which the liberal Kadets tended to draw) and those educated elites in the urban professions and intelligentsias (from which the Bolsheviks and Social Democrats tended to draw).

Inclusionary and exclusionary policies directed at minority nobilities and at their opportunities for social mobility were important in terms of political mobilizations. Non-Russians comprised an important contingent of the noble estate: only 0.87 percent of Russians were classified as hereditary nobles in 1897, 5.29 percent of Georgians and 4.41 percent of Poles were considered hereditary nobility, followed by Lithuanians, Tatars, Azerbaijanis, and Germans (Kappeler 1992: 328). So in proportional terms, far more Georgians and Poles were hereditary nobles than Russians, whereas Georgians, Germans, and Russians had the highest proportion of personal nobles in the empire (Bauer et al. 1991: 202–3). Latterly these impoverished Polish landed elites of the *kresy* (or western borderlands), déclassé Georgian landed nobles, and Lithuanian landed aristocrats became leaders of nationalist, socialist, and other radical political mobilizations. Even within Bolshevism, déclassé Georgian nobles were the most significant noble contingent next to the Russians.

More specifically, there was great differentiation within the non-Russian nobilities in terms of their privileges vis-à-vis the state and in their assimilation or imperialization into the Russian nobility. Some were so fully incorporated that they became, in effect, upper-class minorities in the Russian nation. In fact cultural-linguistic differences between minority nobles and their lower social strata coethnics were often greater than those between nobles of different ethnicities. But by the last years of the empire, ethnicity became most problematic for rural nobles, so urgent linguistic, cultural, and even religious acculturation was common. Multiethnic strata of the nobility became, in effect, a kind of *Staatsvolk*: the Lithuanian Tatar nobility was often Russified or Polonized; Russian noble families were full of Turko-Tataric names, they found a certain status affinity with the Polish gentry, they often Polonized, and they even converted to Catholicism; and landed Ukrainian nobles married ethnic Russians, Russified, and often lost any local or regional identity (Rieber 1994: 61; Weeks 1996: 104; Velychenko 1997: 415). Indeed the near-complete co-optation and integration of the Ukrainian gentry into the Russian *dvorianstvo* was a defining feature of Tsarist rule in Ukraine and an important element that gave shape to their political movements.

In short, Tsarist privileges were accorded unevenly and depended on local ethnopolitics. In the Lithuanian provinces, Lithuanian Tatars ("Muslim nobles") lived in Grodno and Vilna, owned land, and spoke Polish or Russian. But unlike the Polish *szlachta*, they were regarded as loyal to the state and so remained untaxed, with full privileges (Weeks 1996: 90). Generally, Polish nobles' claims to estate status were treated less liberally than Georgians' claims. Like Ukrainian nobles, Georgian nobles were also fully incorporated, although their degree of Russification, cultural and linguistic, remained more circumscribed. And unlike the Polish *szlachta* with landed interests who were severely repressed after the 1830 and 1863 rebellions, the Georgian nobility, after their rebellions of the first third of the nineteenth century, were reincorporated – a testament to their perceived compatibility with the imperial state's ideals and interests, as well as evidence of their importance to the state's need for loyal elites in the Caucasus. Georgian nobles' failure to resist the state's emancipation settlements beyond initial petitions also illustrated the degree to which they had been successfully integrated into the Tsarist hierarchy (Suny 1994: 110). These differences partly explain why Polish civil and military elites in imperial service were sent elsewhere in the empire, whereas Georgian civil and military service elites were assigned to the Caucasus.

Fourth, while the state regarded religion as the bulwark of social stability and an effective instrument of social control, Orthodoxy was not a universalist religion but an ethnically Russian one, and so its ability to proselytize and convert always remained limited (Lieven 2000). For example, even in competition with Buddhism, Orthodoxy fared poorly among Siberian Buriats because Buddhism could tolerate the coexistence of shamanism whereas Orthodoxy could not (Hundley 2010). Outside the Russian core, Orthodoxy always had a weak social hold – including among converted Muslims and indigenous peoples or the newly Christianized (*novokreshchenye*) in the Volga-Urals (Werth 2002). As an imperial instrument of social cohesion, then, Orthodoxy had only weak assimilatory power. Moreover, whereas it was historically easy to tolerate religious differences, by the last decades of the empire, the weakening of religious ascriptions in favor of more ethnicized ones made the tolerance of difference that much more difficult.

The empire's religions and religious elites had been seen in terms Edward Gibbon would have appreciated: tolerated as socially useful to pacify and control their populations, to maintain metrical books, to mobilize the lower classes for imperial military service, and generally to provide stability and moral regulation in the borderlands. But this, too, varied by region and ethnopolitical context. So while some traditional religious elites were supported by the Russian state in their battles against reformers (Muslims in the southeastern borderlands and Volga-Urals [Geraci 2001b] and Orthodox Jews in the Pale [Crews 2003]), Catholics and Uniates were hit hard by cultural and religious exclusions (Staliunas 2007). And despite the fact that the Russian Empire had more than 20 million Muslims – more than lived under Ottoman rule – it was not until the very last years of the empire that the state viewed its Muslim subjects in something other than religious terms – as nationalities, minorities, or political problems. On the southeastern frontier, Tsarist administrators had not repressed or ignored Muslims, but rather forged tactical alliances with key social and religious elites within Muslim society. This permitted the Russian state to assume responsibility for policing its subjects while acting as a patron and guardian of the Muslim faith – and this often meant intervening on behalf of orthodox Islam in the face of reformist challenges (Crews 2003). But generally the Russian state had nonuniform, scattered, and often contradictory policies toward its various Muslim subjects.

Tsarist elites also ruled their religious subjects in an often class-differentiated way: where religious affiliation cross-cut ethnicity or nationality, as it did in the northwest borderlands, for instance, administrators tended to view religion as the most important ascriptive criteria for peasants. In part this was because they considered religious conversion more difficult than linguistic assimilation, and in part because peasant conversions were seen as genuine, while middle-class conversions were viewed with suspicion (Staliunas 2004: 282–3). The Russian state's struggle with apostasy among the Volga-Urals populations was also caught in a tension between encouraging conversion to Orthodoxy as irreversible and hereditary and trying to demonstrate imperial tolerance for religious diversity (Werth 2002). At the same time, encounters between Orthodox missionaries and colonizers in the Kazakh Steppe, and among the nomadic populations, generated ambiguities about whether missionaries considered Muslim Kazakhs an ethnic group, a nationality, or a religious group to be Russified, assimilated, or converted – an ascriptive tension that effectively mirrored their own ambiguously defined Russianness (Geraci 2001b). Generally, however, it was the educationally and linguistically Russified, reformist, or secular elites of the empire's religious groups that were regarded as the greatest threat to the state, not the most orthodox or traditional. Jewish Zionists, Bundists, *maskilim*, and socialists, as well as Tataric *jadidists* and pan-Turkic groupings of the Russified literary and urbane Tatar and Azerbaijani intelligentsias, were arguably the most powerful oppositional groupings. For its part, the imperial state viewed this in almost the same way: Russian administrators feared pan-Turkism as a threat to the political unity of the empire far more than they worried about Islamic religious "fanaticism" and insularity, and they feared the "rationalist, venal, faceless" Jewish *kosmopolit* far more than the religiosity of the Jewish Hasidim (Kreindler 1977: 110–11; Löwe 1993: 75–6; Werth 2002).

Finally, clerical estate membership analyzed by nationality is revealing. The discrepancy between those national minorities occupationally in the clergy and those permitted entrance into the privileged, official clerical estate reveals the limits of the state's religious tolerance at the level of elites. In 1897, occupationally 4.11 percent of Kalmyks (Buddhists) were in the clerical profession, 1.32 percent of Jews, 1.13 percent of Georgians, 0.95 percent of Armenians, 0.77 percent of Greeks, 0.52 percent of Ukrainians, and 0.35 percent of Poles; yet in terms of official membership in the clerical estate with all the privileges it comported, 2.18 percent of Georgian clergy, or almost double those occupationally in the clergy, were admitted, 1.30 percent of Armenians (again more than occupation), 0.83 percent of Greeks (nearly all), and 0.26 percent of Ukrainians (about one-half). Pointedly *excluded* were Kalmyks, Jews, and Poles whose estate membership was reduced to 0.04 percent (Iuzhalov 1904: 456–7; Bauer et al. 1991: 167–74, 203–4). In other words, non-Christian or non-Orthodox Buddhist, Jewish, and Catholic clerical elites were excluded.

Burdens of Empire and Routes to Political Radicalism

In combination, then, these four broad imperial strategies or policy patterns directly affected the Bolsheviks, who derived almost entirely from those social locations the left side of Table 2.1. Significantly, other leftist mobilizations were similarly products of these socioethnic locations, whereas the rightist, conservative groupings were products of those social locations on the right side of the table. So the Bolsheviks' social composition – (upper) middle class nationalities and ethnic Russian peasant-workers – closely approximated the empire's general patterns of social mobility and radicalism from the 1870s onward.

The overall effect of these imperial strategies of inclusion and exclusion was that the costs of empire tended to fall disproportionately on certain socioethnic groups. It is generally argued that the most significant intelligentsias in the empire were Russian, Jewish, Polish, and Armenian – and political mobilizations reflected this. Together these four intelligentsias constituted the core of the early organizers of both socialist and nationalist political movements. In fact there was a strong relationship between membership in the middle classes and political activism, as there is, of course, with most political or revolutionary mobilizations. But there was still a nationality policy component to this. Each intelligentsia responded to different local or regional ethnopolitics. For instance, the Jewish and Armenian intelligentsias were both diasporic, highly urbanized, highly educated, and each produced well-organized radical political groups of considerable sophistication. But because the empire's Jews were far more geographically dispersed, because of the differential strengths of religious Jewish religious identities (Hasidism in the northeast versus its relative absence in the southwest), and because of language debates over the use of Yiddish, Hebrew, or Russian, Jewish politics on the whole invoked greater regional ethnopolitical complexity than did Armenian politics. Moreover, unlike *inorodtsy* Jews who were historically ambivalent in their relationship to the Tsarist state, Armenians were Christians in a Christian empire and historically loyalist until very late in the nineteenth century. In short, religiously, geographically, linguistically, and in their relationship to the Tsarist state, the Jewish intelligentsia was less homogeneous than the Armenian one, so Armenian political radicalism did not have the fractures or the variety that Jewish politics had.

Put differently, political radicalism and key mobilizations emerged from very specific social locations across the Russian Empire, moving beyond simply middle-class radicalism: those socioethnic interstices of imperial society that most politically threatened imperial rule or unity, or that were relied on to provide its economic foundation, produced the most political radicalism. This suggests that many of the empirical findings regarding the Bolsheviks, as well as elements of the analytical framing offered here, might be true – with qualifications – of other radical groups such as the Mensheviks, the SRs, or the Liberal Constitutional Democrats (Kadets). While there is no systematic comparative study of the composition of the political movements in late Imperial Russia, certain features of the leadership elites and of their bases of appeal can be assembled from various works (Martov, Maslov, and Potresov 1912; Spiridovich 1918; Fischer 1958; Perrie 1972; Levin 1973; Birth 1974; Pinchuk 1974; Rosenberg 1974; Lane 1975; Zaionchkovskii 1976; Hildermeier 1978; Kappeler 1979; Pipes 1990; Haberer 1995).[3] Table 2.2 compares features of the Bolshevik's socioethnic composition with those of other key political parties in the last decades of the Russian Empire, from the most radical SRs to the most conservative rightist URP (Union of Russian People) or Black Hundreds.

Two observations can be offered in terms of the political groupings' comparative compositions. First, the leaderships were distinguished by age, status/ class, social mobility, inclusion or exclusion into the imperial state, and, less tangibly, temperament. For instance, most of the Octobrists and URP in the Fourth Duma were between thirty-six and fifty-five years old, whereas most SDs were between thirty and forty years old; socialists had a déclassé dimension to their social experiences, whereas liberal Kadets on the whole did not; the Black Hundreds and Octobrists (and also elements of the Kadets) tended to draw from establishment elements of the middle and upper intelligentsia more firmly integrated into imperial professional and state bureaucracies, whereas the SRs and SDs had more ambiguous status definitions; non-Russian socialists tended to be more assimilated than non-Russian liberals. Among the leftist groupings, the Bolsheviks were younger, more déclassé gentry, and more working-class Russian than the Mensheviks, but they also had more *assimilated* non-Russians from across the empire than the Mensheviks or the Kadets. Party compositions changed, too, with shifting political events. For instance, the Kadets were initially a party of liberal professionals and intellectuals, but they eventually came to incorporate more of the bourgeoisie as it identified with commercial and industrial interests, and even with the military (Rosenberg 1974).

The groupings were also distinguished regionally or geographically: the Bolsheviks tended to draw from Moscow and the central industrial areas, from the Volga and Urals (or west of the St. Petersburg-Astrakhan line), whereas the Mensheviks drew from the Caucasus, Minsk, Kharkov, and Odessa (or east of the Astrakhan-St. Petersburg line) (Lane 1975: 41). The Bolsheviks drew from Russian-speaking areas and areas of rapid growth, taking root among the more traditional Russian working class than the Mensheviks, which drew from more

---

[3] These data sets are not strictly comparable, nor could they be even in a single synthetic work given the unevenness of the historical material available for the different groupings.

TABLE 2.2: *Socioethnic Composition of the Main Political Parties Near the End of the Russian Empire*

Party	Leadership	Base
Socialist Revolutionaries	Middle class, lower intelligentsia; multiethnic, some Jews; students in Moscow, teachers in villages	Russian peasants distrustful of (Russian) landowners; rural immigrants to cities, uprooted peasants
Bolsheviks	Middle-class nationalities, lower urban, rural intelligentsia; young; Russian working class; more Russian and gentry than Mensheviks; many Jews	Urban workers, rural immigrants to cities, uprooted peasants; popular among Latvian lower classes; popular in borderland cities and provincial villages in Russia
Mensheviks	Middle-class nationalities, urban lower, middle intelligentsia; more minorities than Bolsheviks; highly multiethnic, notable Jewish presence	Urban workers, rural immigrants, uprooted peasants; more middle class than Bolsheviks; popular in borderland cities esp. among Georgians and Jews
Kadets	Middle class, middle intelligentsia, and professionals; more cultural intelligentsia than parties further left; intellectuals, academics, and lawyers; notable Jewish	Successful in St. Petersburg, Moscow; Jewish, Polish, Armenian, Muslim support in borderlands to counter rightist nationalism; lots of middle-class membership
Octobrists	Ethnic Russians, Baltic and Volga Germans; rural gentry; new, rising urban wealthy; Moscow merchant intelligentsia; propertied; older	Popular in borderlands among Russians; nationalist elites in old provincial capitals; Russian bankers, industrialists, landowners, large capitalists
Black Hundreds (URP)	Aristocrats, monarchists; older; nationalists and anti-Semites	Appealed to peasants and workers in southern provinces carrying out pogroms

economically depressed areas with older and smaller factories; the Bolsheviks were strongest where industry was Russian-owned, and the Mensheviks where it was more foreign-owned (Lane 1975: 211–13). But what distinguished both was the very large number of men of gentry origin.

Second, if the various leaderships drew from different segments of the intelligentsia and upper strata, bringing with them different sets of social resources, they also had different relationships to the imperial state. The leadership profiles are consistent with the empire's patterns of inclusion and exclusion schematized in Table 2.1. Those socioethnic groups inside imperial professional and state bureaucracies tended to support rightist parties, or parties loyal to the monarchy whose members were propertied and sought to hold the empire together through a conservative nationalism in fear of social revolution. These tended to be members of the traditional Russian ruling class who retained their hold on power until the end. As the traditional core of the landowning elite – largely ethnic Russian, Russianized, or of German origin – they had an enormous stake in landowning, and rural local government and diplomacy were their main areas of activity (Lieven 1989: ch. 2). By contrast, those socioethnic groups excluded, repressed, or subject to Russification joined the center or left parties, united in antistatist opposition. Very importantly, no significant political party of the left or right sought to breakup the empire.

In other words – and this is a key substantive claim of this book – the ethnic Russian lower classes in the empire's core and the middling/upper classes of the empire's capitals and borderlands appear in the center-left parties in disproportionate numbers. Conversely, the ethnic Russian middling/upper classes and the peasants and workers of the national minorities typically joined rightist nationalist parties in the case of the former (especially in the borderlands) or they had not been politicized by state exclusions or Russification – and so they were available for later nationalist mobilizations (e.g., non-Russian peasants). There were obviously significant exceptions – some Jews, and some lower-middle-class Russians in provincial capitals – but on the whole the socioethnic composition and imperial geography of the main political groupings is consistent with the argument offered here for the Bolsheviks: lower-class Russians and (upper) middle-class national minorities disproportionately sustained the burdens of empire in the decades before the Revolution, so their presence was disproportionately reflected in antistate, leftist groupings. The empirical evidence suggests that conservatism coalesced around Russian ethnicity, while a convergence of interest brought ethnic minorities (and their nationalisms) into alignment with the multiethnic, supranational socialist parties (see also Suny 2000: 491). Socialist class radicalism, in other words, was as related to the burdens of empire as it was to industrialism.

Goldstone (1991: chs. 2, 3, esp. 109, 227–8) showed that generally patterns of social mobility preceding revolutions involve *absorption* (upward mobility of newcomers with expansion of elite hierarchies), *turnover* (downward mobility of traditional elites' loss of position), and *displacement* (elite exclusion by newcomers). This argument was not made in connection with the Russian Revolution. But as I argue, in the Russian Empire, midcentury openings and expansions of imperial bureaucracies allowed the upward mobility of ethnic minority middle classes, but the ethnic closures of the 1880s blocked

certain ethnic minorities, while repression of the Russian urban working classes intensified. This accords with the timing and sequencing of the social mobilizations: radicalism was initially characterized by the influx of minority middling classes excluded from professional and official hierarchies, followed by the subsequent entry of excluded Russian lower classes in the years of labor repression and reaction.

In a multiethnic autocratic empire, then, both class (capitalism/economy) and status (politics) conflicts were almost entirely organized around ethnicity. Tsarist elites responded with Russification, centralization, and an exclusionary Russian nationalism. Against this, the Bolshevik mobilization inverted social identities and redefined social conflict. As an empire-sensitive intelligentsia, the Bolsheviks offered on the one hand de-Russification, ethnic decentralization, and a quasi-erasure of Russianness as an identity category with content. On the other hand, they offered political centralization based on class – a new, and as yet unstable, social identity marker. Bolshevism's class universalism offered an alternative *rossiiskii* representation or experiential narrative, an effective mobilizational response to key sources of old regime conflict, exclusion, and marginalization.

Conclusion

The social processes associated with modernization on the one hand and imperial policies or strategies of rule on the other combined to dismantle much of the foundation of late imperial society's traditional ethnic and status hierarchies. The state increased its reliance on ethnic forms of identification to control elections to the Duma and to police social radicalism, entwining ethnicity and surveillance in a kind of ethnic essentialism. As domestic stability and geopolitical survival became entwined with multiethnicity, imperial politics ethnicized. These shifts were also reflected in rightist and leftist (socialist and nationalist) politics, which increasingly invoked nation (*natsional'nost'*) in their political demands. New social identities were in the offing, and so, too, were the possibilities of new social solidarities and the prospects for fundamentally restructured political alignments. Haimson (1988: 2) famously argued that a confusion and scrambling of social identities also meant a certain "fragility and potential explosiveness of social relationships." Classically, identity ambiguities in the transition from a society of stable and established hierarchical socioethnic ranking to one of vaguely defined, though presumably symmetrical, social relationships generates social conflict (Gould 2003). And new political mobilizations could tap into these newly constituting social identities, as well as address some of the conflicts generated by shifting social alignments. Bolshevism's distinctive socioethnic composition, then, gave it a powerful set of social resources with which to construct alternative identities and solidarities: by mobilizing "vertical" ethnic groups along "horizontal" class lines, it effectively competed with, and incorporated, emerging nationalist politics. But even more significantly, this kind of social moment also generates the need for a "conservative" ideology to protect threatened statuses and resolve disputed power relationships in ways that maintain elements of the status quo – one that could protect and reconstruct the empire and positions within it. This conservatism was a significant part of Bolshevism's appeal, as I show in subsequent chapters.

Moreover, with traditional social categories of estate and religion in retreat, by the latter decades of the Russian Empire, ethnicity and nationality emerged as the fulcrum around which identity and politics were organized. This built on already existing ethnic, cultural, and religious communities around which class-based political movements organized, as traditional social hierarchies gave way to new ones. But as importantly, the Russian Empire was finding its ethnic Russianness – and this began to influence most social, bureaucratic, and ethnic minority policies. Loyalty to the state became increasingly tied to ethnicity, as it decoupled from *soslovie*; even religious differences were gradually transformed into ethnic differences. Often the objective was not assimilation; rather it was to protect the stability of the empire and to prevent the influence of upper-class minorities over lower or peasant classes of the coethnics or of other ethnic groups, especially in the borderlands (Ascher 2001: 302–24, 393). Generally policies were designed to protect ethnic Russians of the upper classes, though not those of the lower social classes. The state increasingly aligned itself with Russian nationalism, which was often xenophobic, and homogenizing policies intensified. Indeed Nicholas II complained that the Second Duma had failed because there were too many non-Russians in it. With the subsequent Russianization of the Duma from 1909 (itself prompted by ethnic and demographic restrictions), by 1912–13, rightists and nationalists became the key, cohesive bloc in the Fourth Duma (Anfimov and Korelin 1995: 254).

The Bolsheviks' revolutionary mobilization – both in its narrative and in its membership – reflected a clear grasp of the ethnic and Russian nationalist tensions of late imperial society. As Slezkine (1994: 434–5) noted, for the Bolsheviks, "Russian" would be empty of content – other than historically problematic associations with great Russian "chauvinism," bureaucratic and coercive control, or imperial arrogance: "a Russian could benefit from being a proletarian, a non-Russian could benefit from being a non-Russian." As ethnicity and socioethnic status became the most problematized social identities in late imperial Russia, a social and political movement framed around class emerged. In this new framing, socioethnic particularism was not only acceptable, but also celebrated. The new problematic identity – class – had not yet been fully articulated or widely accepted, except as the framing of antistate, leftist radical mobilizations.

Therefore Bolshevism's social composition, and the social locations across the empire from which the Bolshevik movement emerged, suggests that the class-based socialist mobilization was, in effect, the product of marginalizations experienced in very specific socioethnic imperial coordinates. In the complex

imperial mosaic of ethnic and class grievances, individuals in those socioethnic interstices hardest hit by imperial policies were radicalized by socioethnic
exclusions or oppressive policies and organized a political mobilization around
a constructed class unity – a class unity that emerged out of, and effectively
built on, substantial socioethnic diversity.

IMPERIAL STRATEGIES AND ROUTES
TO RADICALISM IN CONTEXTS

The six chapters that comprise Part II elaborate the Bolsheviks' social experiences and their varying routes to political radicalism. In these biographical reconstructions, I have been mindful of (1) the incentives, constraints, and possibilities of individual social locations or socioethnic niches across the Russian Empire; (2) the intersectional experiences of class and ethnopolitics in each specific region; (3) the available political groupings on offer in each context, as well as the relative attractions of each; (4) and the ways in which all of these interacted with, or were structured by, Tsarist policies.

Each chapter contains two overlapping arguments. First, it offers a substantive, social explanation based on an empirical contextualization of the Bolsheviks. Second, it relates their political radicalism to the theoretical categories outlined in Chapter 2 that organized Tsarist policies. These categories direct attention to specific social coordinates for radicalism within the architecture of imperial rule, but by themselves they do not tell us very much about Bolshevism's precise appeal at a specific location or for those specific individuals – the substantive, socioethnic contexts do much of that work. Latvians and Ukrainians generally had different relationships to the empire for reasons specific to the region's social and political realities, but these contextual variables might be obscured from view if seen simply through broad policy categories; and yet there was a certain architecture in the Russian Empire's policies toward its diversity, and this did contribute to shared dimensions of experience across the realm's many contexts, although this, too, would be obscured if we only considered radicalism through a regional or local lens. In other words, imperial strategies structured identities, relationships, and radicalisms, but they did so differently across regional, ethnic, and class contexts.

So, for instance, Chapter 3 argues that problematic assimilation and ethnocultural marginality in difficult ethnopolitical contexts made a Russian-inflected socialism particularly attractive. A socially ascriptive Jewishness was an existential reality profoundly shaped by imperial policies, and Russian socialism's class universalism became a radical assimilation option. This was underpinned by Tsarist policies of assimilatory Russification, by repressive policies of social control that entwined ascriptive Jewishness with strategies of surveillance and "measurement," and by the exclusions or dissimilatory Russifications aimed

at those social locations with the greatest levels of assimilation and social
mobility – the educated Jewish middle classes.

Chapter 4 explores three Polish and Lithuanian Bolsheviks. Their biographies and paths from nationalism to Russianized socialism are suggestive of
the central tension between nation and class that characterized the borderlands
between the Habsburg and Russian empires, or between the third and fourth
time zones of nationalism. Here, class-universalist politics found greater affinity
with socioethnically marginalized elites as one moved eastward, where nationalisms were less politically developed. This argument is embedded in three
related sets of imperial strategies: the dissimilatory effects of Russification and
educational policies toward Polish landed elites and Lithuanian Catholics; status particularistic policies that otherwise split middle-class elites; and strategies
of social control and surveillance that targeted ethnic and confessional elites.

The Ukrainian Bolsheviks are considered in Chapter 5. The substantive finding is that Bolshevism was an unpopular political option in perhaps the most
ethnically challenging and politically volatile region of the empire (which also
included much of the Pale of Settlement), but that its membership was highly
multiethnic. I argue that Russified socialist internationalism, Ukrainian nationalism, and Russian rightist politics were different responses to the same ethnopolitical tensions. These responses were shaped by (1) imperial strategies
of bureaucratic incorporation or assimilatory Russification (which created an
imperialized assimilation and a generalized russophilia among many educated
Ukrainians); by (2) culturally repressive attempts to divide and rule, or dissimilatory Russification; and (3) by discordant integrative-exclusionary policies
that had the effect of splitting the middle strata.

In contrast to the marginal character of Bolshevism in Ukraine, Latvian
Bolshevism was the most popular political option, as Chapter 6 shows. This
reflected the ways in which marginalized cultural elites in "smaller" cultures on
the empire's borderlands found Russian-inflected, *rossiiskii* radicalism attractive: it offered a political route out of their subordinate position in the Baltics'
socioethnic ranking. Latvian politics had an extensive civic associational base
around which to mobilize, along with a russified, literate, and ethnically diverse
working class in one of the empire's most industrialized cities. Two key imperial strategies underpinned these dynamics: assimilatory Russification policies
in education, and a set of particularly brutal suppressions and army reprisals after 1905. Combined, they created a *rossiiskii*-oriented segment of the
Latvia's middle and working classes that was at once russified and politically
repressed.

Radicalism in the South Caucasus was more complicated. Chapter 7 shows
that Bolshevism was the weakest of the radical groupings, making the Georgian,
Armenian, and Azerbaijani Bolsheviks quite marginal. The region did not produce real internationalists – as had Latvia or Ukraine – but Bolshevik politics did offer a "good imperial ideal" or *rossiiskii* imaginary, underpinned by
geopolitical insecurities among borderlands minorities, and by high levels of
dependence on the Russian state for political, economic, and status protections

or privileges. This argument is analytically framed against two sets of entwined imperial strategies: dissimilatory Russification, or status particularistic policies of ethnic or religious exclusion that affected rising middle classes and descending landed nobilities; and the incorporation of minority elites into the empire's civil and military hierarchies, combined with the traditional protections of the higher commercial estates.

Finally, Chapter 8 explores the radicalization of ethnic Russian Bolsheviks. The argument is that their imperial identities and social experiences provided an important limiting condition to Bolshevism's core identity. The ethnic Russians were not nationalists: their radicalism had a universalist, ethnically tolerant, and *rossiiskii* quality – something that importantly distinguished them from the Russianizing and homogenizing character of Tsarist elites and Russian nationalist politics. In large measure, this was shaped by imperial policies: the failure of the assimilatory Russification of the empire's lower-class Russians and substantial portions of its middle class; the ways in which Tsarist policies of social ascription and repression were bound up with worries about the fragility of Russianness; and the ambiguous policy implications of Orthodox, Russian, and imperial identities. In combination, these gave the ethnic Russian Bolsheviks a commitment to a *rossiiskii* politics that fought illiberalism but did not seek the empire's dissolution.

3

The Jewish Bolsheviks

This chapter offers biographical sketches of the Jews of the Bolshevik revolutionary elite. It explores how their commitments to socialist universalism were influenced by experiences and identities as Jews. It examines the ways in which ambiguities of assimilation, ethnic exclusion, and socioethnic marginality influenced their attraction to Bolshevism's revolutionary politics. The traditional argument has been that the Bolsheviks of Jewish origins were highly assimilated "non-Jewish Jews," and that their Jewishness played no role in their political radicalism. Instead, the claim is made that for the Jewish Bolsheviks, ascriptive Jewishness was a social fact, mediated by ethnopolitical context, and a dimension of varying significance to their revolutionary politics.

The Jewish Bolsheviks were implicated in each of the four patterns discussed in Chapter 2. As middle-class minorities caught in difficult local ethnopolitics, imperial bureaucracies such as the *advokatura* were particularly appealing; the empire's educational institutions were viewed as venues not just for assimilation, but for social mobility, ultimately creating Russified Jews against a backdrop of general rightlessness and exclusion; as the nineteenth century came to a close, even fully assimilated Jews became *inorodsty* – a politicized, ascriptive identity subject to intrusive state policing, surveillance, and social control; and as midcentury openings gave way to dissimilatory Russification, imperial policies targeted educated, middle-class minority intelligentsias, making the Jewish Bolsheviks an especially vulnerable socioethnic group.

Taking together these patterns of socioethnic exclusion – assimilatory Russification in educational institutions, repressive policies of social control and policing, and targeted policies of exclusion or dissimilatory Russification – the central argument of this chapter is that for this elite, Russian socialism had become a radical assimilation option. The Russian socialist movement, and particularly its class universalism, served as a key social ally, experientially validating assimilated identities in a context of political illiberalism and in the absence of ethnocultural belonging. Bolshevism was organizationally ecumenical, and generally *anti-* anti-Semitic, as it provided identity, position, dignity, and a social home to assimilating but socioethnically marginalized

Jews. A commitment to socialist universalist politics was not only a product of assimilation; it could also be evidence of assimilation's failure. But their biographies and political radicalism also concretize the most general claim of this book: perhaps more than any other ethnic group, the disconnect between the narrative of the revolutionary ideology and the experiences of its social carriers was resolved with greater urgency and ambivalence among Jewish socialists. Their biographies underscore with the greatest clarity the ethnic underpinnings of a class-universalist ideology and the way in which the revolutionary narrative socially embedded among those who experienced an uneasy, politically marginalized yet Russified and imperialized existence. The degree to which they were class, versus ethnically, politicized, and the extent to which this mattered to the content and direction of their revolutionary activism, was emblematic of the dilemmas of educated ethnic minorities across the illiberal and nationalizing empire more generally. Moreover, their routes through various forms of radicalism – nationalist, socialist, and internationalist – and their difficult social identities as Russifying, middling-class elites politically singled out by the imperial state demonstrate how a revolutionary class narrative appealed most strongly to those paying the heaviest political costs, or sustaining the greatest burdens of empire, and for whom Bolshevism's revolutionary ideology and its universalist political vision offered an alternative representation, or form of imperial protection, precisely where Tsarism was failing.

With few exceptions, the ethnoreligious dimensions of Jewish Bolshevik identities and their impact on their political radicalism have not been carefully explored (Brym 1978; Frankel 1981; Schapiro 1986). Wistrich (1976, 1979, 1982) analyzed the relationship between Jews and socialism, and his early work argued that Jewish socialists – including those who thought their Jewishness irrelevant to their identities – had sought ethnically neutral social worlds inside a socialist universalism. In a recent biography of Lenin in which Lenin's Jewish great-grandfather is discussed, Service writes that many Jews became Marxists precisely to escape their Jewish origins (Service 2000: 28–9, 153–4). Yet despite the enormous scholarly literature on Bolshevism and the Russian Revolution, this nevertheless remains an assertion – rather widely acknowledged but empirically unsubstantiated. In part this may be because of the sensitive equivalence of communism with the "Judeo-Bolshevik conspiracy," and so the concern with providing empirical support for the historically fascist claim. If the mixed reception to Alexander Solzhenitsyn's (2001) recent high-profile account of Russian Jewry, *Dvesti let vmeste* (Two Hundred Years Together), testifies to the continued sensitivity of the issue, then Slezkine's (2004: ch. 3) recent argument that Soviet Bolshevism was profoundly shaped by the Jewish exodus from the Pale of Settlement certainly frames the issue more boldly. Moving beyond the acknowledgment of Jewish overrepresentation in Bolshevism, then, this chapter tries to specify more precisely how and why Jewishness mattered to their Bolshevik radicalism, and what this said about the Bolshevik mobilization.

The empirical core of the chapter situates the Jewish Bolsheviks in three diverse sociocultural contexts in the Russian Empire and offers a comparative account of how, for each context, class and status intersected with the anti-Semitisms of the middle and professional classes, official state anti-Semitism and exclusion, and violent populist pogroms. However a caveat is in order at the outset. While my claim is that the universalism of Russian socialism and the actual experience of being a socialist activist offered identity and a social home to these Jewish Bolsheviks, it was not the only option that could do so. Liberalism, too, offered a competing and powerful universalist option for the empire's Jews, something I briefly address in the concluding section.

Imperial Strategies and Jewish Radicalism

While Jewish representation in Russian Social Democracy was slightly higher within Menshevism, the number of Jews in the Bolshevik elite during the early state-building years was nevertheless considerable. Of the ninety-three Bolsheviks, at least fifteen were of Jewish background.[1] It is important to state immediately that Bolshevism was decidedly not "Jewish"; Jews were overrepresented against their numbers in the wider population, but so too were Latvians and Caucasians. Nonetheless Jews were, numerically and politically, the most important ethnic contingent after the Russians.[2]

In social origin, the Jewish Bolsheviks derived from the classic *Bildungsbürgertum* and *Besitzbürgertum*, broadly conceived: free professions employed or licensed by the state, merchants, small property owners, and petty capitalists. Of the eleven for whom there is reliable information, five could be nominally categorized within the personal nobles, distinguished citizens, or merchant *sosloviia* – the most exclusive urban, middle-, and upper-middle-class strata comprising slightly more than 1.5 percent of the empire's Jews (Bauer et al. 1991: 198, 200). Three were from the educated middle classes and three were from the propertied/commercial middle class: Emilian Yaroslavsky's, Lev Kamenev's, and Grigori Sokolnikov's fathers were in the employ of the imperial state as, respectively a teacher, a railway engineer, and a medical doctor. Trotsky's father was a well-off middling property owner, and Uritsky's and Ioffe's families were wealthy merchants. Five Bolsheviks were of classic lower-middle-class (*meshchanstvo*) origin, their fathers being skilled artisans (Piatnitsky, Sverdlov, Zelensky), teachers (Yaroslavsky), or shopkeepers (Zinoviev). Only the Ukrainian Jew Kaganovich was from the poor peasantry.

Occupationally the Jewish Bolsheviks were artisans, lower-middle-class clerks and technicians, lawyers, journalists, economists, and doctors. Four were in the free professions, two in journalism, one was in the sciences, and four

---

[1] They were: Radek, Trotsky, Kamenev, Zinoviev, Kaganovich, Ioffe, Uritsky, Piatnitsky, Yaroslavsky, Sverdlov, Zelensky, Gusev, Sokolnikov, Lashevich, and Morozov. The last two are not explored here because of limited reliable data, and Radek is discussed in Chapter 4.

[2] In the revolutionary years there were many Jews in the Bolshevik hierarchy and in the lower levels of the Party, including 16% to 20% of the CCs and 25% to 30% of the Politburos.

were artisans. Crucially, however, unlike their fathers none of these Bolsheviks were employed by the imperial state. And, again unlike their fathers, none was engaged in capitalist or commercial pursuits. Eleven attended *Realschule*, *gimnaziia*, or technical school, and six attended postsecondary institutes or university. Additionally, not only were they among the best educated of all the ethnic groups in the Bolshevik elite, but they were also better educated than the imperial population as a whole and than the empire's Jews in particular (for imperial figures, see Bauer et al. 1991: 93–4, 411–12). This was important because it not only socially and culturally distanced them from most of the empire's Jews, but also paradoxically distanced them from the largely illiterate surrounding Russian and Ukrainian populations, highlighting Russification's potent dissimilatory effects. In short, this placed them squarely on the exclusionary-repressive side of imperial policies outlined in Table 2.1 in Chapter 2.

Because most of these Bolsheviks were from the middle classes, it is here that we need to explore the relationship between their class origins and their Jewishness, or the intersectional experience of class and ethnicity and how this facilitated the appeal of a Russian-inflected revolutionary politics. In a social context of general rightlessness and dependence on ad hoc state privileges, job-hungry, educated Russian urban professionals tended toward illiberal rightist and nationalist politics laced with anti-Semitism. Jews had not especially feared the old *Landespatriotismus* of the empire's local aristocracies, and often found in them social allies with similar commitments to empire for which Jewish *Reichespatriotismus* was sufficient social capital for integration. But the modern political and ethnic nationalisms of the new Russian middle classes, which developed in opposition to imperial centralism and in competition with educated Jews, were also accompanied by new strains of anti-Semitism. Russian middle class and professional pressures on imperial elites for Jewish restrictions were thereby vocal, consistent, and influential (Baberowski 1995). The effect was to raise the bar for middle-class assimilation even higher. Indeed as the empire's emergent multiethnic middle classes competed for social mobility and preferments from the state (Kappeler 1992: 220–1), there were so many assimilated Jews in the Justice Ministry in the 1880s that Jewish lawyers were themselves compelled to take part in discussions about excluding Jews from the *advokatura* (Baberowski 1995: 498–9). These were not just imperial exclusions of minorities, but exclusions of minorities whose efforts at assimilation had promised entry into the middle classes.

So in a pattern typical of Imperial Russia, Jewish access, preferments, and protections were in the hands of the central, Russian state.[3] Here social mobility was easier than in provincial-level employment because of fears

[3] This is evident when Jewish employment in imperial level service is compared to that in local government, provincial administration, or non-imperial civil service: in 1897, 5% of Jews were employed in government, in contrast to only 0.17% in local, *zemstvo*, or provincial civil service. The pattern remains when considered in terms of rural/urban and by region: 5.83% of rural Jews and 7.15% of urban Jews were employed by the state; 2.90% (rural) and 3.62% (urban) were in state-licensed free professions. By contrast, 0.22% of rural Jews and 0.22% of urban

of Jewish control of provincial associations and legislative assemblies and Jewish "exploitation" of local peasantries (Pomeranz 1999: 253, 256). In fact, social mobility had been relatively ethnically open for educated or propertied middle-class Jews of the 1860s generation (that of the Bolsheviks' parents), but it was marked by a notable dependence on the imperial state for access and professional licensing. Between 1856 and 1879, rights of residence were extended to certain Jewish merchants, graduates of *gimnazii, Realschulen,* and universities, incorporated artisans, and apprentices; members of the first guild with university education could enter state service, and Jews could become licensed lawyers and judges; and after 1879 graduates of higher educational institutions could elect, and be elected to, provincial assemblies (Kaznelson and Günzburg 1912–14: 622; Kappeler 1992: 220–4; Löwe 1993: 94; Klier 1995: 29). The Bolsheviks' fathers had found social mobility within the guarantees of these state liberalizations. And given that social mobility was almost singularly predicated on assimilation, Russification had held clear attractions for both the *Bildungsbürgertum* and the *Besitzbürgertum* in the 1860s and 1870s.

Importantly, this selective easing of Jewish restrictions (and the adoption of new ones) significantly contributed to social or class differentiation within Jewish society itself. Even assimilation and Russification blurred certain ethnocultural and social boundaries while drawing new ones. Linguistic Russification meant higher educational levels and increased literacy rates (on St. Petersburg, see Nathans 1996: 189). Jews increasingly acquired a secular Russian education in the empire's elite schools, which not only culturally marked them off from the social world of the *shtetljude,* but also from the surrounding Russian and Ukrainian populations. Indeed, in the late nineteenth century, even Jewish converts were still widely considered to be "of Jewish descent" (*iz evreiskogo proiskhozhdeniia*). In the end, neither Russification, nor apostasy, nor atheism could fully transcend ethnocultural boundaries. Intermarriage may have done so, but exceedingly low intermarriage rates (except among revolutionaries) stand as evidence of the social distances between Jews and others, and cultural codes remained boundary markers despite high levels of assimilation (Nathans 1996: 194–6, 200–1).

In a reversal of midcentury liberalizations, by the 1880s and 1890s policies of ethnic exclusion blocked the generation of educated assimilated Jews that included the Bolsheviks. This set in motion the classic Tocquevillian dynamic of rising expectations. It is difficult to prioritize the causal influences on the imperial state's ethnic, religious, and racialist exclusion of Jews. Certainly official anti-Semitism deepened in the reaction post-1905: in 1908, the *numerus clausus,* or percentage norms, was made into Statute Law by the Council of Ministers, and by 1912–13, rightists and nationalists were a key and cohesive

Jews were employed locally. In Lithuania-Belarusia, 6.25% were employed by the central state, while 0.16% were employed in provincial civil service; in Ukraine, it was 4.49% and 0.18%, respectively; in "New Russia," 4.83% and 0.15%; and in the Baltics, it was 2.86% and 0.18% (all figures from Bauer et al. 1991: 179, 189–92, 329–38).

bloc in the Duma, deepening the political tenor of anti-Semitism (for party breakdown of the Fourth Duma, see Anfimov and Korelin 1995: 254). Whether or not the state's anti-Semitism was tied to a fractured, conservative modernization (Löwe 1993), so important was the Jewish question in the mind of the state, that the Minister of Interior Pleve believed that the empire's greatest problem was the "Jewish question" – above the "worker's question," the "peasant question," and the "school's question."

Jewish policies, however, were ambiguous in their application. For instance, the entwined relationship between old regime anti-Semitism and old regime anticapitalism made southern industry especially vulnerable to the state's anti-Semitism: although the Tsar's ministers were keen to limit Jewish corporate ownership in southern Russia's coal industry and its supporting railroad infrastructure, by 1914, state officials began to equate corporate enterprise with Jewish influence and implemented restrictions accordingly (McCaffray 1996: 210; see also Hillmann and Aven 2011). On the other hand, in the War Ministry, the impact of this anti-Semitism was more muted: here pragmatism, not ideology, prevailed in the Ministry's Jewish policies because of an acute awareness of the multiethnicity of the geopolitically sensitive borderlands (Petrovsky-Shtern 2002).

Given this combination of factors – fear of social radicalism, ambiguous ancien regime anti-Semitism, interethnic competition, and middle-class anti-Semitism – by the late 1880s, the Russian state blocked even assimilated Jews from key sources of social mobility on ethnic, religious, and even racialist grounds (Avrutin 2007). Consistent with imperial strategies of splitting the middle strata, and as outlined in Table 2.1 of Chapter 2, the liberal professions of law and medicine had been especially important venues for social advancement, but they were now blocked by entrance quotas. And the application of the *numerus clausus* from 1887 had considerably limited social mobility, with perhaps its greatest impact in the *gimnazii*. This caused a bifurcation within the Jewish intelligentsia between those able to receive a Russian education (legally or via bribery) and those forced to study abroad (Hausmann 1993: 509–31; Nathans 2002: 269–70, 272; Avrutin 2010, on various forms of evasion and subversion). These policies had important effects on the Jewish Bolsheviks. In short, the social openings of their parents' generation were becoming ethnically closed as blocked mobility was occurring within the very middling-class social worlds into which a new Jewish generation was assimilating.

Therefore their class origins, occupations, and blocked social mobility raise the question of class alienation as "rootless" intellectuals and the degree to which their Jewishness mattered to their political radicalism. Indeed the precise causal relationship between Jewishness, radicalism, and class alienation remains contentious. Did Russian socialist revolutionary politics have a particular Jewish appeal, as may have been true of an earlier cohort of Jewish socialists attracted to the Populist movement (Haberer 1995)? Or were Jewish revolutionaries "non-Jewish Jews" (Deutscher 1968; Schapiro 1968)? Although Solzhenitsyn's (2001: 237) account considers mostly assimilated, Russified

Jews for their disproportionate contribution to 1917, his more general claim
that Jews were overrepresented in Russia's revolutionary movements is, on the
whole, empirically accurate (see also Slezkine 2004: ch. 3, esp. 150–2). The
response, of course, is Richard Pipes' (2000): Jews were also overrepresented
in the Tsarist Empire as doctors, lawyers, chemists, and so forth – and these
distinctions were no doubt related. But Pipes commits an empirical error in
reverse in his assertion that "the high percentage of Jews in the ranks of the
revolutionaries only serves to demonstrate that Jews who abandon their religion and turn their backs on their people become uprooted and hence capable
of the wildest excesses" (Pipes 2000). There were plenty of educated, assimilated (and apostate) Jews who were not radical revolutionaries.

The most influential position has been that Jewish radicalism was the same
in inspiration as that of ethnic Russian revolutionaries because they were anyway assimilated non-Jewish Jews. That is, it was their class identities in the
alienated intelligentsia that mattered, not their Jewishness (Schapiro 1968).
This finds some support, as I show, among the *russkie evrei* in this elite. And
this may have been a function of the degree of social embeddedness within
traditional Jewish social worlds: Bundists were the most deeply embedded,
then Mensheviks, and least of all Bolshevik Jews, who were the most assimilated and Russified (Brym 1978). Or double alienations could also have been
operating, an elision between alienation from Jewish society and from Russian
middle-class society (Frankel 1981).

Interestingly, however, these explanations stand in sharp contrast to the
thinking at the time. Unnerved by radicalism in the universities, most Tsarist
elites considered the high numbers of Jews in the empire's educational institutions to be causally responsible for revolutionary unrest, and they reacted by
targeting educated, assimilating Jews with ethnically repressive measures. In
response, Finance Minister Sergei Witte took the view that it was precisely
this kind of ethnically specific oppression that was itself responsible for much
Jewish radicalism (Witte 1921: 377–9, 381; Hargrave 2004: 42 and passim
for a wider discussion). Similarly, in retrospective discussions, the Russian
Bolshevik Molotov also attributed the high number of Jewish revolutionaries
to their having been "insulted, injured, and oppressed" (Chuev 1991: 272–3).
Despite these differences, the implication was that Jews were radicalized *as*
Jews. And at a minimum, the notion that Jewish revolutionaries confronted
their Jewishness after the 1881 pogroms deserves consideration (Frankel 1981;
Haberer 1992).

Three observations can be offered. First, although most of the empire's
poorer Jews tended, on the whole, toward conservatism, in certain respects
middle-class Jewish radicalism is rather overdetermined. Because political society was essentially urban and middle class, high levels of Jewish urbanization and education facilitated the radicalization into political mobilizations
of the growing Jewish intelligentsia, something also true of the Armenian,
Polish, and Russian intelligentsias. Middle-class, educated Jews were absorbing the Russian intelligentsia's concerns, sociabilities, and forms of dissent, and

this Jewish Bolshevik cohort was no exception. Politicization as assimilated middling-class *intelligenty* was important. To young educated Jews, universalist rationalism and imperial Russian high culture were a single attractive experience; St. Petersburg – the most Europeanized city in the empire – seemed quintessentially Russian to Jews arriving from the Pale (see quotes in Nathans 1996: 181). They experienced no distinction between being Russified and being *kosmopolit*.

Of course this directly countered the reality: Russian identity was ethnicizing, vilifying the alien, foreign *kosmopolit*, and inclusion was becoming racialized (Rogger 1986: 36; Weinerman 1994; Avrutin 2007). But the cosmopolitan, urban, mobile, literate, and culturally modular Jew, as Slezkine's (2004) thesis argues, was becoming the emblem of successful modernity, embodying the shift from agraria to capitalist industria. This also meant that those socioeconomic and cultural achievements that went unrecognized were experienced as acutely humiliating once the comparator of success began to include universalized standards of meritocracy. In this, "the Jewish problem was a distillation of the general intelligentsia predicament," or the more general middle-class predicament in illiberal contexts (Slezkine 2004: 339). Yet this still leaves open the question of where, how, and to what extent they were radicalized and politically mobilized as Jews – and where, how, and to what extent they were radicalized as part of the intelligentsia.

A second observation is that class differences were not especially determinative of radicalism since the revolutionary movement drew from both working and middle-class milieux nearly equally: Jewish students of working-class background did support the revolutionary groups at higher rates than the sons of medium capitalists, but the difference was relatively insignificant – 63 percent to 56 percent, respectively (Halevy 1976: 65). This proportion also roughly held for the Jews within the Bolshevik elite. But educated Jews were disproportionately present in the leadership strata of various Russian revolutionary movements, Social Democracy included, because of high levels of education.

Third, while an existential sense of belonging may have been on offer in the Russian socialist groupings (this is Haberer's 1995 argument for the pre-1880s generation of Jewish Populists), the force of Witte's observation that Jewish radicalism occurred within a variety of ethnopolitical contexts needs emphasis. It was within an assimilated and assimilating, educated, and urbanized intelligentsia milieu that these Bolsheviks confronted vicious – if "civic" – middle-class and official anti-Semitism and social exclusion. To many Jews, official ethnic quotas were more of an affront and a greater source of animus toward the Russian state than pogroms (Nathans 2002: 269). Imperial strategies of ethnic exclusion and dissimilatory Russification strongly shaped middling-class Jewish radicalism. It was impossible to be a Jew in late Imperial Russia and not know it. The desire to assimilate itself demanded this minimalist recognition, if only in self-conscious name changes, which attempted to erase socially stigmatized, ascribed identities. It may be that on the whole they experienced their ethnicity more profoundly than the manner in which they experienced their class – not least because even being an assimilated Jew in these decades meant a deeply ambiguous negotiated social existence between cultural worlds. It required constant vigilance of newly created boundaries, and it generated complex moral and political dilemmas. Assimilation in the face of (sometimes vicious) ethnopolitical and ethnocultural exclusion feels like an existential and personal problem of the highest order. Identities in this social world could not but impinge on one's politics. In other words, radicalization and assimilation were grounded in a particular political sociology, and it was more common in those socioethnic locations in the imperial tapestry characterized by ethnic tensions and marginality within assimilating social worlds.

The Jewish Bolsheviks' Social Worlds

Whereas ethnic identity and political radicalism were deeply entwined across the Russian Empire, Jewish "national" diversity meant that the experience of ethnic marginality caused particularly poignant identity dilemmas in the search for a social existence beyond anti-Semitism and ethnonationalism. Reflective of the ethnonational diversity of the empire, most of the Jewish Bolsheviks came from the Lithuanian and Ukrainian provinces of the Pale of Settlement – some of the most ethnically mixed regions and cities of the empire – and in socioeconomic and ethnopolitical relationships with Ukrainians, Lithuanians, Poles, and Russians. A number came from the Russian interior. In this respect the regional diversity of the Jewish experience was quite distinctive among the empire's constituent nationalities, and therefore implicated relations between ethnonational groups as much as it did Tsarist policies toward any single group (Klier, Avrutin, and Rabinovitch 2003). The promise of access to – and then exclusion from – imperial educational institutions, the entwining of ascriptive Jewishness with the Russian state's systems of social control and surveillance, and the tension between social mobility and Russificatory exclusions, all contributed to the shape and content of Jewish socialist radicalism. So here socialism's appeal was not its messianic content, but its secularism, its anti-nationalism, and its implicit imperial-minded or *rossiiskii* political imaginary.

Piatnitsky and Jewish Socialist Radicalism in Multiethnic Lithuania
Iosif Aronovich Piatnitsky, a party name obtained while in emigration in Germany (Piatnitskaia 1993: 5), was a Lithuanian Jewish artisan who became a Bolshevik after years of activism in the Jewish Bund and in Polish and German Social Democracy. He was born in 1882 in Vilkmerge, and as the son of a carpenter he belonged to the skilled working class that made up 44 percent of the city's population (Iuzhalov 1904: 456; *Evreiskoe naselenie Rossii* 1970: 35). The northwest Pale had relatively small and weak native middle classes, and Jewish capital dominated almost every field of production. There was relatively mild anti-Semitism compared to the Ukrainian provinces. Jewish and Lithuanian communities in Vilna remained religiously, culturally, and linguistically distinct. Among Vilna's urban Jewish artisans, acculturation to Polish

or Lithuanian was neither attractive nor necessary. Jewish neighborhoods were generally Yiddish-speaking and the educated Jewish intelligentsia spoke Russian or German, or both (Plassarand and Minczeles 1996: 67–79). In the northwest Pale, there was relatively ample social space for Jewish culture – and Jewish socialist political movements – to thrive; urbanized Jews far outweighed the social presence of Lithuanians and Belarusians.

Piatnitsky was a half-assimilated autodidactic member of the petty intelligentsia with ties to both the Vilna artisanal milieu and to the Russified *intelligenty* of the socialist political parties. His position within both worlds, and the fact that he spoke Yiddish, Russian, and some French and German, made Polish, German, and Russian Social Democracy at once attractive and possible. In 1896, at age fourteen, Piatnitsky was working as an apprentice at a tailor's shop when his brothers, who were involved in the labor movement, brought home political exiles. This initiated his radicalism as a "politically educated worker" (Piatnitskii 1933: 15; Prokhorov 1969–78: 293). Pressures of proletarianization were affecting Vilna's artisans, who constituted 90 percent of the Jewish workers in the region, so Piatnitsky made his way to Kovno where he joined Jewish Bundist circles. He associated not with his own tailor's trade, but with the more numerous and better-organized carpenters' union (Piatnitskii 1933: 16–17). Piatnitsky was involved in the legal trade unions, but soon went to Vilna to become secretary and treasurer of the illegal Ladies Tailor Trade.

Piatnitsky was committed to ethnic cooperation within these emerging multiethnic working classes. By 1900, both socialist internationalist mobilization and Jewish nationalist movements thrived in the northern Pale, with the Bund the most important of the synthetic movements – at once recruiting among Russians, Jews, and Poles (see examples in Zalevskii 1912: 215–16). Piatnitsky (erroneously) believed that the Bund remained aloof to non-Jewish workers and that this hampered their efforts to organize a single trade across ethnicities (Piatnitskii 1933: 26). But in fact, one of the most significant imperatives of Bundist politics at the time was the need for inter-ethnic cooperation (Zalevskii 1912: 211–13; Frankel 1981: 144–8).[4] There was fear that political revolutionary action by Jews as Jews might trigger anti-Semitism. That Jewish workers were employed in small shops may have made them easier to organize or mobilize, but the antecedent reason for Bundist and Jewish success in cities like Vilna and Kovno was that where Jews were either a very large minority or a minority among other minorities, Jewish radical politics could work either alone or in alliance with others without provoking anti-Semitism. But where Jews were only a relatively small minority, and therefore more conspicuous, or where other workers were not active, Jewish workers would not organize for fear of anti-Semitic reprisals. Therefore the largest Jewish actions took place in large cities (Vilna, Odessa, Kovno, and Minsk) with ethnically mixed working classes, and only if all the

---

[4] HIAPO, Box 206, Index Nos. XVIIIa–XVIIIc, Index XVIIIa, Folder 3, Circular No. 17393, November 18, 1902 on Fifth Congress discussions on the need for interethnic organization.

ethnic groups were radicalized. Indeed the most significant lesson of the 1905 revolutions for many socialist elites was a confirmation of internationalism as multiethnic, working-class organization or as *rossiiskii* mobilization. Both Piatnitsky's pattern of activism and his autobiographical account reflect this sense of urgency around ethnic cooperation.

The second reason for Piatnitsky's sense of the need for interethnic cooperation was that after 1905, Bundism became more significant than Zionism, assisted by the fact that the language of Zionism was Hebrew and the Jewish working classes spoke Yiddish (Frankel 1981: 132–3, 158–60). The shift from Russian to Yiddish as the linguistic and cultural basis of the party's literature allowed greater appeal to the Jewish artisanry (Zalevskii 1912: 220). With this, the previous Bundist leadership of Russian-speaking, ex-*gimnaziia* graduates ceded to a new Bundist elite comprised of ex-yeshiva Jews with a better command of Yiddish. It also meant that the movement adopted more ethnic policies. The Bund became at once more international because its Yiddish-speaking rank and file lived in islands among different nations in the region, and more ethnic because the switch to Yiddish entailed a general switch in cultural orientation from Russian to Jewish (Frankel 1981: 173–86, 190–250; Zimmerman 2004). Piatnitsky was increasingly affected by these linguistic and cultural changes in the socialist revolutionary organizations and in the ethnic balkanization of the region. His linguistic skills were untypical and marginality accorded him a different kind of access. Socialized and radicalized before the shift from Russian to Yiddish, he continued to equate internationalist radical politics with Russian social democracy, not with the Yiddish Bund.

After 1905, in the second edition of his autobiography, Piatnitsky wrote that he was not officially a Bundist during this period and had no clear political affiliation: "[I]f I were asked to what organization I then belonged I could not answer as definitively as I could [now]" (Piatnitskii 1933: 20). Yet his involvement in the Bund remained considerable: he transported literature for the Bund, assisted striking Bundists, carried materials for *Iskra* through Bund connections, distributed leaflets for Piłsudski's nationalist PPS (Polish Socialist Party), and attended Bundist meetings and celebrations (Piatnitskii 1933: 24–7). According to official accounts, Piatnitsky joined the RSDLP in 1898 at age sixteen (Prokhorov 1969–78: 293). His membership was likely only nominal, and largely through Bundism, because the RSDLP did not penetrate the area until 1905, and because his own account details numerous contacts with Bund sections and Bundists in Vilkmerge and Kovno at least until 1903 (Piatnitskii 1933: 24–8, 34, 49–50). At best it would be true to say that he was active in several national/ethnic groupings at more or less the same time. Piatnitsky had contacts with the PPS between 1899 and 1900, while remaining active in the Bund, and this despite the fact that the Bund and the PPS were in direct competition for workers. As a member of Lenin's *Iskra* group after 1901, Piatnitsky continued to attend Bundist celebrations and to rely on Bundist contacts as well as activists in the PPS. Ideological commitments and identities were still fluid and multiple; they had not yet balkanized into ethnic blocs. Political radicalism was not yet a dichotomized choice between socialist universalism and an ethnic or Jewish particularism.

But Piatnitsky's radicalism was also not limited to Bundism or to Lithuania. While in prison in Kiev in 1902, he came into contact with *Iskra* prisoners and Ukrainian Socialist Revolutionaries. On his escape from a Kiev prison in 1903, he was active in the German Social Democratic Party and smuggled literature across the border from Tilsit as he worked in its illegal printing offices. In Tilsit, while working for the German Socialists, he also assisted the national-ist Lithuanian Social Democrats (LSDP) in smuggling religious literature and pamphlets across the border, and he worked with the Mensheviks (Piatnitskii 1933: 40–50, 52–6, 60–1).[5] Between 1903 and 1905, Zionism was an attractive option for disillusioned Bundists, challenging the Bund in the northwest prov-inces just as it had separated from Russian Social Democracy (Tobias 1972). But Zionism was portrayed as a movement of the Jewish capitalist middle class, something that a half-assimilated socialist radical like Piatnitsky could countenance only with difficulty. Piatnitsky's multiparty membership lacked a clearly articulated ideological position and it reflected the organizational toler-ance of the early years of revolutionary activism in Lithuania. But it still would have been too restricted within the Zionist groupings as they were then config-ured. His early political activism and ethnocultural orientations now commit-ted him to a socialist internationalism and not to a Jewish particularism, which increasingly even the Bund began to represent.

Piatnitsky therefore moved in and out of ethnic socialist mobilizations with relative ease, and although he never severed connections with the Bund, his urgency regarding cross-ethnic alliances only intensified with the pogroms in 1905. He witnessed pogrom violence and assisted in the Bund's Jewish defense effort with the future Jewish Bolshevik Iakov Gusev (Drabkin). Accustomed to the relative absence of anti-Semitism, once confronted with it, he identified both as a Jew and as a socialist internationalist. In his experiences these were not incompatible. Although pogromism was notably absent in the northwest provinces, for young, "conscious" Jews, "there was virtually no way a Jewish youngster could escape appreciating the civil liabilities of his Jewishness or avoid a sense of outrage" (Tobias 1972: 12). As we will see in connection with Gusev, Piatnitsky's involvement with the Bund's self-defense units in Odessa in 1905's revolutionary events continued to strengthen his commitment to inter-ethnic organizational alliances, in working with Bolsheviks, Bundists, Armenian Dashnaks (a nationalist party), and SRs. Piatnitsky went to Paris in 1912 just as the city became an important Bolshevik center, and he was subsequently arrested, exiled to Siberia, and released as a Bolshevik with the Revolution (Piatnitskii 1933: 173–6, 208; Prokhorov 1969–78: 293).

Piatnitsky repeatedly emphasized the cosmopolitan nature of his political involvements when he recounted 1905 events, when he described activism in Kovno, in Kiev prisons, in Leipzig between 1909 and 1912 among Poles,

[5] HIAPO, Index No. XIIIb(1), Box 123, Folder 1E, Outgoing Dispatch No.1080, 3/16 July 1913.

Lithuanians, and Jews, and in activism in German socialism in Austria and Berlin (Piatnitskii 1933: 80–8, 129, 144, 164–72). As with so many revolutionaries, he had a mixed marriage: his wife (whose first husband had been a petty officer in the Russian Army) was the daughter of an Orthodox priest and a Polish noblewoman (Piatnitskaia 1993: 6). Piatnitsky's early radicalism in Lithuania had allowed comparatively wide social space for combining Jewishness and socialism, but his own linguistic abilities allowed him to straddle ethnocultural worlds, and therefore permitted entry and exit in a variety of socialist revolutionary groupings – the German, the Polish, the Jewish, and the Russian. Assimilation had comparatively little urgency. And yet, as these groupings began finding their ethnic identities and became more restrictive, Bolshevism's Russian-inflected socialist mobilization remained ethnically open to an openly Jewish socialist like Piatnitsky.

Urgencies and Ambiguities of Jewish Assimilation and Radicalism in Ukraine

The biographies and political radicalism of the five Ukrainian Jews highlight ethnocultural worlds very different from Piatnitsky's Vilna. Ukrainian Jewry was socioeconomically and culturally differentiated, and assimilation was both more necessary and more ambiguous. These experiences were reflected in the early radicalism of this elite and in the great appeal of Russian and *rossiiskii*-oriented socialist movements. Although not from a "fanatically religious" family, Lazar Moiseevich Kaganovich spoke Yiddish in the home. His biography reflected the social world of the poor rural Jew in the Ukrainian countryside, with Jewishness invoked in the context of both violent anti-Semitism and socioeconomic tensions. Known as Stalin's "iron commissar," Kaganovich was a rural worker with little formal education, born to a farming family in 1893 near Chernobyl. Rural Jews were few outside the colonies, so this family was rather atypical. And unlike most Jewish Bolsheviks who had extensive periods of exile and emigration, Kaganovich had not lived outside Ukraine before 1917. Largely self-educated, he often made grammatical mistakes in his writing (Marcucci 1997: 21; Davies et al. 2003: 31), but he had a command of Russian, Ukrainian, and Yiddish.

Kaganovich's socioeconomic circumstances were materially difficult and made even more severe with the early death of his father (Kaganovich 1996: 20–3, 30–1). He left school at thirteen and found work in Kiev, though not before several periods of unemployment and a brief spell in the Tsarist army. Through his brother, who had been a Bolshevik since 1905, and in a village state school, Kaganovich was exposed to radical publications and to the literatures of Kiev – Gogol, Nekrasov, Tolstoy, and Shevchenko (Kaganovich 1996: 26–8, 30–1, 34–8). In this intellectual exit from rural Ukraine he barely distinguished between what was culturally Ukrainian from what was Russian. In some senses Russian and Ukrainian literatures represented the same sort of middle-class social world for the rural Jew. This stood in sharp contrast to the assimilation of the urban Kievan Jew Mikhail Uritsky (Moisei Solomonovich

Boretskii) or the Odessa Jew Trotsky, for whom the Ukrainian and the Russian were very distinct cultural options, comporting different social experiences.

Underlying the sociology of Kaganovich's early radicalism were emerging nationalist movements and populist anti-Jewish pogroms. Kaganovich (1996: 26, 41, 61) retrospectively wrote of exploitative Jewish capitalism, and he juxtaposed poor colonists and the lack of rights for small Jewish farmers against the wealth of Kiev's Jewish financiers. And indeed, once in power, Kaganovich became an unflinching proponent of class war, implementing purges of regional party organizations, railways and heavy industry, and attacking kulaks and intelligentsia. Even allowing for embellished post hoc reconstructions, there was clearly increasing socioeconomic differentiation within Ukrainian Jewry, to which Kaganovich was sensitive.

Just as importantly, however, Jewishness was experienced against these ethnic tensions. Kaganovich wrote that Jews experienced tensions between Ukrainians and Russians as pogroms, while in contrast, the Russian socialist revolutionary movement spearheaded the struggle of all oppressed nationalities under Tsarism (Kaganovich 1996: 46–7, 83–7). Socialist rhetoric aside, Russian socialist political activism did offer an organizational and political antidote to the excesses of both ethnonationalist particularism and capitalist exploitation. Interestingly, Kaganovich never calls the rightness of the empire into question. So he became a Bolshevik in 1911 in Kiev in the leatherworkers union. Recent scholarship suggests that he became a Bolshevik "out of conviction," and that he was "immensely proud of his proletarian origin" (Davies 2003: 22–34). Indeed, Marcucci (1997: 24) argues that despite Kaganovich's estrangement from his social origins in a Jewish cobbler family in a small Ukrainian village, these formative experiences nevertheless left significant imprints on his biography. Political opportunity, organizational proximity, and unemployment also have to be given causal importance, but there is nevertheless something to this. Bolshevik socialist radicalism allowed Kaganovich to cultivate his class origins while submerging his ethnic Jewishness. In the Bolshevik mobilization he was a class revolutionary first and an ethnic second. Bolshevik activism held distinctly nonethnic appeals; it permitted, and even encouraged in a noneducated rural Jew the development of a non-Jewish, assimilated identity. In this context, a largely self-read, poorly employed Ukrainian Jew could easily privilege his class over his ethnicity in a Russian-inflected radical mobilization.

Kaganovich's biographer believed that not only was his youth immersed in the pogromism endemic to the region, but also that the family likely experienced violence in the wave that swept the Gomel area in 1904 (Marcucci 1997: 19). Young Jews who experienced or witnessed violent anti-Semitism, particularly sons of poor rural Jews or those of the Jewish lower middle classes, often attempted to "survive unnoticed" or to "carry the burden passively" (Wistrich 1976: 178). This was a version of self-hatred born out of a sense of self-preservation. It caused Kaganovich to actively distance himself from his Jewish origins (Davies et al. 2003: 36), but it was precisely his Jewishness that was the important motivator for his political radicalism. He was a hard-line supporter of the purges (Conquest 1968: 34–6, 634), and as Secretary of the Ukrainian Party from 1925, he vigorously pushed through policies of Ukrainianization and grain requisitioning, actions for which he became the target of anti-Semitic attacks. In many of his appointments and policies he stoked anti-Semitism, but it was clearly something he did not mind (Davies et al. 2003: 32). Kaganovich rose to prominence as Stalin's closest deputy in the 1920s and 1930s and became the only Jew in Stalin's Politburo to survive the purges (Khlevniuk et al. 2001), in part because of his anti-Jewish ruthlessness: Beria's (2001: 164) son wrote that "between a gifted Jew and a mediocre Russian, Kaganovich always chose the Russian" because of concerns over "personal safety." Whether true or not, his Bolshevik brother committed suicide to avoid execution in the anti-Semitic paranoia.

In significant ways, Kaganovich's experiences in rural, working-class Ukraine differed from those of the four remaining Ukrainian Jews (Uritsky, Trotsky, Grigorii Zinoviev [Ovsei-Gershchen Radomyslskii], and Adolf Ioffe), and so their Jewishness was differently invoked. For them, anti-Semitism was experienced within the educated, assimilated middle classes – a very different social world. Uritsky was Chairman of the Petrograd Cheka that ordered executions of counterrevolutionaries (though he opposed the policy) just before an SR assassinated him in 1918 (Leggett 1981: 105; Granat 1989: 734). He was radicalized as part of a highly educated, culturally Russified Polish-Jewish elite in Kiev. Uritsky was born in 1873 to an Orthodox Jewish merchant family in Cherkassy, a city whose population was 37 percent Jewish (*Evreiskoe naselenie Rossii* 1970: 34; Granat 1989: 734; Bauer et al. 1991: 216–17). Although the family's actual financial status is unclear, the use of "merchant" in official biographies and in Okhrana police records suggests that they were at least nominally members of the privileged merchant estate, a small but influential capitalist middle class in Ukraine.[6] Yet relative impoverishment and status reversal followed the death of Uritsky's father, and Uritsky had to give lessons to pay *gimnaziia* fees.

The late 1880s and early 1890s were especially difficult for Kiev's Jews. Kiev's 1881–84 pogroms were among the most violent in the empire (Klier and Lambroza 1992: 43), and its paper, the *Kievlian*, was the empire's most Judeophobic periodical (Klier 1995: 182, 206). Associational life in Kiev was ethnically complex and delicate, and its tensions were expressed in both ethnically specific and multiethnic associations as they drew in middle- and working-class Jews (Meir 2003, 2006). Middle-class anti-Semitism was pervasive, affecting Russified, educated Jews in the urban liberal professions. In this social world, Uritsky was raised on the Talmud; his mother had wanted

---

[6] On Uritsky's merchant estate status, see Prokhorov 1969–78: 78; HIAPO, Index Cards, reference to Outgoing Dispatch No. 242, dated 1916, notes that he was the "son of a merchant." The actual social condition of those in the merchant estate is difficult to ascertain with precision because, despite official categorization, many may also have been included as relatively poor petty traders.

him to become a rabbi, but the assimilative power of Russian culture in the classical *gimnazii* was strong (Granat 1989: 734). His radicalism dates to his years in *gimnaziia* when he joined Russian socialist radical circles in Cherkassy in the 1880s, followed by activism at Kiev University in the 1890s. His admittance to Kiev's Law Faculty was itself remarkable because of the Jewish percentage quotas. Kiev University was almost entirely comprised of students of upper- and middle-class origin, and the key way around the percentage norms was via bribery or some form of circumvention (Avrutin 2010, on the general phenomenon).

While in university, Uritsky was attracted to both the PPS and the Kiev-based Ukrainian Socialist Democratic Union Spilka (the youth wing of the Ukrainian SDs) – activism not mentioned in official or unofficial biographies but documented in Okhrana arrest records.[7] Jews often joined the Spilka because it rejected nationalism and condemned Jewish persecutions (see Meir 2006). Kiev was at the center of both Polish and Ukrainian radicalism, and Uritsky was attracted to both. Surrounded by an elite culture alternatively dominated by Polish and Russian, assimilation would be different than it was for the artisan Piatnitsky in Lithuanian Vilna, or for Kaganovich in rural Ukraine. Severe ethnic tensions meant that Jewish life had limited social space for political organization, and so Russification held clear attractions for Kiev's ethnic minorities (Bauer et al. 1991: 415; Beauvois 1993: 285–6). Linguistically, Polish socialism retained German for much of its literature, and Uritsky was proficient in German.[8] At this time the PPS had not yet found its ethnic identity and was then still open enough to include assimilated Jews.

Uritsky's activism in the Ukrainian Spilka is less well documented. Despite high levels of Russification among educated Jews, and despite the fact that Kievan Jews were largely indifferent to Jewish culture, they were often perceived by Ukrainians and Russians as too "*proches des Polonais*" (Beauvois 1993: 311–15; Hamm 1993: 120–1; Meir 2006). There had historically been some affinity between Kiev's Ukrainian and Polish political radicals. Although 90 percent of the 1863 revolutionaries in Kiev and Volhynia were ethnic Poles, politically dissatisfied Russians and Ukrainians also joined them. In turn, many Poles were active in the Kiev Societies of Ukrainians, and they supported Ukrainian cultural rights, something which only "fueled the paranoia of Kiev's small but active Russian Nationalist Club" (Hamm 1993: 80). So Polish Kievians had a significant social presence but a notable political impotence (Beauvois 1993: 275–6).

The Ukrainian socialist movement's position on Jewry was ambivalent, and Ukrainian-Jewish relations were contentious. The leftist Ukrainian SD Party combined socialism and nationalism in the manner of the PPS, but when it

---

[7] Information in HIAPO, Index Cards, reference to Outgoing Dispatch No. 242, 1916.
[8] In fact, Uritsky and Trotsky corresponded in German; see correspondence dated 12/11/1914, *Boris I Nicolaevsky Collection*, Hoover Institution Archives, Box 185, Accession No. 63013 8.41/44, Series No. 119, Folder 17.

became more nationalist (as did the PPS), Jews were marginalized (although the PPS did have a Jewish wing). My sense is that Uritsky's Ukrainian activism was part of a deeper imperial commitment. He was culturally Polish and Russian, not Ukrainian, but it was common for Jews to ally with Poles, prompting a deep-rooted distrust of Jewish intellectuals on the part of the Ukrainian nationalist intelligentsia who viewed them as lackeys of the Polish *szlachta* or of the Russian state (Klier 1995: 110–11). Jewish intellectuals in Ukraine were a minority increasingly caught between two anti-Semitic nationalisms, and this is what may have motivated Uritsky. This typically manifested in political alliance with the culturally dominant Polish or with the statist Russian. While Ukrainian nationalists argued that Russified Jews in radical parties only strengthened their centralist tendencies showing indifference to local differences (Frankel 1981: 218–19), Polish socialism and RSDLP-allied Ukrainian socialism offered Uritsky an organizational, radical form of an imperial, multi-ethnic vision, a response to Polish and Ukrainian nationalisms alike.

Uritsky obtained a law degree in 1897 (Granat 1989: 734), yet its value was diminished by the fact that by then Jews had been almost entirely excluded from the Russian *advokatura*. The *advokatura* had historically been open to all regardless of ethnic or religious origin, and so it had become a crucial venue for mobility and social position for educated and assimilating Jews (Baberowski 1995: 498–9; Pomeranz 1999: 251–2). But the Russification of the once ethnically open *advokatura* blocked this venue of Jewish social mobility (Kucherov 1966: 222). Unable to practice law, Uritsky joined the imperial army in 1897 or 1898 (Granat 1989: 734).[9] His stay may have been as little as eight days – it ended because of his record of radicalism – and this triggered arrest, imprisonment, exile, and emigration.[10] This would not have been uncommon: Russian-Jewish loyalty and patriotism were notable, and until 1917 Russia's Jews largely supported the imperial army (Petrovsky-Shtern 2009b: ch. 5). As a wartime émigré and Menshevik from 1903, Uritsky was involved in Trotsky's *Nashe Slovo* and Mezhraionka group, becoming a Bolshevik with Trotsky. Uritsky's initial political radicalism was as an assimilating Jew, excluded from middle-class possibilities by the imperial state's ethnic policies. His eventual attraction to Russian socialism, first Menshevism then Bolshevism, remained an option that gave these experiences political and organizational expression.

Like Uritsky, Zinoviev, Trotsky, and Ioffe were of the same generation of educated, urbane, and Europeanized middle-class Jews. Zinoviev was born in

---

[9] This is omitted from official biographies. He served as a *vol'nopredeliaiushchiisiia* (loosely translated as a "non-draftee") – a person with secondary education serving terms in the Tsarist army under privileged conditions.

[10] Uritsky was exiled to Iakutsk in 1899. After participation in events in 1905 in St. Petersburg and Krasnoiarsk, he was arrested in 1906 and again exiled. He spent several years in emigration before 1914. Documented in Okhrana records: HIAPO, Index Card File referencing dispatches: 1226, 1222, 1363, 594, 757, 979, 994, 6100, 22, 157, 940, 1134, 118, 1451, 1680, 1128, 913; *Nicolaevsky Collection*, Box 185, Accession No. 63013 8.41/44, Series 119, Folder 17, Letters dated November 14, 1913 and August 13, 1913.

1883 in Elizavetgrad, to owners of a small milk firm. The family was not especially well off, so Zinoviev worked at a young age to contribute to the family's keep (Granat 1989: 418). Trotsky was born to a family of wealthy landowner farmers (Trotsky 1970: 5–7; Granat 1989: 720), and Ioffe was born in 1883 to a family of wealthy merchants from Simferopol (Crimea). Owners of the transport and postal services in the Crimea, they owned a home in Moscow, and carried the title "hereditary distinguished citizen," because Ioffe's father was considered a "favorite Jew" of Witte's (Prokhorov 1969–78: 390; Granat 1989: 422; Joffe 1995: 3; Ioffe 1997: 29). They were Karaites, a small Jewish sect of Lutsk (Volhynia), Troki (Lithuania), and the Crimea, with a lineage culturally distinct from the Yiddish-speaking Jews of the Pale and notably tolerated by the imperial state (Klier 1995: 10). This made Ioffe's Jewishness unique among the Bolsheviks.

Zinoviev, Trotsky, and Ioffe were active in European socialist revolutionary politics in addition to the Russian émigré colonies, so their political radicalism and assimilation highlight the world of émigré *Ostjuden* in Central Europe. Zinoviev first became involved in radical circles in the late 1890s (Nodgot 1990: 59). He was home-educated to pass the examination for the *gimnaziia* maturity certificate and was forced to continue his studies abroad – a pattern typical of thousands of Russian Jewish students who were excluded from Russian universities because of percentage norms, political radicalism, or both (Nodgot 1990: 59). First arrested in 1901, Zinoviev emigrated to Berlin, and then to Paris, Geneva, and Berne, always associating himself after 1903 with Lenin and the Bolsheviks.[11] Under police surveillance, in Paris, Zinoviev edited the Russian SD's central publication.[12] He became active in German and Swiss Social Democracy while studying at Berne University's Chemistry and Law Faculties (Granat 1989: 418–19).[13] At the outbreak of the Great War he was in Galicia with Lenin and the Zimmerwald Left, and he became co-editor-in-chief of *Pravda* at the time of the Revolution (Granat 1989: 419–20).

Ioffe's political radicalism similarly began while in *gimnaziia* in the late 1890s as the labor movement was taking off in the area. By 1899, he was active in Social Democratic circles in Simferopol, devoting part of his family's wealth to the cause (Granat 1989: 422). Ioffe's ability to enter *gimnaziia* despite the Jewish quotas may testify both to his Karaite status and to his family's financial ability to circumvent regulations. In 1902, he joined the RSDLP, was labeled politically unreliable, barred from entering any Russian university, and finally left for Berlin to continue his studies (Granat 1989: 422). On the evidence, his exclusion was not on the basis of his Jewishness, but rather his

---

[11] *Granat* has it in 1903, but in his 1934 autobiography he wrote that he met Lenin in 1902; Nodgot 1990: 59, and note 3.
[12] HIAPO, Box 198, Index XVIId–XVIIh, Index XVIIe, Folder 5, Spravka No. 36.
[13] He was arrested in Petersburg in 1908, and this was followed by a period of surveillance in Elizavetgrad. By August 1908, he was at the RSDLP plenum in Geneva, and in 1909 in Paris. HIAPO, Box 198, Index Nos. XVIId–XVIIh, Index No. XVIIe, Folder 5, 'Spravka,' No. 36; Box 198, Index Nos.XVIId–XVIIh, Index XVIIe, Folder 4, No. 1000, Paris June 20/July 3, 1913.

record of political radicalism. This initiated many years in emigration: he was in Berlin in 1903 to study medicine, and there he joined the German Social Democratic Party (Ioffe 1997: 30). Deported in 1906 or 1907, Ioffe went to Zurich to study law and joined the Swiss Socialist Party (Granat 1989: 422–3; Joffe 1995: 4). He was in Vienna in Trotsky's Vienna club between 1908 and 1912, working on *Pravda* (Ioffe 1997: 31–2). And between 1912 and 1917, Ioffe was imprisoned in Odessa and in exile in Siberia, where he worked for the first time as a physician and from where he wrote a series of letters that testified to his fragile nervous state, prefiguring later nervous breakdowns (Granat 1989: 423; Joffe 1995: 6).[14]

If Zinoviev's early radicalism was linked to Lenin, Ioffe's early radicalism as an émigré in Central Europe was, like Uritsky's, closely connected to Trotsky. Trotsky's life is so well known that I only highlight two relevant aspects of his identity and early radicalism: the ambiguities of Jewish middle-class assimilation in Ukraine (in contrast with that of Kaganovich's poor, rural Jewish acculturation) and his later experiences as an émigré in Central Europe (Granat 1989: 720–1). Like most agricultural Jews in the Steppe, Trotsky's family was semi-Russified and spoke a combination of Ukrainian and Russian (Deutscher 1954: 7; Trotsky 1970: 18). Trotsky's father had bought and leased land in a German-Jewish farming colony in Kherson province (Trotsky 1970: 5–7; Granat 1989: 720). Deutscher (1954: 5–6) observed that Trotsky's family was "illiterate, indifferent to religion ... [appearing] almost completely un-Jewish." Though hit hard by the agricultural crises of the 1880s, the Bronsteins became wealthy landowner-farmers.

Trotsky was sent to a Yiddish-speaking *kheder* in a local German-Jewish colony near Kherson. He failed entrance into an Odessa *gimnaziia* in 1887, although it is not clear if it was because of the *numerus clausus*, but he was admitted in 1888 to a Russified, liberal, multiethnic German-Lutheran *Realschule*, a springboard to Odessa's Jewish Europeanized intelligentsia (Trotsky 1970: 45–6). Trotsky then studied at the Mathematics Faculty as an *auditeur libre* (Granat 1989: 720), but by 1897 he organized workers in Marxist circles. Trotsky became a Menshevik in 1909 after editing *Pravda* and the Ukrainian Spilka's journal in Lwöw (on the latter, see account in Granat 1989: 722).

Unlike Kaganovich's early influences, Yiddish was not spoken in Trotsky's home. And unlike Ioffe's Jewish family life (Ioffe 1997: 29), Trotsky's autobiography was more concerned to stress his father as a privileged kulak who mistreated the farm laborers than any sense of Jewishness (Wistrich 1976: 192). Trotsky famously wrote: "[I]n my mental equipment, nationality never occupied an independent place, as it was felt but little in everyday life. ... The language of my family and household was Russian-Ukrainian ... [and] I was not

---

[14] HIAPO, Index XIIIb(1), Box 122, Folder 1A; Ioffe's prison letters from Odessa in *Nicolaevsky Collection*, Box 186, Series 119, Folder 9 and Box 41, Accession No. 63013 8.41/44, Series 16, Folder 30; for Ioffe's famous suicide letter, see Box 627, Accession No. 63013 8.41/44, Series 276, Folder A.

personally affected by the [Jewish percentage] restrictions … national inequality probably was one of the underlying causes of my dissatisfaction with the existing order, but it … never played a leading part – not even a recognized one – in the list of my grievances" (Trotsky 1970: 86–7).

Given such clarity of denial of Jewishness, much has been written about whether or not Trotsky had a "Jewish complex." His often quoted exclamation, "I am not a Jew, I am an internationalist," has been contested for its display of contrived indifference to his Jewish origins (see, inter alia, Wistrich 1976, 1979; Pipes 2000). Trotsky may have been indifferent to his Jewishness, but he was not unaware of it, and neither was he unaware of wider anti-Semitism in Russia or elsewhere. Plenty of autobiographical evidence of Jews' experiences across the empire's educational institutions suggests that anti-Semitism existed even in elite secondary schools, albeit often in subtle and indirect forms, and that Jewish students tended to form friendships and networks (mirroring their residential patterns) with other Jewish students. In choosing a name for his passport (used in police surveillance, among other things) in 1902, Trotsky went with the name "Trotskii" because it seemed noncommittal from the standpoint of race – an important recognition that Jews were arrested at higher rates than Russians (Medvedev 1983: 155; Granat 1989: 720–1). As a foreign correspondent for *Kievskaia Mysl* among Serbian, Bulgarian, and Rumanian nationalists and socialists during the war, he wrote polemically and movingly of the Romanian "Jewish question" and its anti-Semitism, in descriptions that could easily have applied to his own Russia (Deutscher 1954: 202–27; Trotsky 1970: 226–9; Weissman and Williams 1982: especially 226, 229, 230).

Trotsky's Jewishness was less important in his early life than in his later career as a Bolshevik – when he become "the *zhid* Trotsky" in anti-Bolshevik propaganda, for example – but even as an avowed non-Jewish Jew he must have been keenly aware of a certain ascriptive Jewishness, if only by actively choosing to disavow it. Here we encounter a subtle and suggestive difference between Kaganovich's erasure of his ethnic roots and Trotsky's: for the uneducated, rural Ukrainian Jew Kaganovich, there was, as noted, a certain self-hatred born out of a sense of self-preservation, as direct experiences of violent anti-Semitism had taught him how to "survive unnoticed"; for the educated middle-class Trotsky, self-hatred was tied to middle-class assimilation that made him acutely aware of Gentile sensibilities and sociabilities. It was perhaps, as Wistrich (1976: 8) suggested, part of a wider youthful nihilism, a "general attitude of negation, iconoclasm, non-conformism, rebellion." And yet it was Trotsky who changed his name, not Kaganovich.

The most common claim has been that Trotsky had found intellectual attraction in Marxism's scientific universalism. Deutscher (1968: 27, 35–6) thought that living on the borderlines of ethnicities – that is, being a Jew in the Russian Empire – had given Trotsky a certain cognitive privilege: "in society but not of it," Trotsky could "see societies in flux" and "comprehend great movements." Trotsky's own account held that his innate rationalism had prompted within him a search for universal laws and basic regularities, "the supremacy of the general over the particular experience, of law over fact, of theory over personal experience," which socialism's universalist historicism provided (Deutscher 1968: 35; Wistrich 1976: 192; 1979: 16).

While Trotsky's preference for socialism's "Roman universalism over Greek parochialism" may have been as much a product of circumstance (Wistrich 1976: 192) or psychological predilection, it may also be that both Deutscher's and Trotsky's accounts are perhaps too strictly intellectualist: there was also, I think, an attraction to certain ideas because he lacked a certain ethnocultural belonging. In Central Europe, for many Germanized Jewish liberals like Karl Popper, the antidote to the more nuanced and less direct anti-Semitism felt in educated, middle-class milieux had been an uncompromising liberal assimilationism (but for an account of an entirely unique response, see Hall 2010 on Ernest Gellner). Indeed Popper's biographer suggests that this call for assimilation itself worryingly bordered on anti-Semitism (Hacohen 1999: 110, 145–6). Similarly for a young educated Trotsky, it was through assimilation or Russification that he could experiment with forming his identity, and it was in the choice of a universalist revolutionary ideology and a classless, international society that he could find both intellectual and existential belonging independent of ethnic roots. Whether the need to dissolve ethnic origins was born out of a need for self-preservation or out of a radical, iconoclastic nihilism, for both Trotsky and Kaganovich the practical, political solution to "Jewishness" was in the socialist assimilationism of a class-universalist radical mobilization.

Between 1907 and 1914, Trotsky, like Ioffe and Zinoviev, lived in Vienna and Berlin in intellectual community with Austrian and German socialists. He wrote disdainfully of Austrian Marxism and the Herr Doktors, but he was deeply impressed by the then more internationalist German Socialist movement. Certainly Europeanized, multilingual, and urbane, Trotsky, Ioffe, and Zinoviev were in communities with other Europeanized and acculturating Jews. And often the language in the Vienna cafés was Viennese-German and Yiddish, a subtle reinforcement of acculturating Jews' acculturation with other acculturating Jews. Yet there was in this social world not only a familiarity but also a subtle complicity: in contrast to Kaganovich's pride in his class origins, as sons of wealthy Jewish capitalists they sought to submerge, repudiate, or compensate for both their ethnic *and* class roots.

But Russian Jews in these émigré colonies experienced their identities, both private and political, in even more ambiguous ways. Trotsky, Ioffe, Uritsky, and Zinoviev were well aware of their status as exiles and émigrés; schooled in Tsarist prisons and Siberian hard labor, they were a contrast to the refined and more intellectualist Viennese socialists who plotted revolution over cups of tea. As émigrés, they were aware of their *Ostjuden* status, making identity dilemmas even more complex and their own Russified assimilation even more ambiguous. In this social world there was an implicit sense of hierarchy, or the superiority of the Jews of Vienna and Berlin. Joseph Roth movingly wrote of the intense antipathy that Viennese Jews felt for their (in his case) Galician coreligionists. Within assimilated Viennese Jewish circles, *Ostjuden* were of a discernibly different status (Wistrich 1982: 219). In some ways Trotsky responded as had German-Jewish liberals: a general disdain for the "backward" *Ostjuden* only intensified their insecurities over where and whether they belonged, and therefore prompted a greater urgency to assimilation.

Russkie Evrei: *Radicalism and Russification in the Russian Interior*
Unlike Lithuanian and Ukrainian Jews, *russkie evrei* lived in more homogenous ethnocultural worlds. The term *russkie evrei*, or Russian Jew, was first used in the 1850s. Though comparatively few, they were products of what Nathans (2002) terms "selective emancipation" from the Pale of Settlement through access to imperial educational and employment opportunities in the Russian heartland. Sokolnikov (Brilliant), Iakov Sverdlov (Morshevich Solomon), Lev Kamenev (Borosovich Resonfeld), Zelensky, and Gusev's fathers were all employed by the imperial state, enabling them to live in Saratov, Nizhny Novgorod, and Moscow. Some went to great pains to stress their atheism (Gusev and Yaroslavsky) and their complete erasure of any Jewishness (Sverdlov). But others openly identified themselves as Jews: Kamenev in Bundist activism and Sokolnikov as the victim of anti-Semitism.

The assimilated identities of the Russian Jews and anti-Semitic experiences in the Russian interior differed from those of Lithuanian and Ukrainian Jews. In the educated middle-class world of the Russian *gimnazii* in Moscow, anti-Semitism was subtle: disturbing glances, minor exclusions, and harassments. Russian *gimnazii* did have anti-Semitism of the "civic" kind, where allusions to race were seen by Jews merely as rude; as Iulii Martov wrote, prejudices were rife in secondary schools, giving rise to a "spontaneous view of ourselves as an inferior race" (quoted in Wistrich 1976: 178), although anti-Semitism was generally much less pronounced in student milieux (Nathans 2002: ch. 6).

This was the case for Sokolnikov. He wrote that he was forced to confront his Jewishness in the context of the more nuanced anti-Semitism of a Moscow *gimnaziia* (Granat 1989: 681). Sokolnikov's ability to attend a Moscow *gimnaziia* reflected his family's privileged social status and general integration: they lived in Ukraine, but his father was employed by the imperial state as a medical doctor on the railroads, so he was allowed in the Russian interior. Sokolnikov studied the classics, attended politically oriented study circles, and was active in the SRs. In 1905, he became a Bolshevik. Sokolnikov was arrested in 1909 and imprisoned in Boutyrka before exile to Enisei (Granat 1989: 682). Unable to attend Russian university because of a combination of radicalism and Jewish quotas, he studied law in Paris where he obtained a doctorate in economics. Sokolnikov was later active in the Swiss Socialist Party (Granat 1989: 682–3).[15]

In contrast to Sokolnikov's experiences of "civic anti-Semitism" as an assimilating middle-class Russian Jew, Gusev's sense of Jewishness was awakened

---

[15] HIAPO, Index XIIIb (1), Box 126, 1G, Outgoing dispatch No. 1412, December 3/16, 1915.

early and violently. He was born in a settlement in Riazan, the son of school-teachers; at age four, Gusev was beaten in the street as a "*zhid*," of which he later wrote – somewhat incredibly – that for the first time he became dissatisfied with the existing order (Granat 1989: 399). His family moved near Saratov where he wrote that the "spirit of fanaticism" pervaded several of the village taverns, and at age sixteen he witnessed what he believed to be a pogrom (Granat 1989: 399). Gusev's autobiography is one of the few in which there are extensive references to anti-Jewish violence, something he believed was organized by the Tsarist state. He "saw a merger of blood and vodka," a reference to innkeeping and the liquor trade, one of the most prevalent occupations of village Jews. He was required to read the Jewish prayer books and the Bible, and subsequently wrote of his hatred and aversion to Hebrew and of his disgust with God and religion (Granat 1989: 399). This was remedied when he entered radical circles in *Realschule*. As part of a rebellion against the experiences of Jewishness, he was captivated by French literature and by Darwinism, with the consequence that in 1891, Gusev was temporarily expelled from *Realschule* for preaching atheism.

Gusev's early religious training and identity as a Jew was experientially entwined with the violent anti-Semitism surrounding him. He completed *Realschule* in 1892, but he was initially denied admission to the St. Petersburg Technological Institute because of "increased competition among Jews," a reference to the *numerus clausus* (Granat 1989: 399–400).[16] His ethnicity – not his radicalism – blocked entry into university. Unemployment followed, and during a brief eight-month position in a bank, Gusev came into contact with *Narodnaia volia* radicals, read *Capital*, and joined SR circles – unsurprising because he would anyway have had limited access to specifically Jewish political movements (Granat 1989: 400).

Gusev found refuge from Jewishness in these Russian-inflected radical mobilizations. Jewish radicalism in *rossiiskii* or imperial-minded movements should not be underestimated: there were significant numbers of "Jewish Jews" in Russian Populist and SR movements of the 1880s (Haberer 1995: ch. 10). At the time of his early radicalism with *Narodnaia volia*, the general position of the socialist populist movement was that pogrom violence was a product of the character of the regime. Gusev joined these groups at a time when they were undergoing important transformations. Although *Narodnaia volia* had failed in 1881 to adequately respond to the pogroms because of latent slavophilic and judeophobic tendencies, the general position of *Zemlia i Volia* (its predecessor) of St. Petersburg had been (1) a rejection of Jews as a minority, (2) a condemnation of pogroms on the grounds that pogrom violence stoked national antagonisms at the expense of a peoples' revolution, and (3) a reiteration of the need for solidarity among workers across religions, nationalities, and ethnicities (Mishkinsky 1992). So Gusev's early radicalism drew him to

---

[16] Other sources say he entered the Institute immediately; see Prokhorov 1969–78: 460–1 and Lazitch 1986: 160. The latter may have used the Prokhorov account. I use Gusev's.

radical political movements that not only largely repudiated anti-Semitism but also, and more significantly, allowed him to cultivate an existentially much needed non-Jewish identity in the Russian interior.

Gusev was admitted to the St. Petersburg Technological Institute in 1896, and after several years' activity as an SR joined the RSDLP, officially becoming a Bolshevik in 1903 (Kopanev 1967: 311; Prokhorov 1969–78: 460–1; Granat 1989: 400). Although this was mentioned only in passing in his autobiography, and not at all in official sources, Gusev was deeply involved, *as a Bolshevik*, in the protection of Jews in Odessa during the 1905–06 pogroms. The sketchy accounts are contained in Piatnitsky's memoirs, as they worked together for the Odessa SDs (Piatnitskii 1933: ch. 4). Gusev had been involved in student Bolshevik organizations in Odessa and in the technical apparatus of the Odessa committee (Piatnitskii 1933: 76–7). Already Bolsheviks, Gusev and Piatnitsky worked closely with the Bundist self-defense organizations. The 1905 confrontations in Odessa were between the forces of reaction (Black Hundreds) and the forces of revolution (the socialist parties) (Weinberg 1992: 259). Yet it was precisely because Jews were prominent in the leftist parties that they also became targets of both reactionary social forces and of a state that feared social revolution. Odessa's manufacturing was mostly small-scale, with committees representing Mensheviks, Bund, SRs, Armenian Dashnaks, and Bolsheviks. Bundists, SRs, Mensheviks, Bolsheviks, Poale-Zionists, and Dashnaks organized federated joint resistance and set up defensive armed detachments. According to Piatnitsky, they were impeded by the fact that police, Cossacks, and cavalry defended the pogromists, and on the second day of the pogroms Gusev terminated Bolshevik involvement because they were "losing too many comrades" (Piatnitskii 1933: 86–8). By 1909, Gusev had experienced beatings as a "*zhid*," prison, surveillance, unemployment, anti-Jewish percentage norms, pogrom violence, and emigration. These experiences came at a price: he suffered from a prolonged nervous breakdown between 1909 and 1917, which incapacitated him until the revolution released him from it (Lazitch 1986: 160; Granat 1989: 401).

In contrast to Sokolnikov and Gusev, the early radicalism of the remaining Russian Jews – Sverdlov, Kamenev, Zelensky, and Emilian Yaroslavsky (Gubelman) – invoked Jewishness only tangentially; their politicization was perhaps more closely tied to easy access to radical political circles and to unemployment. Before his death of Spanish flu in 1919, Sverdlov was the key organizational figure around Lenin between 1913 and 1918. Zelensky was less known. Both were from the large Jewish *meshchanstvo*, but that their families lived in Nizhny Novogorod and Saratov, respectively, suggests that they took advantage of social openings that allowed skilled Jewish artisans to reside in the Russian interior. Zelensky was born in 1890 into a lower-middle-class family: his father was a tailor and soldier in the imperial army, and Zelensky himself became a tailor after completing elementary school (Prokhorov 1969–78: 453; Granat 1989: 417). While little is known of his social circumstances, he worked closely with Kamenev and was active in the SDs from the age of sixteen. This resulted in years of arrest, imprisonment, surveillance, and exile until 1917.

Sverdlov, by contrast, began his political activities at age seventeen in Nizhny Novgorod, where he was involved with the SRs through his brothers (one of whom was adopted by Gorky). He was born in 1885 in relatively cosmopolitan and progressive Nizhny Novgorod. His father, a skilled engraver and owner of a printing shop, lead an impoverished but assimilated lower-middle-class existence. Sverdlov attended a classical *gimnaziia*, but after four years could no longer afford the fees as the family's material circumstances deteriorated (Granat 1989: 651). He subsequently worked as an apprentice in a pharmacy and did clandestine party work in Sormovo.

The SRs were the older tradition in the area, following the populists. According to his biographer, Sverdlov's failure to secure steady, gainful employment was the main reason for his becoming a professional revolutionary in Sormovo factories (Duval 1971: 36). This seems a fair assessment, but his family's radicalism (his family's apartment was a depot for illegal literature and armaments [Duval 1971: 19; Granat 1989: 651]) and relatively easy access to radical political mobilizations must also be given causal roles. Later revolutionary activism brought him to the Urals and long periods of administrative exile in Tomsk and Turkhansk (see Plotnikov 1976 on Sverdlov's exile), where he taught Russian to non-Russian and native peoples.

Sverdlov always identified himself as Russian and he married a Russian woman. In explaining why he never joined the Bund, he wrote, "I never felt a nationalist yoke or was persecuted as a Jew. In fact during the first days of Kishinev pogrom I felt nothing which separated me from the attitude of the non-Jewish population" (quoted in Duval 1971: 53).[17] These were relatively ethnically neutral social spaces, so that attitude would have been indifference. Sverdlov had apparently never faced anti-Semitism or persecution as a Jew either in Nizhny Novgorod or while engaged in party work in the Urals. This seems consistent with the historical scholarship: anti-Semitism was common in the western provinces, Poland, and the Pale, but less so among most ethnic Russians of the interior who had only the most minimal contact with Jews. Yet Sverdlov was not insensitive to anti-Semitism: he later opposed Trotsky's appointment as Commissar of Internal Affairs because he thought the latter's Jewish background problematic for such a post.

Similarly, Kamenev and Yaroslavsky's parents were also political radicals: Kamenev was born in Moscow in 1883 to parents who had themselves been radical students in the 1870s. Born in 1878, Yaroslavsky was radicalized in a penal colony in Chita, which was comprised of deportees, convicts, and political

---

[17] Whether Sverdlov felt himself Jewish or not, even Jews regarded him as such: the poem "I am a Jew" by the Yiddish poet Itsik Gefer, who was later repressed with the Jewish anti-Fascist Committee, read: "On my pride in Sverdlov I depend, And on Kaganovich, Stalin's friend," (quoted in Rubenstein and Naumov 2001: 2–13).

prisoners forced by the courts to settle in remote areas after completing prison sentences. Yaroslavsky's father was a skilled furrier and then became a teacher; his mother had an elementary school education (Prokhorov 1969–78: 558; Granat 1989: 785). In fact, the Chita colony's radicals from the 1860s through the 1880s were primarily of petty bourgeois origin (Granat 1989: 785). It does not appear that it was his families' Jewish origin that placed them there, but rather their radicalism: members of his mother's family had joined the revolutionary Decembrists in the 1820s.

Like Sokolnikov, Kamenev felt himself Jewish, but for Yaroslavsky, as with Sverdlov, Jewishness was not a claimed identity. Indeed Yaroslavsky often referred to Jews in the third person. Kamenev was a converted "half-Jew" – his father was Jewish and his mother Russian. Although his parents' mixed marriage would have entailed the conversion of his father,[18] thereby diluting the son's Jewishness, Kamenev would later be active in the Jewish Bund anyway. His father had been educated at St. Petersburg Technical Institute, and worked as an engineer in a nail factory, and later, when the family moved to Vilna, as a railroad mechanic (Granat 1989: 427). In Vilna, Kamenev worked summers in a factory as a joiner and locksmith and attended *gimnaziia* until age thirteen when the family moved to Tiflis because of his father's employment with the state railroad.

Yaroslavsky and Kamenev were active in other radical groups prior to becoming Bolsheviks. Like Piatnitsky, in Vilna, Kamenev had been simultaneously active in the Bund and in the RSDLP. He was not from a devout family, but clearly he felt himself sufficiently Jewish for Bundist activism. Kamenev completed secondary school in Tiflis and continued his activities in Marxist circles in the Caucasus around 1903 (Granat 1989: 427; Donkov 1990: 90). In Tiflis, the political options for young radicals were the SRs and SDs. Kamenev chose the latter and worked with cobblers and railroad workers in Nakhalova, although it is unclear whether he was a Bolshevik at the time, given that the Mensheviks were the predominant party in the region, and there was anyway no practical organizational divide between them and the Bolsheviks (Granat 1989: 427). But he worked with Georgian SDs in an organizationally *rossiiskii*, multiethnic mobilization (Jones 2005: 123). He was expelled from *gimnaziia* for political radicalism with admonitions from school authorities, and subsequently had a difficult time gaining admittance to university. He continually petitioned the Minister of Public Education for the right to enter university and was finally admitted to Moscow University Law Faculty in search of a political career. He continued revolutionary activism, however, and so he was again expelled and deported to Siberia. The evidence suggests that it was his record of radicalism, not his Jewish origin, that had caused these difficulties (Haupt and Marie 1969: 40).

---

[18] I thank the late John Klier for this observation.

Similarly inescapably influenced by his surroundings, Yaroslavsky's first political involvement, like Gusev's, was with *Narodnaia volia*, the first radical groups in the area before the SDs. After attending state elementary schools, Yaroslavsky attended *gimnaziia*. At age nine he worked as a bookbinder and then for a pharmacist and as a legal clerk (Granat 1989: 785). In 1898, the year he joined the SDs at age twenty, he sat an exam to become a pharmacist's assistant, something he was unable to pursue because of trouble with the authorities. He therefore began organizing SD circles of workers on the Transbaikal Railroad (Prokhorov 1969–78: 558; Granat 1989: 785).

Both Yaroslavsky and Kamenev had difficulties finding employment because of their radicalism. In 1902, after expulsion from university, arrest, and Siberian exile, emigration remained Kamenev's only option. In Paris he met Lenin and began to write for the *Iskra*, but his activism with the Jewish Bund continued even while in emigration: at a Bundist reunion, Kamenev met his future wife – Trotsky's sister. This was followed by arrest, imprisonment, police surveillance, and another failed attempt to reenter university (Granat 1989: 428). So Kamenev immersed himself in revolutionary work in the Caucasus, Moscow, and St. Petersburg. After a 1908 arrest, he was in Geneva with Lenin to edit the Bolshevik paper *Proletarii*. During the Great War and then the Revolution, Kamenev was in Zurich, Kracow, Paris, Finland, and Siberian exile. He was caught in the Finnish civil war and imprisoned by the Whites until 1918 (Granat 1989: 429–30).[19] Similarly, after a brief time in Berlin and Paris, Yaroslavsky was arrested during 1905 revolutionary events and in 1907 he was sentenced to five years hard labor (Granat 1989: 787).[20] Between 1898 and 1901, he served in the Tsarist army in the Eighteenth Siberian Rifleman's Regiment. His immediate postrevolutionary writings notably revolved around antireligious party work (Iaroslavskii 1925: esp. 278–84).

In sum, then, the Russian Jews' early radicalism and identities highlight the continued ascriptive significance of the *russkie evrei*, despite assimilation and Russification in the Russian interior (Dubnow, Kaznelson, and Günzburg 1912–14, vol. III: 336–7). While Sokolnikov, Gusev, and Kamenev articulated their Jewishness through Bundist activism, or in activism against violent anti-Semitism, Sverdlov and Yaroslavsky vigorously claimed Russianness. All but Zelensky had been active in revolutionary movements other than Bolshevism, and yet all six became Bolsheviks long before 1917. Whereas certain imperial policies of "selective emancipation" allowed the residential and educational incorporation of delimited categories of Jews, other Tsarist strategies of dissimilatory Russification or exclusion stigmatized identity ascriptions; and strategies of measurement, social control, and surveillance ensured that even the most thoroughly assimilated would be politicized.

---

[19] See also HIAPO, Index XIIIb (7), Box 124, Folder 1F, Outgoing dispatches No. 1276, 7/20 Aug. 1913.
[20] See correspondence on his Siberian exile, *Nicolaevsky Collection*, Box 441, Series 288, Folder 3.

The Liberal Universalist Option

A Russian-inflected socialist universalism, however, was not the only non-Jewish political option on offer. Liberal universalism was also available. The relationships among Jewish exclusion, assimilation, and attraction to universalist revolutionary ideologies were neither unique nor uncomplicated. Russian Jews' political activism in populist and socialist mobilizations sought the equality of ethnically neutral social worlds inside a universalist socialism. But if universalism, as Cynthia Ozick (quoted in Stanislawski 2001: 9) has written, is "the ultimate Jewish parochialism," it is one that in its fundamentals adheres to more general universalist claims of political modernity (Slezkine 2004). The so-called Jewish predicament embodied not only specific, ethnically Jewish realities; it was also emblematic of the requirements of a meritocratic, universalist modern society. This makes it difficult to disentangle middle-class intelligentsia sources of radicalism from ethnic ones, particularly in an illiberal multiethnic – but Russianizing – empire.

Crucially, then, assimilation requires social allies, and this was a sociological condition not met in the ethnopolitical climate of late Imperial Russia. As Ernest Gellner (1998: 82) put it, "a Jew in *lederhosen* does not become a Tyrolean": one can claim assimilation, but it is only if Tyroleans recognize you as one of their own that one goes from coexistence to integration (on Gellner's own response, see Hall 2010). Without the necessary social allies, even the most articulate liberal universalism is too weak to defend assimilation (one lesson of Hacohen 2000). The social and political weakness of Russian liberalism and the growing strength of the nationalist movements (including the *Staatsvolk* variety) made social allies for assimilation hard to come by. In certain respects, for Jewish assimilation the differences between liberal universalist politics and the socialist universalism of the left were less ideological than they were a matter of political context and sociological possibility.

Russian liberalism as a political option, for instance, was anchored in different generational and social locations, and it was politically weak as it was outflanked by extremist politics. Liberalism remained centrist and statist, socialism class-based and internationalist; and whereas Jewish liberalism remained Jewish, Russian Jewish socialism on the whole sought to submerge its Jewishness. While Russian liberal politics broadened in the early 1900s from its previously gentry and *zemstvo* social bases to include much of the professional middle classes and intelligentsia, and although it did turn leftward, it was nevertheless matched on one side by growing Russian (and minority) nationalisms and on the other by increasingly powerful socialist mobilizational politics. Of course the social and political weakness of the moderate, liberal middle of the political spectrum was not singular to Russia, but it was perhaps most consequential here: Tsarism's increasingly intransigent and repressive policies coupled with populist pogrom violence discredited moderate opposition and strengthened political extremism.

For the Jewish Bolsheviks' generation coming of political age in the late 1880s and 1890s, socialist political radicalism (like Zionism) offered a distinct youthful appeal: its Russian-inflected ideological narrative combined the attractiveness of Russian culture with the class-universalist promise of erasing distinctions between Jew and Gentile in a spirit of true equality, and it experientially located all of this within a particularly potent youth culture of self-sacrifice. Slezkine (2004: 173) captures it nicely: "[S]uspended between the illegitimate patriarchies of family and autocracy, they created a durable youth culture imbued with intense millenarian expectation, powerful internal cohesion, and a self-worship so passionate it could be consummated only through self-immolation. ... [The] temple of youth ...was both very large and very welcoming." Institutionally and organizationally the multiethnic, all-Russian socialist parties also mirrored the empire itself, and experientially provided a response to the sociopolitical tensions of ethnonationalist particularism. Bolshevism became the mobilizational product of certain ethnopolitical isolation and organizational marginalization. This is crucial for understanding this particular Bolshevik elite's attraction to socialism over liberalism.

Moreover, the social profile of Jewish liberalism at the turn of the century differed from that of Jewish socialism in several important respects – and it did so in ways that mirror those outlined in Chapter 2, Table 2.2. It was, on the one hand, more intellectual, culturalist, and upper-middle-class in composition (see, for instance, Fischer 1958; Gassenschmidt 1995). Liberalism tended, in other words, to attract different segments of the Jewish intelligentsia, broadly defined, and there may have been more of a déclassé element within the socialist movement. Liberalism's activists were funneled from different social locations, based on slightly different relationships to the imperial state, and they drew from less problematic socioethnic positions. Among other things, this gave liberal political movements a different set of social resources. And because of its late development, Russian-Jewish liberalism was less assimilationist than acculturationist, so it generally retained religious dimensions of identity (Gassenschmidt 1995: 136–40). Jewish liberals were more articulately and openly Jewish in identity than were Jewish socialists, and this also made it less appealing to assimilating Jewish youth.

Conclusion

Thus ethnopolitical realities and Tsarist imperial strategies combined to give Jewish assimilation an urgent and fragile character: ancien regime Judeophobia, the Jew as *inorodets*, the ethnicization of Russian national identities, social control as public and private coercion, the anti-Semitism of the rising middling classes, and the fears and humiliations of pogroms – and latterly even the growing anti-Semitism in the upper eschelons of the military during the war years (on the latter, see Petrovsky-Shtern 2009b: ch. 5) – all combined to create particular illiberal social worlds. These were not subtle exclusions. A generalized culture of anti-Semitism, both private and official, permeated these social locations. For Gusev, Kaganovich, and Piatnitsky, violent anti-Semitism was direct and unambiguous; for Sokolnikov and Uritsky, exclusion was more "civic," and for Trotsky it involved complex identity dilemmas. The effects of these kinds of exclusions and social fears on identity construction require more sustained reflection: as Brym and Ryvkina (1994: 31) have shown in a different context, merely the fear or anxiety of anti-Semitism can make one "more Jewish." At a minimum, social fears and indignities had an immediate impact on the cultivation of young identities, and on careers and social mobility, particularly for these assimilating Jews who crossed ethnocultural worlds. In turn, these dynamics funneled them into socialist radicalism.

Yet repression and exclusion were not a break on assimilation. For many Jews, neither pogroms nor ethnic quotas relented assimilatory trends and Russian-inflected political mobilizations continued to appeal. While the fathers suffered the emotional break with Judaism, the sons wrestled with the construction of a new identity, somewhere between acculturation and assimilation in organizationally more *rossiiskii* environments.[21] More importantly, assimilation was not a guarantee of anything. The tensions induced by self-conscious attempts to realize assimilated belonging made identities and radicalism more ambiguous and complex, particularly because most were in their teens when their radicalism initiated, making the need for social and personal integration especially acute. In their uneasy mix of ethnic exclusion and assimilation's desire for inclusion, a Russian-inflected universalist revolutionary movement proved experientially appealing.

In middle-class contexts, the lived experience of Jewishness was most often submerged. And Tsarist identity regime strategies had their social effects: Jews had had decades of practice circumventing or negotiating bureaucratic intricacies, or petitioning authorities around identification documents (the adoption of surnames, passports, censuses, birth/marriage certificates, military service records, etc.), in order to use legal codes to their advantage, and to nevertheless participate in imperial civil society, or to evade conscription or endure military service (Petrovsky-Shtern 2009b; Avrutin 2010). But in particular the association of Jews as victims of pogroms and ethnic quotas was almost a source of shame and embarrassment. This was especially true for educated upper-middle- and middle-class Jews like Trotsky, Uritsky, Sokolnikov, or Ioffe. For the sons of lower-middle-class Jews in Russified milieux, or for those confronted with violent anti-Semitism (Kaganovich, Sverdlov, Gusev, and Piatnitsky), the response tended to be either a stoic embrace or a fierce repudiation of Jewishness. In comparatively more tolerant Vilna where Jews had wider cultural and social space, Piatnitsky and Kamenev felt this less acutely or obviously than the Southern Ukrainian Jews. On the whole, however, belonging was everywhere given a particular urgency, and this placed high social costs on an articulated Jewish identity. Anti-Semitism was affecting precisely the assimilated, educated

---

[21] I owe also this point to John Klier.

middling-class milieux that were making them Russian. In a sense Witte was only half-right: Tsarist ethnic exclusions *had* contributed to the radicalization of the empire's Jews, but it was the humiliation of assimilating Jews' exclusions from particular working- and middle-class milieu that gave ethnic radicalism certain direction and content. In these social worlds, Jewishness as a social identity was inescapably overdetermined.

Unlike the atmosphere prevalent in wider society, in the all-Russian revolutionary groups Jews and Gentiles could coexist within a different value system where Jews were accepted as equals (Haberer 1992). New social identities and new social solidarities redefined both assimilation (or the costs of entry) and Jewishness. In effect, this provided the institutional framework against which their Jewishness was mediated: in certain cases it allowed erasure of their ethnic origins (Sverdlov), whereas in others it permitted socialist expression as Jews (Gusev and Piatnitsky). Nathans (2002: 249) is no doubt right when he writes: "[T]he comparatively tolerant attitude toward Jews among radical students [in the 1860s–1870s universities] prefigured and contributed to that within the revolutionary movement as a whole, where individuals of Jewish background gained extraordinary access." Complex ethnic identities were simplified in the Russian socialist revolutionary movement, mainly because the issue was either ignored or submerged. Apart from other considerations, explicit anti-Semitism inside the revolutionary movement would have been denounced as reactionary, nationalist chauvinism. This was why an imperial-minded, *rossiiskii*, or universalist narrative resonated and the lived experience inside Bolshevism's mobilization matched it.

For all its collectivism, Bolshevism paradoxically individualized identities in one key sense: it accepted individuals as revolutionaries first and as ethnics second. Jews from the entire spectrum of assimilation/acculturation/identity retention found accommodation: Jewish socialists like Piatnitsky and Kamenev, a self-proclaimed non-Jew like Sverdlov, and the deeply ambiguous Jewishness of Kaganovich were equally accepted without identity costs. In short, a variety of Jewish experience was accommodated in early Bolshevism. It offered acceptance and allowed social space to cultivate or work out tensions within ethnic identities, for "Jewish" and "non-Jewish" Jews alike. Their Bolshevism was the institutional product of ethnopolitical and organizational isolation. Although Bolshevism was not devoid of anti-Semitism, it is generally accepted that there was comparatively little anti-Semitism inside the SD revolutionary movements.

Apart from the ideological equivalence of nationalist (anti-Semitic) chauvinism with reactionary politics, two other sociological considerations also bear consideration. First, as we will see in Chapter 8, several of the ethnic Russians within Bolshevism were of service gentry or noble origins, so they embodied a particular kind of paternalist morality that was neither anti-Semitic nor nationalist. The Russian Bolsheviks were not ethnic nationalists. Moreover, Lenin and Dzierżyński were, if not exactly Judeophiles, nearly so. Dzierżyński's close friendships in the Bund and his relationships with Jewish women were well known; Lenin's great-grandfather was an apostate Jew and an anti-Semite, but Lenin himself admired Jews as a particularly gifted race (Service 2000: 17–18, 28, 470; see Petrovsky-Shtern 2010 on Lenin's Jewish roots), welcoming Zinoviev, Kamenev, and later Trotsky as his closest associates; and this importantly set an ethnically neutral – if not ethnically tolerant – culture inside Bolshevism's revolutionary organization.

Second, and as important, intermarriage rates between Jews and Russians were low in wider society, but they were remarkably high within the socialist radical groupings. In part this was because of the high number of Jewish women in the revolutionary movement, most of who were from assimilated urban milieux (on the latter point, see Fiesler 1989: 213). Beside Dzierżyński, Trotsky's second wife was Russian, Piatnitsky's wife was Russo-Polish, Sverdlov's and Zinoviev's wives were Russian, and just within the early Bolshevik elite, Molotov, Rykov, Voroshilov, Andreev, Kirov, Bukharin (second wife), Kosarev, and Kalinin were all ethnic Russians with Jewish wives.[22] There was a particular acceptance of both assimilation and Jewishness within the culture of Russian or *rossiiskii* radical socialist mobilizations that was lacking in wider society.

In sum, then, several of the imperial strategies outlined in Chapter 2 implicated the Jewish Bolsheviks. The most important were those that entwined an ascriptive Jewishness with the regime's policies of surveillance and social control, and those dissimilatory Russification policies of socioethnic exclusion targeting precisely those social locations of greatest Jewish assimilation and social mobility: the educational institutions and the middle-class liberal professions. Against this, Russian Bolshevism provided a dignified – if temporary – universalist social home to a number of young Jewish activists marginalized by ethnonationalist exclusions of assimilating, middling-class milieux. Bolshevism offered an alternative form of imperial protection precisely where Tsarism was failing. But Bolshevik socialism was vulnerable to the exigencies of nation-state building – it too Russianized, making Jews among its first victims (Schapiro 1968: 288 on the last point).

---

[22] On the search for Jewish wives among the Moscow party elite in the 1952 anti-Jewish trials, see Rubenstein and Naumov 2001: 282 and Slezkine 2004: 179–80.

4

The Polish and Lithuanian Bolsheviks

This chapter examines in some depth the political biographies of three key Polish and Lithuanian Bolsheviks: Vincus Mickevičius-Kapsukas, Feliks Dzierżyński, and Karl Radek.[1] Dzierżyński and Radek were two of the best-known Bolsheviks, even though neither was Russian and both were radicalized in the Polish imperial borderlands. A key theoretician and brilliant polemicist, the Galician Jew Radek became one of the most famous victims of Stalin's Show Trials in a public fall from grace. By contrast, the Polish Catholic Dzierżyński attained heroic status: as the founder of the Soviet Cheka (forerunner of the KGB), his name became synonymous with terror. And although less well known, Kapsukas was the most influential Lithuanian Bolshevik in the immediate postrevolutionary years. In Russian Poland, Dzierżyński became a Polish nationalist in response to Tsarist Russification; in Austrian Galicia, the Jewish Radek became a Polish nationalist in search of the kind of assimilation that Dzierżyński rejected; and in Tsarist Lithuania, Kapsukas became a Lithuanian nationalist in a rejection of both Polish and Russian influences. Yet in these imperial borderlands all three made the political migration from Lithuanian or Polish nationalist movements to *rossiiskii*-inflected and class-universalist mobilizations.

Their revolutionary politics concretize three key analytical claims of this book. First, problematic biographies prompted paths from activism in nationalist movements, to exclusion because of the movements' ethnopolitics, and finally to a Russified socialist mobilization. Second, the mobilizational effect of cross-class alliances, which allowed the movement to reach into the social resources of both ethnic networks and class communities, effectively broadened the movement in contexts of ethnic ranking and allowed it to compete with nationalist movements. Third, Russianized socialist ideology was not generally popular in these regions, but because it was rooted in key cultural frameworks, it spoke to grievances specific to particular elites (i.e., ethnic exclusion

---

[1] There were two other relevant Bolsheviks – the Russified Pole Stanislav Kosior and the Belarusian Aleksei Kiselev. I do not discuss them here because there is a dearth of reliable biographical data.

and downward mobility), and so it protected and even elevated the status of key declining elites by guaranteeing their place in an empire-building political mobilization.

The entire spectrum of radical options (nationalism, socialist nationalism, and socialist internationalism) was available in these regions, so the narrative framings of ethnicity and class were the most complex, especially where internationalism was initially the least popular option. This allows explicit theorization of the nationalities problem in the revolutionary socialist movement – that of reconciling national identities with class politics – by exploring socialist internationalism's appeal across complex ethnic/class configurations at the historical moment in which heterogeneous imperial realms were becoming homogeneous nation-states (see also Rieber 2001), and it underscores the importance of connecting nationalist mobilizations to other forms of contentious politics (McAdam 2001: 234).

The substantive argument of this chapter, then, is that these biographies suggest a specific relationship between nation and class in terms of political radicalism: moving eastward, from Gellner's third to fourth nationalist time zone, the center of gravity of radical politics shifted from nation to class, particularly in imperial borderlands. As Kapsukas's, Radek's, and Dzierżyński's biographies excluded them from Polish and Lithuanian nationalist groups, Russian socialism in its internationalist and *rossiiskii* Bolshevik variant became attractive. This means that a class-universalist political mobilization tended to find greater affinity in imperial borderlands than in places that experienced a more developed nation-building process (e.g., Congress Poland). Ethnically excluded or problematically assimilated minorities were more susceptible to socioethnic tensions and to geopolitical insecurities in the empire's multiethnic borderlands. So it was here that the socialist internationalist movement was the most appealing revolutionary ideology. In more homogeneous contexts, with more advanced nation-building processes, nationalism tended to undermine universalist ideological mobilization; here separatist or nationalist (even if socialist) revolutionary politics became the more appealing radical option.[2] But in the Tsarist borderlands, nationalisms were less politically articulated, allowing a class-internationalist revolutionary mobilization to take hold among elites in particular social locations or socioethnic, imperial coordinates.

This argument is analytically embedded in three key imperial strategies outlined in Chapter 2. The social experiences and radicalizations of the Bolsheviks in the Polish-Lithuanian borderlands reflected (1) the dissimilatory effects of Russification, (2) repressive but particularistic policies of socioethnic exclusion of non-Russian landed nobilities, or the splitting of middle-class elites, and (3) the radicalizing effects of the state's identity policies, social surveillance regimes, or other ascriptive forms of social control. For instance, Dzierżyński's route to Russianized socialist radicalism was mapped by repressive policies,

---

[2] I thank Dingxin Zhao for suggestions on this point.

which specifically targeted rural, educated Poles of the northwest, most notably in the form of Russification; and Kapsukas's experiences reflected a culturally marginalized middle-class activism, drawn to Russian socialism's universalist, *rossiiskii* inclusiveness.

Imperial Strategies in the Western Borderlands

The contexts for these Bolsheviks were three: Congress Poland, the Tsarist western provinces (or the *kresy*) of the Polish right-bank Ukraine, and Austrian Galicia. In the ten ethnically Polish provinces of Congress Poland, the only significant non-Polish ethnicity was Jewish, and to a lesser extent German; here ethnic Russians were conspicuous by their absence. There were no Bolsheviks from Congress Poland. The ethnically mixed Polish-Lithuanian borderlands did not have a single predominant nationality: Lithuanians, Belarusians, Poles, and Jews were present in large numbers, and there was a relatively small ethnic Russian presence. But these multiethnic borderlands produced four Bolsheviks: Dzierżyński, Kapsukas, Kiselev (Belarusian), and Piatnitsky. The third Polish region in the empire was southwest or right-bank Ukraine (Kiev, Podolia, Volhynia), administratively subordinated to the Governor-General of Kiev. No single nationality predominated, yet unlike Congress Poland and the *kresy*, these *gubernii* did have a significant ethnic Russian social presence. The non-Russians in these provinces, particularly Poles and Ukrainians, were among the most Russified minorities of the borderlands. Two Bolsheviks, the Polish Kosior and Uritsky (discussed in Chapter 3), came from this region. The final Polish region I consider is Habsburg Austrian Galicia. In ethnic composition, western Galicia was similar to Congress Poland with a majority of Poles, and with Jews as the only significant minority; eastern Galicia had Poles, Jews, and a substantial Ukrainian minority. Whereas Polish language and culture were repressed in Tsarist Polish lands, Polish culture was on the political ascendancy in comparatively liberal Austrian Galicia.

The imperial strategies outlined in Chapter 2 took a particular inflection in the western borderlands as differences in regional ethnic composition contributed to differences in political rule, administration, and Russification (the next paragraphs are drawn from Leslie 1963; Thaden 1981, 1984; Weeks 1994, 1996; Rodkiewicz 1998; Snyder 2003; Staliunas 2007). Patterns of ethnic exclusion and dissimilatory Russification were most notable. They reflected a set of ad hoc strategies that combined repressive Russification with attempts to induce social mobility. The result was that certain socioethnic niches became most vulnerable. For instance, the 1830–31 Polish insurrections caused official Russia to view the Polish gentry or *dvorianstvo* of Congress Poland, the northwest borderlands, and right-bank Ukraine as disloyal and irredentist subjects. But anti-Polish policies varied by region. In Congress Poland, the response was tighter administrative control and the beginnings of Russification, quickly making Congress Poland the most bureaucratically administered region of the empire. The state also dismantled Polish educational institutions: schools run by the clergy were closed, Russian was introduced as the language of instruction, and by 1839, the Polish educational system was placed under the Curator of the Warsaw Education Region, itself administratively dependent on St. Petersburg. The center of cultural Russification was right-bank Ukraine, while in the Lithuanian northwest, Vilna University was closed in 1832, and Russian was made the language of administration, courts, and schools in 1834. In 1836, Russian *gimnazii* were opened in Grodno and Vilna as Russian teachers replaced Polish teachers in the *gimnazii* and the teaching of Polish ceased. Because these dissimilationist or segregationist measures were intended to undermine the sons of the disloyal Polish *szlachta* by targeting elite secondary institutions and universities, most lower-class Poles remained unaffected. By 1857, Polish land confiscation had reduced much of the petty *szlachta* to the ranks of peasant and townsmen, impoverishing much of the Polish nobility in the western *gubernii*, but the Polish landowning class nevertheless continued as a powerful political and cultural force in the borderlands.

The empire's nationality policies shifted after the 1863 Polish rebellions, and any residual policies of cooperating with local elites were abandoned. The Lithuanian and Belarusian provinces were targeted for Russification, but not with a set of ethnically based, coherent assimilationist policies. Because of an inability to find a stable definition of Russianness, and because of a poorly coordinated imperial bureaucracy, Russifying bureaucrats in the borderlands enacted policies that lacked an ethnically assimilationist focus (Dolbilov 2004). So status-particularist policies split emergent middle classes and coethnic nobilities from peasants. The Russian state sought (1) to court Polish, Ukrainian, and Belarusian peasants as Slavs generally viewed as loyal to the Tsar, (2) to prevent alliances between Polish *szlachta* and Ukrainian intellectuals, (3) to protect Ukrainian, Belarusian, and Lithuanian peasants from Polonization and Polish influence, and (4) to court the Jews as a counterweight to the Poles on the view that, if granted civic rights, they would be less disloyal than Poles (Weeks 1996: 58, 60, 63–4, 71–2). To the extent that these policies were divide and rule, they were meant largely to divide Polish *szlachta* from peasants and lower orders, culturally and linguistically (see Table 2.1, Chapter 2).

This translated into a series of conflicting but politically consequential policies that shaped subsequent mobilizations by funneling certain socioethnic niches into leftist political radicalizations. Specifically, the most consequential social reforms involved agrarian relations between Polish landowners (affecting Dzierżyński's family) and Belarusian or Lithuanian peasants (affecting Kapsukas's family). The solution to the land question was the most radical where the insurrections were the most intense. According to contemporary accounts, Polish gentry land confiscations and a series of restrictive regulations on property rights were especially harshly felt in the western *gubernii* (Tyszkiewicz 1895: 14–38). The interdiction of December 1865 provoked particular gentry resentment by precluding anyone of Polish descent from purchasing land that was now sold to Russian landowners (Tyszkiewicz 1895: 14–20, 26–8). Polish landed elites were also undermined by peasant emancipation as

Polish, Lithuanian, and Belarusian peasants received emancipation settlements more generous than those granted the Russian peasantry.

In effect, peasant emancipation and agrarian reform in Congress Poland after the 1863 insurrections reversed years of Tsarist policy: rather than seek accommodation with the propertied and noble classes – as had been the usual policy with many ethnic minorities across the empire – now the aim was to court non-Russian (including Polish) peasantries and Jews in the western borderlands at the expense of the propertied classes, and to counter Polonization with Russification (Leslie 1963: 376–8). Russification further intensified between 1883 and 1897, particularly in the educational system. Educational Russification was extended from the middle classes and elites to primary education, and therefore to the peasantries and lower social classes, particularly because the absence of *zemstva* meant that the needs of rural and primary education had not been met (cf. Thaden 1984: 226–7; Weeks 1996: 101; Rodkiewicz 1998). Moreover, imperial elites worried most about Polish cultural and economic power over local peasantries (Weeks 1996: 99–100), and about Jewish "economic exploitation." So a number of Russificatory linguistic measures were enacted between 1864 and 1869 designed to limit Polish and introduce Russian in administration, *gimnazii*, and other public domains. With the Russification of Warsaw University in 1869, Polish was relegated to minority linguistic status and educational institutions were placed under Russian local control (Tyszkiewicz 1895: 52–3, 58–60, 158, and passim; Weeks 1996: 98–100). And given that the Catholic clergy and Jews were both viewed as highly seditious, Church lands and monasteries were confiscated, clergy control over education was limited with the removal of Polish language, and Church administration was placed under the Russian Ministry of the Interior (Tyszkiewicz 1895).

In short, and as outlined in Chapter 2, Polish elites were not repressed or incorporated as an ethnic group, but instead in imperialist particularist fashion as an upper-status minority, affecting them differently than the Polish lower classes. This had implications for radical mobilizations because in these efforts, Tsarist borderland policy created not only widespread Polish (and eventually Lithuanian, Belarusian, and Ukrainian) resentment, but also undermined the Russian state's ability to govern because of its failure to allow provincial or local political institutions to thrive. Official Russia's fear of seditious Polish *szlachta* and nobility had caused them (not without dissension) to withhold local government or *zemstva* to prevent any provincial Polish civil and political society. But this rendered imperial rule, and especially Russification, tremendously difficult without the cooperation of local *szlachta* and without a sizable ethnic Russian social presence. This also effectively undermined the Polish educated political class, just as the Polish *szlachta* had been undermined by Russification and land confiscation. Educated middle-class Poles had to seek bureaucratic and political careers in the imperial bureaucracy because they were excluded from local provincial positions, leaving a very thin local gentry and educated segment of Polish society to respond to rising Lithuanian, Belarusian, and Ukrainian national movements.

Additionally, religion and religious conversion had been important criteria for Russification policies in the 1860s (Staliunas 2004: 280–1), although policies turned on a linguistically defined ethnic identity by the late 1880s. Yet from 1880 to 1905, Lithuania/Belarusia was not Russified in the sense of cultural transformation; policies were more pragmatic because thoroughgoing cultural assimilation was seen as too radical. Here again, imperial religious policies were class and status differentiated. Other than ethnoreligiously exclusionary policies toward Polish landowners and Catholic clergy (e.g., Dzierżyński and Kapsukas), there was no real activist nationality policy toward loyal and conservative Polish peasants (Weeks 2001; Staliunas 2004). And the social composition of subsequent revolutionary political mobilizations reflected this divergence.

Put differently, the aim was not cultural Russification per se, but rather an alteration of the ethnocultural status of the region. Even Russification policies toward Lithuanians were a by-product of anti-Polish, anti-Catholic drives, and underpinned by an assumption that Lithuanian culture was anyway thin and so it would inevitably give way to assimilation. The Lithuanian nationalist movement, then, developed as a result of both repression and neglect (Weeks 2001). Lithuanians were seen as a cultural-status group, while for religious purposes Poles were seen as a potentially viable nation, and therefore their influence had to be reduced. Policies were characterized less by modernist understandings of nationalism and more by the traditionalist imperial loyalty characteristic of a deeply conservative dynastic polity. Whether characterized as bureaucratic nationalism (Rodkiewicz 1998) or as bureaucratic Russification (Dolbilov 2004), imperial policies reflected patterns outlined in Chapter 2: (1) they were not coherent, modern assimilationist strategies, in part because of the absence of a consistent definition of Russianness; (2) they variously sought to strengthen Russianness and weaken Polishness in order to maintain social order in the borderlands; (3) they differentially affected Lithuanians, Jews, and Ukrainians given the primary concern with Russianness in the borderlands; and (4) they displayed a general neglect of the peasantry and the intellectual proletariat of peasant origin, which would form the basis of Lithuanian, Belarusian, and Ukrainian nationalist movements (on this last point, see especially Rodkiewicz 1998).

So, Polish, Ukrainian, Jewish, and Lithuanian became as much political categories as ethnic ones. Ethnic identities became politicized and securitized in insecure imperial borderlands. Imperial strategies did not just involve ethnic exclusion of minorities, but particularist status exclusions and inclusions of certain middle-class and noble minorities, funneling them into leftist political mobilizations. Nationalists and pan-Slavists worried about pan-Germanism and events of 1871 and saw the need for a more unified and coherent national Russian response, while the Polish rebellions had sensitized official Russia to the state-threatening potential of Ukrainian separatism (Seton-Watson 1967: 410–12; Hosking 1997: 367–8, 374–6). Tsarist policy in Congress Poland – where nation-building was more advanced – was driven primarily by geopolitical worries of Polish separatism, which gave policies both a harsher Russificatory component to ensure loyalty and an excessively bureaucratic component to maintain social control. Here nationalist movements were more attractive than socialist internationalist mobilizations, as we will see with Dzierżyński. In contrast, Tsarist policy in the western *gubernii,* especially in the Lithuanian provinces where nation-building processes were in their earlier phases, was also broadly geopolitically motivated; it was more centrally concerned with Polish *dvorianstvo*'s cultural and political influence and irredentism, and so it privileged Russificatory policies and land confiscation over administrative centralization. Here socialist radical mobilizations were more varied and included both internationalist and ethnically inflected politics, as we will see with Kapsukas.

Kapsukas and Cultural Lithuanian Radicalism

Kapsukas's political radicalism traveled from an anticlerical Lithuanian nationalism, to a union of Polish and Lithuanian socialists, to Lithuanian socialism, to Lithuanian-Russian socialist union, and finally to an anti-Lithuanian, Russified Bolshevism. His route to Bolshevism through these ideologically varied political movements reflected the appeal of a class-universalist mobilization in a context of complex biographies, ethnopolitical exclusions, and marginalizations. In Bolshevism Kapsukas could be considered a revolutionary first and an ethnic minority second.

Polish Culture, the Russian State, and Lithuanian Nationalism

Kapsukas was born in 1880 in Budvieciai in the rural and predominantly ethnically Lithuanian Suvalkija (Užnemuné) region near the Prussian border. His family was among the prosperous, quasi-aristocratic landowners of Užnemuné. After the 1807 Treaty of Tilsit, the region became part of the newly created Duchy of Warsaw, and with the Napoleonic Code, serfdom was abolished early, thereby setting the conditions for the development of the region on a course distinct from that of the rest of Lithuania (Strazas 1996: 43–5). The Russian state generally viewed Lithuanians as hardworking and potentially patriotic agriculturalists whose anti-Polish feelings were to be encouraged (Weeks 1996: 67, 121). After the 1863 Polish insurrections, two decrees permitted Lithuanian peasants to purchase the lands they used without further obligations to the Polish *szlachta.* Over time, this kind of progressive legislation (at Polish gentry expense) created a relatively well-off and socially differentiated Lithuanian peasantry compared to the Russian peasantry, particularly in Užnemuné; it created a class of landless peasants who migrated to the cities as well as a small, quasi-aristocratic, prosperous Lithuanian landowning rural elite (Sabaliunas 1990: 5; Strazas 1996b: 47, 57–8). Kapsukas's social origins derived from the latter.

Kapsukas's family was able to allow him to study for the priesthood. The most important Lithuanian Catholic educational centers were the Marijampolé

Gymnasium and the Catholic Theological Seminary in Seinai (Sejny). Kapsukas attended Marijampolé between 1890 and 1897 before enrolling in the Seminary (Suziedelis 1970–78: 39). Both in *gimnaziia* and at the Seminary, Kapsukas was active in the anticlerical, liberal Lithuanian nationalism that was a product of the Catholic school system. The Lithuanian intelligentsia and the religious-cultural phase of early Lithuanian nationalism emerged in Marijampolé and in the Seinai Seminary, or within the Polonized elite Catholic system where there was still autonomous cultural space outside the Russified state system. For decades, the language of instruction had been Polish, with the result that most of the priests-in-training – sons of prosperous Lithuanian land-owners – became moderate-to-radical secular or religious nationalists, rebelling against the pervasive religious use of Polish. Although designed to undermine Polish cultural influence, Tsarist measures against the Catholic Church and the Polish *szlachta* had directly but unintentionally politicized the emerging Catholic (and secular) Lithuanian intelligentsia.

After 1863, non-state parish schools were closed, and in state schools Russian was made the language of instruction. In status-particularist policies of dissimilatory Russification, by 1897, state schools became instruments of Russification, Lithuanian was banned in both instruction and informal conversation, and only graduates of Orthodox seminaries were employed as teachers. The press ban on Lithuanian books (extended to include all religious books and anything in Polish-Latin script) required that they be published in Cyrillic. It affected all educational institutions and most of the Lithuanian press. Imperial strategies sought both de-Polonization and Russified assimilation (Staliunas 2007: 304). One important result was that Lithuanian resentment was now directed not only at Polish imperialism, but at Russian imperialism as well. Another consequence was the famous book smugglers movement that drew together students, intellectuals, radicals, and various professions united against linguistic Russification: religious and other books were printed in East Prussia where there was a sizable historic (albeit Lutheran) Lithuanian community, and smuggled across Tsarist borders (Zalevskii 1912: 180–1). As an active nationalist, Kapsukas took part in this book smugglers movement.

But in the ethnically homogeneous but Polonized Lithuanian religious schools, and away from the multiethnic capitals, the Lithuanian intelligentsia was in largest part also the Užnemuné intelligentsia – by the end of the century, 114 of the 235 leading nationalists came from Kapsukas's region (Strazas 1996b: 52). And by the time he joined the Lithuanian nationalist movement in 1890, the church-dominated phase of Lithuanian nationalism had already ceded to a nationalist-socialist agenda with the infusion of Marxist socialism. So Kapsukas was politicized during the last years of the cultural, anticlerical phase of Lithuanian nationalism. In 1898, he was expelled from the Seminary because of his political activities and denied permission to enroll in a Russian university. So in 1902, he immigrated to Switzerland to audit courses in economics and sociology at Bern University. Already an avowed nationalist, Kapsukas – literally Little Kapsas – considered himself a follower of the great

Kapsas Vincas Kudirka, who wrote on Lithuanian patriotism and democracy (Suziedelis 1970–78: 39). Kapsukas wrote for *Ukininkas* in 1901–02, and in 1902 he coedited *Varpas* (Strazas 1996a: 42–4). *Varpas*, together with *Auszra* and *Ukininkas*, were the most important underground Lithuanian papers between 1883 and 1905, and both were published in East Prussia and smuggled into Lithuania. Essentially secular in approach, these cultural, literary, and historical publications also positioned themselves on political currents as they tried to move away from clerical control (Zalevskii 1912: 181; Strazas 1996a: 34–6).

Yet the nationalists' problem was that ethnic Lithuanians were a minority in most of the Lithuanian *gubernii*.[3] Jews, Poles, and Russians dominated Lithuania's cities, leaving Lithuanian society a pyramid without a top, given that much of the Lithuanian aristocracy was also Polonized (Strazas 1996a, part 2: 38). But the small, cultural nationalist intelligentsia created an urban or social Lithuanian presence through its nationalist press, and Kapsukas was at the center of this movement (Zalevskii 1912: 181). During Kapsukas's nationalist political activism in the early 1890s, social democracy was a significant force in Lithuania, particularly in the form of the Social Democratic Party of Lithuania (LSDP, *Lietvuvos socialdemokratu partija*). The lineage of the LSDP owed much to Jewish socialists and particularly to the Bund and its forerunners, but it was also influenced by German, Austrian, and Polish socialism, as shown later in the chapter in connection with Dzierżyński (Zalevskii 1912: 182–3; Sabaliunas 1990: 15–18).[4] By 1904–05, Kapsukas was a liberal nationalist and one of the most influential figures in the LSDP: he was on its Central Committee between 1905 and 1907 and organized workers on a multiethnic basis (Suziedelis 1970–78: 39; Sabaliunas 1990: 33, 48–56, 113).[5]

Students had founded the LSDP as a Lithuanian political movement that espoused socialism. But they mostly used Polish as its working language because the student founders were descendants of Lithuania's nobility and did not speak Lithuanian. Indeed, the future Bolshevik Dzierżyński had attended the LSDP's creation congress as its youth representative. As a Pole, he eventually left the party because of its separatist program, but at the time the LSDP was ethnically mixed, its publications were in Lithuanian, Polish, Yiddish, and German, reflecting its multiethnic leadership, and it promoted liberal nationalism on a generally socialist platform (Sabaliunas 1990: 28–9). Its membership was comprised of urban workers, students, and professionals, so until 1902 no effort was made to reach into the Lithuanian countryside where most ethnic

---

[3] In 1897, Grodno *guberniia* was 2.1% Lithuanian, Vilna *guberniia* 17.48% Lithuanian, and Kovno, where Lithuanians were a majority, 66.02%. The rest were Jews, Poles, Belarusians, and Russians.

[4] The PPS had a chapter in Vilna as of 1892, but refused to accept Lithuanian workers because of their separatist tendencies.

[5] In October 1905, 40,000 demonstrators took part in strikes in Kovno, Vilna, and other Lithuanian cities in sympathy with Russian workers. They were organized by the Bund and LSDP, with leaflets published in Polish, Lithuanian, Yiddish, and Russian (Zalevskii 1912: 185).

Lithuanians lived. Importantly, because the party's liberal founders sought political autonomy and the eventual creation of an independent Lithuanian state, their politics necessarily de-emphasized class radicalism (Sabaliunas 1990: 10).

By 1905, intergroup ties were created beyond the usual tactical collaborations: the Polish Socialist Party (PPS) branch in Lithuania merged several of its city chapters with those of the LSDP, but not in border cities like Białystok where there were too many Polish workers who strongly identified with the Polish-PPS, or in Brest, which had Jewish and Polish followings and where the LSDP did not want a merger for fear of diluting Lithuanian influence. So until 1914, the LSDP tried to attract Jewish workers and it established relations with the Bund with some success: in 1907, of the LSDP's 2,310 members, 380 were Jewish, mostly from Grodno and Vilna. Jewish workers in the Lithuanian party were granted autonomous status and Yiddish literature. Alliances with LSDP and the Latvians were also relatively easy, with chapters in Riga, Mitau (Jelgava), and Liepāja, and 500 active members (figures in Sabaliunas 1990: 99–105).

So where tactical mobilizational alliances occurred, it was for organizational reasons, and nationalities questions were set aside. Yet while Kapsukas was a member of the LSDP's CC, there was little accord between the LSDP and the RSDLP because of differences over the national question. Although the middle-level leadership of the LSDP wanted a merger with the Russian party in 1906, the elite, including Kapsukas, did not (Sabaliunas 1990: 108–10). Kapsukas was adamantly nationalist in his position and unwilling to cede any ground to the RSDLP or to a Russified socialist ideological movement.

Ethnic Politics, Emigration, and Bolshevik Socialism

But revolutionary events of 1905, the subsequent Stolypin reaction, and the concomitant Duma elections changed the landscape and shifted the center of gravity within the LSDP. From 1896, the LSDP had wanted an autonomous Republic of Lithuania in federal arrangement with its neighbors; the Bund wanted Jewish cultural autonomy; the national question was still almost nonexistent in Latvia; the Social Democratic Party of Poland and Lithuania (or SDKPiL) was increasingly Luxemburgist in its position; and the PPS was increasingly nationalist. In other words, the ethnic and national socialist mobilizations of the Polish-Lithuanian territories had become irrevocably balkanized. Against this, the LSDP revived a position that had been submerged in Lithuanian socialism from the beginning: they stressed that Lithuanian workers were more advanced than Russian workers, who were not deemed ready for socialism. The Russian socialist leadership, too, was deemed "backward," and in turning to a more west European orientation, the LSDP elite – Kapsukas foremost among them – prioritized the national over the social.[6] Kapsukas argued

---

[6] Indeed, the LSDP was not admitted into the Second International until 1923 because of its separatist platform, which had also alienated Dzierżyński after 1905.

that workers would follow their class interests only in an ethnically distinct Lithuania (Sabaliunas 1990: 122–3). Put differently, socialism could now only be actualized through a movement that *embraced* Lithuanian nationalism.

The multiethnic LSDP leadership had, in effect, ceded to a position of ethnic unity. Moreover, arrests and repression in the cities forced the LSDP into the ethnically homogeneous countryside and away from multiethnic Vilna. Although the LSDP leadership was 52 percent middle class and 32 percent working class, with the activism of students, intellectuals, educated professionals, and labor union leaders, and as evidenced by the 1906 Duma elections, wider support came from the countryside where Lithuanian peasants elected five Lithuanian SDs to the 1907 Duma (Sabaliunas 1990: 115–16). Rural Lithuanian support prompted the elite to change the party's working language from Polish to Lithuanian. This pattern resembled that of the Bundist leadership, with similar immediate effect: Polish speaking LSDP elites were de facto excluded while Lithuanian-speaking elites ascended. Dzierżyński left and Kapsukas rose to the CC. After 1900, then, the LSDP focused less on multiethnic urban workers and more on Lithuanian farm labor and small landholders, pivoting to attract ethnic rural support for their rank and file, privileging nation over class in their mobilizational narrative, and ethnicizing Lithuanian radical politics.

This marked an important contextual shift within which to situate Kapsukas's revolutionary politics. In recruiting in the rural areas where most ethnic Lithuanians resided, the LSDP now drew support from the village farmer, their student offspring, and artisans. It gradually began to penetrate the two largest rural strata: agricultural workers and urban peasants. Kapsukas was himself part of the rural upper bourgeoisie, so this rural cross-class coalition building created a certain alliance between farmers and socialists. But it was a political union, not an ideological one. The issue of land ownership had caused deep rifts, and when farmers with landed estates broke away, the LSDP's class strategy shifted to the poorest, largest agricultural sector, the so-called village proletariat (Sabaliunas 1990: 129–31). In reality, however, there was very little revolution among these rural strata, and language problems with Polish and Belarusian peasantries surfaced: the LSDP intelligentsia had greater affinity with rural landowners than with agricultural workers, something that structurally undercut its socialist claims. Kapsukas found himself at the heart of these linguistic and cultural cross-currents within the Lithuanian socialist movement, just as his activism in 1905–06 triggered years of exile and imprisonment. Between 1906 and 1914, arrest, exile, and resettlement had thinned the LSDP leadership, and this included Kapsukas. He spent time in Lithuanian, Polish, and Russian prisons; in 1910–11, while in a Warsaw prison, he came into contact with members of the SDKPiL, Dzierżyński's new party, and he was influenced by its Polish members (Sabaliunas 1990: 33, 93–4). But when Kapsukas was exiled to Vladimir and Krasnoiarsk in Russia, he gravitated toward Russian socialism under the influence of the Jewish Bolshevik Sverdlov.

As older LSDP elites remained committed to their nationalist positions, younger radicals, deeply impressed by Russian revolutionary events in 1905–07, viewed nationalism as an obstacle to closer LSDP and RSDLP ties (Sabaliunas 1990: 118–19). The federalist and autonomist wings of the LSDP solidified, and Kapsukas embraced the more radical, federalist option. Indeed a number of Lithuanian Social Democrats moved closer to the Bolsheviks and the RSDLP. It was increasingly obvious that the LSDP elite had too many Lithuanian and Polish intellectuals, and its appeal was too segmented to effectively broaden the social base of its mobilizational efforts. Significantly for Kapsukas, most of the LSDP intellectual elite also pursued cultural, literary, and foreign interests in literary societies, Lithuanian library groups, museums, and other cultural groupings. This set the cultural elite in Lithuanian social democracy apart from the professional elite of revolutionaries, and Kapsukas was quickly marginalized from the former given the shifting social alignments within the movement.

In short, not having the cultural capabilities to remain a "Lithuanian" socialist, Kapsukas was excluded by its ethnic politics. That is, socioethnic niches and differential cultural capabilities funneled him into particular mobilizations: as early as 1901, Kapsukas had published a few second-rate articles combining literary criticism with Marxist analysis, and sat on the margins of Lithuanian (socialist) cultural and literary society. It may have been that his embrace of Bolshevism "made him an outcast in Lithuania" (Sabaliunas 1990: 145), but it may also have been that he embraced Bolshevism precisely because he was something of a cultural outsider among Lithuanian intellectuals.

Not all Lithuanian nationalists became political nationalists, however. After the Russian state's repressive reaction and through the war years, Lithuanian intellectual-cultural elites, both socialist and nationalist, turned inward and focused on Lithuanian national-cultural pursuits; indeed, a number of the remaining LSDP organizations were nestled among the Lithuanian diasporas in Latvia, Britain, and the United States. On his return from exile in 1913, and marginalized from Lithuanian cultural politics, Kapsukas gravitated toward this Lithuanian diaspora and joined its intellectual émigrés.[7] In 1913 Kapsukas edited Lithuanian socialist papers in Philadelphia during a six-month stay in the United States, and on his return he edited papers in Latvia (Suziedelis 1970–78: 40; Lazitch 1986: 320).

Lithuanian colonies were notably concentrated in Scotland's Lanarkshire industrial belt, especially around the mines, factories, and iron foundries. They became important cultural and intellectual centers for activist intellectual émigrés like Kapsukas. They published the weekly *Rankpelnis* (The Laborer) in Glasgow between 1907 and 1923 (White 1975: 2), and it became the leading organ of the LSDP during the war. Kapsukas took over its editorship between 1915 and 1916, while also editing *Socialdemokratas*, the journal of the Foreign

---

[7] Riga had 35,000 Lithuanian emigrants and St. Petersburg had 30,000. Between 1869 and 1914, more than 300,000 Lithuanians left for the United States, especially New York, Boston, Philadelphia, and Chicago (Strazas 1996a: 67–8).

Bureau of the LSDP. He moved to Glasgow in 1915, and "for at least part of the war years Bellshill [Glasgow] became the main center of Lithuanian socialism" (White 1975: 4–5). Kapsukas's editorship of *Rankpelnis* and *Socialdemokratas* meant that they took hard internationalist and antiwar positions. During the war, Kapsukas also penned several articles for the British socialist press in attempts to raise awareness of the oppressive conditions caused by Tsarist rule, and he did this in cooperation with the Russian Jewish Literary Society in London (White 1975: 5–6). But it was also during the war – and in emigration – that Kapsukas became a Bolshevik.

His internationalism hardened his antinationalist stance following the Revolution, and he took active part in Bolshevik efforts to Russify and centralize Lithuania and Belarusia as head of the government of the Lithuanian Soviet Republic (until the Polish army ousted it in 1919). In 1920, Kapsukas returned to Lithuania with the Russian forces until activities were forced underground. As a member of the Lithuanian Communist Party and director of its underground activity in Lithuania, Kapsukas had between 700 and 900 followers in 1921, although nearly two-thirds were not ethnic Lithuanian (Suziedelis 1970–78: 40). But by then Kapsukas's antinationalist activism had an additional source: those Lithuanian socialists who had been nationalists were eager to dissociate themselves from nationalism (White 1990: 95). It was only in the 1920s and 1930s that the Bolshevik Kapsukas received recognition – of the Soviet type – for his reviews and essays on Lithuanian literature's aesthetic role and national character.

In short, frustrated and marginalized by Lithuanian cultural nationalism, Kapsukas finally found a literary home critiquing Lithuanian culture from within Russian Bolshevism. Kapsukas had brought a distinctive set of cultural and social resources to Bolshevik activism – those of the wealthy and Polonized Lithuanian landed rural bourgeoisie. Initially radicalized as a nationalist in response to the socioethnic exclusions of Polish and Russian rule, he was excluded from the Lithuanian nationalist movement's ethnopolitics, and in years of emigration became an internationalist and finally a Russianized Bolshevik. His route to Bolshevik radicalism was emblematic of the ways in which minority elites in particular socioethnic niches of imperial society were marginalized not only by Tsarist policies, but also by regional ethnopolitics, and their experiences eventually found political expression in leftist, *rossiiskii* or imperial-minded radical mobilizations.

Dzierżyński and Déclassé Polish Gentry Radicalism

Originating from the same region, Dzierżyński wove in and out of many of the same circles as had Kapsukas. Dzierżyński's radicalism reflected the ethnopolitical exclusion of the declining Polish petty nobility of the rural Polish-Lithuanian borderlands. Radek wrote that Dzierżyński had rejected Polish nationalism for internationalism because social proximity to the Lithuanian peasantry, and agitation among Polish and Jewish workers in Lithuania, had estranged him from the ideals of the Polish nobility (Radek 1935: 100, 110). And yet while Tsarist repression and the ethnopolitics of the borderlands created by growing nationalisms were most important, Dzierżyński's origins in the impoverished Polish *szlachta* were also influential to his early nationalism and to his later internationalism. Here, too, imperial policies of ethnic exclusion and dissimilatory Russification targeted minority nobilities in a particularly repressive fashion; in protecting the empire, however, socialist *rossiiskii* political mobilizations offered not only a universalist inclusiveness of an idealized empire, but also status protection and identity or community for elites marginalized by ethnonationalist politics and nationalizing policies.

Early Radicalization and Polish Nationalism
From the 1870s, sons of the rural Polish landowning classes migrated to the cities to seek alternative professions. With limited sources of social mobility, they found positions in urban society as petty civil servants in the lower-level imperial bureaucracies; some went into private business, the free professions, or earned subsistence wages in literary work and journalism. They constituted a disproportionately large intelligentsia; sons of the borderland Polish gentry comprised about two-thirds of those urbanites with proof of noble lineage in 1897. Much of Russian Poland's urban intelligentsia therefore embodied the cultural and political attitudes of the Polish gentry of Polish-Lithuanian imperial borderlands.

Dzierżyński was a product of this period of political and social change. His family had been affected by the state's punitive socioethnic policies in the Polish borderlands in which ethnopolitical repression also contributed to a déclassé experience. Agrarian reform, the confiscation of Polish lands, and sustained Russification under Tsar Alexander III (1881–94) vacillated between repression as Catholics and repression as Poles, but both were punitive in intent (Weeks 1994). Several decades of undermining Polish cultural control of the region had important effects on educational and administrative elites, on the church clergy, and on the landowning gentry itself. Consequently, Dzierżyński's generation of Polish petty nobility or rural intelligentsia became the most politically oppressed social group in the western borderlands, and among them emerged most of the leaders of the Polish socialist and nationalist movements, including the leader of the Polish Socialist Party, Józef Piłsudski (Snyder 1997). Because of ethnic dispersal and political repression, the ideologies of this generation of Polish intelligentsia reflected most clearly deep political tensions between socialism and nationalism – or between class and nation – though in multiethnic Vilna some, like Dzierżyński, absorbed Jewish socialists' internationalism.

Dzierżyński's father was an educated landowner and his mother was from a wealthy, educated intelligentsia family (Blobaum 1984: 22–4). They felt the diminishment of their middle-gentry status on their Lithuanian estate, as his father could only find employment as an instructor in a remote Taganrog *gimnaziia* despite a degree in mathematics and physics from St. Petersburg University. Though not wealthy, the family was not impoverished either: the father's state pension combined with the leasing of the property to Belarusian peasants rendered a comfortable existence (Strobel 1974: 126–7; Dzerzhinskii 1984 [1902]: 3–6).[8] Dzierżyński's mother raised him a patriot, insisting on the importance of the Catholic Church in saving Poland from Tsarist Russification. In fact, raised on a rural Lithuanian estate on Polish nationalist romanticism, Dzierżyński later told Kapsukas that after his father's death in 1882, the home became so nationalistic that as a young boy he had dreamed of killing Muscovites (Blobaum 1984: 22–4).

Dzierżyński was sent to a Vilna *gimnaziia* where his first political activism took form. As outlined in Chapter 2, the empire's *gimnazii* were among the most important venues for Russification of the sons of Polish gentry and intelligentsia (on suppression of Polish, see Rodkiewicz 1998: 166–72). Entrance exams required knowledge of Russian, and signs abounded advising that the use of Polish was prohibited even outside the classroom, as was the study of Polish literature and history. By the late 1880s, several decades of Russification had humiliatingly reduced the status of Polish language and culture. This was a generation of adolescents that experienced the political exclusion of educational humiliation; forced to publicly despise the culture of their fathers, they turned to ideas that offered the promise of radical political transformation, nationalist and socialist (Snyder 1997: 239–40).

Against this background, Dzierżyński's pre-Bolshevik radicalism had roughly four phases: Polish nationalism, Lithuanian Social Democracy, Polish Social Democracy, and Polish-Lithuanian Social Democracy. His Polish nationalist phase began in 1887. A romantic-nationalist reaction against positivism was already under way when Dzierżyński entered *gimnaziia*, so his earliest activity was in Catholic patriotic circles of Young Poland, a response to the oppressive Russificatory atmosphere in these secondary institutions, and part of his desire to enter the Seminary (Blobaum 1984: 18, 24–5, 32). Though he otherwise received excellent marks in *gimnaziia*, Dzierżyński's Russian skills were evidently poor and left him with a bitter experience of Russification. This may have been a form of passive resistance to Russification (as Blobaum suggests), but Dzierżyński had been radicalized even before coming into direct contact with Tsarist oppression: nurtured on Polish nationalism and anti-Tsarist sentiment, he had been socialized to the resentment of the dislocated Polish gentry under Russian rule even before *gimnaziia*. Vilna's multiethnic urban setting and political atmosphere, and the *gimnaziia* setting, merely rendered the humiliation more apparent and provided the organizational opportunities with which to express it in nationalist mobilizations absent in rural Lithuania.[9]

---

[8] In 1921, Dzierżyński claimed he was from a petty *szlachta* family – a fact subsequently deleted from official accounts (Granat 1989: 407).

[9] Dzierżyński's brothers never became radicals, however: one attended St. Petersburg University, another a Veterinary Institute, a third Moscow University, and a fourth a St. Petersburg *gimnaziia*, HIAPO, Box 162, Index No. XIIId(2), Processing Intelligence, Folder 2A, Headquarters Circular No. 4317, June 26, 1902.

The second phase of Dzierżyński's radicalism involved both Polish socialism and Lithuanian social democracy. In his seventh year of *gimnaziia*, Dzierżyński entered socialist political circles loosely tied to the PPS, marking a move from Polish nationalism to a vague Polish nationalist socialism. Between 1890 and 1919, Polish Marxism was something of a conduit or arena of exchange between Europe and Russia, with the PPS calling for Polish independence in a program modeled on that of the German Social Democratic Party (SPD). In 1893, Polish socialism was warring between its nationalist and internationalist wings, when Dzierżyński was active in the PPS circles of Vilna's *gimnazii*. An essentially Polish party with a chapter in Vilna, the PPS was premised on the belief that Lithuania was a Polish province with no legitimate separatist claim to autonomy (Blobaum 1984: 32; Granat 1989: 407; Sabaliunas 1990: 18). In the early 1890s, it also promoted the idea that a Polish proletariat transcended ethnolinguistic boundaries and comprised both Polish and Yiddish-speaking Jewish workers (Zimmerman 2004). But the PPS had very little support among Polish workers in Vilna and it was slowly eclipsed by the secular, socialist reformism of Lithuanian social democracy. As we saw with Kapsukas, the founders of the LSDP were linguistically and culturally Polonized descendants of Lithuania's nobility. Partly because in 1894 Lithuanian socialism had lots of early contacts with Jewish Bundists, it was also open to educated Polonized Lithuanians and to Polish radicals, making it attractive to both Kapsukas and Dzierżyński in the same moment (Strobel 1974: 101–9, 124, 127).

By early 1895, Dzierżyński began to organize artisans, craftsmen, and factory apprentices in Lithuanian SD circles. But he fell into more frequent conflicts with *gimnaziia* authorities and was eventually expelled. He entered Vilna's political life and agitated among workers for the Vilna LSDP, organizing strikes in conjunction with Jewish socialists (Granat 1989: 407; Sabaliunas 1990: 25, though there is an earlier dating in Strazas 1996a: 43). As noted in Chapter 3 in connection with Piatnitsky, because Vilna's labor force was multiethnic in small workshops and handicraft enterprises, organizing effective strikes required interethnic cooperation. The best organized were the Jewish socialists anxious to involve Polish or Lithuanian workers in citywide strikes to avoid anti-Semitism. Jewish socialists' aspiration to empire-wide socialist organizations so persuaded Dzierżyński that he began to study Yiddish to work more effectively among Vilna's Jewish workers. Very few among the Jewish socialist intelligentsia in Vilna themselves spoke Yiddish because most were Russified and assimilated, so, as Radek wrote, "it was a great joke to us that [in] the headquarters of Polish Social Democracy, which contained quite a number of Jews, only Dzierżyński, former gentleman of Poland, and Catholic, could read Yiddish!" (Radek 1935: 100). Russian had been difficult for him, but somehow Yiddish came much easier.

Dzierżyński formed a chapter of the LSDP in Kovno in 1897, the PPS chapter having collapsed because of repression (Granat 1989: 407). He set up an illegal printing press to publish a Polish underground paper that stressed interethnic labor alliances (Prokhorov 1969–78: 482; Dzerzhinskii 1977: 16–26),

as he turned to his Jewish friends and contacts for assistance (Tobias 1972: 102–3). Importantly, then, both Piatnitsky (a Jewish artisan) and Dzierżyński (a Polish *intelligent*) wrote on the urgent need for interethnic cooperation in Vilna and stressed the importance of multiethnic class alliances (Piatnitskii 1933: ch. 6; Dzerzhinskii 1977: 49–52). In 1894, Dzierżyński pointedly renounced his Catholicism, but not his Polish nationalist commitments and remained opposed to any form of Lithuanian autonomy.

Official biographies state that on joining Lithuanian circles, Dzierżyński adhered to their left or non-nationalist wing; he himself wrote that in these years, he studied Marxist literature and adopted its anti-nationalist position (Prokhorov 1969–78: 482; Granat 1989: 407). Yet Dzierżyński opposed Lithuanian nationalist aspirations quite apart from his Marxist orientation. He had had very little contact with Lithuanian peasants or factory workers, or those ethnic Lithuanians most implicated in Polish-Lithuanian socioeconomic relations, and he had been remarkably and consistently indifferent to Lithuanian, Belarusian, and Polish peasants alike. Dzierżyński's opposition to Lithuanian nationalist politics did not so much invoke his socioeconomic identity as an impoverished Polish gentry-landowner, I think, as his gentry-intellectual experiences as a Pole in Russifying Vilna. Ethnopolitical exclusion created by nation-building might have mattered more. Lithuanian socialist movements had initially been a political alliance between Polonized Lithuanian nobles, intellectuals, and aristocrats and similarly oppressed descendants of the Polish petty nobility – so both Dzierżyński and Kapsukas were in the same political movement. Imperial policies of assimilatory Russification had radicalized them. But as the Lithuanian intelligentsia found and asserted its cultural identity vis-à-vis the cultural dominance of the Polish rural gentry, it eventually privileged Lithuanian cultural autonomy from Polish influence over common socialist and anti-Russian political aspirations.

As the Lithuanian LSDP elite demanded to be treated as a distinct entity free of Polish influence, the right or national wing of the party came to the fore. At the same time, Polish socialism was finding *its* national identity as the movement's leadership constituted itself around opposition to Lithuanian separatism from historic Poland. In short, Polish socialism in its "patriotic" form and Lithuanian socialism in its "patriotic" form became mutually exclusive: the Polish-Lithuanian-Belarusian borderlands were becoming ethnolinguistically balkanized into their respective nationalities and nationalist political mobilizations. Dzierżyński found himself marginalized by competing socialist ethnopolitics. Paradoxically, however, ethnopolitical marginality also meant that he had more of an elective affinity with Russified Vilna Jews than with ethnic Poles of urban Poland. This was an affinity he increasingly cultivated, and it nurtured a universalist, *rossiiskii*-oriented commitment to multiethnicity.

It also meant that he was slowly excluded from provincial political parties and nationalist attachments and so he gravitated toward internationalist cosmopolitan political movements to redefine himself. In addition to the descendants of the rural Polish nobility, Russified Jews were the other social group

finding themselves squeezed between nationalizing socialisms and ethnicizing socialist movements. The entwined development of Polish and Jewish socialisms in the 1890s in Vilna was significant in shaping Dzierżyński's radical politics (on the PPS and early Bund in this regard, see Zimmerman 2004). In this, the cultural and intellectual influence of Jewish socialists' cosmopolitanism on Dzierżyński was significant. He was intimately involved with Jewish socialists in Vilna, many of whom later became Bundists. Indeed his affairs with, and marriages to, Jewish women were well known: Dzierżyński married twice to Jewish revolutionaries.

Whereas one of his biographers argued that Dzierżyński's close relations with Jewish socialists affected his internationalism (Blobaum 1984: 34), his socioethnic origins also militated against an ability to embrace either Polish or Lithuanian national socialisms, anyway forcing him into an internationalist, multiethnic socialism. Moreover, the PPS, the LSDP, and the Bundists came into conflict over attempts to recruit the same workers – Jews, Poles, and Lithuanians in borderland cities (Strobel 1974: 128–30). The multiethnic character of the working classes in these cities was distinctive because there were no large industrial factories with highly concentrated homogeneous labor bases; urban labor of the borderlands was small-scale, comprised mostly of handicraft shops that tended to employ co-ethnics. For the socialist and nationalist intelligentsias, then, the narrower the linguistic and cultural affiliation of the working classes, the more limited their political influence. The converse was also true: internationalist, cosmopolitan affiliations broadened the social base of the organization. Dzierżyński's moves from Polish patriotism to the PPS to Polish-Lithuanian alliance in the early LSDP were profoundly affected by intimate friendships with Jewish socialists – but they were also a result of the ethnopolitical limitations of his sociocultural origins.

Dzierżyński was arrested in 1898 and exiled to Viatka *guberniia*, where he worked in a printing cloth factory, and from which he escaped in 1899.[10] Exile took a severe physical toll on him, and he was exempted from service in the Imperial Army because of poor health (Prokhorov 1969–78: 482). But his emotional state was more debilitating. Intense political activism often prevented Dzierżyński from bouts of depression, fueled by a determination that the Russian state would "pay for everything" (Dzerzhinskii 2002: 132). In letters from prison during this period he wrote that life in freedom had no meaning, while life in prison gave his existence meaning and purpose (Dzerzhinskii 1984: 7–8). Only in the moral strength needed to "protect against the foulness of modern society" did he see himself as "transcending the humdrum of everyday life" and creating a "bright future" against the "hell of contemporary life" (Dzerzhinskii 2002: 133, 213, 219). Part of Dzierżyński's identity was indeed premised on an aestheticization of suffering, on a heroic combination of salvationism and fatalism (Dzerzhinskii 2002: 40, 77–8, 104, 154, 277).

---

[10] On his 1898 arrest and exile, see HIAPO, Box 126, Index No. XIIId(2), Processing Intelligence, Folder 2A, Headquarters Circular, Warning Lists, Circular No. 4317, July 26, 1902.

Socialist Internationalism to Russian Bolshevism

On his return from exile, Dzierżyński's political radicalism entered its third, most internationalist phase – indeed one that grew distinctly reactive to growing nationalist socialisms. Dzierżyński now thought that nationalist claims in Lithuanian socialism were on the ascendancy and so he deserted the party (Strobel 1974: 132–9). In 1897, the same year as the founding of the Bund in Vilna, the Polish National Democratic Party (*Endecja*) was founded under Roman Dmowski's leadership with a clear nationalist platform. Meanwhile in the PPS, too, a nationalist narrative gained priority over socialism. So excluded by socialist ethnopolitics, in 1899 Dzierżyński and Rosa Luxemburg founded the Social Democracy of the Kingdom of Poland and Lithuania (SDKPiL), which called for Polish and Lithuanian autonomy within a Russian federation. Dzierżyński's SDKPiL de facto recognized the legitimacy of imperial boundaries. He then went to Warsaw to reestablish contacts with Polish social democrats and with friends in the Vilna Bundist organization (Granat 1989: 408). With his Bundist contacts Dzierżyński worked among factory workers to counter the rightist PPS, whose patriotism he thought divided Polish workers from Russian and Jewish workers (Blobaum 1984: 61–4).[11] His SDKPiL had already concretized the political imaginary of a universalist, nonethnicized empire.

Dzierżyński then returned to Vilna to merge Warsaw and Vilna groups on the basis of Polish and Lithuanian unity in a cosmopolitan, *rossiiskaia* federation. Along with other national socialist political movements, the SDKPiL formed a loose federation with the RSDLP. The merger caused considerable controversy, and Dzierżyński was insistent on a centralized organization, opposing his Bundist friends' demands for recognition of their Jewishness and requests for special status within the RSDLP (Blobaum 1984: 90–1). Although intimately involved with Jewish socialists and deeply influenced by Jewish internationalism, Dzierżyński was clearly at odds with Bundist nationalism. He could make common cause with Jewish socialists as long as they were socialists first and Jews second, but as they found their ethnic identities, he could not easily follow. Similarly, as Polish socialist mobilizations began to give precedence to nationalist demands over workers' (class) demands, Dzierżyński's social and organizational base in the multiethnic borderlands could only problematically be incorporated. Dzierżyński's internationalism was increasingly a response to isolation from growing nationalisms and nationalizing socialisms; socialist universalism increasingly came to reside with Polish émigrés and further east among Russian socialist internationalists. Class slowly gave way to nation in the empire's western borderlands.

Dzierżyński's position on Polish nationalism was Luxemburgist, embracing "organic incorporation"; he agreed with her that the problem was not the SDKPiL's position on the national question, but rather the RSDLP's Leninist concessions to self-determination (Blobaum 1984: 94). Dzierżyński, and more

---

[11] HIAPO, Box 162, Index No. XIIId(2), Processing Intelligence, Folder 2A, Headquarters Circular No. 4317, June 26, 1902.

generally the Polish and Jewish émigré Left, viewed concessions to nationalist separatism as undermining their position and strengthening Dmowski and Piłsudski's parties. Not a theoretician by nature, Dzierżyński came at the issue pragmatically: Polish and Lithuanian nationalist political mobilization would only weaken radicalism in areas that were ethnically mixed because workers of different nationalities would not see their mutual interests, thereby making strike organization more difficult. Even in socialist organizations *rossiiskii* integrity had to be maintained. Cosmopolitanism was becoming a social precondition for an effective socialist mobilization; socialism was struggling to transcend ethnonational boundaries not only because of the consolidation of Polish and Lithuanian nationalisms, but also because of Jewish claims to national recognition.

Dzierżyński was arrested in Warsaw, and after a period in the Warsaw Citadel he was exiled to Iakutsk in Eastern Siberia (Dzerzhinskii 1984: 35–8). He famously escaped by swimming across the Lena River – despite pneumonia and tuberculosis for which he spent time in a sanatorium (Strobel 1974: 175; Dzerzhinskii 2002: 163–74).[12] Dzierżyński described his existence as painful and miserable, and only political activism could prevent him from sinking into yet another depression. He wrote of his hatred "for all injustice, crime, drunkenness, depravity, excess, extravagance … I detest oppression, fratricidal strife and national discord … I want to see humanity surrounded with love, to warm it and cleanse it of the filth of modern life" (Dzerzhinskii 2002: 147).

On release, Dzierżyński edited the SDKPiL's radical paper in Kraków and Zakopane under Austria's more lenient rule (Zalevskii 1912: 157–8, 162; Dzerzhinskii 1977: 40–4).[13] He was again imprisoned in the Warsaw Citadel and released with the October Manifesto (Dzerzhinskii 1984: 69–70; Granat 1989: 408). Yet the SDKPiL's factory organization was by now no longer a political sect, but a mass party (Blobaum 1995: 134–7),[14] and concessions had to be made to the national question, as the SDKPiL, and Dzierżyński, conceded to certain guarantees of cultural development, such as national schools and freedom to use native languages in Poland. After the 1905 revolutions underscored the growing importance of nationalism, socialists became clearer about their ethnopolitical affinities: the PPS-Left aligned with the Mensheviks and the Bund, while SDKPiL internationalists moved closer to the Bolsheviks. The former more explicitly retained their particularistic ethnic identities, while the latter ignored diversity and emphasized stricter internationalism.

By focusing more narrowly on ethnically Polish workers in 1905, the PPS had cut itself off from the revolutionary potential in Russia, while the SDKPiL, with its almost entirely Polonized Jewish intellectual leadership, had flourished and increased its base. Crucially, Dzierżyński and other Polish socialists saw

---

[12] Well documented by the Okhrana in the *Boris I. Nicolaevsky Collection*, Hoover Institution Archives, Box 88 Accession No. 63013, 8.41/44, Series 54, Folder 28.

[13] On its publications, HIAPO, Index XIIIb(1), Box 121, Folder 1G, Outgoing Dispatches.

[14] Its organizational structure as seen by the Okhrana, HIAPO, Box 208, Index XIX, Folder 12B, 1909.

in 1905 a vindication of internationalism, believing that the strength of Polish social democracy lay in its connection to a *rossiiskii*-minded, universalist labor radicalism in conjunction with the Russian working class. This belief was reinforced by the fact that in 1905 student and strike activity in Warsaw had involved Polish, Jewish, and Russian students in common struggle over Polish rights in education. Interethnic cooperation in 1905 had vindicated a more strident socialist universalism over the nationalizing socialist parties, and Dzierżyński followed Luxemburg, not Lenin, on the national question (Strobel 1974: 172, 262). But he carefully balanced his political commitment to internationalism with a continued affection for Polish culture: writing to his brother from the Warsaw Citadel in late 1905, Dzierżyński asked to be sent a copy of Mickiewicz's *Pan Tadeusz* (Dzerzhinskii 2002: 192–6).

Dzierżyński's assessment proved tactically correct in the short run: the years of Tsarist reaction between 1905 and 1911 were the years of peak SDKPiL influence among Polish, German, and Jewish workers, including a large influx of factory proletariat (Zalevskii 1912: 168). The SDKPiL's influence in 1906–07 as a mass party just smaller than the PPS was truly multiethnic. In the longer term, however, Duma elections and political reaction in Russia had galvanized national over labor radicalism. And the National Democrats' autonomist-separatist platform eclipsed the socialist parties with their cultural organizations (Zalevskii 1912: 164–6, 169–71).

The Russian state stripped Dzierżyński of his privileges deriving from noble birth and permanently exiled him to Siberia. But his prolonged absence resulting from imprisonment and exile in the years of Tsarist reaction caused his activism to turn inward for justification, and with that, the perceived scope of his enormous sacrifice grew beyond the multiethnic working classes – to all of humanity (Zalevskii 1912: 168, 174). The more limited the actual influence of his activism, the more the sacrifice became an internal one, and the wider the perceived objective needed to justify the struggle. He wrote that his suffering was justified, and that his choice of a life in prison was right because it felt "an organic necessity"; it was his own "inner requirement" to sacrifice his own needs for the good of greater humanity (Dzerzhinskii 2002: 86–7, 184). In the years in which socialist revolution seemed the least likely, faith in its inevitability justified both his suffering and his political identity.

On release, Dzierżyński had wanted affiliation with the RSDLP while retaining sole organizational privileges over multiethnic regions of Poland and Lithuania. His politics were still antinationalist, those of the Polish gentry of the multiethnic borderlands with an implicit commitment to the integrity of imperial territories. But in 1911, the SDKPiL suffered internal splits and the PPS came to dominate the Polish labor movement; the SDKPiL's strident internationalism had slowly marginalized not only some of its leadership, but its following as well. Its multiethnic membership began to find their respective ethnic identities. SDKPiL membership dropped and the leadership migrated to Germany where they found a more suitable leftist home in the German-dominated International.

But in 1912, Dzierżyński was exiled and spent the war years in chains in a labor camp. He was moved to a Moscow prison but remained hospitalized because the chains had caused severe cramping in his legs, and he now faced the prospect of amputation (Dzerzhinskii 1984: 219–59 on correspondence during this period). When the Provisional Government proclaimed an amnesty for all political prisoners, Dzierżyński was released, but by this time he was unable to stand. There is no doubt that his extensive period of personal and physical struggle reinforced in Dzierżyński his attitude toward suffering. Although there were moments of sobriety – in 1914 he wrote of the "senselessness of my present life" (Dzerzhinskii 2002: 247) – his writings generally reflected an aesthetic fatalism, claiming that a life in prison was a destiny not only to be accepted but embraced (Dzerzhinskii 1984: 249–50).

The SDKPiL was already thinned because of mobilization and conscription of younger members into the imperial army, but with events of 1917, its base shifted from Poland to Russia. The Polish Communist Party was constructed on Russian, not Polish, soil with the merger of Dzierżyński's SDKPiL and the small but influential PPS-Left – both with their antinationalist positions intact. Dzierżyński had planned to return to Poland, but his close ties to Lenin assisted his position in the Bolshevik ranks. The early revolutionary years fired the belief that Russian events should be nurtured so that they might spill over into Poland, hence Dzierżyński's active involvement in the Russian Revolution: he became a Bolshevik in 1917 through contacts with Lenin. His Bolshevik activism briefly implicated him in Polish affairs in the Polish-Soviet War, on Brest-Litovsk he opposed Lenin on the national question and on the terms of the German treaty, and his defense of the socialist revolution during the Civil War was unmatched.

It may not be necessary to invoke his internationalism to understand his identity shift from Polish to Russian socialism. It may have been that internationalist principles again followed his transfer of loyalty rather than produced it. Early and continued influence of the Jewish socialist movement on Dzierżyński was profound, as his biographer wrote: "[H]is love affairs with Jewish women were more than just circumstantial; they were the logical outcome of a man which had been possessed of a certain way of seeing the world" (Blobaum 1984: 225). While no doubt true, I would also suggest a slightly different emphasis. From his early embrace of Polish radicalism, Dzierżyński had rejected Lithuanian nationalist socialism, Polish nationalist socialism, and Bundist cultural autonomism. He was attracted to Lithuanian socialism before it found its national identity or ethnic core; he was attracted to Polish socialism in its cosmopolitan, not in its nationalist, variant; and his efforts toward alliances between Polish, Lithuanian, Jewish, and Russian labor groupings consistently privileged internationalism over national labor radicalism. Even though he opposed the dismemberment of the empire in the terms of Brest-Litovsk, he abstained from the final vote, not ultimately committing himself to the internationalism of the Left Communists (as would Radek) because it was a cosmopolitan vision too far beyond empire. Although initially a Polish nationalist in response to Tsarist Russification, now Dzierżyński embraced a Russianized or national version of Bolshevism, although he understood this as imperial nationalism, not as an ethnic Russian nationalism. This was not consistent with pure internationalist principles.

In short, Dzierżyński's socialist universalism had clear imperial borders. So his various political alignments were not a rejection of his social, national, and religious backgrounds, but rather their embodiment: an impoverished Polish gentry-intellectual of the multiethnic borderlands, it was ethnonationalist marginality (Lithuanian, Jewish, and even Polish) and imperial policies of social exclusion that threatened identity, belonging, and position. Though ethnopolitical and social dislocation and political repression had characterized the Polish intelligentsia more generally, and though they disproportionately paid the costs of empire, Dzierżyński liminally sat on the empire's ethnocultural borders – neither fully within Polish urban culture nor fully within the Lithuanian Vilna milieu. He was among a *rossiiskii*, imperial-minded minority elite, socially blocked by dissimilatory Russification, in search of a politics that could protect their status and position within a reconstructed universalist or *rossiiskii*-oriented project. Radicalism in socialist internationalism offered such a way of creating a new social identity in a morally noble universalist politics, but his socialist universalism had to have territorial boundaries if one was to have true power within it.

Radek's Jewish Assimilation and Radicalism in Galicia

Radek's socialist universalism was a product of a different set of ethnopolitical dynamics outside Imperial Russia. Persecuted by Stalin as a "cosmopolitan Jew," Radek, according to A.J. Cummings (1935: xi–xii), was at heart a Polish Jew: "[W]hen he wished to speak words of endearment to women, they would be Polish words ... but for revolutionary matters he thought in German." Radek could work in several languages, but he was a Jew who could not speak Yiddish and a Bolshevik who barely spoke Russian. An Austrian citizen, Radek was a Polish-Galician Jew who flirted with Catholicism, became a Bolshevik in 1917, and a Spartacist in Germany in 1918. And he was a Polish Jew who arrived at Russian Bolshevism through German socialism (Möller 1976).

To his biographers, Radek was the embodiment of the *vaterlandslos* cosmopolitan: never identifying himself as a Jew, he had no national or ethnic affiliation other than his Jewishness and no consistent values other than his commitment to internationalism and to urbanism; he was a Jewish cosmopolitan whose lack of national identity permitted him to move in and out of socialist groupings and embrace socialist internationalism where *Vaterland* could be transcended (Lerner 1970: viii, 174–5; Tuck 1988: 19). There is certainly a great deal to this view. And yet, as with Dzierżyński, the antinationalist language of internationalism's mobilizational narrative should not be taken for the *experience* of the *vaterlandslos*. He was not one of Deutscher's "non-Jewish Jews": as we saw in Chapter 3, ascriptive Jewishness for most Jews was a social fact that consistently challenged claims to assimilation. Despite Radek's writings on the virtues of internationalism, he actually desired a national homeland. Judging from his political activities, internationalism may not have been a first choice, but either a second-best alternative or a necessity. Far from rejecting national cultures, on the biographical evidence Radek continually tried to embrace them.

Galician Jewish Assimilation to Polish Nationalism

Radek was born Sobelsohn in 1885 in Lwów (Granat 1989: 593). Much of Radek's early radicalism embodied the cultural and political orientations of the rising, secular Galician Jewish middle class in the last decades of the century. Galicia was politically more moderate than Russian Poland and the borderlands, but because of its socioeconomic underdevelopment and Lwów's cultural diversity, the secularized Jewish intelligentsia's assimilation was rendered more difficult; the Galician Jewish professional and commercial elite (Radek's family) struggled in midcentury as Austrian citizens for Jewish rights based on a German cultural assimilation and an anti-Polish loyalty to the empire (Mendelsohn 1969, 1971: 521–2).

The Sobelsohn's Austrophilism aspired to posts in the Austrian civil service: restrictions on Jewish occupations in Galicia were removed in 1860, and after 1867, the Austrian civil service was opened to all nationalities, Jews included (Wandruszka and Urbanitsch 1980: 893). They settled among the emancipated Jews of the city, and Radek's father assumed a position in the post office while his uncles held positions in the Austrian civil service and in the army (Granat 1989: 593). The Sobelsohns aspired to an acculturated Jewish middle-class existence, free from the *shtetl* as fully integrated Austrian citizens. Both as beneficiaries of the Austrian state and as secular Jews, they preferred the universalist and humanitarian ideals of German literature and philosophy to the Catholicism, anti-Semitism, and clericalism of Polish culture, even though they spoke both German and Polish at home (Steffen and Wiemers 1977: 14). The family's German-oriented Austrophilism, like that of many others, continued through the end of the empire (and arguably beyond), despite the fact that after the Ausgleich, Polonization was rapid and thorough. As the Polish majority in Galicia was granted self-rule, German Lemberg became Polish Lwów, causing a rupture in the provinces' ruling culture and forcing secular Jews to deal with Polish nationalists rather than German-speaking Austrian officials. Peace had to be made with Polish rule, as political necessity required. For those like Radek, born after the 1860s, accommodation was achieved in schools. So Radek's cultural capabilities had a certain duality. Although the family was thoroughly culturally Germanized, Radek was importantly the first to become linguistically Polonized (Granat 1989: 593).

A key aspect of Radek's initial switch in cultural orientation and his family's persistent Austrophilism is worth highlighting because of its implications for his revolutionary politics. Despite Galicia's Polonization, a significant portion of middle-class Jews persisted in their rejection of Polish culture and insisted that their children be raised Germanized Austrians, as they continued to send them to German *Gymnasien* and universities (Mendelsohn 1969: 579, nt. 8; Wandruszka and Urbanitsch 1980: 924). This suggests that perhaps something other than access to social mobility based on assimilation was operating. Part of the dynamic may lie in the cultural choices and orientations on offer. Polish culture, history, and language, though now the center of political gravity in Galicia, were considered those of a politically defeated nation-state whose temporary ascendance in Galicia was the result of a benevolent and liberal dynasty. More importantly, Polish culture was enveloped in the anti-Semitic Catholic Church, and a uninational, Catholic Polish Galicia could only be feared by even acculturationist Jews. In other words, for a number of middle-class Galician Jews, fears of a Catholic anti-Semitic Polish province proved more important than the possibilities for social mobility that Polonization could bring – hence the Sobelsohns' persistent German Austrophilism.

But Lwów also became an important center of the Ukrainian nationalist movement, largely as a result of Tsarist oppression on the other side of the border. Polish cultural dominance was threatened, and Eastern Galician Jews were caught between competing Polish and Ukrainian national movements. One important consequence was that Polonized or Germanized Galician Jews, and Radek among them, tended to align culturally with the antinationalist socialist Left, first in Polish groupings and then in German or Austrian groupings, but far less so with Jewish groups. So as a conspicuous cultural minority caught between often violent Ukrainian anti-Semitic nationalism and clerical Polish nationalism, Jewish cultural and political orientations tended to privilege the imperial state's language and culture, and the socialist leftism of the Polish Left (SDKPiL) and German Socialism (SPD) over Austrian Socialism (SPÖ). By the 1880s, both Polish cultural-political and Jewish (Hebrew and Yiddish) associations made their appearance. This was assisted by the fact that Galicia was particularly fertile soil for Polish-oriented nationalist and socialist associational life, more so because of Russian Poland's oppressive political atmosphere. In 1892, Polish Social Democracy, in 1895, the Polish Peasant Party, and in 1895, Polish National Democracy were all active recruiters in Austrian Galicia (McCagg 1989: 182)

So although the Sobelsohns continued to hold all things Polish in contempt, Radek's early radicalization rejected his family's German-Austrian cultural orientation, turning to the culture that he had been taught to hate: the romanticism of Polish nationalism. He rejected both the class and ethnic background of the Jewish petty bourgeoisie (Tuck 1988: 168). Radek chose to adopt Polish culture as his own despite – and even in part because of – its Catholicism. In fact, Radek was so taken with the romanticism of Polish nationalism that he considered converting to Catholicism in order to be more fully involved in the Polish nationalist cause (Granat 1989: 593). So in *Gymnasium* Radek was, as had been Dzierżyński, a Polish patriot, attracted to Mickiewicz.

Here was the crux of identity formation for marginalized minority elites in multiethnic imperial cultures: although from different social locations, both

Radek and Dzierżyński found similar political groupings attractive because of the shared or common dimensions in their social experiences and ethnopolitical contexts. Radek was a petty bourgeois Galician Jew and Dzierżyński a Catholic Polish gentry-intellectual of rural Lithuania, yet both turned to Polish nationalism. In 1869, the year that Polish was banned in secondary schools in Russian Poland, it became the official language for administration and courts in Austrian Galicia, with its school system becoming quickly Polonized (Weeks 1996: 100–2). While for Dzierżyński Polish nationalism was a response to Tsarist Russification, for Radek Polish nationalism represented an historical and romantic irredentist struggle against the Austrian government. Dzierżyński's earliest radicalism followed his mother and the Polish nationalism of the déclassé Polish gentry, whereas Radek's earliest radicalism constituted a rebellion against his acculturated Austrianophile civil servant family. But in both cases, by the 1890s, Polish nationalism was increasingly tied to socialism.

Radek's Polish nationalist radicalism drew him closer to socialism as he developed an antipathy to the Austrian bureaucracy (Granat 1989: 593–4). For *Gymnasium* students in the 1880s, Polish nationalism held out a different identity than it had for their parents: "[F]ar from being exclusive and anti-Semitic, [it] appeared to offer an honorable place within its ranks for Polish Jews" (Mendelsohn 1971: 524). A vision of Jews – "Poles of the Mosaic persuasion" – and Poles fighting oppression together represented the essence of Polish nationalism at this moment. Indeed, Radek's writings reflect a period in which he viewed Polish patriotic circles as the united struggles of Polish workers in Austria, Prussia, and Russia, all under the banner of "Patriotism, Democracy, Socialism" (Granat 1989: 594).

After his father's death, the Sobelsohns moved to Tarnów because Radek's mother regarded it as less East European and more Austrian than Lwów (Granat 1989: 594). Tarnów had no international press, so while in *Gymnasium*, Radek read the Kraków organ of the Polish Social Democratic Party (PPSD), which combined Polish nationalism and Polish socialism. He joined the party. The PPSD was by now Austrian Poland's version of the PPS in Russian Poland. Radek met his first workers at age fourteen, and he combined membership in patriotic circles with membership in neo-socialist circles. Radek also read novels about Polish students' struggles to preserve their national identity under the Russification of Tsarist *gimnazii*, such as the *The Labor of Sisyphus*, published in 1898 about a nationalist Polish boy named Andrzej Radek. Radek began to construct his political identity and dropped his own German-Jewish Sobelsohn (Granat 1989: 594–5).

Two observations are worth making about Radek and Dzierżyński's elective affinities to Polish nationalism, their early identity formation, and their routes to radical politics. First, Polish nationalism, as Radek and other middle-class Polish urbanites understood it, was now intimately connected to socialist doctrine and tied to the problems of the Polish peasantry in the face of perceived collusion between the Austrian state and the Polish landowning nobility. This was far different from Polish nationalism as conceived by Dzierżyński and other déclassé Polish gentry in the Lithuanian-Belarusian borderlands. Their concerns had little to do with peasant exploitation, but a great deal to do with Tsarist Russification and political oppression. In other words, Radek's early Polish nationalism was the product of acculturation – a Polonized Jewish youth swept up by the romanticism and belonging and possibilities of Polish freedom to transcend his Jewishness. In contrast, Dzierżyński's early Polish nationalism was the product of the exclusion of a Polish gentry-intellectual forced to submit to the humiliation of Russian rule.

Secondly and relatedly, just as Dzierżyński's identification with Polish patriotism was intimately related to his social experience as Polish petty nobility in the borderlands, so too might Radek's have been related to his social experience in Galicia. After the death of Radek's father, the family's middle-class existence was threatened, and his mother, a kindergarten teacher, struggled to support them in Tarnów (Granat 1989: 593). From the Austrian rising, middle-class civil servant family that the Sobelsohns were in Lwów, in Tarnów they had become a financially struggling family in the social milieux of the city's artisans and lower classes. Even though the city was more Germanized than Lwów in keeping with the family's cultural orientation, and though Tarnów's Jewish population was more modern, the Sobelsohns' social existence still suffered a reversal, and the struggles of their now lower-middle-class experience may have made Radek more receptive to the class conflicts inside Polish nationalism. So both Radek and Dzierżyński also had a particular déclassé dimension to their ethnopolitical exclusion.

Like Dzierżyński, Radek was also expelled from *Gymnasium* for his political radicalism. Radek enrolled in the *Gymnasium* in Kraków where he continued his studies and his activism with socialist groups of the PPSD. In 1897, the SPÖ had reorganized on a federative basis and its Galician section had become officially Polish, insisting that its members be "international" in the Polish language. So Polonized Jewish socialists in Galicia generally joined Polish parties, often their left wings. Even Austrian socialism in Galicia was Polish. But Radek was not attracted to Austrian groupings. Nor was he attracted to Jewish groupings, socialist or nationalist, and indeed very few were. Radek's political radicalism thus far was neither Jewish nor fully socialist, and far from internationalist. Polish socialist movements *and* Polish nationalist movements, whether PPS, PPSD, or SDKP, were still open enough to attract acculturated Polonized Jews. Yet this would not last long as the PPS moved rightward: it became increasingly anti-Semitic as it chose between nation and class (Hagen 1996; Porter 2000).

German Socialism to Bolshevik Internationalism

Radek's vistas opened beyond Austrian Galicia and in 1903 he met, and liked, the by then legendary Dzierżyński who was in Kraków setting up a new SDKPiL section (Granat 1989: 596). Radek's biographer writes that Radek was moved by Dzierżyński's renunciation of his social background – a privileged, Catholic

Polish gentry rejecting Polish independence in order to join the socialist cause – with the Russian movement no less. He argues that Radek questioned the PPSD's possibilities, and began to see Polish socialism as an international force in itself, and not merely as a tactic for achieving Polish independence (Lerner 1970: 7–9).

Yet this may be conflating the causes of his radicalization with the content of the ideology he espoused. As we have seen, Dzierżyński's radicalism was not a renunciation of his social origins or experience, but an expression of it. The same might be said of Radek. In the same year that he met Dzierżyński, Radek went to Zurich and found work as a librarian.[15] He joined Dzierżyński's SDKPiL as an émigré member and was immediately introduced into the Second International, which was at the time fighting the revisionist versus revolutionary battles of Eduard Bernstein and Rosa Luxemburg. Although Radek was no doubt attracted to the idea of socialist internationalism as a value necessitating the abandonment of Polish nationalism (Granat 1989: 595), this may have been a consequence of the dynamics within the political groupings as they structured his options.

Specifically, the PPSD in Austrian Galicia had been attractive to Radek, but in Zurich its political scope appeared limiting. Indeed, localism was Galician radical politics' defining feature (McCagg 1989: 185–6). Moreover, the rivalry between the nationalist PPS and the internationalist SDKPiL had intensified between 1901 and 1903. And the nationalist strain in the PPS was becoming increasingly more exclusionary and anti-Semitic – the PPS sat to the right of most European socialist parties. This sent most Polish Jewish socialists, already more attracted to Polish movements of the Left than they were to Jewish groupings, into even more leftist and cosmopolitan Polish groupings, such as Dzierżyński's SDKPiL. In short, the internationalist SDKPiL (in federation with the Russian Social Democracy) offered greater political vistas than Galician politics for Radek's considerable talents, and for an assimilating Jew it offered an escape from an increasingly ethnicized politics inside Polish socialism. In effect, Radek was simultaneously a member of the RSDLP, federated SDKPiL, and Galician Social Democracy. The fact that he belonged to a leftist internationalist Polish grouping in Russian Poland and a nationally minded Polish grouping in Austrian Poland at the same time said as much about Radek's cultural modularity as it did about ethnopolitics within and across socialist and nationalist political mobilizations.

Radek had also been writing on the Galician peasantry, but he came to the realization that revolutionary potential lay instead with the working class in Russian Poland (Granat 1989: 596). With the outbreak of the 1905 Revolutions, Radek made his way to SDKPiL headquarters in Warsaw (on his activities there, see Steffen and Wiemers 1977: 17–20). The following year he was arrested, began studying Russian, and became a regular contributor to

---

[15] He may also briefly have been a student (Möller 1976: 23), although this was not included in the semiofficial *Granat*.

the German leftist press (Granat 1989: 597–8). As his relations with German socialism deepened, Radek's writings became increasingly critical of calls for Polish independence. He also remained active in the SDKPiL during 1907 and 1908. But as the SDKPiL's constituent nationalities balkanized politically, its multiethnic leadership, Radek included, drifted into the German-dominated International, which in these years was full of leftist Polish (and Polish-Jewish) émigrés who felt increasingly ethnically squeezed by the growing nationalism of Polish socialism. The center of gravity for leftist Polish socialists was now Germany, and Radek consciously abandoned his Polish orientation and relied on his Germanized Jewish background.

Radek began to write on colonialism and imperialism during the first Balkan Crisis, and he edited the SDKPiL's journal in Berlin (Granat 1989: 597–8). He became a regular contributor to the *Leipziger Volkszeitung* (the most important organ of the German Left) and *Die Neue Zeit*, moving to Leipzig to immerse himself in German socialism (Granat 1989: 597–8). But the SDKPiL was in disarray and in decline.[16] The SPD also began to lose its stridency as revisionism prevailed and participation in parliamentary elections dominated its agenda: German Social Democracy, too, was finding its national home. In response, the German Left, which now included nearly all the Jewish leftist émigré members of the Russian-Polish-Lithuanian SDKPiL (Luxemburg, Leo Jogiches, and Radek), formed a loose-knit group; the nucleus of the German-based internationalist Left was increasingly dominated by Polish-Jewish intellectuals with affiliations to both the SPD Left and the leftist SDKPiL. In other words, the more Polish-Jewish émigrés were marginalized by Polish and German socialist mobilizations, the more cosmopolitan political parties became attractive to them. Ultimately this was a more radical, class cosmopolitanism than Dzierżyński's, not least because most Jewish socialist émigrés located anti-Semitism within class relations and not within the very nations into which they sought assimilation.

Immediately preceding the war, Radek's multiparty activism openly reflected uneasiness with the nationalist tendencies of the socialist political mobilizations and ambivalent membership status.[17] Shortly after the SDKPiL split into the Berlin and Warsaw factions in 1911, Radek was expelled from the Berlin group. German socialists regarded Radek as too Bohemian, sloppy, and irresponsible (Lerner 1970: 19). Some of the subtext of this was clearly anti-Semitic, as Radek's appearance and behavior seemed too Jewish. But he had slowly been gravitating toward a new group, the Bremen Left radicals, *l'enfant terrible* of German socialism. He began writing for the *Bremen Bürgerzeitung*, the most radical and anti-revisionist paper

---

[16] The factionalism of the Polish parties – and Radek's part in it – was not missed by the Tsarist Okhrana, HIAPO, Box 208, XIX, Polish Revolutionaries, Index XIX, Folder 6, Doc. No. 1017, July 30/August 12, 1911 and Box 208, Index XIX, Folder 123, dispatch 1912.

[17] Documented in Okhrana surveillance records in HIAPO, Box 708, Index XIX, Polish Revolutionaries, Index XIX, Folder 6, Circular No. 1017, Paris, July 30/August 12, 1911, and Circular No. 14053, December 12, 1909.

in Germany. Radek's personal credentials and integrity came under attack when he was accused of embezzling money from the SDKPiL. A commission set up by Dzierżyński investigated the "Radek Case": he was found guilty, and Dzierżyński's activist purity led him to conclude that Radek should not be allowed membership in *any* socialist party (Lerner 1970: 28–9; Blobaum 1984: 207–8). Radek's expulsion from the SDKPiL was followed by expulsion from the SPD. Then the SPD expelled him on the grounds that he had tenuous membership credentials and because he had already been repudiated by the SDKPiL. So the only party that welcomed Radek was the Bremen Left Radicals (Möller 1976: 19–22).

In Berlin at the declaration of war, Radek was shocked that German Social Democracy became imperialist and more concerned with national fatherland than with class revolution (Granat 1989: 601–2). The realities of ethnonationalist attachments over socialist ones hit the Jewish émigrés hard and continually prompted searches for ever-more inclusive internationalist, cosmopolitan organizations. In 1914, Radek was an Austrian citizen and liable for military service, so he went to Switzerland and began writing for the largest socialist paper there, the *Berner Tagwacht*, which opposed the war and sympathized with the Second Internationalist Left (Granat 1989: 603). Disillusioned, and in response to growing national identities of the socialist movements, Radek gravitated to the nucleus of internationalism, which during the war was among the Russian émigré-dominated Left. The Russian émigré colonies in Switzerland were actually quite eclectic and cosmopolitan in membership, but more importantly, they were now the only internationalists willing to accept marginalized Jewish radicals. And it was not hard to see why: after fifty years of socialist internationalism, it was famously still possible to seat all the internationalists for the Zimmerwald antiwar conference in just four train coaches. Radek wrote for them in the Second International press. Although he held to Luxemburg's position on the national question and not to Lenin's, and although he had no real interest in Russian socialism, he cultivated a relationship with Lenin on an antiwar basis. Radek was now a Bolshevik: only the Bolsheviks had supported his membership in the International.

He was in Sweden during Russian revolutionary events, and he continued to regard Russian events with dispassion, singularly focusing on their relevance to world revolution (Möller 1976: 28–9). In this, his understanding differed markedly from those Bolsheviks who had begun to see the revolution in more Russian terms. Once again his leftist internationalism was a product of personal, ethnopolitical, and organizational isolation. As the Revolution slowly found its Russian national character, however, Radek reconfirmed his commitment to a radical internationalism. As the Bolshevik leadership accepted the terms of Brest-Litovsk that dismembered the empire, Radek deserted and clung to his leftist internationalism, not simply because of an intrinsic belief in world revolution, but perhaps also because as a Galician Jew who could barely speak Russian he now found himself slowly marginalized from an obviously Russifying socialist revolution.

So initially Radek turned from Russian events back to German politics in 1918. After the collapse of the German government, he was involved with the German Spartacists. Radek's return to the German Left now had gravitas: he was a Bolshevik, from the only country to have had a proper revolution. In 1919, he was captured and placed in solitary confinement by the German government (see discussion on this episode in Carr 1951). His isolation from Russian and German politics at this crucial time reinforced his international-ism – by now at home in the Comintern – and which in the 1920s was a refuge for ethnopolitically isolated Jewish radicals. Until 1924, the language of the Comintern had been German, which Trotsky, Lenin, and Radek knew with var-ious degrees of proficiency. But with Zinoviev's ascendancy in the Comintern and Stalin's ascension in Soviet Russia, the shift from German socialist inter-nationalism to a Russianized Soviet internationalism with anti-Semitic under-tones was clear, and Radek, among other Jewish leftists, would find himself excluded from a now Russianized International (on his own thinking in these years, see Radek 2000). The Comintern, too, was failing as a refuge from eth-nopolitics. Radek's desire to belong had carried him from Polish nationalism to Polish socialism (until it became nationalist), to the then more ethnically open German socialism, which dominated the International (until it became imperialist), and finally to Bolshevism's internationalist proletarian revolution (until it became Russian).

Conclusion

These three biographies are emblematic of the identity dilemmas inherent in the reconciliation of ethnicity with class within Bolshevik's revolutionary nar-rative and, more concretely, within its mobilizational politics. As ethnicity was politicized, and as Jews and Poles remained conflicted in their assimilation-ism, their biographies underscore revolutionary socialism's contested ability to transcend ethnic boundaries (Zimmerman 2004: 274–5). Politically excluded or problematically assimilated minorities were acutely vulnerable to both class and ethnic tensions in ethnically ranked borderlands, sitting at once at the intersection of class and ethnicity in terms of social stratification and at the intersection of nationalism and empire in terms of political change. Because of the ways in which class and ethnicity intersected in these multiethnic bor-derlands, these three revolutionaries' ethnopolitical exclusions were entwined with a particular status or class decline. Experientially, this tension made them receptive to the class conflicts within Polish and Lithuanian radical politics and to the ethnic grievances channeled by the socialist revolutionary narrative. Radek's Polish nationalism was the product of acculturation – a Polonized Jewish youth swept up by the romanticism and possibilities of Polish freedom to transcend his Jewishness. Dzierżyński's was the product of the exclusion of a Polish gentry-intellectual forced to submit to the humiliation of Russian rule. And Kapsukas's exclusion was cultural: incapable of meeting the high standards of the Lithuanian cultural elite, he was receptive to the possibility of a Russified, socialist critique of Lithuanian culture.

But as importantly, they highlight some of the key policies or strategies adopted by the Russian state, which contributed to both the content and direction of minority elites' routes to political radicalism. Dzierżyński was the product of dissimilatory Russification, repressiveness, and the increasing salience of ethnic markers in the state's policies of surveillance and social control, especially the ethnic repressions that caused the rural Polish landed elite of the western borderlands to disproportionately bear the political burdens of empire's integrity. Kapsukas similarly experienced dissimilatory Russification – albeit linguistically less viciously and more as a religious minority – but his marginalization from Lithuanian cultural nationalism made *rossiiskii* routes to radicalism experientially attractive. And although Radek was radicalized outside the Russian Empire, social exclusion and ethnocultural marginality in the face of ethnicizing socialist movements in the empire's borderlands, as well as his own problematic assimilation, caused him to move eastward into *rossiiskii*, leftist mobilizations, which welcomed him as a revolutionary first and as a non-Russian second.

Yet the subtle differences in their social experiences and in their routes to radicalism are also suggestive of the effects of imperial strategies on the many socioethnic niches in the imperial tapestry – or, put differently, on their varying elective affinities with a Russian-inflected Bolshevism. For instance, both Radek and Dzierżyński had a particular déclassé dimension in their ethnopolitical exclusion: just as Dzierżyński's identification with Polish patriotism was bound up with his social experience as Polish petty nobility in the borderlands, so too Radek's was related to his family's petty bourgeois experience in Galicia. One of Dzierżyński's biographers claimed that he was constitutionally "in need of a cause, of a categorical imperative," a claim Dzierżyński came close to making himself (Leggett 1981: 251; Dzerzhinskii 2002: 25, 40, 48, 87, 142, 149, 293, and passim). And yet Dzierżyński had less of an identity problem than did Radek: Dzierżyński's was more a concern over political orientation and social position, whereas Radek's persistent ambiguities over assimilation meant that political orientation was more directly related to his social identity. Dzierżyński's socialist universalism was therefore less radical than Radek's. His universalist vision was contained within the limits of empire, as befitted the moral politics of a segment of the borderland gentry; his Bolshevism defended a state-bounded universalism determined to control any particularistic threat, and Dzierżyński eventually became a ferocious Russifier. By contrast, Radek's socialist internationalism became purer, radicalizing with successive ethnic exclusions. But his desire for an assimilated belonging caused him to repeatedly underestimate the persistence of anti-Semitism as he ultimately fell victim to a Russifying, anti-Semitic socialism. Radek's political migrations embodied the failure of recognized assimilation in the context of nation-building processes and the identity politics of Jews as imperial nation (on the latter concept, see

Klier 2003). His was not a rejection of his Jewish declining petit bourgeois background (as Tuck 1988: 168 argues), but rather its political expression.

By contrast, Kapsukas's radicalism brought him from Lithuanian national- ism – anti-Polish, anti-Russian, and anticlerical – to Polish-Lithuanian socialism, to Lithuanian socialism, and finally to Bolshevism, where he would eventually advocate for Lithuania's cultural Russification. Each political shift was struc- tured by cultural and linguistic shifts in the various political mobilizations. Bolshevism's *rossiiskii* inclusiveness offered access, ethnic belonging, and polit- ical status to an aspiring but culturally marginalized activist like Kapsukas. He was also, eventually, drawn to its antinationalism – once he had repudiated his own nationalist activism.

These three biographies and political migrations, therefore, illustrate the degree to which socialism succeeded in transcending ethnic and national boundaries only in the Tsarist Russian "fourth time zone." The appeal of uni- versalist ideologies, in this case socialist internationalism, was contingent on the strength of nationalism: socialist internationalism had a narrower social base where nationalism was more politically articulate, because a more developed nationalism tended to undermine universalist ideologies. As 1914 approached, in the "third time zone," nations became organizationally more powerful than class, so for excluded ethnic minorities with problematic biographies the radi- cal option was no longer universalism, but some form of nationalism. Further east, however, the political center of gravity was reversed: nationalist move- ments were generally in their early cultural-autonomist phases, with as yet very weakly articulated political claims, making universalist socialism a potent radical force. Radek's, Kapsukas's, and Dzierżyński's problematic biographies embodied these tensions in their social identities and reconciled them in a polit- ical radicalism that traveled eastward from Lithuanian and Polish nationalisms to an imperial-minded, if Russianized, class universalism.

5

The Ukrainian Bolsheviks

An assumption often articulated by Ukrainian nationalists in exile concerning Ukrainian revolutionary politics under Tsarist rule is that Ukrainians were excluded, repressed, or relegated to minority status under the Russian rule. But as noted in Chapter 2, Tsarist elites rarely conceived of the empire's constituent minorities – and in this case the Ukrainians – in wholesale ethnic terms. Instead they constructed both conciliatory and repressive policies differentially targeted at specific groups: peasants, nobility, cultural elites, liberal professions, civil service, or military elites. Actually the majority of educated Ukrainians were not excluded, but rather co-opted into the imperial state and bureaucracy. Indeed, Russified Ukrainians were so common that Max Weber (1989: 129–52) observed that most of the Ukrainian intelligentsia hardly questioned imperial unity or Russian hegemony because of their absorption into its bureaucracies.

A key strategy outlined in Table 2.1, Chapter 2 – the integration of certain middle- and upper-class minority elites into the empire's civil and military bureaucracies – contributed a particular assimilationism to their political radicalism. That is, the bureaucratic assimilation of sections of the Ukrainian intelligentsia had important effects on the ethnic composition and ideological character of the radical political mobilizations that emerged in Ukraine. Socialist revolutionary movements, for instance, had a certain social strength in the Ukrainian provinces, but so did nationalist movements. Tsarist Ukraine produced some of the most virulent nationalist mobilizations (Russian, Ukrainian, Polish, and Jewish), but also some of the most internationalist, socialist ones (Russian, Ukrainian, and Jewish). These were related in one of the most problematically and violently multiethnic regions of the empire, which also included the Jewish Pale. After 1905, the left bank and southern provinces (squarely within the Pale) became strongholds of nationalist and rightist parties, of anti-Semitism, and of Polonophobia (Klier and Lambroza 1992: 43, 194; Lohr 2003: ch. 4). And the internationalist movements responded in tandem by moving further to the left. In other words, a key substantive argument of this chapter is that in the Ukrainian regions the same ethnopolitical conditions and Tsarist strategies of bureaucratic incorporation – resulting in imperial-minded assimilation – shaped the character of both nationalist or rightist mobilizations and socialist internationalist ones. They were different responses to the same socioethnic tensions. And here is where both sides of Table 2.1 in Chapter 2 on leftist and rightist mobilizations emerged in direct conflict.

It is important to note immediately that Bolshevism had little support in the Ukraine in 1917, particularly among ethnic Ukrainians. There were eight Ukrainians in the Bolshevik elite, a significant underrepresentation as compared to their proportion of the empire's population.[1] From a labor force of nearly 2 million, in 1918 the Bolsheviks were merely 4,000–5,000 strong (mostly in the Donetsk industrial region), while the Ukrainian SRs had more than 300,000 members. Importantly, ethnic Russians and Jews comprised nearly 75 percent of the Ukrainian Bolshevik party (all figures in Subtelny 1994: 348–9). This gives some sense of the exceptionality of Ukrainians within Bolshevism. In fact the leaderships of the three Bolshevik Ukrainian factions were ethnically mixed: the Kharkov-Ekaterinoslav group was led by Rightists Emmanuil Kviring (son of a German colonist) and Fedora Sergeev (Russian), the Leftists in Kiev were led by Georgi Piatakov (Ukrainian-born Russian) and Evgenia Bosh (Jewish), and the Centrists were led by Nicolai (Mykola) Skrypnyk (Ukrainian). So the key question for understanding how imperial policies shaped Ukrainian Bolshevik routes to political radicalism is not only how and why the few Ukrainians who came to Bolshevism did so, but also how and why the small Ukrainian Bolshevik revolutionary mobilization was able to hold together Russians, Jews, Germans, and Ukrainians among its members.

A second claim relates to imperial strategies of dissimilatory Russification and status-particularistic policies of socioethnic exclusion. In response to Ukraine's complex ethnopolitics, the battles within Ukrainian Bolshevism were between the internationalists who conceived of an unconditional unity within the imperial state as a way to counter nationalist movements (Nikolai [Nikolay] Krestinsky, Dmitri [Dmitry] Manuilsky) and those who conceived of cultural autonomy within the empire as a way to counter Russian centralism (Skrypnyk). This tension was emblematic of the wider political struggles in the ethnically complex Ukrainian territories. So in these very difficult multiethnic environments nationalist political movements (liberal separatist, rightist, or xenophobic) and socialist politics (nationalist and internationalist) were also simply different ideological and organizational products within Bolshevism of the same socioethnic and political tensions.

This is also suggestive of the wider claims of this book. Most immediately, the Ukrainian Bolsheviks' biographies highlight the ways in which socialism's revolutionary, Russian-inflected ideology organized materially: it drew in, consolidated, and funneled the cultural and social resources of Russified workers and Russified educated elites into common cause with the region's ethnic Russians and excluded non-Russians. It did this by offering a narrative

---

[1] I do not explore Matvei Muranov because of insufficient biographical sources. Alexandra Kollontai was also part Ukrainian. Her father was Ukrainian and her mother Finnish.

of ethnic inclusion – and the experience of a concrete movement to go with it – that struck chords in their particular Russified yet politically marginalized social experiences. Russian-inflected socialism was an antidote for certain elites caught within problematic socioethnic frameworks and social locations characterized by Russification and socioethnic tensions. This particular composition, and the resources they brought into the mobilization, allowed it to compete organizationally with Ukraine's narrower nationalist mobilizations. Moreover, regardless of their position on Ukrainian nationalism's ideological continuum, these Bolsheviks sought noncolonial, but territorially *rossiiskii*, political arrangements and geopolitical commitments. A largely Russified Ukrainian intelligentsia and working class emerged from the empire's borderlands committed to reconstructing a Russian-inflected, universalist state.

Imperial Strategies and Ukrainian Radicalism

Because of the discussion on Ukrainian radicalism developed later in this chapter, it is useful to distinguish the socioethnic and political differences between Cossack left-bank Ukraine and the formerly Polish right-bank provinces west of the Dnieper (the following paragraphs draw from Kohut 1988; Beauvois 1993; Szporluk 1997; Kuromiya 1998; Kappeler et al. 2003; Lohr 2003; Miller 2003; Snyder 2003; Brown 2004). Left-bank Ukraine was the site of the Cossack-led state, the Hetmanate, with significant autonomy and cultural distinctiveness until its abolition in 1763. By the mid-1830s, the Hetmanate was institutionally absorbed into the empire, most notably through the co-optation of Ukrainian nobles, Cossacks, burghers, clergy, and peasantry – the former into the Russian *dvorianstvo* and imperial bureaucracies. Ukrainian rural elites were almost entirely Russified by the early nineteenth century. By contrast, Russia's share of partitioned Poland was the Dnieper's right-bank Ukrainian provinces of Kiev (Kyiv), Podolia, and Volhynia. Most Ukrainians were incorporated as peasants, Polonized nobles, landed gentry, or *meshchane* and merchants in Kiev.

By the 1830s, then, most of the Ukrainian territories were imperially administered as nine *gubernii*.[2] But midcentury, reforms of provincial governments – *zemstva* assemblies and municipal government – differentially affected the Ukrainian regions depending on their socioethnic composition. Because *zemstva* were introduced in some of the left-bank provinces where Polish landed elites were fewer (Kharkov, Chernigov [Chernihiv]), a provincial political and civil society developed in contrast to the right-bank provinces (where Polish *szlachta* still dominated), and where reforms were largely withheld, blocking an important venue for social mobility.

The different modes of incorporation, historical trajectories, and socioethnic structures of the left and right banks gave rise to different regional political

---

[2] These included the four left-bank provinces – Chernigov, Kharkov, Poltava, and Ekaterinoslav – and Kherson, and Taurida (Crimea).

identities and radical mobilizations. The left-bank (Chernigov, Ekaterinoslav, Kharkov, and Poltava) provinces urbanized slowly and retained their histori-cally indigenous elite, so Ukrainian national identity was relatively weak. By contrast, in the more socioeconomically advanced right-bank provinces, the nobility supported Russian nationalists (in opposition to left-bank Ukrainian calls for cultural rights), while acute competition for seasonal work among peasants made them more receptive to the nationalist message inside Ukrainian socialism (for context past and present, on Volhynia, see Brown 2004). So dif-ferences in socioeconomic development were a key source of divergent pat-terns of radicalization. But equally important were the regions' respective ethnopolitics, and the fact that the territorial Ukrainian provinces were nearly coterminous with the Jewish Pale of Settlement – something that permanently and consequentially entwined Jewish and Ukrainian political developments under Tsarist rule.[3] The empire's worst anti-Semitic violence took place in the Ukrainian provinces, but these same provinces also produced the greatest num-ber of socialist internationalists – two distinctions that I argue are related. And the fact that more Bolsheviks – of all ethnicities and social strata – were radicalized in the territorial provinces of the Ukraine than in any other region of the empire suggests that revolutionary politics in these provinces had a dis-tinctive underpinning.

These are important considerations given that the Ukrainian Bolsheviks' political radicalization reflected these dynamics: those Bolsheviks from the Polish-dominated right bank (and Mogilev) were the most internationalist in political activism, whereas those from the old Cossack lands and the industri-alizing south, where *starshyna* (officerships or military elite) traditions with regional identities persisted, were more conflicted in their socialist-nationalist politics. So I situate them within three closely related Tsarist strategies drawn from Chapter 2, which directly impinged on the early radicalization of the Ukrainian Bolsheviks: (1) Tsarist cultural repression of Ukrainian elites and restrictions on Ukrainian language and literature in attempts at divide and rule through dissimilatory Russification; (2) policies directed at inclusion, assimila-tory Russification, or imperial bureaucratic incorporation, which contributed to a generalized Russophilia among many middle-class Ukrainians; and (3) the splitting of the Ukrainian middle classes through combinations of integrative and exclusionary imperial strategies.

First, the Russian state had historically supported Ukrainian culture because of its potential anti-Polish value, but as the nineteenth century progressed, wor-ries emerged of alliances between Polish *szlachta* and Ukrainian intellectuals; concerns emerged of Polish influence over Ukrainian and Slavic peasantries (as well as the concomitant desire to encourage the Ukrainian peasantry as a poten-tial ally) (Weeks 1996: 123–5); anxieties developed about the ethnoreligious and

---

[3] In addition to the Polish-Lithuanian-Belarusian provinces (Minsk, Kovno, Vilna, Mogilev, and Vitebsk) and Bessarabia (after 1812), the Pale included Ukrainian Volhynia, Podolia, Kiev (except the city of Kiev), Ekaterinoslav, Kherson, Crimea (Taurida), Poltava, and Chernigov.

linguistic minoritization of ethnic Russians (Kappeler 1993: 76–7; Saunders 1995); fears grew of the radicalizing influences of social revolutionaries and educated elites on Slavic peasantries; and a concomitant desire to strengthen Russian assimilation potential in the borderlands similarly grew (Miller 2003). All of these prompted the language, publication, and cultural restrictions of the 1863 Valuev Circular and the 1876 Ems Edict. Yet most educated Ukrainians (and nearly all the peasantry) were in practical terms minimally affected by these language restrictions as most were linguistically Russified or bilingual anyway and most of the peasantry had low levels of literacy. Tsarist language laws practically – and arguably intentionally – implicated only a small but influential minority of Ukrainian cultural elites. Moreover, these language policies were not primarily intended to Russify or integrate these Ukrainian elites, but rather to exclude or dissimilate them in order to strengthen a Russian cultural presence, particularly in view of the fact that a competing Polish high culture had potentially strong assimilatory power as an attractive and vibrant alternative to the imperial Russian. Of the Ukrainian Bolsheviks, Skrypnyk was the most affected by these exclusions.

A second relevant feature of the imperial state's Ukrainian policies was its strategies of bureaucratic incorporation or integration, resulting in substantial levels of voluntary Russification and the creation of an imperial-minded elite. The Russian state incorporated a substantial segment of educated Ukrainians (some Russified, but most bilingual) into the imperial civil and military bureaucracies even after the introduction of language policies (Velychenko 1995, 2000). The Ukrainian gentry had been almost entirely co-opted into the Tsarist *dvorianstvo*,[4] and in such large numbers that Russian nobles complained of the careerism of the "creeping Little Russians." But this also mitigated the effects of the loss of regional or local institutions (Velychenko 1997: 421–9). As early as 1835, no political privileges had distinguished Russian officers, administrators, and merchants from their Ukrainian counterparts. Some 1.4 million Ukrainians Russified between the 1860s and 1890s, as much of educated Ukrainian society was siphoned off into imperial bureaucracies and Russianized in the process (Subtelny 1994: 204–5; Saunders 1995: 193). Privileged and Russianized Ukrainians began to associate Ukrainian Cossack culture with anarchy and lawlessness and contrasted it to the civic inclusiveness and order of the imperial state. So they consistently supported state centralization and were often strongly assimilationist. Beside access to careers, positions, titles, wealth, and land, another important advantage of empire for some Ukrainian elites was its geopolitical value: only inside the Russian Empire could the Hetmanate cope with its traditional enemies – Poles, Tatars, and Turks (Kohut 1988: 261–3).

---

[4] For instance, in 1785, *dvorianstvo* rights were granted to Cossack officers, and these rights were elevated to those of the Polish-Lithuanian *szlachta*, prompting Ukrainian *szlachta* to switch to *dvorianstvo* status, which now allowed access to careers in civil and military imperial bureaucracies. Additionally, Ukrainian peasants were enserfed for the first time in 1783 to the delight of the landed Ukrainian gentry (Kohut 1988: 237–56).

A certain Ukrainian patriotism did continue, however, because of a historical capacity for holding different loyalties simultaneously (Tsarist, imperialist,
Hetmanate, and noble estate), and because Hetmanate traditionalists retained
both a loyalty to the Tsar and an active desire for Ukrainian autonomy, often
resisting total assimilation (Kohut 1988: 266–7).

The Ukrainian clergy, too, was easily reconciled to Russian rule as shared
Orthodoxy meant shared culture: they were heavily Russified, wrote to each
other in Russian, spoke Russian at home, and even preached village sermons
in Russian (Kohut 1988: 295; Kappeler 1993: 78–9). Following notables,
Cossacks, and clergy (and setting aside the peasantry), the middling strata of
burghers, artisans, and merchants were also integrated. Typically weak and
outnumbered in most Ukrainian cities and towns by Jews, Poles, or Russians,
they were folded into what essentially became ethnically mixed *meshchanstvo*
and artisan classes. In an effort to resist ethnic monopolies, Kiev's guilds were
organized by profession, not by nationality; Ukrainian artisan guilds (especially in the building trades) included large numbers of Russians and Jews
and became de facto Russified or *rossiiskii* in character. This had the effect of
simultaneously strengthening and diluting Ukrainian (and Jewish and Russian)
identities in both status and corporative structures as well as in associational
life (for a discussion on Kiev, see Meir 2006).

All of this had an important influence on the tensions within Ukrainian
radical political mobilizations, both nationalist and socialist. As a result of
inconsistent imperial strategies of minority elite co-optation, ethnic exclusion,
and dissimilatory Russification, high levels of acculturation-Russification were
as important in shaping Ukrainian radicalism as were repressive or illiberal
state policies. Much Ukrainian politicization was distinctive because of its
abiding assimilationism and willing integrationism. In the under-administered
Ukrainian provinces, the Russian-Ukrainian assimilation barrier was quite low,
in fact, with porous and easily culturally recognizable languages and religions,
which facilitated Ukrainian peasant and worker Russification (Miller 2003: ch.
7 and p. 252). Ukraine's loss of distinct identity was indeed perhaps more complete than any other region of the empire (Hosking 1997: 26–7). And it was a
process of imperial integration that occurred with remarkably little resistance
on the part of the Ukrainian gentry, and with more than a notion of political
expediency. So while the strength of Ukrainian identity and Russophilia in the
left-bank provinces contrasted with the virulence of that of many right-bank
Kievian cultural elites, overall Russification and Russophilia remained pronounced among Ukrainians. And this was finely calibrated across both nationalist and socialist movements.

The immediate consequences for Bolshevism's revolutionary politics were
similarly complex. The cultural intelligentsia's motivating fear was cultural
minoritization in the face of its own Russophilic elites' imperial-mindedness.
Ukrainian nationalists battled pro-imperialist, Russified Ukrainians, and
Russified educated Ukrainians in the socialist movements battled Ukrainian
nationalism as much, if not more, than Russian state policies. Put differently,

Ukrainian nationalist and socialist movements defined themselves in opposition to each other as much as in opposition to the Russian state. Ukrainian nationalists (the Ukrainian People's Party) were defensive in viewing the primary threat as the persistence of voluntary cultural assimilation and Russification among Ukrainians. And Russified Ukrainians (socialists in the RSDLP or the SRs, and national socialists in the Ukrainian Social Democratic Party) sought with equal motivation to protect their new, Russified social identities. For them, a commitment to Russified social identities – and so to a form of *rossiiskii* politics – made the all-Russian socialist mobilizations highly attractive. These intricate socioethnic contexts, experienced most acutely in the Pale's provinces, produced the most internationalist socialists. This was as much in response to local nationalisms (including those of their co-ethnics) as it was to illiberal Russian centralism. So high levels of Russification and/or Russophilia, the ranked and ambiguously assimilated ethnicities in the Pale's territories and their respective nationalisms, and a commitment to internationalist socialism were of a piece for Ukrainian socialist internationalists: left Communist and internationalist Bolsheviks were more numerous in Ukraine than in any other part of the empire.

Third and finally, Tsarist elites pursued more specific inclusionary and exclusionary policies toward educated Ukrainians: they encouraged social mobility through imperial state service while trying to limit the number of commoners made noblemen. The very specific ways in which Tsarist imperial policies split the Ukrainian middle strata had important effects not only on their radicalization, but also on the direction and content of their political movements. By the turn of the century, there were five distinct strata within the Ukrainian middling and petty noble classes: (1) a small cultural, intellectual, and academic elite, many of whom were in exile; (2) the liberal or free professions, many in the employ of *zemstva*; (3) a substantial strata of Ukrainians in the employ of the imperial state as bureaucrats and civil servants in middling and low-level positions in the Ukraine and elsewhere; (4) a nobility, including service nobles in higher imperial posts; and (5) bureaucrats in the imperial military bureaucracy and army. Of the eight Ukrainian Bolsheviks, five came from these middle strata.

Of these five strata, the last three were de facto Russified and co-opted into the imperial state to varying extents. The second group, those Ukrainians in the free professions (statisticians, teachers, agronomists, and engineers) were often in the employ of the *zemstva*, which were introduced in the left-bank and southern provinces where local Russian landowning and propertied presence was deemed sufficient to introduce the assemblies (e.g., Kherson, Kharkov, Ekaterinoslav, and Poltava). Only the first strata, the small cultural and intellectual elite, were the most nationalist politically, and they came primarily from the right-bank provinces, particularly Kiev.

Tsarist imperial strategies contributed to the splitting of these middling strata. As noted in Chapter 2, Table 2.1, the state repressed the cultural and humanist elite and generally conciliated those Ukrainians in the imperial civil service and the peasantry. The incorporation of noble and educated Ukrainians into the imperial bureaucracy contributed to their Russification and created dual-identity educated elites. The composition of the Tsarist local imperial bureaucracy suggests that in absolute terms, Russians dominated the bureaucracies of the Ukrainian provinces in a manner out of proportion to their share in the population, at least through 1897. But those Ukrainians who *could* qualify for government jobs (that is, educated, literate, non-peasant urban dwellers, nobles, and honorary citizens) *were* so employed. For every nine Ukrainians with higher education, there was one ranking administrator, whereas for Russians the ratio was twenty to one. But by the late nineteenth century, not only were more than half of middling-level imperial posts across the empire held by Russified Ukrainians, but there was actually a shortage of educated, literate Ukrainians to fill them (Robbins 1987; Anfimov and Korelin 1995; Velychenko 1995: 197).[5] Ukrainians staffed more than half of the middling-level government positions. (Ukrainian underrepresentation in absolute terms was largely the result of the patronage appointment and promotion system, as lower postings were more dependent on clientalist appointments than the higher posts). And there was little evidence of ethnic discrimination given that the percentages of Ukrainian administrators corresponded very closely to the percentage of Ukrainian urban dwellers and noblemen who declared their native language Ukrainian. By these measures, then, middle-class Ukrainians were less alienated from the Russian state, and better integrated into the imperial bureaucracies, than were middle-class Russians (Saunders 1995; Velychenko 2000).

So the small Ukrainian middling and noble strata, or loosely the intelligentsia, were split between those whose Russification and interests lay within the imperial state – or those whose occupations contributed to dual identities and interests – and the best-known, the intellectuals who had been fully excluded with neither occupational anchor nor imperial incorporation in Ukraine itself. These different social locations most consequentially determined receptivity to socialist and nationalist political mobilizations, as was the case with the Bolsheviks Alexsandr Tsiurupa, Manuilsky, Skrypnyk, and Krestinsky.

Moreover, Tsarist elites were as concerned with vertical associations between social and ethnic strata as they were with horizontal coethnic associations, so splitting cultural elites of any ethnicity from peasants of any ethnicity was generally practiced throughout the empire. But this meant that politics became greatly ethnicized, because ethnic ranking in the Ukrainian provinces was anyway strongly pronounced: Ukrainians were the vast majority of the peasantry; Poles, Russians, and Jews comprised the urban middle classes; Russians and Ukrainians (and some Poles) the bureaucrats; and Russians and Poles (and few Russified Ukrainians) the landed elites. And it lay atop a set of already

[5] Tsarist bureaucratic needs were so acute that in 1897 there were 5,631 Ukrainians serving outside Ukraine and 16,129 Russians and Germans serving in Ukraine. Even if all the former replaced the latter, the Ukrainian provinces would have had 10,498 positions unfilled – and insufficient numbers of educated Ukrainians to fill them (Velychenko 1995: 204).

highly complex capitalist relationships. In the 1890s, Ukrainian peasant and peasant-worker politicizations in the southern industries were affected by the enormous influx of Russian, Jewish, Tatar, and Armenian workers, while Ukrainian peasants in the right-bank provinces were politicized in economic competition with Polish and Jewish workers. These different socioethnic contexts, together with imperial policies designed to prevent vertical (ethnic) and horizontal (class) associations, contributed to the differential appeals of socialist and national socialist politics – something concretized in the radicalism of the Ukrainian Bolshevik workers Grigori Petrovsky (Hryhorii Petrovs'kyi), Dmitri Lebed', and Vlas Chubar'. I consider their radicalizations after a discussion of Tsiurupa's *zemstvo* radicalism.

Tsiurupa and Zemstvo Radicalism

Together with Skrypnyk, Tsiurupa was part of the oldest generation of Ukrainian Bolsheviks, and among the most educated. Born in Kherson in 1870, Tsiurupa was the son of a municipal government official in Aleshki. The family was comfortable as part of these incorporated, educated middling strata of Ukrainians. After the death of his father when Tsiurupa was young, the family moved to Kherson. Tsiurupa graduated from Kherson Agricultural College and began a career as an agronomist and statistician (Prokhorov 1969–78: 611–12; Granat 1989: 750). His level of education placed him among the 0.36 percent of Ukrainians with more than elementary education, and occupationally either a member of the free professions (only 0.46 percent of all Ukrainians) or a government employee (0.61 percent of Ukrainians); by estate membership, and depending on his civil service rank, he was likely in the upper levels of the *meshchanstvo*, which comprised 5.69 percent of Ukrainians, and where most *zemstvo* statisticians would have been classified (Bauer et al. 1991: 107, 157, 198, 329).

There is no mention of political activism until he attended Kherson's Agricultural College, where in 1891 Tsiurupa organized student Marxist circles. He was arrested for these activities in 1893, with six months imprisonment and four years of police surveillance followed by another period of imprisonment in 1895 (Prokhorov 1969–78: 611–12). His first student radicalism coincided with the famines of 1891–92 in which *zemstvo* statisticians and agronomists were directly involved in providing assistance to the peasantry (Johnson 1982: 347). This no doubt influenced Tsiurupa, yet prison and surveillance did not prevent him from completing his studies and obtaining employment in 1893 as a *zemstvo* statistician.

Tsiurupa's pre-Bolshevik radicalism should be contextualized within the radicalism and reformist politics of the *zemstva* more generally. Budget and personnel problems hindered *zemstva* functioning (Starr 1992: 304–6), but they employed trained experts – mostly doctors, teachers, engineers, agronomists, and statisticians. *Zemstvo* statisticians were charged with gathering information from peasants and landlords to assess the causes of poverty and indebtedness, and to provide data on which to base land reform. After 1893, *zemstvo* statisticians' assessments prompted clashes with *zemstvo* gentry and government officials. In the left-bank and southern Ukrainian provinces, the *zemstva* were up to 75 percent noble and gentry landowner in composition; they were only mildly liberal and consistently closed ranks with conservatives in the face of challenges to their position, moving to the right during periods of reaction (Manning 1982: 143–55). But by the 1880s and 1890s, *zemstvo* experts like Tsiurupa were radical, liberal, or socialist reformers, often combining professional activity with political activism. And because their mandate involved local issues such as building roads, rural education, and irrigation techniques, they were sensitive to Ukrainian-specific issues. They also tended to be more interested in self-government and decentralization than in cultural or national issues per se. But most importantly, *zemstvo* employment provided educated Ukrainians a local venue for social mobility.

Tsiurupa's career as a *zemstvo* statistician-agronomist spanned more than two decades: he worked as a statistician for the Kherson *zemstvo* from 1893 to 1895, in Simbirsk in 1896, in Ufa from 1897 to 1901, in Kharkov and Tula in 1901 (during the peasant unrest of 1902 in Kharkov and Poltava), and from 1905 as an agronomist in Ufa (Granat 1989: 750). *Zemstvo* statisticians and agronomists, in particular, were the most involved in radical politics, and they were especially influential during the periods in which statistical activity flourished in the mid-1880s, between 1906 and 1914, and in the 1890s in clashes with conservatives (Johnson 1982: 344–50; Manning 1982: 141–3). Political activism within the context of his work brought Tsiurupa to the RSDLP in 1898. Although most *zemstvo* statisticians spent their entire careers in one locality, Tsiurupa was among the few who were highly mobile, something that was most likely related to his student political activism: those who had been in oppositional circles in student days, or who had engaged in conflicts with officials, were labeled unreliable and were therefore moved around. (Repeated arrests were common because they were rarely underground and therefore easily traceable within the bureaucracy). Yet despite this mobility, political radicals like Tsiurupa performed the same work and remained statisticians throughout their careers (Johnson 1982: 352–4, 357).

In his capacity as a *zemstvo* professional, Tsiurupa published articles and studies on the rural economy of the Lower Volga and on demographic trends and landownership in Ufa. At the same time, and also like most *zemstvo* experts, he was deeply involved in political activities *as a statistician*: in 1901, as a member of the Kharkov Committee of the RSDLP, Tsiurupa led a strike of statisticians (Granat 1989: 750). Activist statisticians contributed articles to populist and liberal journals and attended public demonstrations, although none of this prevented them from taking part in the *zemstvo* bureaucracy (Johnson 1982: 353, 356–7). Followed by the Tsarist police, Tsiurupa fled to Tula, was arrested in 1902 and exiled for three years in Olonets (Prokhorov 1969–78: 611–12; Granat 1989: 750). Tsiurupa took part in the revolution in Ufa in 1905 and was again arrested. It was common for *zemstvo* activists to take part in political strikes in 1905, but elected (gentry) *zemstvo* deputies retaliated with widespread dismissals (Manning 1982: 141), so it took Tsiurupa three years to secure a position as an agronomist for the Tsarist provincial food administration in Ufa – a post he held until 1915 (Prokhorov 1969–78: 611–12).

As a government statistician-agronomist, Tsiurupa's daily work implicated him directly in the lives and experiences of rural Russian and Ukrainian peasants and landowners – a rarity among Bolsheviks in the region. No doubt political activism in Russian socialist groups in the southern Ukraine and in central and north Russia nurtured in him certain ideological prejudices about the peasantry. But the prejudices of his occupation also carried distinctive sociological assumptions about the peasantry: *zemstva* statisticians tended to be idealists, they were typically young and poorly paid, and they would have found more profitable careers in private practice. In fact, for many young radicals, *zemstvo* service was a *consequence* of youthful radicalism, and this seemed to have been especially true of the statisticians, who had a reputation for being been politically unreliable in the eyes of the state (Johnson 1982: 354). To opt for *zemstvo* employment would itself have been a mark of young idealism, so conservatives stereotyped them as political unreliables and subversives, while liberals and socialists (including Lenin) considered them naive and prejudiced (Johnson 1982: 343). Most *zemstvo* statisticians tended to view the peasantry as an undifferentiated mass, overlooking its substantial economic differentiation and polarization, and strong idealist sympathies for traditional craft production and village communes caused them to underestimate the influence of capitalism in the countryside (Johnson 1982: 358–9). In the end, then, the discrepancy between the social economy of the peasantry as seen by a *zemstvo* agronomist-statistician and the Marxist sociology of the peasantry as seen by a committed socialist was not great.

Arguably Tsiurupa's practical experiences organized at least some of his political thinking. More than twenty years of employment in the Tsarist imperial and provincial bureaucracies as an agronomist-statistician in *zemstva* and in the Tsarist food administration during the war produced a view of the state as incompetent, inefficient, and corrupt in its agrarian policies – and an equally impressive and totalistic view of the peasantry as an undifferentiated mass whose problems could be solved through a commune writ large (on the general phenomenon, see Johnson 1982). So after 1921, when crisis conditions abated, Tsiurupa helped implement – with reservations, because it meant a diminishment of his own position as Commissar of Food – NEP programs, Gosplan, and, as Commissar of Foreign and Domestic Trade, all centralized planning. Nevertheless, his route to Bolshevik political mobilization was shaped by his service in the imperial *zemstva* bureaucracy. Given his social location, Tsiurupa's politics involved the assimilation that imperial access accorded, a rather unique sensitivity (at least among the Bolsheviks) to the conditions of the peasantry, and an antistate politics that meant that his radicalism traveled from a generally liberal critique to a socialist one.

Petrovsky, Lebed', Chubar': Russified Worker Radicalism in left-bank Ukraine

If Tsiurupa's *zemstvo* radicalism within the imperial bureaucracy was largely limited to rural issues, Petrovsky's, Lebed's, and Chubar's social experiences and socioethnic locations made them receptive to socialism's more classic working-class appeal in Ukraine. Petrovsky's father left and Lebed's father died, so both struggled early in poverty. This interrupted their studies by forcing them into manual labor, and it made them available to social democratic radical workers' circles in the factories, which only occasionally and inconsistently highlighted their Ukrainian identities. Chubar' identified more strongly as a Ukrainian, although there is some limited evidence that he may have been a Ukrainian Jew. But Kaganovich frequently clashed with Chubar' because of the latter's Ukrainian nationalism (Medvedev 1983: 117), and Stalin, too, famously thought Chubar' (and the Ukrainian Pole Kosior) guilty of Ukrainian nationalism. I briefly contextualize each before drawing some conclusions.

Petrovsky was born in 1877 in Kharkov to a very poor family of artisans.[6] His father was a tailor and his mother was a laundress. In a general account of his childhood as one characterized by misery and privation, when Petrovsky was three his father left the family, and a violent stepfather raised him (Granat 1989: 581). Because of the family's financial circumstances, Petrovsky worked while in secondary school from age eleven as a locksmith, machine lathe operator, and in other piecework in shops and guilds (Prokhorov 1969–78: 488–9; Granat 1989: 581). Official sources say he joined the CP in 1897, at age nineteen, through the Ekaterinoslav Union of Struggle for the Emancipation of the Working Class, or one of the earliest all-Russian socialist radical groups (Prokhorov 1969–78: 488–9).[7] But Petrovsky had been working since 1889, and he dated his activism among workers to 1895; he had previously been expelled from seminary in Kharkov for political activity, so he already had at least several years of political activism before 1897 (Granat 1989: 581).

Lebed' was born in 1893 in the village of Nikolaevka in Ekaterinoslav *guberniia* to a peasant-worker family. His father was a *chernorabochii*, or "black worker" – one of those workers who assumed the most dangerous unskilled-labor jobs. He died when Lebed' was fifteen years old; this left the family in difficult financial circumstances and caused Lebed' to leave the local railway school in search of employment (Granat 1989: 491). He had already been involved in small-scale, anarchist-terrorist skirmishes along with other student radicals, such as stealing revolvers, holding-up Jewish vodka shops, and handing out illegal brochures and leaflets. He subsequently described this activism in the anarcho-terrorist movement as heroic, on the belief that single individual acts could explode capitalism out of existence (Granat 1989: 491).

---

[6] Or 1878, depending on the source; compare Granat 1989: 581 and Prokhorov 1969–78: 488.

[7] See the account in "Piatnitsa," February 4, 1938, No. 29, in Nicolaevsky Collection, Box 796, Accession No. 63013 8.41/44, Series 291, Folder 11.

In semirural Ukraine, capitalism was most often Jewish, and indeed vodka shops were mostly Jewish-run and typically associated with the "exploitation" of rural Ukrainians. This of course suggests that anti-Semitism may have had some background dimension here in Lebed's early radicalism, something I explore and contextualize later in the chapter.

But if Lebed's radicalism likely skirted an element of anti-Semitism, Chubar's implicated him in Ukrainian-Jewish tensions in a different way. Born in 1891 in a Ukrainian village in Ekaterinoslav *guberniia*, Chubar's parents were illiterate small-scale Ukrainian farmers (Prokhorov 1969–78: 239; Granat 1989: 759). His political activism began at age thirteen when he proclaimed himself an atheist under Darwin's influence. The next year he joined radical circles and was arrested and beaten by the police (Granat 1989: 759). With the support of a *zemstvo* stipend, private lessons, and work at a local railroad shop, between 1904 and 1911 he attended the Aleksandrovosk Mechanical and Technical School. It is unclear whether he completed schooling, but he worked as a plumber, metalworker, fitter in a boiler plant, farm day laborer, and day laborer on the railways, among intermittent periods of unemployment (Prokhorov 1969–78: 239; Granat 1989: 759). Under a teacher's influence, Chubar' became actively involved in Populist and SR groups with whom he organized Ukrainian peasants and conducted organizational work. But life in Aleksandrovsk and in the railroad workshops exposed him to Social Democratic workers' groups, and he became a Bolshevik in 1907.

In sum, then, for all three of these Bolsheviks, employment in these southern industrial cities easily lent itself to political activism, and there was some diversity of groupings from which to choose. Petrovsky wrote in considerable detail of the difficulties of his own extremely low wages and long hours, conditions that would equally have held for Lebed' and Chubar'. In 1895–96, Petrovsky's daily work experiences included strikes and confrontations between workers and employers, which were frequent; he wrote of "living in fear of the tyranny of the chief assembler or worse, the police" (Granat 1989: 581). Petrovsky's description of his involvement in an 1898 Briansky Factory mutiny, where workers stormed the gates and were beaten back by guards, emphasizes the arbitrariness of factory administration and the brutality of the repressions (Granat 1989: 582).

The scholarly evidence substantiates much of this. The Donbas area was the multiethnic heart of the southern coal-mining and metallurgical industries (Kuromiya 1998).[8] Russian was the language of the cities, but the less educated spoke a blended Ukrainian-Russian dialect (Kuromiya 1998: 42). Miners in the Donbas were generally peasants, landless, single, and seasonal workers. They migrated in large numbers to the Donbas in search of opportunity, making its industrial centers the fastest-growing areas of the empire. Local mine operators offered a number of inducements to attract Ukrainian and Russian peasants

---

[8] The Donbas population was 52.4% Ukrainian, 28.7% Russian, and the remainder were Greeks, Germans, Jews, Tatars, Belarusians, and Poles (Kuromiya 1998: 41).

from the surrounding villages: comparatively high wages, free housing and heating coal, and train tickets to the Donets Basin. An Injured Miner's Fund had even been established in the mid-1880s. Although barrack housing and heating was also provided, conditions were barely acceptable. Yet even with these inducements, the great boom of the 1890s meant that the local workforce was still insufficient, and many of the European-educated engineer-managers understood that they needed to improve workers' conditions in terms of education, health, and living quarters (McCaffray 1996: ch. 5). Whereas housing and living conditions were only between 5 percent and 9 percent of strike grievances, far more significant concerns were wages and terms of payment – that is, money with which to secure more adequate housing (McCaffray 1996: 104–5). So as classic socialist analyses have it, working conditions have to be given an important role in these Ukrainian Bolsheviks' radicalizations.

So, too, does the availability of radical groupings. Like Petrovsky, in 1905, Lebed' was similarly active in various radical groupings around the Dnieper, a number of which were Menshevik organized. He joined the SDs in 1909, and by 1910 he considered himself a "class conscious worker" (Prokhorov 1969–78: 231; Granat 1989: 491). Although Lebed' studied Marxism in workers' groups, he excelled in practical revolutionary work (Granat 1989: 492). Not well versed in the debates of the Russian social democratic movement, including those between Bolshevism and Menshevism, Lebed's labeling of his involvement in the radical groups was loose: radicalism was radicalism and it was exciting and heroic – and it also confused the dates of his political affiliations with his activism. But notably absent from Petrovsky's and Lebed's accounts are explicit discussions of their ethnic experiences, or the ethnic or identity dimensions in their political radicalism. So in a pattern of traditional worker radicalization, they were receptive to the class or capitalist narratives of the socialist brochures circulated at workers' evening meetings.

And yet Chubar's early biography and his political trajectory suggest that several background ethnic dimensions were, in fact, operating in these industrial Ukrainian provinces. And this, too, accords with the scholarly literature. Because Petrovsky, Lebed', and Chubar' were among the relatively small class of ethnic Ukrainian urban workers in the industrial cities of the south, we should be as precise as possible in situating them within their respective social and ethnic contexts.[9] Petrovsky, Lebed', and Chubar' worked in Ekaterinoslav and Kharkov, the two principal urban centers in the Ukraine, which were only 7.31 percent Ukrainian (by nationality), and only 4.78 percent of Ukrainians (by mother tongue) were employed in manufacturing (Bauer et al. 1991: 156, 277). In 1897, the proportion of Russian industrial workers to Ukrainian workers in Kharkov was 2.5:1, and in Ekaterinoslav it was more than 4:1. By the 1890s, industrial growth in the Donetsk Basin and southeastern Ukraine

---

[9] Matvei Muranov could also be included here, but reliable information on him is sparse. He was born in 1893 to a peasant family and became a worker in Kharkov. He was active among railroad workers (Prokhorov 1969–78: 121–2).

prompted substantial migrations of ethnic Russians in search of work. Among the most experienced workers in heavy industry, only 25 percent of coal miners and 30 percent of metallurgical workers were ethnic Ukrainians (Subtelny 1994: 272). But the levels of linguistic Russification – if not social acculturation – were extremely high among Ukrainian workers. Indeed, in Kharkov and Ekaterinoslav, respectively, more than 39 percent and 40 percent of ethnic Ukrainians could read Russian (Bauer et al. 1991: 413). In fact, using linguistic criteria alone, it was exceedingly difficult to tell who was ethnically Ukrainian and who was ethnically Russian (Miller 2003: 252). And although the numbers of ethnic Ukrainian workers in the cities of the south were comparatively small, of those who were literate, rates of Russian-language literacy were substantial.

And yet there were tensions between Ukrainians and Russians. The Russian Bolshevik Kliment Voroshilov, working in the Donbas, wrote of his identification with his barracks' community or *zemliachestva* (same family clan, or village) and made little claim to wider political visions (Kuromiya 1998: 54, 64), but he also wrote of tensions between Ukrainians and Russians (Voroshilov 1968: 121–2, 67). They lived in relatively distinct villages and relations were strained in cities and workers' settlements: workers regularly fought and insulted each other, and violence was common (Kuromiya 1998: 42–3). Lebed', Petrovsky, and Chubar', then, came from within these comparatively small strata of Russian-literate, ethnic Ukrainian workers in the southern cities, and their experiences were characterized by these tensions and acculturations. For the few ethnic Ukrainians in the urban industrialized south, radicalization was of a piece with their social acculturation into an essentially Russified industrial milieu.

That they were attracted to *rossiiskii*, or even specifically Russian, radical workers' movements is therefore hardly surprising. Both Petrovsky and Lebed' were involved in the Russian-inflected Emancipation of Labor Group in Ekaterinoslav because of daily involvement, socialization, and radicalization with ethnic Russian workers in factories. Unlike some multiethnic cities of the western borderlands, in which ethnicity and class co-stratified (i.e., the commercial class was German and the workers were Latvian), in the Ukrainian south and the left bank, both capital *and* labor were primarily Russian – with important qualifications that I discuss in the section that follows. This created a situation in the Ukrainian cities where ethnic Russian workers – the majority of the urban labor force – were to a great extent organized by Russian SDs against ethnic Russian industrialists and capital. So part of the strength of Russian socialist or class mobilizations of worker radicalism in these industrial cities was that they rendered ethnicity for the most part irrelevant, and class conflicts appeared much clearer. The presence of both Russian capital and Russian workers diluted ethnic divisions, and Ukrainians simply did not have sufficient access to Ukrainian-only radical groupings in these industrial contexts. In short, for the comparatively few Russified Ukrainian workers, activism in all-Russian groupings was almost inevitable.

Thus the political fault lines were not between Ukrainians and Russians, but ethnopolitics did involve an important Jewish dimension. Strains of anti-Semitism made their mark in this industrializing milieu where the most complex relationships were with Jews. Very specifically, in 1905, anti-Jewish pogromists destroyed Chubar's student apartment in Aleksandrovosk, prompting him to return to political activism with the SRs (Granat 1989: 759). This of course raises the strong possibility that he was Jewish – something that I have not been able to verify with any other documentation, so I still default him as Ukrainian. Yet this was nevertheless a startling incident to include in his autobiography. He may have been a highly assimilated Ukrainian Jew – in the minority to be sure, in identifying not with the imperial Russian but with the "colonial" Ukrainian (for a general discussion of this "anti-imperial choice," see Petrovsky-Shtern 2009a). Because of the complexity of triangulated ethnic politics in the Ukraine, Jewish assimilation could, and sometimes did, cause Jews who were regarded by Ukrainians as aligned with the imperial government to instead ally with Ukrainians in common resistance to Tsarist oppression (Meir 2006: 483). Chubar's integration into Ukrainian society, then, would have been initially facilitated by the village peasant occupation of his family, and from working so extensively with the SRs among the Ukrainian peasantry.

As was likely with Lebed', the Ukrainian village peasantry, peasant-workers, some urban, lower-middle classes (*meshchane*), and migrants from Russian provinces were among the worst perpetrators of anti-Jewish violence and pogroms in 1905, with Kiev, Kherson, and Ekaterinoslav the most affected cities (Klier and Lambroza 1992: 43, 194; Wynn 1992: ch. 7; Kuromiya 1998: 43–8 on pogromism in the Donbas in 1892, 1903, and 1905). Ukrainian and Russian workers resented Jews more than any other capitalist group, to the point where anti-Semitism had become an ideologically binding force (Wynn 1992: 62–5). In addition to shared religious backgrounds, Ukrainian and Russian workers could often find common cause against Jewish small and large capitalism. Against this, the *rossiiskii* socialist revolutionary movements, the SRs and SDs, organizationally offered multiethnic, umbrella political mobilizations, with a proportionally large number of Jews, Poles, and Russified Ukrainians (see Perrie 1972 on the SRs; Haberer 1995 on the Populists). And indeed Jews in these social locations viewed these political mobilizations as the best defense against both Ukrainian and Russian nationalist excesses. But they nevertheless contained inevitable tensions that resulted from holding together in a single mobilization Russified Ukrainians, Russified Jews, and Russians – all against a background of often violent ethnopolitics.

To put this differently, commitments to Russian-inflected revolutionary movements were highly dependent on context and social location. Economic histories of the Dnieper railroad workers, for instance, suggest that those who launched southern Russia's coal industry and its supporting railroad infrastructure were themselves ethnically and socially mixed. In the last decades of the nineteenth century, Cossacks, Jews, Ukrainians, Russians, merchants, nobles, engineers, technical intelligentsia, and even female landowners were involved in the coal industry (McCaffray 1996: 24). And yet it was especially vulnerable to the virulent strain of anti-Semitism emanating from Nicholas II's government: although Russian elites were keen to limit Jewish participation in corporate ownership, by 1914 state officials had begun to equate corporate enterprise with Jewish (and foreign) influence (McCaffray 1996: 210). Restrictions on Jews and Poles in the southern industries had increased after 1880, and although Jews could move with relative ease in Ekaterinoslav province (within the Pale), they could not own or rent land in the Don region. In 1899, Jews were forced to leave the Donbas port cities of Taganrog and Rostov-on-Don. And yet many of the engineer-managers of these southern coal-mining and railroad industries were Jewish or German. Foreign capital drove industrial development in the Donbas, where foreign and Russian capitalists lived lavishly (Kuromiya 1998: 49). In Kharkov, Jewish capital was negligible, but in Ekaterinoslav where both Lebed' and Petrovsky worked and where they were politically active, Jewish capital comprised about one-third of the total, behind Russian capital (Bauer et al. 1991: 452). Here Jewish workers constituted a significant portion of the industrial labor force. So because of the strength of anti-Semitism in these social locations, Jewish workers tended to organize in all-Russian SD groupings rather than in specifically Jewish groups (unlike Jewish activism in the Vilna Bund, for instance). This goes some way to understanding the sources of the multiethnic composition of these political mobilizations in the Ukraine in which Chubar', Lebed', and Petrovsky were active.

But the radical groupings were in constant flux, and growing industrialization and imperial repressions of political activists also had their effects. After four years of political activism, in 1899 Petrovsky was called into military service in the imperial army, although poor health forced him to leave (Granat 1989: 582). After finding work in a Kharkov steam engine factory, he began revolutionary work in Nicolaev workers' circles for the Social Democrats. From there he went to Ekaterinoslav and again worked with the SDs until his arrest. Petrovsky spent more than a year in solitary confinement in prison, and on release found employment in the Donets mine pits in workers' settlements until another arrest in 1903 (Granat 1989: 582). Petrovsky organized the Ekaterinoslav soviet and city strike committee during 1905 revolutionary events (Prokhorov 1969–78: 488–9).

To contextualize his activism, then, revolutionary events in Ekaterinoslav in 1905 were initially limited and traditional in terms of their economic demands. Yet competition between Bolsheviks, Mensheviks, Bundists, and Anarchists was intensified and they ratcheted up political and antigovernment demands. As strike activity produced few results, workers grew frustrated and anti-Jewish sentiment among Russians and Ukrainians surfaced, particularly among factory workers in the industrial neighborhoods. Just as the government issued its October Manifesto – seemingly the political victory that the revolutionaries had been seeking – the Ekaterinoslav soviet, of which Petrovsky was a key figure (Granat 1989: 582), called off the political general strikes. Pogroms followed the Manifesto across the Donbas, in the steel towns and in the mining settlements. Ekaterinoslav consequently had the greatest economic property damage, as strikes and pogroms moved out in waves along the railroad lines and at railroad stations.

These two groups in the Ukrainian provinces – Russified Ukrainian day laborers or peasant-workers and ethnic Russian workers and day laborers – had been the shock troops of pogromism in 1880, and they were so again in 1905. The enemies were now more all-encompassing, however: the capitalist, the state, and Jews. Rightist xenophobia toward foreign-owned industry and Jews also underlay the violence and strike activity, often targeting "*yhids and democrats.*" The rightist Black Hundreds' conflation of *yhid* and democrat was significant and complex because it implied that Jews and Russified Ukrainian socialists like Petrovsky, Lebed', and Chubar' belonged to the same revolutionary movement, something reinforced by the fact that poor urban Jewish workers and craftsmen tended toward all-Russian parties, primarily the urban-based SDs. So without minimizing the presence of anti-Semitism – which Lebed's early anarchism involved, which Petrovsky would have experienced around him, and of which Chubar' may have been a victim – and in contrast to Ukrainian workers in the sugar factories in the right-bank provinces where intense ethnic competition made them more receptive to nationalist revolutionary politics, industrial workers in the left-bank and southeastern Ukraine had generally weaker Ukrainian and stronger Russified identities. So they were typically politicized in the socialist mobilizations on that basis. This also stood in contrast to the social locations that funneled the radicalization of educated Ukrainians like Manuilsky or Krestinsky: politicized in non-Russian and non-proletarian contexts, attraction to Russian socialism derived from a different kind of Russification and different ethnopolitical exigencies, as we will see.

So although the Donbas labor movement was not easily organized because of the geographic mobility of its workforce and because of its ethnic diversity, southern industrialists were among the most organized in the empire (Kuromiya 1998: 51–64). Oppositional politics was therefore class-focused and particularistic. Ethnic cooperation between Ukrainian and Russian workers in the southern Ukraine was also made easier by the war, as strikes and radicalism increased, and as they became increasingly antistatist in thrust. Lebed's Ekaterinoslav group formally joined the Ukrainian Social Democrats and accordingly adopted an antiwar internationalist position. Imperialist accounts were easy to sell to Dnieper workers: industrialists had started the war in their pursuit of profits. For Lebed', Chubar', and Petrovsky – and for most Ukrainian and Russian workers – the war was experienced as an extension of their already formidable economic hardships. Given their already high levels of Russification, however, economic imperialism seemed more persuasive for workers already implicated in labor disputes on a daily basis than did vague national or political motives. Class conflict was clearer, as it was with the ethnic Russians in the Russian interior.

During the reaction that followed the social unrest of 1905, Petrovsky worked in factories in Germany until his return to Russia in 1911–12. In 1912, Lebed' came into contact with Ukrainian Bolsheviks, and he organized for the Fourth Duma elections where Petrovsky became the Ukrainian Bolshevik delegate with Lebed's assistance. In fact, Lebed' and Petrovsky developed a close and enduring friendship in their common politicization as Russified Ukrainian workers among ethnic Russians. In 1916, Lebed' was drafted into the Imperial Army in the 228 Regiment in Ekaterinoslav, where he served for only three months, also because of poor health; this led to further strike organizing among Ekaterinoslav railroad workers, followed by imprisonment and eventually administrative exile (Granat 1989: 493). Chubar', too, was drafted into the army in 1915–16 and then sent to a weapons factory as a lathe operator in Petrograd until the Revolution (Granat 1989: 759). All three had been drafted – if briefly – into the imperial army.

In sum, then, the Ukrainian SD movement was distinctive as it reflected both the socioethnic complexity of the industrializing region and the differential impacts on these locations of assimilation, anti-Semitism, and the state's repression of workers. At the level of the worker, particularly the railroad worker who moved with great frequency along the rail lines, it meant that Russified Ukrainians were organizing with other Ukrainians, but they were doing so in the company of other Russified Ukrainians, as we have seen with these Bolsheviks. Therefore there may have been little occasion to call into question the tension in this social identity, and despite certain ambiguities there was a generally accepted naturalness of alliance between ethnic Russians and Russified Ukrainians.

But there was nevertheless a contradiction that was difficult for the socialist mobilizations to address: the political violence of the lower classes in the Donbas meant that (Russified) Ukrainian and Russian workers were active participants in pogromism, carrying a reactionary politics into some socialist movements that also had Jewish members. So the SD mobilizations – and particularly the Bolsheviks – forbade terrorist violence, sending many would-be recruits to the SRs and Anarchists. So the two kinds of mobilizations – SR/Anarchist and SD – were largely similar in social and ethnic composition, but they differed at least in this crucial respect of tolerance for ethnic or anti-Jewish violence (Kappeler 1979; Kuromiya 1998: 62–7).

Skrypnyk: Ukrainian Radicalism, Nationalist and Socialist

Unlike these workers' passive assimilation and social acculturation in working-class milieux in Ukraine's south, educated Ukrainians confronted a more explicit nationalist politics. If socioethnic tensions across the Ukrainian regions produced both activists in nationalist/rightist and socialist political mobilizations, as I argue, they also produced those who sought to navigate a radicalism between Ukrainian nationalism on the one hand and Russian/imperial centralism on the other. This, too, was a distinctive feature of Ukrainian minority elites' routes to radicalism. Skrypnyk became one such Bolshevik. Best known for his post-1917 promotion of Ukrainian language and literature in the face of Soviet Russification, Skrypnyk was considered an Old Bolshevik, a friend of Lenin's, and among the last Bolshevik supporters of national communism in Ukraine. Skrypnyk was also one of the most important and prolific writers in the revolutionary cohort, with a spell on *Pravda*'s editorial board during the war. After 1921, his role in the de-Russification or Ukrainianization of the Ukraine led to charges of "national deviationism," and he eventually committed suicide in 1933 in protest of Moscow's policies in Ukraine. More than any other Ukrainian Bolshevik, Skrypnyk opposed Russian centralism and Russification as imperialist. Usually considered a representative of Ukrainian national communism, his nationalism reflected his Kharkov left-bank roots. He was not an émigré nationalist product of Kiev and exile, and though an internationalist who opposed Russification, his internationalism was not European or a product of the right-bank provinces (as was initially Manuilsky's). Skrypnyk's radical politics navigated between two opposing pressures: Russian chauvinism (centralism) and Ukrainian nationalism (separatism).

He was born in 1872 in a village in Ekaterinoslav *guberniia* to a Ukrainian railroad clerk (Granat 1989: 669).[10] His mother was a trained midwife. His father, a telegraph operator and subsequently assistant stationmaster, was uneducated but as an employee of the state railways he was among the 0.38 percent of Ukrainian-speakers occupationally considered administrative-government employees (Granat 1989: 668; on imperial figures, see Bauer et al. 1991: 277). Skrypnyk wrote that his family had an "uneasy and restless relationship" with the landowning classes, most of whom were ethnic Russians. His parents had been loosely involved in the revolutionary movements in the 1850s and 1860s in Kharkov, and Skrypnyk felt he was nurtured on "a discontent with the established order" (Granat 1989: 668). But this discontent was likely less a reflection of nationalist discontent than a desire for more local rule (on this general argument, see Hechter 2000): his family was semi-Russified and spoke a Ukrainian-Russian hybrid by virtue of their state employment, yet they retained a certain ambivalence toward the Russian and Polish propertied classes. This dualism in social identity was typical of low-level Ukrainian civil servants. One of Skrypnyk's early passions was hearing about his family's revolutionary tradition: a Polish noble famously killed his great-great-grandfather, a Zaporozhian Cossack, for participation in Cossack insurrections in the eighteenth century, something Skrypnyk contextualized against the wars of liberation, general Ukrainian history, and Shevchenko's poetry (Granat 1989: 668). This was a relatively traditional Ukrainian identity that reflected more the regionalism of the historical Cossack left-bank lands rather than a modern,

[10] Although Okhrana sources (I think erroneously) dated his birth to 1880; HIAPO, Box 162, Index No. XIIId(2) Processing Intelligence, Folder 24A, HQ Circular No. 3918, Warning Lists, June 6, 1902.

ethnicized Ukrainian national identity as it developed in the urbanized context of Polish, Jewish, and Russian right-bank Kiev.

Skrypnyk wrote that his early cultural and political development differed from that of most Russian revolutionaries because of his rural isolation: in the 1880s, his father's employment with the railways meant that the family was transferred every six months across rural southeastern Ukrainian villages where there were no local revolutionaries. So Skrypnyk procured books and reading materials from railroad employees, Polish revolutionaries, and old Decembrists (Granat 1989: 668–9). He considered himself a member of the RSDLP as of 1897, at the relatively old (for a revolutionary) age of twenty-five. Skrypnyk attended village primary schools (most likely run by *zemstva*) and was expelled from *Realschule* for radicalism. But he attended another *Realschule* in Kursk as an external, suggesting that prior to becoming a Social Democrat, Skrypnyk had had at least ten years of political activism (Granat 1989: 669).

The content and direction of this earlier radicalism is hard to precise because it invoked both a cultural Cossack-Ukrainian identity and an imperial-Russian education in *Realschule*. His earliest activism was among the Ukrainian peasantry; he propagandized under the pretext of spreading Ukrainian folk songs, but his political ideas were, by his own admission, very unclear (Granat 1989: 669). Although mentioned only briefly and without much qualification in his autobiography, Skrypnyk's first exposure to organized revolutionaries was among Galician Ukrainian radicals, which obviously invoked a certain dimension of Ukrainianness, if only cultural or linguistic. Skrypnyk wrote that his conversion to Marxism was difficult: after reading Ricardo, Marx, and Kautsky, he read the Erfurt Program of the German Social Democrats "in Galician translation" and thereafter considered himself a Marxist (Granat 1989: 669).

The political movements available to Skrypnyk by the 1890s were also dualist Ukrainian and Russian in political identity and content, and importantly multiethnic in their leaderships. In 1893, ethnic Russians in Kiev led the Russian Group of Social Democrats, the first relatively stable Marxist group in Ukraine. Other groups appeared in Odessa, Kharkov, and Ekaterinoslav. Ethnic Ukrainians were very rare in these early political movements, and in composition most early socialism in Ukraine's cities was Russian, Jewish, and Polish (Subtelny 1994: 290–1). In this respect, early Ukrainian socialist mobilizations resembled those of the early Lithuanian socialists of the LSDP, as we saw with Kapsukas and Dzierżyński, and as we will see with the South Caucasians. For instance, the Socialist Revolutionary Party was formed in 1901, mixing populism, socialism, and political terrorism in its opposition to both the Ukrainian "colonial" relationship with Russia and to Ukrainian separatism (White 2007). So the party's Russified internationalism was ambivalent. Its ethnic and class composition was very similar to that of the SDs or the SRs (see Perrie 1972). The largely liberal and constitutionalist members of the *zemstva* formed the Union of Liberation in 1904 and later became the Kadets. Finally, ultra-rightist groups such as the Black Hundreds and the Russian Nationalist Party were very active in Ukraine (Kappeler 1979; on the latter's role, see Lohr 2003:

22–7). Also important were the Ukrainian nationalist movement, especially in Poltava *guberniia*, where its strength was in direct proportion to the weakness of the Tsarist administrative bureaucracy (Velychenko 2001; see discussion in Miller 2003: 143–4) and the Kiev Club of Russian Nationalists, a prominent nationalist grouping embedded within Kiev's associational life (Meir 2006). Significantly, the Kadets, the SRs, and the SDs consistently attracted Jews and Russified or Russophile Ukrainians.

So these were Skrypnyk's early options. And while his first activism had a greater Ukrainian component, by 1900 he had enrolled in the St. Petersburg Technological Institute, where he joined the Social Democrats (this was before the formal Bolshevik/Menshevik split) (Granat 1989: 669).[11] But he moved fluidly between the SR and SD movements. Between 1901 and 1917, Skrypnyk was arrested fifteen times, exiled seven times (from which he escaped three times), and was sentenced to death (in abstentia) for organizing an armed uprising. During a period in exile in Iakoutsk he met Uritsky and Dzierżyński, and while in Saratov he worked both for the SDs and SRs (Granat 1989: 670). In these years he worked as an *Iskra* agent while employed as a technical draftsman in committees in Saratov; and he organized students and workers for both the SRs and SDs because there was a lot of collaboration between them in the Urals. Skrypnyk also worked among textile workers in the Urals and in Perm, where he tried to siphon off SRs to the SDs (Granat 1989: 670). While in Odessa in 1903–04, he worked with other non-SD organizations. Skrypnyk moved from city to city during the years of reaction as he edited revolutionary journals with Krestinsky and Stuchka. After 1913, he joined the editorial board of *Pravda*. He was arrested but eventually secured employment as an accountant in a bank in St. Petersburg while he organized workers (Granat 1989: 672–3).

What we know from Skrypnyk's political radicalism, then, accords with left-bank and Ukrainian-based radical movements more generally: they were multiethnic in leadership, uneasily combined elements of Russian-centralism with Ukrainian autonomy, and were often Menshevik or SR in sympathy. Skrypnyk finally came to Bolshevism as a Menshevik with Trotsky, but both had arrived initially through the Ukrainian Spilka, or the Ukrainian Social Democratic Union. Though Ukrainian, Spilka had many ethnic Russian and Jewish members (the Bolsheviks Uritsky and Trotsky, for instance) and its publications were mostly in Russian. It accepted the RSDLP's platform on the nationalities question and advocated an all-Russian unity of socialist national and Russian groupings.[12] Pragmatically stressing trade unionism,

---

[11] HIAPO, Box 162, Index No. XIIId(2) Processing Intelligence, Folder 24A, HQ Circular No. 3918, Warning Lists, dated, June 6, 1902.

[12] Ukrainian parties developed rapidly in the 1890s and 1900s. In 1900, Polish students sympathetic to the Ukrainian cause founded the Ukrainian Socialist Party in Kiev. The Ukrainian Revolutionary Party (RUP) was founded in 1900 in Kharkov by Ukrainian and Ukrainophile students, which because of internal differences (mostly battles between liberals, nationalists, and socialists over the proper combination of national to social) split into a number of parties. The

its membership was substantial prior to, and during, 1905, particularly in Poltava, Kharkov, and Ekaterinoslav *gubernii*. But it was decimated by the state repressions that followed. Although Spilka condemned Ukrainian nationalism, its very raison d'etre was premised on at least a territorially distinct Ukrainianness – a belief Skrypnyk shared – as the radical movements wrestled with both centralist-federalist and autonomist organizational narratives in order to attract more activists across the Ukrainian territories.

So in his more than twenty years of political radicalism before 1917, Skrypnyk had organized strikes and engaged in political activism in Kazan, Perm, Ekaterinoslav, St. Petersburg, Saratov, Samara, Kharkov, Kursk, Ekaterinburg, Odessa, Riga, Krasnoiarsk, and other cities in the Volga region (Prokhorov 1969–78: 530; Lazitch 1986: 432–3; Granat 1989: 669–74). He had been a member of the SDs (Menshevik, then Bolshevik), Ukrainian Social Democracy (Spilka), the SRs, and an early amorphous Galician Ukrainian grouping. His *rossiiskii* or all-Russian political radicalism was substantial, albeit limited to Ukraine and Russia and to the time spent in exile and prisons in Siberia. Skrypnyk's political trajectory had moved from loose, culturally Ukrainian groupings, to Ukrainian-Russian groups with multiethnic leaderships, to Menshevism, and finally to Bolshevism. His political commitments were never rigid, and he could hold incompatible identities in tension without much need to resolve them. This derived in part from his social location, from the traditional multiple identities of Ukrainian elites in the left-bank provinces, and in part from its ambiguous relationship to the imperial state. And this, too, contributed to his particular internationalist socialism: he prioritized the development of national culture within an imperial or *rossiiskii*-oriented framework – a socialist Ukraine closely associated with Soviet Russia – but with equal status to develop its own cultural institutions.

In 1917, Skrypnyk became a member of the Petrograd Military Revolutionary Council, and secretary of labor and industry of Ukraine (Prokhorov 1969–78: 530). Aside from posts in the Comintern, the remainder of his post-1917 career was closely entwined with Soviet life in Ukraine. Bolshevism continued to have few ethnic Ukrainians in the Ukrainian party: in 1922, more than half of the party was Russian and Russified Ukrainians, and the First Secretaries were usually non-Ukrainians: Piatakov (Russian), Kviring (German), Kosior (Polish), and Kaganovich (Jewish). Remarkably, Ukrainians only formed a majority of the party in 1927 (Bilinsky 1978: 108). For Skrypnyk, then, national self-determination in the context of the Revolution was synonymous with national cultural liberation. His internationalism was less a response to local nationalisms than it was an attempt to hold Russian chauvinism and Russification in check in the pursuit of a noncolonial imperial ideal. Fearful of

RUP had called for an independent Ukraine with support from *gimnaziia* students. It constituted the core of the future Ukrainian socialist party, but with the splits in 1902, its right wing formed the Ukrainian People's Party, a nationalist party with small doses of socialism (Zalevskii 1912: 201–6).

Great Russian nationalism, and in defense of Ukrainian rights against a centralizing Russian state, he called for the de-Russification of the party, education, and the civil service. After 1927, as Ukrainian Commissar for Education, Skrypnyk forged the CP(b)U's policy on Ukrainian literature, writing in 1929, "[W]e are building Ukrainian national culture because we are internationalists" (Luckyj 1956: 185). So he allied with the decentralizers because he opposed both Stalin's Russian centralism and Trotsky's internationalist centralism (Bilinsky 1978: 114).

In fact, the contrasts among Skrypnyk, the Lithuanian Kapsukas, and the Pole Dzierżyński on these issues are revealing. As imperial-minded as Dzierżyński, Skrypnyk's position derived from a different set of social experiences and political relationships to the Russian state – that is, from subtly different elective affinities. And whereas Skrypnyk wanted to divorce politics from aesthetics, Kapsukas sought a politicization of all aesthetics. But Kapsukas's had been a mediocre literary talent, marginalized from the Lithuanian cultural elite when they formed the core of Lithuanian nationalism – hence his subsequent internationalism. Skrypnyk, however, had achieved enormous intellectual stature, and so had greater cultural self-confidence. He embraced a political radicalism that ultimately reflected the tensions and ambiguities of the social locations of which he was a product: semi-Russified, educated left-bank Ukraine.

Krestinsky, Manuilsky: Internationalism and the Multiethnic Western Provinces

Born in the same year, Krestinsky and Manuilsky were Russified Ukrainians; both were from the multiethnic western provinces of the Pale and both were initially politically active against nationalist separatism in any form. But whereas Krestinsky remained an avid internationalist, Manuilsky's internationalism eventually ceded to an imperialist Russian centralism. And their fates as Bolsheviks reflected these differences. Krestinsky forged a diplomatic career as a Bolshevik, most notably as the Soviet delegate to Berlin – which became the basis for Stalin's later accusations that he was a Gestapo agent (Haupt 1969: 150). Despite pleas of innocence to charges of collaboration with Trotsky, Krestinsky confessed and was shot in 1938. Manuilsky, on the other hand, became one of the very few non-Russian Old Bolsheviks to survive the purges with both career and reputation intact.

Krestinsky was born in 1883 in Mogilev to Ukrainian parents from Chernigov (Belarusia). His father was a *gimnaziia* teacher in Mogilev and Vilna, and Krestinsky was no doubt fluent in Russian because by this time most *gimnazii* in the *kresy* were completely Russified. Krestinsky's father had himself been active in the nihilist movement, and according to Krestinsky, his mother was a "petty intellectual" and political activist in the Populist movement (Granat 1989: 462). That their activism was in populist and not nationalist groups is also evidence of the family's Russification. In fact, the Russian Bolshevik Molotov (Chuev 1991: 198–9) subsequently claimed that Krestinsky was "not

much of a Bolshevik"; he was "a former Jew, but he was probably baptized
... perhaps I am wrong, a baron [of the landed gentry], surely a baron." [13]
Apart from his parents' influence, Krestinsky also attributed his early radicalism to a teacher at the *gimnaziia* in Vilna who was a Social Democrat (Granat
1989: 462). In contrast to Dzierżyński's Polish experience in a Russified Vilna
gimnaziia, which had contributed to his early Polish nationalist radicalism,
the likelihood was that the Ukrainian Krestinsky would already have been
highly Russified anyway, and his activism in Vilna's Social Democratic circles
between 1897 and 1901 flowed from this cultural access. As noted in Chapter
4, the memberships and the leaderships in these socialist movements were initially very ethnically mixed, comprising Russians, Jews, Poles, Latvians, and
Lithuanians. Krestinsky was among the few Ukrainians in Vilna; both the city
and its *gimnaziia* were largely Polish, Russian, and Jewish, so he was also one
of the few Ukrainians in the region's political movements. But his Russified or
assimilated status and his family's middle-class social position meant that he
found a certain affinity with other Russified minorities in Vilna.

In 1901, Krestinsky entered the Law Faculty at St. Petersburg University.
He became a member of the Social Democratic Party in 1903 in its Vilna section (Granat 1989: 462). He was arrested in 1904, prohibited from residing
in St. Petersburg, and sentenced to two administrative exiles to Vilna (Granat
1989: 463). Much like the Pole Dzierżyński, the Lithuanian Kapsukas, and
the Jewish Piatnitsky, Krestinsky's radicalism was limited to the cities of
the Polish-Lithuanian *kresy* – Vilna, Vitebsk, Kovno, and St. Petersburg. He
became a Bolshevik after 1905. Several more arrests in Vilna and Vitebsk did
not prevent him from completing his degree, and in 1907 Krestinsky returned
to St. Petersburg to work as a lawyer until 1917 (Prokhorov 1969–78: 393–4;
Granat 1989: 462). Little is known about his successful ten-year employment as
a lawyer in St. Petersburg, most likely as a member of the St. Petersburg branch
of the *advokatura*. This was one of the three recognized bar associations in
Russia, but because of its restrictions on Jews after 1889, it was Russified and
nationalizing. But it was also a comparatively progressive estate governed by
an ethos of public, not state, service. So for those like Krestinsky, professional
commitments and political activism functioned compatibly.

Manuilsky was also born in 1883, but in rural Kremenets in Volhynia
guberniia near the Galician border. His father was a Ukrainian Orthodox cleric
or rural scribe, although official biographies claim his parents were peasants
(compare Prokhorov 1969–78: 340 and Lazitch 1986: 295 with Granat 1989:
793 and the omission in Suiarko 1979). His father was likely semi-Russified;
Ukrainian priests and scribes were well treated by local Russian authorities

---

[13] Ukrainian minorization in Vilna and Chernigov also meant that the vast majority of the intelligentsia and petty officials in these cities were Polish or Jewish, and by the last decades of the
century most of the teachers were ethnic Russians brought in from the interior (Weeks 1996:
78). So it is of course possible that Krestinsky was of highly Russified Jewish origin, but this,
too, is murky in the sources.

as potential allies against Poles and Jews (Weeks 1996: 109). The family was typical of the small but rising Ukrainian intelligentsia: by 1900, most educated Ukrainians were sons of burghers, professionals, or clerics, and only 20–25 percent were of gentry-noble origin (Subtelny 1994: 271). Because of the Russian state's concern with local Polish influence and with Jewish "exploitation," particularly in the rural areas, *zemstva* were not introduced and language and property-owning restrictions applied in full force (Lohr 2003). Some of these policies benefited Ukrainians, however, especially in terms of access to local civil service and administrative posts, and as noted earlier, even minimally educated Ukrainians who sought positions in the provincial or imperial bureaucracy were able to find them. This was the case with Manuilsky's father. Imperial strategies of excluding Poles and Jews resulted in the co-optation of more educated Ukrainians into regional bureaucracies.

Moreover, right-bank Volhynia was multiethnic, albeit slightly less so in the rural villages. Religiously it was largely Orthodox Ukrainian and Russian (70.52 percent), with minority populations of Jews (13.31 percent), Catholic Poles, Belarusians, and Ukrainians (9.93 percent), and Protestant German colonists (5.08 percent). Only 7.8 percent of the population was urbanized, mostly Jews, and indeed Kremenets was 30 percent to 50 percent Jewish (figures from Iuzhalov 1904: 453, 456–7; Brown 2004 for wider context). This, too, is important for understanding the content and direction of Manuilsky's early politicization. After attending village school, Manuilsky was transferred to a Russified but multiethnic (Russian, Jewish, Polish, and Ukrainian) *gimnaziia* in Ostrog, where he gave lessons to earn his way (Suiarko 1979: 5; Granat 1989: 793). His radicalism began here in student circles under the influence of the Russian revolutionary Marxism of university students in Kiev and St. Petersburg, and specifically under the influence of the most famously Russified Ukrainian, Maxim Gorky (Suiarko 1979: 5–6). Part of the regional strength and appeal of Russian socialism in these multiethnic and multiconfessional southwestern cities lay precisely in the effects of this ethnic diversity: most Jews were Russified in response to rural Ukrainian anti-Semitism and to urban Polish anti-Semitism, and it was the most urbanized, educated Ukrainians who, by virtue of the local socioethnic composition of the region, had no alternative but to attend Russian imperial educational institutions, *gimnazii* and *Realschulen*.

Although obviously Russified, Manuilsky still maintained a vague Ukrainian identity and an intellectual awareness of – and interest in – Volhynia's historic importance as a center for Orthdoxy and religious book publishing (Suiarko 1979: 6). Ukrainian roots and a Russified existence were compatible identities, and Ukrainian nationalist movements (even if socialist) were less appealing given Manuilsky's religious and linguistic identification with imperial Russia. His drift into *rossiiskii* and even ethnically Russian groups was facilitated by the surrounding presence of sometimes violent anti-Semitism, the multiethnicity of Kremenets's highly combustible ethnopolitics, and a very devout Orthodox home life. This imperial-minded Russianness remained central to his worldview for the remainder of his life.

In 1903, Manuilsky enrolled in the Philological Faculty at St. Petersburg University and joined Russian SD radical groupings (Suiarko 1979: 6–7; Granat 1989: 793–4). Already a Bolshevik, in 1904 Manuilsky was arrested and beaten for his participation in protests against the war in Japan. He took part in the 1905–06 revolutions in St. Petersburg, Dvinsk (Vitebsk *guberniia*), and Kronstadt, and in 1906 he was again arrested, deported, and sentenced to five years' exile in Iakutsk; he escaped and continued work in the party committee in Kiev (Granat 1989: 794). Both official Soviet biographies and the authorized *Granat* biography recount Manuilsky's period of emigration in Paris beginning in 1907, and although the reasons for his exile are left unclear, it was likely connected to the Tsarist repressions in Russia (Prokhorov 1969–78: 794; Lazitch 1986: 295). By 1907, the state's post-1905 revolution reaction had set in with mass arrests of revolutionaries, but so too had the strength of the Black Hundreds or ultra-rightist groups, comprised largely of ethnic Russians and Russified Ukrainians who took part in the reaction against Jews and Ukrainian nationalists. The Black Hundreds' militias had emerged in the fall of 1905 to defend the monarchy from radical students, Jews, socialists, and non-Russians in efforts to make "Russia one and indivisible" (Hosking 1997: 439–40). They were particularly strong in St. Petersburg in 1905, so for Manuilsky these years of reaction may have been experienced in social unrest and ethnic exclusiveness as much as in state persecution (for a brief account of his experiences in this context, see Suiarko 1979: 10).

By 1905, at least three revolutionary political mobilizations had evolved from the defunct RUP: the Radical-Democratic Party (the Ukrainian equivalent to the Russian Kadets), the Ukrainian Social Democratic Party (Spilka), in loose association with the RSDLP but combining socialism and national autonomy in the manner of the Polish PPS, and the rightist Ukrainian People's Party, similar to the Polish National Democrats – nationalist and highly anti-Semitic. So the Ukrainian parties began to resemble their Polish counterparts, with similar consequences: given the growing strength of the nationalist groups, the socialist parties began to find their national identities. Ukrainian socialism, too, was finding its ethnic core. This had immediate effects on those Russified Ukrainians in the all-Russian parties like Manuilsky. They had defined their Russified political identities in opposition to the growing peasant-worker appeal of Ukrainian socialist movements more than they had in opposition to Ukrainian nationalist movements. Russified Ukrainian socialist activism was now caught between the non-Russified Ukrainian left and a Ukrainian ethnic nationalism.

At the core of this tension among the Polish mobilizations was also a debate around solutions to the geopolitical "Polish problem" and the opposing internationalism of Polish socialism's most important elites and allies, the Jews, who themselves sought to transcend this growing political ethnicization. Among Ukrainians, similar political tensions reflected different social and cultural roots: at the heart of tensions between the national-socialists, the nationalists, and the internationalists (or those in the *rossiiskii* and all-Russian parties) was simply the social fact of very high levels of Russification, Russophilia, and imperial-mindedness among Ukrainians themselves. Tsarist strategies had their unintended effects.

After 1905, activist Ukrainians with the highest levels of Russification were the most implicated in Russian Social Democratic groups. This was as true of Manuilsky and Krestinsky as it was in working-class contexts with Lebed' and Petrovsky. They increasingly found themselves in common political mobilization with both non-Ukrainians – Russians, Jews, and Germans – and with other, similarly Russified Ukrainians, also with weaker ethnic ascriptions. And these non-Russians and Russified Ukrainians became the core of the Bolsheviks in the Ukraine in the crucial 1917–21 revolutionary years. It is worth noting, too, that with the exception of Chubar' and Tsiurupa, Manuilsky and the other Ukrainian Bolsheviks profiled here remained indifferent to the plight of the Ukrainian peasantry, and almost all of their activism was limited to non-Ukrainian urban workers in Ukraine and in cities across the empire. As we will see, this was a pattern similar to that of the Georgian Bolsheviks. In short, despite their rural Ukrainian roots, political radicalization for most involved identification with non-Ukrainian urban workers. Local ethnopolitics and the differential impact of imperial strategies of incorporation and exclusion had shaped both the content and direction of political radicalism in these specific social locations.

The years of reaction in Tsarist Russia, then, began Manuilsky's years in emigration: between 1907 and 1912, he was in Paris and Geneva, as a member of Lenin's *Vpered* group (Prokhorov 1969–78: 340). In 1910, he completed legal studies at the Sorbonne while organizing French workers (Suiarko 1979: 11).[14] Manuilsky's political organizing brought him into contact with a Jewish Social Democrat from St. Petersburg, G. A. Alexinsky, something for which Lenin had him expelled from *Vpered*.[15] Like the Polish Bolshevik Dzierżyński, Manuilsky's close collaboration with Jewish socialists while in emigration also strengthened his internationalism. He worked with SRs, Anarchists, and Mensheviks, and although he wrote primarily for Russian socialist papers like *Golos* (which he cofounded), during the war he also wrote for Trotsky's *Nashe slovo* and subscribed to its internationalist, pacifist views (Granat 1989: 795). Here Manuilsky first explicitly theorized his internationalism, the potential for workers' revolutions among the French and German working classes, and the imperialist character of the war. But in practical activism Manuilsky straddled the Bolshevik-Menshevik divide, an apt expression of both his Ukrainian-Russian early experiences and his time in cosmopolitan European emigration with European socialists who were more Menshevik in orientation.

---

[14] HIAPO, Index XIIIb(1), Box 125, Folder 1H, Outgoing Dispatch No. 1532, November 6/19, 1914.

[15] Collaboration with Alexinsky documented in HIAPO, Index XIIIb(1), Box 125, Folder 1G, Outgoing Dispatch No. 1314, August 7/20, 1914; activities in *Vpered* and conflict relations Lenin are documented in detail in Suiarko 1978: 11–14.

Meanwhile, Krestinsky remained in Russia and took active part in the Duma elections in 1912. He was deported in 1914 to administrative exile in the Urals and Ekaterinburg, where he was politically active in the soviet before his election to the Constituent Assembly for Perm (Prokhorov 1969–78: 393–4; Granat 1989: 463). Together with the Crimean Jew Ioffe and the Pole Dzierżyński, as a Left Communist Krestinsky abstained from the crucial vote on Brest-Litovsk that de facto dismembered the empire. Nevertheless, consistent with Leninist tolerance in the early years, he was reelected to the CC in 1918 and appointed Commissioner of Finance from 1918 to 1921. In 1919, he was elected to the Politburo and Orgburo (Haupt 1969: 149).

Manuilsky, too, was part of the internationalist Left in 1917, and in May he was on the second sealed train that followed Lenin to Russia, although he continued to belong to Trotsky's *Mezhraionka* group until its merger with the Bolsheviks (Granat 1989: 259). Now Manuilsky's shift in political commitment from a Europeanized internationalism to Russian centralism reflected events in Ukraine during the war and revolutionary period, which unfolded with dizzying rapidity and complexity: three Ukrainian governments were attempted, power in Kiev changed five times, and the Bolsheviks, among others, invaded the Ukraine three times.[16] Lenin understood the need to win

---

[16] Ukrainian Progressives, a small, liberal grouping, led the first Central Rada government in Kiev between March 1917 and April 1918. Membership included Ukrainian moderates, SDs (including a few Bolsheviks), and SRs; in composition it was petty intelligentsia, teachers, lower clergy, students, bureaucrats, and *zemstvo* officials. Because its objectives were national-cultural, Russian conservatives, socialists, and Jews – that is, all urban minorities in Ukrainian cities – generally opposed it. But in July 1917, Russian and Jewish parties joined, so that at its peak non-Ukrainians held between one-third and one-fourth of the Rada's 822 seats (Frankel 1988: 265). After considerable hesitation, the Kerensky government recognized the Rada as legitimate. Opposition to the Rada came from Russified urban Ukrainians, like Manuilsky, despite the fact that linguistic Russification was so pervasive that all prominent persons in the Rada spoke Russian fluently (Reshetar 1952: 137–8). In defying Russian imperialism the Rada had miscalculated German imperialism, and the German government disbanded the Rada in 1918.

The second Ukrainian government was in the southern old Cossack lands – the Hetmanate. It was a government of what amounted to propertied interests in the left bank and southern provinces, or those who had a stake in maintaining the social order. It had many ethnic Russians in its ministries, and despite its attempts to Ukrainianize education, Ukrainian national socialists and nationalists opposed the Hetmanate and viewed the government as only very thinly Ukrainian with deep Russian interests. Also highly dependent on support from the German government, the Hetmanate lasted eight months.

In 1918, a third Ukrainian government took the form of the nationalist Directory. The Bolsheviks were split in 1918 between Skrypnyk and the Kiev faction who considered it essential that the Ukrainian party have a high degree of autonomy, and those of the Ekaterinoslav faction who wanted greater centralist control. In the event, while Rakovskii and Manuilsky were dispatched by Lenin to negotiate with the Directory, the Bolsheviks under Antonov-Ovseenko invaded the Ukraine a second time, and in 1919 Kharkov fell to the Bolsheviks. Leftist Ukrainian Social Democrats and leftist SRs (Borotbists) then joined the Bolsheviks. In good imperialist fashion, Lenin appointed Christian Rakovskii, a Romanian-Bulgarian, to head this Ukrainian government. Rakovskii expressed concern that his not being Ukrainian might pose difficulties. "Could not he unearth a Ukrainian grandmother among his ancestors to establish

the support of the nationalities because by this time he viewed the greatest obstacle to revolution to be Russian chauvinism, even within Bolshevism. In December 1919, the Bolsheviks (with a 3.5-million-strong Red Army led by 50,000 Tsarist Army officers) formed a third Soviet government, the Ukrainian Socialist Soviet Republic, and because of the terms of Brest-Litovsk, it was nominally distinct from the Russian CP and putatively treated as sovereign. This new and more nationally conciliatory Soviet government brought in a large number of Ukrainian Bolsheviks, including Manuilsky. Their political fortunes as Bolsheviks necessarily entailed *both* a degree of Russian central-ization *and* an acknowledgment of their Ukrainianness. If it was true before the war and the Revolution that the less Ukrainian the politics, the greater its social base, now it was that the more Ukrainian the politics, the greater its social base. The paradox was that to the extent that Ukrainian socialists were acting in the interests of socialism, they were also working in the interests of Russia. After two Bolshevik failures in Ukraine, Manuilsky said: "Each year we equip a successive troupe for the Ukraine which, after making a tour there, returns to Moscow in the autumn" (quote in Subtelny 1994: 365). Manuilsky's internationalism quickly ceded to a Russian centralism as it reflected the ambi-guities inherent in his imperial-minded Ukrainian or *rossiiskii* identities.

As First Secretary of the Ukrainian Communist Party, and with the Revolution now at stake, Manuilsky took an increasingly Stalinist view of Russian cen-tralism. The political lines were acrimoniously drawn between those like Skrypnyk, a leading figure in all three Soviet governments, who became avowed anti-centralists in defense of Ukrainian autonomy and Ukrainianization as a way of making Bolshevism more attractive, and those like Manuilsky who were considered "red imperialists." *Korenizatsiia* policies of the 1920s were in line with Skrypnyk's more culturally Ukrainian politics, but in 1933 it was Manuilsky who, in tenacious defense of a *rossiiskii* identity, launched the party purge in Ukraine, accusing Skrypnyk, among others, of nationalist conspir-acy. Manuilsky's internationalism had morphed into a Russian centralism in battles against Ukrainian separatism, but it was even more ferocious against Skrypnyk's Ukrainian autonomy within the new Soviet Empire.

Conclusion

The Ukrainian provinces produced not only the most Bolsheviks – of any eth-nicity – but also the most conflicted Bolsheviks in terms of the ethnic and class dimensions of their political commitments. Compared to the rest of the empire, the most ethnic nationalist (both Russian and Ukrainian) and

his legitimacy?" was Lenin's reply (Conte 1989: 146). This (second Soviet) Rakovskii govern-ment lasted ten months, in part because it alienated the Left (the Ukrainian SDs). The Rakovskii government, too, was comprised mainly of non-Ukrainians, primarily Russians and Jews. The Bolsheviks had also vastly underestimated the importance of the peasantry and the countryside because of a focus on Ukraine's urban centers; as a result, they had a very small and unstable social base (for a general discussion, see Eley 1988: 205–46).

class-internationalist (Russian, Jewish, and Ukrainian) emerged from the same provinces that also had the most violent ethnopolitics and anti-Semitic pogromism. These were arguably products of the same set of social and political dynamics. Liberal and socialist universalisms have distinctive appeal in contexts of deep ethnic or nationalist diversity (cf. Gellner 1998: Hacohen 2000; Hall 2010). So nationalism, internationalism, and socialism were, in effect, alternative responses to the same ethnic and geopolitical tensions characteristic of the borderlands. Put differently, Bolshevism in Ukraine was an ideological and organizational product of the same socioethnic and political tensions that produced the nationalist and rightist political movements. The combustability of these social locations funneled activism into divergent politics (see Table 2.2, Chapter 2). Imperial policies of incorporation and exclusion, together with the effects of industrialization, set in motion social and political dynamics in these social locations that variously funneled politics into leftist and rightist, nationalist, socialist, and international mobilizations.

Mindful of the ways in which imperial strategies and patterns of inclusion/exclusion interacted and shaped socioethnic experiences and ethnopolitics, I highlighted three key imperial strategies that affected the Ukrainian Bolsheviks: those policies of dissimilatory Russification, particularly in cultural exclusions targeted at cultural elites and intellectuals; the ways in which educated Ukrainians were also incorporated or included – and thereby Russified – in the empire's bureaucracies and civil service, particularly those in the upper intelligentsia; and the more status-particularistic policies of inclusion/exclusion that made certain socioethnic locations especially vulnerable, splitting emergent middle strata and noble elites (e.g., *zemstvo* employees versus intellectuals). These had important effects, as we have seen, on the high levels of Russification and *rossiiskii* identification of the Ukrainian Bolsheviks.

More specifically, the appeal of a Russian-inflected socialism for the Ukrainian Bolsheviks was a function of high levels of assimilation and Russification in a context of illiberal and violent ethnopolitics. Elites from an already *rossiiskii*-oriented and Russified working class and intelligentsia joined a movement that had a core empire-saving political imaginary. Antinationalist, ecumenical, and anti-Russian, socialist universalism was most appealing in these social locations where ethnic and religious tensions were especially threatening. Russified Ukrainians, conscious of their cultural roots, sought either internationalism or Ukrainian autonomy within a *rossiiskii* political framework, but after 1905 those with the strongest ties to the all-Russian groups (Manuilsky, Lebed', Krestinsky, and Petrovsky) found affinity with radicalized non-Ukrainians (Russians, Jews, and Germans). These *rossiiskii*-oriented revolutionaries became the core Bolsheviks in the Ukraine, both a validation of Ukrainian cultural identities and a check on the Russian nationalism that increasingly defined Tsarism. In the competition between class and ethnicity, a multiethnic socialism offered an antidote to the complex meshing of both ethnic and class grievances. High levels of Russification, complex ethnopolitics, and the appeal of Bolshevik socialism's class-universalism were of a piece.

In the end, a Russian-inflected, class-universalist, *rossiiskii* movement appealed because of the ethnopolitics of local nationalisms. Russified or dual-identity Ukrainians confronted Jewish, Russian, Polish, and Ukrainian nationalisms on the one hand and the Russian Empire's centralism on the other. The development of Ukrainian identities was closely bound up with the development of Russian identities, just as Russianness was often defined against non-Russianness. Indeed, the agents of Russification could alter both their self-identities and their understandings of Russianness (Miller 2002 for a discussion; Lohr 2003). These identities and assimilation tensions found expression in the leftist, *rossiiskii* radical movements, where the line separating Bolshevik internationalists and Bolshevik (Russian) nationalists was often blurred (for example, see White 2007 on the SRs).

Just like the role of associational civic life in Russia more generally, all-Russian or *rossiiskii*-minded political movements could serve as neutral social and political space for Jews, Ukrainians, and Russians. In part this was because Ukrainians dominated Ukraine only in a demographic sense. Russians, Jews, and Poles dominated urban, economic, political, and civic life. So *Russified* Ukrainians found a particularly neutral *rossiiskii* organizational framework in which experiential belonging came with no identity costs. Moreover, organizationally the Bolshevik mobilization in Ukraine drew together Russified Ukrainians, Jews, and Russians into multiethnic common cause because a Russian-inflected class-universalism ideologically organized their common Russified experiences against a background of socioeconomic marginalization. More than with other non-Russian groups in this elite, then, these Ukrainian Bolsheviks were radicalized in purer class terms.

6

The Latvian Bolsheviks

Famously providing the Rifles regiments during the 1917 revolutionary seizure of power, Latvians were disproportionately represented in the Bolshevik elite – there were six. Yet despite its enormous influence, the Latvian party elite was actually quite small and close-knit, with shared backgrounds and lots of inter-marriages. A rural element was also notable, represented by the propertied Latvian rural bourgeoisie (Petr Stuchka [Pēteris Stučka, Peter Stutschka] and Ivar Smilga), the rural intelligentsia (Jan Berzins [Jānis Bērziņš-Ziemelis], Karl Danishevskii [Julijs Daniševskis]), and the lower strata of peasants and rural laborers (Jan Rudzutaks and Ivan Lepse). Their socialist internationalism was to the left of Russian Social Democracy and far to the left of the Jewish Bund, in part because it was initially borrowed from Germany, not Russia. But Latvian socialists found strong affinity with Russian Bolshevism, so they must be understood against the sources of both their internationalism and their Russophilia. Latvians never developed a strong non-Bolshevik socialist option. Bolshevik prestige among Latvians was so substantial that it was the only party that continued to exist after the 1905–08 repressions when the others were all but decimated; until 1917, Latvian SDs were the largest component of the RSDLP, with more members than the Russian party (Ezergailis 1983: 23; 1974: 7).[1]

So the central argument of this chapter is that the elective affinity between Bolshevism's revolutionary ideology and its social carriers centrally revolved around the attraction that a Russian-inflected socialism had for elites from the "smaller" cultures in the empire's borderlands; marginalized socioeconomically, but highly Russified and Russophile, they not only sought access to the wider empire and, through it, to Europe, but as an ethnic group subordinate to German control, they saw in a *rossiiskii*-oriented socialism a political ideological

---

[1] Of the four Latvian SD factions in 1917 – Leninist-Bolshevik, Unionist-Bolshevik, Unionist-Menshevik, and Menshevik – the first was the most important. In September, the Bolsheviks had 12,000 members and the Mensheviks had two 2,600. In the first constituent assembly elections in November, the Latvian Bolsheviks defeated the Peasant Union and the Latvian Mensheviks with nearly 72% of the vote overall and more than 67% of the vote in the crucial Riga districts.

escape from their locked, subordinate position in a historic socioethnic rank-ing. More specifically, the Latvian Bolsheviks' revolutionary politics highlight three important claims of this book. First, their ideological mobilization was materially organized around tightly knit socioethnic networks and communi-ties, particularly in rural civic associations, schools, and ethnic institutional life. They drew heavily on these rural social and cultural resources and brought them to bear on their politics. These resources contributed to the movement's vibrant political organization – indeed often outpacing that of the Russian socialist parties – and it gave the movement a wide and deep mobilizational base with which to compete with nationalist mobilizations. Second, if commit-ments to a Russian-inflected revolutionary socialism were context dependent, Latvia provided the ideal social locations for this affinity to take root: for Latvian peasant-workers, a Russian-inflected class narrative found a partic-ular elective affinity in their experiences in Riga's multiethnic working class. Here ethnic backgrounds were effectively subordinated in what amounted to a Russified, multiethnic working-class radicalism in Latvia's cities, Riga most especially. And third, given their high levels of Russification, a Russian-inflected Bolshevism promised a socialist and universalist, *rossiiskii*-oriented political imaginary, one that addressed a key grievance against the imperial state: its aspiration to represent an "imperial ideal" – Russian-inflected but univer-salist – offered an especially resonant political expression for those Latvians that had suffered the brutality of Tsarist repression after 1905.

Of the key imperial strategies identified in Chapter 2, then, two contrib-uted most to the content and direction of Latvian Bolshevik radicalism. First, educated middle-class Latvians were the product of the assimilatory effects of Russification in educational institutions, where radicalism took on a *rossiiskii*-minded quality against a general backdrop of illiberalism. They quintessentially embodied the cultural ambiguities of Russified yet politically marginalized elites. Second, propertied rural Latvian elites were a particularly repressed socioethnic category, one that was specifically targeted by policing, surveillance, and social control. So in response, and to protect their status and position, they sought a politics that could express a "better" form of Tsarism.

Imperial Strategies and Latvian Radicalism

The Baltic provinces were incorporated into the Russian Empire with the eighteenth-century Polish Partitions (the following paragraphs are drawn from Henriksson 1983; Kappeler 1992: 67–70; von Pistolkors 1992; Plakans 1995: ch. 4, 5; Raun 2006). Eastern and southeastern Courland were the most ethnically mixed, with Latvians, Germans, Poles, Jews, Lithuanians, and Belarusians, while the westernmost areas had mainly Latvians and Germans. These provinces were also highly socioethnically stratified: Courland and southern Livland comprised largely Latvian peasants and Latvian urban lower classes; in Estland and northern Livland the peasantry and the urban lower classes were Estonian; and in all three the rural nobility, clergy, and middle and upper-urban classes were German. Baltic cities had Old Believer, Russian Orthodox, and Jewish minorities, and by 1900, Riga also had very substantial and growing Lithuanian and Polish working-class minorities.

As the only Protestant region in the empire, the Baltics had four *Ritterschaften* or noble corporations rooted in German constitutional and *Rechtsstadt* traditions. Because regional nobilities were crucial to Russian administration of its borderlands, estate self-government was guaranteed, the Lutheran Church's position was solidified, and German was the official language of all government and crown offices. The cultural and commercial heart of the Baltic littoral was Riga. It was the fifth-largest city in the empire, after Moscow, St. Petersburg, Warsaw, and Odessa. And as a major metropolis, it had the empire's fourth-largest industrial proletariat, after Moscow, St. Petersburg, and Warsaw (Henriksson 1986: 179; Plakans 1995: 52–4). But equally important for understanding Latvian revolutionary politics and Bolshevism's strength, Riga was also one of the empire's most ethnically, linguistically, and religiously diverse cities.[2]

So two social locations, or socioethnic niches, are important to understanding Bolshevik revolutionary politics: Latvians from the rural educated and propertied bourgeoisie and urban working-class Latvians. Both should be properly contextualized against the social changes of land reform because of its implications for political mobilizations. Under German rule, land reform was introduced in stages in 1804 and 1816, and serfdom was abolished in the Baltic provinces a half-century prior to its abolition in Russia. Baltic peasant reform was only completed in the 1850s and 1860s when peasants were allowed to purchase land. Rural smallownership substantially increased, yet landlessness and the growing indebtedness of those with land also increased, ensuring that peasant unrest and agrarian reform would continue as political issues (Plakans 1995: 87). Because land reform was promised but introduced incrementally, there was an element of social restlessness born of rising expectations, and this was channeled through well-developed rural institutions (Plakans 1981: 219). This permanently entwined the relationship between Latvian rural associational and institutional life and Latvian radical politics – an important feature of subsequent political and Bolshevik mobilizations. Most consequentially, peasant rural courts established in 1816–20 gradually gave rise to a considerable Latvian rural bureaucracy and the effective institutionalization of schools, councils, and treasuries – all linguistically Latvianized. These rural institutions in turn became key social locations for funneling political activism into leftist, multiethnic mobilizations.

---

[2] By 1897, the majority of the Baltic population was Latvian (44.86%) or Estonian (37.10%), but the proportion of Latvians was decreasing: in 1800, Latvians comprised 89.9% of the total population, 68% by 1897, and only 60% in 1914; at midcentury, Germans were 45% of Riga's population, Latvians 31%, and Russians 14% (Bauer et al. 1991: 215, 435; Plakans 1995: 73–4, 88).

More specifically, the terms of the land purchase agreements had resulted in both rural small ownership and peasant landlessness. This resembled the serf emancipations of Polish Lithuania, with similar consequences: substantial socioeconomic differentiation in rural Latvia added a layer of intra-Latvian class conflict to historic Latvian-German tensions, and it provided the mobilizational framework for competing socialist and nationalist movements. This is crucial for understanding class-ethnic tensions and the appeal of socialism in rural Latvia by the 1890s and 1900s, something I explore in the following section in connection with Stuchka and Smilga. Moreover, the emancipation settlements did not tie peasants to repartitional communes as they had in central Russia. So landless peasants migrating to Riga were not seasonal workers as they were in St. Petersburg or Moscow. Latvian peasants instead tended to settle permanently and quickly in the cities, and they rapidly assimilated into a distinctive multiethnic, urban working-class culture. I consider the consequences of this for the nature of Rudzutaks's and Lepse's radicalizations.

Under conditions of rapid industrialization and urbanization, the social positioning of Latvia's ethnicities and multiethnic urban classes were also consequential for radical politics. Germans held the majority of industrial, commercial, proprietary, and professional posts. The German free professions formed a distinctive group: typically educated at Dorpat University, they were pastors, teachers, lawyers, and other educated elites, comprising a peculiarly Baltic German estate with a certain social, professional, and political cohesiveness (Wittram 1973: 141–2; Henriksson 1983: 1–2). A substantial number of ethnic Germans were also part of an urban, lower-middle class of shopkeepers, noncertified artisans and servants, clerks, and minor civil servants.

By contrast, the first ethnic Russians to settle in the Baltics were Old Believers fleeing Tsarist persecution, as well as Russian merchants and peasants. Baltic Russians were socially, occupationally, and religiously diverse: in Riga, more than one-fifth of the city's ethnic Russians were soldiers stationed in local garrisons and therefore not permanent residents; there was a thin layer of civil servants and affluent merchants on par with the Baltic Germans; and there were petty traders, artisans, unskilled laborers, and urbanized peasants. Only 62 percent of Baltic Russians were Orthodox; the remainder were Old Believers. The motley social composition of Riga's Russian community, combined with its substantial Old Believer dissident sectarians, meant that there was a very weak social anchor for Russian nationalism to take hold.

Additionally, in 1881, nearly 12 percent of Riga's population was Jewish, although this is an underestimate because of the difficulty of measuring assimilation. But given that Riga was outside the Pale, given Baltic Germans' generally liberal rule, and given that it was a city to which many Jews migrated, Jewish Germanization would likely have been substantial. Jews had arrived in the Baltics from the Pale of Settlement in the 1800s, and those who were upwardly mobile Germanized within two or three generations. Most were artisans, petty merchants, and tradesmen; by 1897, almost one-third of the Jewish labor force was engaged in commerce and more than one-half was employed in craft production (all figures in Bauer et al. 1991: 355).

Finally, ethnic Latvians comprised the lower urban classes, unskilled laborers, domestic servants, a thin layer of shopkeepers, clerks, the "Latvian trades" – a group of nineteen semiskilled occupations with corporate organization and self-regulatory authority – and a small but growing urban middling class; as a proportion of their population, Latvians had the sixth-largest industrial-manufacturing sector in the empire or 15.60 percent, behind that of Jews (35.37 percent), Germans (25.01 percent), Russians (18.31 percent), Estonians (17.35 percent), Armenians (16.40 percent), and Poles (15.83 percent) (Bauer et al. 1991: 156).[3]

So Riga's very multiethnicity guaranteed that it would in some measure be an imperial Russian city, and its ethnic Russian presence was often decisive in local ethnopolitics. Jews, Poles, and Lithuanians – the ethnic groups whose proportion of Riga's population increased most substantially between 1867 and 1914 – were very influential in radical politics and contributed to the city's linguistic Russification. Riga's cultural and social life was often fragmented along national or ethnic lines: each ethnic group had its own network of clubs, cultural institutions, credit unions, political organizations, charities, and insurance societies (Henriksson 1986: 193). This differed considerably from the ethnic rankings of Polish-Lithuania or Ukraine, for instance, where provincial civil society was almost entirely the purview of the higher-status ethnicities. And this had its effects on the character of socialist political mobilizations.

In fact, a distinctive feature of Baltic social stratification was that upward social mobility, urbanization, and occupational diversity entailed linguistic and cultural Germanization. Latvians entering the "literati" or merchant guilds adopted German names and closely identified with professional circles; Latvian laborers and artisans integrated and were gradually absorbed into the *Kleinburgertum*, often via marriage. Russification, by contrast, typically occurred among Latvian peasants and artisans who were recruited into the Russian army, which was even at the time described as "becoming Russian." The distinction between Latvian and German in Riga was at best blurred, because many for whom German was their daily language spoke Latvian as children and had Latvian-speaking parents. This was facilitated by shared Lutheranism, which made intermarriage even easier. Social mobility and prestige were associated with German, and virtually any education beyond primary school meant the adoption of a non-Latvian language and culture later in life.

But the midcentury emergence of Latvian nationalist mobilizations interpreted Latvian as the linguistic marker of an emerging ethnic status rather than its historical association with a lower social class. These nationalist activists were of divided loyalties: many were married to Germans, wrote more proficiently in German because of their education, had benefitted from German patronage,

---

[3] In 1897, 58.41% of Latvians were employed in agriculture, 15.60% in manufacturing or industry, and 12.23% in domestic service.

and spoke German at home (Plakans 1981: 225; 1995: 92–3). So in the 1860s and 1870s, Latvian nationalists and liberals often welcomed the expansion of Tsarist influence as an antidote to German cultural and political dominance, giving Latvian radicalism a strong Russophilic color (Plakans 1995: 100). They demanded that Russian *zemstva* push back the German *Ritterschaften* and often sought joint Latvian-Russian electoral tickets to oppose German candidates, although this changed after the 1905 Revolution when Baltic Russians closed ranks and began voting with the Germans (Henriksson 1983: 33; 1986: 197). But Latvian nationalism was numerically smaller than Latvian socialism's subsequent strength, so Latvian nationalists turned to new urbanites for recruits (Plakans 1995: 94). Yet by the 1890s, these working-class urbanites were more attracted to the revolutionary narrative inside socialist movements than to that of nationalist politics.

Importantly, nationalists and socialists both drew their resources from the same rich Latvian associational life and extensive rural government, especially in 1905 (Raun 2006). The Latvian societies, associations, and civic institutions, both rural and urban, mirrored the liberal and well-institutionalized character of Baltic German society. There were Latvian mutual aid societies for the urban working classes, literary and teacher organizations for the educated urban classes, merchant corporations for Riga's Latvian commercial-industrial elites, rural institutions for the rural, landed bourgeoisie, and peasant aid societies for the rural poor. Indeed, by 1887, Livland had 231 Latvian organizations (Plakans 1981: 228). Agricultural societies, literacy societies, insurance societies, and rural courts and institutions mushroomed by the late 1880s, raising Latvians' self-confidence and giving rural elites greater voice in courts and councils. And because recordkeeping in these new rural institutions was increasingly in Latvian (Plakans 1995: 95–6), it became the language of communication among an increasingly socially differentiated society.

Put differently, political inclusion and social mobility no longer required Germanization. By the 1890s, rural and urban Latvians viewed Latvian language use pragmatically. This was reinforced by employment in imperial bureaucracies: the empire's civil bureaucracies provided only very limited social mobility for educated Latvians, because most were employed in local Baltic civil service and provincial or rural posts. The Baltic provinces became a closed and insular world, and most official and government posts were within the well-institutionalized Baltic civil and political hierarchies, not in the sparser Russian bureaucracy.[4] This existed alongside the dense associational and institutional life of the rural Latvian bourgeoisie, and in the rural schools and educational networks, particularly given that Russian *zemstva* were not introduced.

---

[4] In 1897, only 0.20% of Riga's Latvians held government posts, substantially less than their empire-wide representation (0.68%) and than their Baltic representation (0.77%) (Bauer et al. 1991: 446). Most Latvians in imperial bureaucracies were not in Riga, but in rural Livland and Courland.

In due course, the richness of Latvian civil society facilitated the emergence of political mobilizations. Members of the growing and socioeconomically differentiated Latvian middle class and land-owning peasantry were funneled through these ethnic networks into a wide variety of radical movements (Raun 2000: 124). By the late 1880s, when socialism was borrowed from Germany, Latvians had clearly demarcated classes, urban and rural: an influential urban merchant/manufacturing middle class and educated professional class, a working class of landless peasants and rural laborers from the countryside, a stratum of skilled urban workers and craftsmen, a well-institutionalized and increasingly self-confident rural bourgeoisie of wealthier farmers and land-owners, a middling stratum of smaller proprietors, and a larger stratum of landless laborers, peasants, and rural artisans. This growing class differentiation among Latvians blunted the effectiveness of purely nationalist mobilizations and opened the way for Latvian socialist radical movements, which were mostly Russian-inflected and multiethnic.

Why this was so turned on the way in which Russian rule asserted itself in the mid-1880s in the form of assimilatory Russification, felt most forcefully in Latvia's educational institutions: as noted in Chapter 2, imperial strategies of Russifying secondary schools in particular reproduced Russian imperial culture in these social locations, and this gave radicalism a distinctive imperial-minded quality. I explore this in detail in connection with the schoolteacher Bolshevik Berzins. But beyond educational Russification, an *ukaz* in 1885 ordered that Riga's military conscription board use Russian instead of German. This was followed in the same year with another *ukaz* designating Russian as the sole language of correspondence between Baltic authorities and the imperial government. In Riga these had the effect of Russifying the city police, for instance, and translators were hired to render official paperwork into Russian (Henriksson 1983: 47–8, 50; von Pistolkors 1992: 398–400). In 1889, the Russian judicial system was introduced in the Baltic provinces, and Russian was made the language of courts, administration, and civil business of local government (Wittram 1973: 218–19). Other initiatives sought to enlarge the Orthodox Church by forcing conversions in mixed marriages (Plakans 1981: 235).

But these policies did not strengthen Latvian nationalism. The Latvian national movement had been in decline from the mid-1880s. Russification was only enforced between 1885 and 1895, and, on the evidence, between 1884 and 1904, Latvian language publications actually increased (Plakans 1995: 101). Latvians entering professional life in the 1890s – as did most of the Latvian Bolsheviks in this elite – were educated in Russian without much resistance and often learned German because it was still necessary for advancement in most of the professions. Russification policies hit *after* the nationalist movements' peak influence, and, as we will see with the Bolsheviks, it did so at a time when the Russian of the imperial state was increasingly seen by culturally sensitive elites as cosmopolitan, enabling access to European culture, and therefore superior to the more "provincial" Latvian.

By contrast, for Baltic Germans, Russification affected mostly those in the educated and professional middle layers of society, effectively breaking the German hold on the provincial civil service and in the professions by displacing them with linguistic restrictions (Henriksson 1986: 183). Many migrated to Germany, but those who remained gravitated to a Baltic German nationalism. German liberalism ceded to a conservative defense of traditional privileges, but they remained loyal to Tsarist Russia. Baltic Germans were frustrated at Russification's illiberalism, but they hardly viewed it as a cultural threat (von Pistholkors 1992: 397–416). Indeed, the post-1905 German-Russian détente revealed the depth of German and Russian commitments to social conservatism. Though Russificatory, Tsarist reforms were equally fearful of the entrance of the lower orders into positions of municipal power. *Zemstva* were withheld here, not because of fear of local political influence and separatism as in the western borderlands, but because of fear of subverting the pragmatically effective and socially conservative Baltic German Diets. Imperial elites' social conservatism took precedence over its desire for Russification.

But the political earthquakes of 1905–08 changed everything. The 1905 Revolution in Latvia and the Tsarist state's brutal reprisals in the rural areas gave the empire's repressive presence in the Baltics a new intensity in its new policies of dissimilatory Russification (Raun 2006). The social and political effects of imperial strategies identified in Chapter 2, which had to do with policing, surveillance, and the brutality of ethnically inflected policies of social control, all dramatically shaped Latvian radicalism's antistatism. The Bolshevik Smilga experienced these reprisals personally. Beside triggering a new wave of antistate radicalism in response to the repressions, two other major social changes resulted. First, Latvian associationalism increased at the expense of German civil society. Second, and more importantly, the Russification of the Baltic civil service – the replacement of Germans with lower-class Russians and Latvians – resulted in imperial career access and greater Russian centralization. Whereas Russification in the 1880s and 1890s had hit education, after 1905 it was targeted at the Baltic civil service to bring the region administratively in line with the rest of the empire by recruiting ethnic Russians from the lower classes (Hagen 1978: 56–62). So using the imperial bureaucracy as a vehicle for social promotion, Latvians gravitated in large numbers into the middle and lower ranks of the Baltic civil service. These shifts hint at the sources of Latvians socialists' attraction to internationalist movements, as politics navigated between the ethnicization of Latvian institutional life on one hand and Russian centralism on the other.

Stuchka: Latvian Socialist Radicalism and Baltic German Liberalism

Stuchka's early political radicalism occurred between the 1860s and the 1880s, before Latvia's Russification, and firmly within the context of liberal Baltic German society, as his activism reflected underlying ethnopolitics. Berzins's radicalization, by contrast, would be almost entirely within a Russificatory context in the late 1880s and 1890s when he entered imperial Russian society – and his activism reflected this as well. These different moments and contexts found expression in the character of their leftist internationalist activism: Stuchka's internationalism was an early means of countering both Latvian nationalism and Russian centralism, but two generations later, Berzins's internationalism was more russophilic, rural in orientation, and Europeanized.

Stuchka, *aka* "Veteran" and "Paragraph," was among the oldest in the Bolshevik elite and a key figure in Latvian Social Democracy, with enormous influence over the Latvian Party in 1917. He was born in 1865 in the rural Koknese district of Livland (Livonija) to a family of prosperous landowners or "Latvian grey barons," part of the new class of propertied rural Latvians, which in the socialist literature after 1905 acquired a highly politicized connotation. Although official biographies claim Stuchka's family were peasants, like Smilga's, they were quite prosperous given that Stuchka attended an elite and private German *Gymnasium* in Riga (on his peasant status, see Prokhorov 1969–78: 15 and Granat 1989: 708; on the *Gymnasium*, see Lazitch 1986: 451).

There is very sparse information on Stuchka's *Gymnasium* years, but quite a lot is known about Riga's German secondary schools more generally. The Baltic school system had expanded significantly in the 1860s and 1870s. Latvian and Estonian were used in primary schools and German was used in secondary and higher education. Stuchka's *Gymnasium* education promised social mobility within Baltic society. There is no evidence that he had any involvement in radical student circles; indeed, before Russification, these schools were generally quiescent. Stuchka was of a generation of educated Latvians exposed neither to the humiliations of Russification, which would hit the Riga German school system after 1886, nor, because of his socioeconomic status, to the growing anti-German nationalism in the Latvian school system of the 1860s and 1870s. He was linguistically and culturally Germanized, but he was also multilingual, with some fluency in Russian, as was the case in most well-to-do Latvian Riga homes.

After completing *Gymnasium*, Stuchka attended the Law Faculty of St. Petersburg University, not "separatist" Dorpat University – a further indication of his integration into not only educated Baltic society but now also into the empire's educational system. After receiving his law degree in 1888, Stuchka worked for nine years as an advocate's associate in Riga (Granat 1989: 708). The fact that he worked in Riga's legal profession, Russified since 1889 and by that time an uneasy combination of Russian and German, was both a testament to his language skills and proof of his successful entry into the privileged German professional classes. But by the 1890s, tensions between localism and cosmopolitanism were deeply felt by those Latvian cultural elites able to access European and Russian cultures. The Baltic world and provincial nationalism had begun to feel too stifling against the more cosmopolitan appeal of the new ideas from Europe, especially Germany, and especially for those educated in St. Petersburg or Germany (Plakans 1981: 255). We see the beginning of the identity fractures of this cultural restlessness in Stuchka, although it is more complete in Berzins. Some of the appeal of European and Russian socialism for Latvian cultural elites in the 1880s and 1890s was its wider cultural vistas – a need more intensely felt by cultural elites in the "smaller" cultures on the empire's peripheries. Most importantly, however, European ideas eclipsed worries about the effects of Russification and crucially introduced a class critique into Baltic society (Plakans 1981: 255–6).

So two important forms of Latvian political radicalism emerged: Latgalian nationalism among the eastern Latvians in Latgale in Vitebsk, and Latvian socialism, or the New Current *Jaunā strāva* (its followers were the *jaunstrāvnieki*). Stuchka was the key figure in Latvian socialist politics, which after 1905 became Latvian Social Democracy. In parallel with his employment as an advocate's associate, between 1888 and 1897, Stuchka was also coeditor of one of the most influential New Current papers, *Dienas Lapa* (The Daily Paper). After 1893, *Dienas Lapa* became the ideological organ of the Latvian democratic intelligentsia and the first major Latvian progressive, non-nationalist journal to offer a Marxist analysis of Baltic socioeconomic conditions (Granat 1989: 708 on Stuchka's involvement; Drizulis 1957: 418 and Plakans 1995: 102–3 on the context). In the 1890s, the Latvian radical intelligentsia was non-nationalist and focused solely on Latvian socioeconomic divisions and income differentials. It centered on the rural landless and poorer urban workers, to the notable exclusion of nationalist politics. In the mobilizational battles between Latvian nationalism and German-inspired socialism, then, a politicized socialism won the day – and this during the height of cultural Russification in the Baltics.

Like Stuchka, most of the *jaunastrāvnieki* were of rural origin. The 1890s group differed from the earlier nationalist intelligentsia because most of the former had been more urban in origin. And whereas the Young Latvians were products of nationalist Dorpat University, the *jaunastrāvnieki* were more likely to be products of St. Petersburg, Moscow, and Zurich Universities (Ezergailis 1974: 4–5). Members of *Dienas Lapa*, Stuchka among them, formed radical workers' groups in Riga, Libau (Liepāja), and Mitau, and they organized strikes, lectures, and work stoppages. But with the labor unrest of 1897, the *jaunstrāvnieki* and other leftist radicals were arrested, exiled, or expelled from the Baltic provinces because of Tsarist reprisals, and as a result many turned against the Russian state for the first time. Some eighty *jaunstrāvnieki* were arrested and eventually brought to trial in 1899. Stuchka was among them. He was sentenced to five years in exile in 1902 and settled in Vitebsk where he continued his political activism. The reprisals not only further radicalized the *Jaunā strāva*, but their revolutionary politics now also attacked the Latvian nationalism of the nationalist Riga Latvian Association (RLA) on socialist, class grounds, because the RLA represented Riga's merchant and propertied interests (Plakans 1995: 103–4).

This context is important for understanding Stuchka's attraction to socialist radicalism as well as his anti-nationalism. Although the municipal reforms of the 1860s and 1870s had allowed Latvians and Russians entry in city council elections, property restrictions on the franchise were still narrow enough to ensure that the social and ethnic composition of Riga city government remained German-dominated between 1877 and 1913 (Henriksson 1986). Latvians had risen economically and culturally, but as late as 1905 they remained politically excluded from provincial government; they had negligible representation in the Riga city council, majorities in only four small towns, and poor representation in city patronage jobs (Henriksson 1986: 196; Plakans 1995: 104–9). It was obvious to them that this political underrepresentation was not commensurate with their newly rising economic status. But middle-class Latvians like Stuchka did not become nationalists, and their routes to political radicalism reflected both these socioeconomic locations and the effects of Tsarist policies. More specifically, different interests developed between the urban Latvian commercial middle class, the cultural activists of the RLA, and the now powerful Latvian rural middle class. And these particularist interests did not coalesce around the Latvian nation, but rather remained local and status particularistic. So, for instance, in local elections, most propertied Riga Latvians supported German tickets – against the Latvian nationalists – in defense of the privileges they had acquired on entering the merchant estate. Indeed, nationalists polemicized that the Latvian defeat in the 1886 municipal elections was the result of the high number of Germanized Riga Latvians who had voted against the Latvian-Russian ticket.

In other words, Latvian electoral victories and failures in town councils represented affluent and propertied Latvian groups, so social reform and progressivist politics were relegated to a secondary position. In 1909, this allowed Stuchka to maintain, through his *Dienas Lapa* editorship, that progressive Latvians, namely the urban and rural lower classes, had nothing to gain from supporting the Latvian national tickets because they represented the Latvian propertied establishment as much as that of the Germans (Henriksson 1986: 196). In this, Stuchka's political radicalism was firmly socialist, drawing on and reinforcing urban and rural class distinctions alike. By 1906, Stuchka had questioned whether the 1905 Revolution was a class or nationalist mobilization, and he concluded that the Latvian bourgeoisie had tied itself to its German counterpart (Ezergailis 1974: 79).

Throughout this period Stuchka was employed as a barrister in St. Petersburg and took part in the trials of many of the 1905 Revolution's participants. But he also remained politically active: he worked on the Latvian journal *Sotsialdemokrat*, and in Riga in 1903 Stuchka founded what would become the Latvian Bolshevik Party, joining its CC at the first congress of the Latvian Social Democratic Workers' Party (LSDWP) in 1904 (Granat 1989: 708). Initially the Latvian Party admitted only ethnic Latvians, but it collaborated with other ethnic groupings in federative committees in the Latvian territories, and eventually their ethnically exclusive membership ceded to a more pluralist one (Plakans 1981: 260–1; 1995: 104). From the beginning it was perhaps the most influential and prestigious regional party because of Riga's extensive industrialization and because of the high literacy rates among the

Latvian lower classes (Raun 2000: 125).[5] In 1906, Stuchka was instrumental in bringing the Latvian party into coalition with the RSDLP as the SDLK (Social Democracy of the Latvian Krai); by 1907, he became the leader of the Latvian Bolsheviks, and in 1914 the party joined the RSDLP on a basis similar to that of the Jewish Bund and the Polish-Lithuanian SDKPiL (Drizulis 1957: 418; see Kalnins 1972: 141–2 for discussion). Stuchka was the most prominent Latvian Marxist theoretician, particularly on agrarian issues (Ezergailis 1974: 70). He also wrote extensively on the national question and on the relationship between nationalism and socialism in Latvia. In fact, along with the Armenian Stepan Shaumian (Chapter 7), Stuchka was one of the few non-Russian Bolsheviks to explicitly address the nationalities question in 1905–06, earlier than Lenin's famous 1913 tract. Indeed, it is possible, as some have speculated, that the ethnic minority borderland Bolsheviks actually led Lenin and the Russians on this question, and not the other way around (Ezergailis 1974: 88).

So how can we understand Stuchka's commitment to a purely class-based political mobilization? The German landowners' part in the 1905 Tsarist army's punitive expeditions had turned large segments of the Latvian intelligentsia against Latvian membership in the empire (Plakans 1981: 266–7). As both Stuchka and Shaumian admitted, the 1905 events in the empire's multiethnic borderlands were largely nationalist-minded mobilizations, and they were important to the extent that they began to transform cultural nationalisms into political nationalisms. Even though they were still some way from being mass movements, socialist activists now had to explicitly counter the nationalist movement. The Jewish Bund had pursued the nationalities question in the RSDLP in 1903, and by 1905, not only nationalist groupings, but also nationalist socialists in the borderlands increasingly won substantial support. As Stuchka wrote, "[W]e are all against nationalism, even when it comes under a socialist label, and as a frightening example we are mentioning the demands of the Bund for national cultural autonomy which is even unacceptable at the Menshevik conferences" (quoted in Ezergailis 1983: 81).

As a result, Stuchka consistently promoted democratic centralism. He maintained this position through 1917 on the grounds that there could not be a free Latvia in an unfree Russia; political autonomy could be carefully circumscribed only in union with a democratic Russia (Ezergailis 1983: 84–5). Ezergailis (1983: 87) wrote, "at both junctures [1905 and 1917] Stuchka... sought escape from the Great Russian chauvanistic bear and from Latvia's own nationalists," and in so doing continually emphasized democracy. This seems true. Stuchka's socialist internationalist politics navigated between Russian centralism and Latvian separatism, and his position changed little between the two revolutions. But given the differences between Latvia in 1906 after the failure of the revolutions and the brutality of Russian nationalist response on the

[5] Its membership went from strength to strength: 2,500 in 1904, 7,000 by June 2005, 18,200 by the October Manifesto in 1905, of which 7,000 were based in Riga (Raun 2006: 51, citing Kalnins' [1972: 134–6] figures).

one hand, and Latvia in 1917 after two years of war and a seemingly successful revolution in Russia on the other, Stuchka's position was held under rationales arguably more cogent to the circumstances.

At both junctures Stuchka emphasized an empire-saving or *rossiiskii*-oriented political imaginary, the replacement of the imperial "prison of nations" with a territorially multiethnic but democratic centralism. For Stuchka, the lesson – and the fear – of 1905 was that the greatest threat to the Latvian socialist movement was Russian chauvinism, not Latvian nationalism. So the appropriate socialist response was Latvian autonomy within a socialist federation. Stuchka's post-1905 fear of Tsarist reaction may not have been misplaced: arguably Latvia was now worryingly leading Russia in revolutionary social dynamic (even Lenin thought so). And Stuchka understood – mostly because he was implicated in it on a professional basis as a practicing lawyer – that 1905 had changed Latvia in practical, institutional terms: Latvians were moving to the fore in provincial and city parliaments and administrations, and electoral ethnic dynamics were shifting rapidly (see also discussion in Raun 2006: 56).

During the 1915–17 period, these fears were geopolitical and pragmatic. German-occupied Courland would be kept by Germany and Latvia and likely be dismembered, so stressing unity was important. Again this was a well-founded (and prophetic) fear given that at Brest-Litovsk the Bolsheviks did offer up Latvia to Germany (Ezergailis 1983: 91, n. 31). German occupation caused the entire Russian bureaucratic structure to flee, prompting Germany to organize a military apparatus for administrative purposes (Page 1959: 28–9). German occupation had insulated Courland and Lithuania from the direct effects of the Russian Revolution, but it opened new possibilities for Latvian local political control, and this threatened to sever Latvia's socialist mobilization from Russian events. In important ways, the greatest obstacle for the Latvian Left was not the Provisional Government or German control, but the rural councils and associations of the propertied Latvian middle class, whose politics virtually ignored rural landless peasants and rural laborers – precisely those most represented in the Latvian infantry units of the Imperial Army. To the rural landless and to the soldiers, it appeared that this landowners' nationalist struggle excluded them.

So the Latvian Bolsheviks seized the radical moment and moved their editorial offices from Petrograd to Riga, and thereby became the de facto leadership of the Latvian Rifles. They proclaimed Latvia's right to secede from Russia, Leninist-style, and promised land to landless peasants and soldiers. A dual administrative power emerged: the SD's landless councils and the autonomous councils of the middle class aligned class divisions with the competing political mobilizations. The Latvian middle classes wanted independence, while peasants and workers sought autonomy within a federated Russia (Page 1959: 66). The latter prevailed and Latvian Bolshevism retained wide support.

But the rapidity of events ensured that the relationship between the nationalist and socialist movements did not stand still. Though he remained committed to Latvian unity with Russia, geopolitics forced another reassessment on

Stuchka. The German Army was deployed in Estonia and Latvia in 1918 when the Bolsheviks signed the Treaty of Brest-Litovsk. German military authorities recognized the nationalist movements, so any Red Army offensive would constitute foreign invasion by the terms of the treaty. Independent Soviet states were created in the path of the Red Army, first in Estonia, then in Lithuania and Latvia. When Lenin asked that Stuchka head a Latvian Provisional Revolutionary Government comprised of key members of the Latvian SD, Stuchka opposed it as a flagrant concession to nationalist separatism. He reluctantly agreed to become a "separatist," however, not least because "the German social-traitors would scream that Soviet Russia did not liberate small nations, but conquered them." Stuchka edited the Latvian Soviet government's manifesto and agreed to a Red Army offensive – which included the Latvian Rifles – so that it could claim to be "a Latvian Army" (discussion and quote in White 1994: 1362–3).

In the wake of the German collapse and evacuation, a communist government was established, headed by Stuchka and Karl Danishevskii, among others. Stuchka proclaimed the independence of Soviet Latvia and declared it part of the Universal Union of Soviet Republics. In a commitment to internationalism, Bolsheviks Kapsukas and Stuchka supported the creation of Soviet states in Estonia, Latvia, Ukraine, Belarusia, and Lithuania. Stuchka imagined these as part of the spreading world revolution; the Communist International was a federation of socialist states, not a collection of parties (White 1994: 1366). So after a tactical concession to a separatist Latvian Soviet government, Stuchka's commitment to internationalism remained substantially intact – if only in the belief that Soviet Latvia was part of an international of states. In practice, however, geopolitics – and the desire to save the Revolution in Russia – had obviously forced Stuchka's socialist internationalism into a nationalist-separatist corner.

In the end, his route to political radicalism had reflected the mobilizational possibilities of the Germanized, educated, rural Latvia milieux of the 1860s to the 1880s, before Tsarist Russification. Socialist internationalism was a political alternative to both Latvian nationalism and Russian imperial centralism. Intra-Latvian class tensions and a growing rural associational life made socialist mobilization relatively attractive because it could counter German dominance. Stuchka's employment as a lawyer in St. Petersburg also had its role in his eventual attraction to a Russian-inflected socialism but so, too, did his commitment to a territorially integral *rossiiskii* empire as the antidote to the perceived conservative nationalism of the Latvian middle classes.

Berzins and Danishevskii: Russophile Socialism and the Latvian Middle Class

If Stuchka was radicalized in a crumbling Latvian-German world, Berzins and Danishevskii were radicalized two decades later in an emerging Latvian-Russian world. The differences in their political radicalism reflected this important shift in the Latvian radical intelligentsia, particularly in terms of the social sources of their socialist internationalism and in the social locations that produced the two generations of Latvian Bolsheviks. Posthumously rehabilitated, Berzins was arrested in 1937 by Stalin as a Latvian nationalist and died in 1938 under unknown circumstances; similarly, Danishevskii died in the purges in 1938 under speculation that he had been a Menshevik before Bolshevism. Berzins's diplomatic career had been considerable: he had served as the Bolshevik ambassador to Switzerland, Finland, and Austria. Danishevskii was a key Latvian Bolshevik orator in 1917, and with Stuchka led in tactical decisions and in writing party resolutions (Ezergailis 1974: 42–3). As a Bolshevik, Danishevskii was a member of the Izkolat (the Executive Committee of the Soviet of Workers', Landless Peasants', and Soldiers' Deputies), the Riga Soviet, the Latvian Social Democratic CC (with Berzins, and as a co-opted Menshevik), and the Soviet Latvian government that Stuchka had established after Brest-Litovsk (Drizulis 1957: 42).

Berzins was born in 1881 in the Cēsis district in Livland, to a family of peasant farmers; Danishevskii, aka "German," was born in 1884, also in rural Livland, and also to a peasant family (Drizulis 1957: 42; Prokhorov 1969–78: 529). Although there is little reliable data on their education, there is general agreement that Danishevskii attended the Moscow Commercial Institute in 1910, but he was expelled in 1912 for radical activity; Berzins attended the Riga Teacher's Seminary (Drizulis 1957: 42 on Danishevskii).[6] Both were socialized in the 1880s and politicized in the 1890s, two decades after Latvian nationalism's mobilizational peak.

Relatively few Latvians of the 1880s generation had experienced either serfdom or the period when social mobility was first experienced by rural Latvians of Stuchka's generation. By the 1890s, German dominance was substantially attenuated, and Latvian intelligentsia's radicalism shifted from its traditional anti-German inspiration to a more Russian-oriented one. So Berzins's and Danishevskii's political radicalizations did not occur during the period of greatest nationalist activity against German rule, as had Stuchka's, but in the early years of Russification with the introduction of Russian language education and curriculum in the early 1880s. Latvian parents in rural districts sent their children to Russian-language schools. The vast majority accepted educational Russification without objection – and often with a certain enthusiasm – because parts of the Latvian intelligentsia welcomed the extension of Russian as a way of diminishing German control over provincial life (Plakans 1981: 241). This would have broadly characterized Berzins's and Danishevskii's schooling.

Indeed, in the last decades of Tsarist rule, the empire appeared attractive to the many thousands of Latvians who emigrated from the Baltics. Many sought imperial venues for education and attended institutes in St. Petersburg or Moscow, as did Danishevskii and as had Stuchka. Although understudied,

---

[6] On Berzins, see HIAPO, Box 210, Indexes XXII-XXIV, Index XXII, Folder 1B, Circular 768, November 11/24, 1915, Paris, on Berzins.

and based mostly on anecdotal evidence, many Latvians with advanced degrees from Russian universities were viewed suspiciously by Baltic Germans, and on their return they experienced some blocked mobility, resulting in an even stronger identification with the empire's Russian language and culture and a generalized commitment to empire (Plakans 1995: 111). Another consequence of this generational shift was that, unlike Stuchka, Berzins and Danishevskii were more fluent in Russian than in German. For the generation educated in the 1880s that reached intellectual maturity in the 1890s and early 1900s, not only advanced education, but also urbanization now meant Russian, not German. So Stuchka had traveled from a well-off, landowning rural family to membership in the Baltic German society as a lawyer, whereas Berzins traveled from a rural, moderately well-off peasant family to membership in the Russified Latvian intelligentsia as a schoolteacher.

The Okhrana files indicate that Berzins was employed as a public or state schoolteacher either in the city or in the rural schools in Livland *guberniia*.[7] Although there is little specific biographical information available outside Latvian-language sources about Berzins's career in Latvia, several general comments can confidently be made about the social and political context of ethnic Latvian teachers in these years. Employment as a state schoolteacher implied that his Russian proficiency would have been good. In 1885, all primary schools in the Baltic provinces were centralized under the St. Petersburg Ministry of Education, and by 1891, all city schools in Riga taught all subjects in Russian. In 1887, Russian was made the language of instruction in certain *Gymnasien* and in 1889 this was extended to private secondary schools (Wittram 1973: 219–20; von Pistolkors 1992: 408–10). By the mid-1890s, all schools in the Baltics had Russian as their official language of instruction, so Latvian schoolteachers were unable to teach if they lacked Russian skills. Although careers in city and rural schools were available, they were blocked to those who had been members of Latvian nationalist organizations or associations (Plakans 1981: 250). So Latvian schoolteachers like Berzins clearly felt the impact of educational Russification.

More professionally trained Latvians became teachers than any other occupation, and most midcentury nationalist efforts had famously been in the teaching professions. Yet as noted, the radicalizing role of Russification among Latvians should not be overstated. Baltic German schools were among the highest quality in the empire, educating the greatest proportion of the population, but Russification of the Riga school system actually allowed Latvians and Jews to make substantial gains (Henriksson 1986: 188–9). What radicalized was not the introduction of Russian per se, but a series of administrative centralizing

---

[7] HIAPO, Box 210, Index XXII–XXVIa, Index XXII, Folder 1B, Circular No. 1274, October 9/22, 1912, Paris, and Circular No. 858, June 27 – July 10, 1912, Paris. These Okhrana reports are the only non-Latvian language sources I found that specify his employment as a Baltic public school teacher. The first is a Livland Okhrana report, the latter an Okhrana translation of intercepted correspondence of the Foreign Bureau of the SDLK. Similar information is repeated in both.

moves that undermined Baltic educational autonomy (cf Hechter 2000 on this dynamic more generally). Since the late 1880s, jurisdictional questions continually arose between local school districts and state governing authorities. These authorities often reserved the right to terminate teachers, something that resulted in hundreds of disputes from the 1890s (Plakans 1981: 240).

The Russification of education caused the most tension between the Russian state and the German *Ritterschaften*, not between Latvians and Russians. So at a 1905 conference of Latvian schoolteachers, the social democrats, not the nationalists, were the leading faction, and they called for greater autonomy within a socialist Russia. They were politicized into a Russian-inflected socialism, not into an anti-German nationalism. Moreover, among the rural Latvian intelligentsia – which was extremely active in the 1905 revolutionary events – rural schoolteachers like Berzins were at the forefront: an estimated 42 percent of rural teachers in Kurland and 31 percent in southern Livland were involved in radical mobilizations (Raun 2006: 56). In keeping with the sources of radicalism of most Latvian schoolteachers, Berzins's politicization was not likely in response to Russification – but there was political restlessness with Tsarist illiberalism and centralization, which chafed all the more in the context of historically liberal Baltic society.

In 1902, at age twenty-one, Berzins joined the Latvian Socialist Party in Riga, which had large numbers of students and teachers in its membership (on CP activism, see Drizulis 1957: 432; Prokhorov 1969–78: 229; for an anecdotal account of party composition, see Granat 1989: 632). In 1903, he was arrested for illegal activities, released, arrested again in 1904, and escaped in 1905. Berzins took part in revolutionary events in Valka (Walk) in 1905–07; he was secretary of the St. Petersburg Committee of the RSDLP in 1907 and a delegate to the London party conference under the name Pavel (Drizulis 1957: 432). Because of severe Tsarist repression in the Baltics after 1905, Berzins's political radicalism in the European émigré community was not only substantial but also at a relatively high level of influence judging by the attention paid to him by the Tsarist Okhrana: abroad, Berzins was on the editorial board and an active contributor to the Latvian Bolshevik publication *Cīņa* (Struggle), to the main organ of the Latvian SDs *Sotsialdemokrat*, to the RSDLP journal *Proletariat*, and he edited the paper of the Foreign Committee of the Latvian party, *Biletens* (Bulletin).[8] More generally, he was simultaneously a member of several SD parties, a reflection of both the complexity of the ethnic socialist parties and of Berzins's Russian-inflected activism. In 1910, he joined the foreign bureau of the RSDLP;[9] he was also secretary of the Foreign Bureau of the Paris group of the SDLK, and in this capacity he was involved in overseeing

[8] The Tsarist Okhrana closely followed his editorial party work in Paris and Europe; see HIAPO, Box 210, Index XXII–XXIVa, Index XXII, Folder 1B, Circular No. 1274 dated October 9/22, 1912, Paris.
[9] See HIAPO, Box 124, Index XIIIb(1), Folder 1E, Outgoing Dispatch, No. 852, April 30/May 13, 1914, Paris.

the transport of materials from Russia (Lazitch 1986: 27).[10] But Berzins's commitment to internationalist socialism had already been underpinned by his employment as a schoolteacher in rural Latvia. Culturally sensitive, yet peripheral and insulated from European political excitement, he saw escape either via imperial Russian or European cultures. Berzins's political activism embodied elements of both.

His commitment to internationalism was further strengthened during the Great War, even though he was in the United States, Europe, and in the Russian interior, not in war-devastated Latvia. For Stuchka, the war and its surrounding geopolitical considerations had pressed him to make nationalist concessions in order to preserve the revolution and Latvia's place in the new *rossiiskii* state. Until this point Berzins's internationalist socialism had been more truly cosmopolitan and abstract, less pragmatically implicated in tactical decisions, as was Stuchka, for instance. Berzins had spent more than nine years in emigration as a key figure in the Latvian socialist émigré community, and he opposed the war as member of the Foreign Bureau of the Latvian branch of the RSDLP.[11] He was among the small but active Latvian socialist community in the United States, as had been the Lithuanian Kapsukas: in 1916–17, Berzins edited the Latvian social democratic paper *Stradnieks* (Worker) in Boston and the Russian leftist internationalist paper *Novii mir* in New York (Drizulis 1957: 432). Latvian socialist antiwar publications abroad called for struggle against Russian autocracy, not national unity, in part because for these political émigrés, Russification seemed a comparatively minor infraction (Plakans 1981: 432). For Kapsukas, Berzins, and Danishevskii, as socialists from small, geopolitically fragile potential states, internationalism during the war was common.[12] But this shifted when the revolution in Russia opened new geostrategic possibilities.

On his return to Russia, Berzins' activism implicated him more immediately among Latvian refugees in the empire's interior. Within six months of the German declaration of war on Russia, the southern part of the Baltic littoral became an active war zone, and the dislocating effects of the German armies in Courland and the southern Latvian territories were most appreciable among rural Latvians (Raun 2000: 126). More than 570,000 refugees had fled or were evacuated from Courland into Livland and Latgale when the German armies advanced and established a military-civilian government (Page 1959: 38–9). The Tsarist government was confronted with nearly three million refugees fleeing into Petrograd and the central Russian provinces from the war-occupied Polish, Lithuanian, and western Latvian territories, posing a considerable problem for the Russian state (Gatrell 1999: 47). By some estimates, Latvian

[10] This according to Paris Okhrana agents; HIAPO, Box 210, Index XXII–XXIVa, Index XXII, Folder 1B, Circular No. 858, June 27–July 10, 1912, Paris, and Box 190, Index XVIb(2), Folder 4, Circular No. 1186, September 18/October 1, 1912, Paris.

[11] See HIAPO, Box 210, Index XXII, Folder 1B, Circular No. 768, November 11/24, 1915, Paris.

[12] At the Thirteenth Conference of the Latvian Party in 1917, Danishevskii stressed the imperialist character of the war (Ezergailis 1974:66–7).

political refugees had up to 260 different organizations in St. Petersburg alone, and as many as 100,000 ethnic Latvians in the imperial capital in 1917, in highly organized SD refugee organizations specifically designed to cater to refugee needs (Ezergailis 1983: 250; White 1990: 100).

Berzins was a key SD figure in Petrograd among these organizers in Prometejs, the national section of the RSDLP(b). Headed by Stuchka and Danishevskii, its main function was to canvass support among Latvian war refugees (White 1990: 93). With the evacuation of factories in the Baltics, more and more Latvian SDs went to Petrograd, even organizing a passport bureau used by Russian radicals. In 1918, the coordination of national left-wing groups in the occupied regions (among Lithuanians, Latvians, Estonians, Belarusians, Ukrainians, Poles, and Finns) was commonly referred to as the Little International, and it created important mobilizational links between the Russian and German Revolutions (White 1994).

Berzins and Danishevskii organized the first soviets in cities and factories among these refugees and Latvian soldiers. Support came primarily from the most desperate and displaced, from unskilled landless peasants, and from substantial numbers of disillusioned soldiers of the Latvian infantry units. The war, German occupation, evacuation, starvation, and disease had created either demoralized soldiers or terrified civilians and uprooted refugees, all easily politicized. In turn, these refugee mobilizations created new frameworks for cultural and political activity for the revolutionary movement (Gatrell 1999: 95, 141). But Latvians in the Russian interior were often mistaken for Germans because they were Lutheran and they had German surnames, something that prompted them to find pride in their Latvianness and a new affection for their "backwoods," linking "refugeedom" with nationality (the term from Gatrell 1999: 142–3). This newly found fondness for Latvia, particularly among cultural elites, was most evident in the ad hoc network of refugee schools. Gatrell (1999: 159–60) hints at the possibility that ethnic dispersion caused by refugeedom gave rise to a fear that Latvianness would be diluted. Although scholarly work on these empirical connections is lacking, for Russified Latvian socialists like Berzins and Danishevskii, the very fact that war suffering funneled many into nationalist mobilization at the very least undermined their socialist mobilization.

In this context, therefore, the need to bind Latvian socialism even more tightly to Russian socialism was acutely felt by Latvian SD activists in Petrograd. The war had caused Stuchka to battle both a growing Latvian institutional presence and Russian centralism in the Latvian territories, but Berzins's and Danishevskii's socialist revolutionary activism in Petrograd among Latvian refugees had to directly contend with the growing Latvian nationalist movement. And yet substantial class-status divisions within Latvian society meant that the interests of the various social strata diverged in both subtle and not so subtle ways. So, too, did their political commitments: wealthier Latvian farmers – the independent and affluent rural middle class – organized as refugees and became the central preoccupation of the nationally minded Latvian

Central Refugee Committee. In contrast, mass evacuations funneled poorer Latvian farmers and agricultural workers from Courland (Kurzeme), and as of July 1915, it also funneled 75,000–145,000 dependants of three-fourths of Riga's Latvian, Polish, Lithuanian, and Jewish factory labor force into the socialist revolutionary mobilizations (Gatrell 1999: 25, 85). One important source of strength of Latvian socialist politics, then, was that they targeted those uprooted Latvian refugees with the *weakest cultural and political identities*, namely impoverished peasants, unemployed rural laborers, displaced factory workers, and disaffected Latvian soldiers in the imperial army.

In sum, Berzins and Danishevskii's social worlds and routes to political radicalism reflected the Russophilic socialism of segments of the rural Latvian middle class as it developed during a period of assimilatory Russification of strategies around educational and imperial administrative opportunities. In these socioethnic locations, intra-Latvian class tensions meant that the socialist internationalism of *rossiiskii* political movements held a distinctive appeal, even more so than nationalist groupings. This was further intensified in the wartime mobilization of the rural poor, displaced laborers, and soldiers.

Rudzutaks and Lepse: Socialist Urban Radicalism in Riga

For the theoretician Stuchka, 1905 had forced a reconciliation of nationalism with socialist radicalism; for Berzins and Danishevskii, 1905 strengthened their internationalism. In contrast, Rudzutaks's and Lepse's experiences in 1905 focus attention on a different socioethnic location: Riga's urban labor. Both were urban working-class Bolsheviks: Lepse was born in 1889 in Riga to a worker father, and Rudzutaks was born in 1887 in Kursisu district in Courland to a family of farmhands and laborers (Prokhorov 1969–78: 346; Granat 1989: 631). There is little reliable biographical information on Lepse, so in this section I focus primarily on Rudzutaks, and through him try to understand and contextualize their social world.[13] While there is vast biographical material on Rudzutaks in Russian, English, and Latvian, as a prominent victim of the purges, the greatest portion refers mainly to his post-1917 political career and not to his prerevolutionary activity. In part this is no doubt also because Rudzutaks spent between 1907 and 1917 in Riga's Central Prison and in Moscow's famed Butyrka Prison, effectively removing him from political activity.

Rudzutaks attended a rural parish school, in all likelihood one of the Lutheran rural schools (Granat 1989: 631), while Lepse received two years

---

[13] Lepse was drafted into the Tsarist army during the war, though official accounts do not specify Latvian Units. Between 20,000 and 25,000 soldiers were initially mobilized in the Latvian territories, with 10,000–15,000 Latvian soldiers killed between 1914 and 1915 when the German armies occupied Kurland south of the Daugava (Dvina) River. At the front, Lepse conducted propaganda work among these soldiers, where he was wounded, and in 1915 he returned to Riga and then Petrograd (Kopanev 1967: 37–8, Prokhorov 1969–78: 346).

of elementary schooling in a Riga city school (Kopanev 1967: 37). Rudzutaks worked as a farmhand and, from age fifteen, as a shepherd for a landowner (Granat 1989: 631). He wrote that he suffered "bitter privations" within an exploitative peasant-landowner relationship, and he focused his resentments on both the Latvian grey barons and the German landed elite. As we saw earlier, the Latvian urban bourgeoisie was indecisive, first siding with the revolutionary forces and then moving to the right to protect their social position from the same revolutionary social forces. In fact, class divisions among Latvians were so pronounced that even the rightist nationalism of the Latvian People's Party applauded the Tsarist government's military tribunals, its anti-Semitism, and the punitive expeditions – of which rural, and often poor, Latvians were the targets. So Rudzutaks had experienced the class tensions between propertied rural elites and the landless peasants or rural laborers in rural Latvia. At age sixteen, without a passport and against his father's wishes, he left the countryside for Riga (Granat 1989: 631–2).

So to contextualize Rudzutaks's subsequent biography is, in effect, to access the social world of Latvia's urban working-class radicalism and to join his radicalism with Lepse's. He was part of the considerable migration of rural Latvians into the city's factories: between 1867 and 1913, Riga's population grew nearly 500 percent as the expanding economy and rural unrest attracted Latvian peasants; between 1890 and 1900, Riga's labor force tripled – only Moscow, St. Petersburg, and Łódź had larger working classes.

But the Latvian peasant migration experience to Riga in search of work in factories was distinctive compared to that of other cities in the empire in at least four ways. First, as noted, peasant emancipation had not tied peasants to repartitional communes, so it weakened their ties to the land and made them more than seasonal workers. The vast majority – Rudzutaks and Lepse among them – settled permanently, abandoning all ties to the countryside. So urban acculturation was more rapid than it was St. Petersburg or Moscow, as we will see in Chapter 8 with the Russian Bolsheviks. Latvian peasant-workers' assimilation was so rapid that the conservative editor of the *Rigasche Rundschau* wrote that in Riga it was difficult to distinguish between former peasants and members of "good society," unlike in other Russian cities where the streets were full of people easily identifiable as rural (Henriksson 1986: 202). Rural Latvian peasants were not especially confronted with their Latvianness in Riga, so they were only very weakly politicized on the basis of this identity. Instead, they acculturated into a particular urban working-class Riga culture: socialist, multiethnic, and Russophilic.

Second, Riga's working-class radicalism was also distinctive because high levels of worker literacy facilitated acculturation and radicalization. Because the Lutheran church, the Baltic aristocracy, and peasant rural communities had consistently maintained effective networks of village and rural schools, the vast majority of Latvian peasant migrants to Riga were already highly literate – much more so than Russian peasants arriving in St. Petersburg, Moscow, or the provincial cities of central Russia. In fact, Riga had the lowest illiteracy rate of any of the major cities in the empire (Bauer et al. 1991: 410–28). But it was also the fourth-largest *industrial* city and the third-largest port city in the empire. So even with its large industrial and shipbuilding labor forces it still had the lowest levels of illiteracy and the highest levels of *Russian* readers.[14] Rudzutaks was among the more than one-third of rural Latvians and two-thirds of urban Latvians who could read Russian – a level of Russian-language literacy on par with that of the empire's Jews. The implications are important for socialist radical mobilizations, because high levels of Russian-literacy facilitated access to Russian socialist mobilizations. This literacy also resulted in an enormous number of publications. Riga had among the largest circulation of newspapers, journals, and periodicals: in 1905–07, there were 107 periodicals in Latvian, of which 63 were daily periodicals and weekly newspapers, and by 1910, there were a record 45 publishing firms in Riga alone, and 75 in the Latvian territories (Plakans 1995: 106). On the specific biographical evidence, we know that Rudzutaks and Lepse easily accessed this literature (Prokhorov 1969–78: 346; Granat 1989: 632).

Third, Rudzutaks and Lepse were metalworkers, the most dominant of the new industries and among the most politically radicalized, organized, and fully mobilized, as we will see in greater depth in Chapter 8 in connection with the ethnic Russian Bolsheviks. With Riga's industrial expansion, dozens of large plants were opened, producing machinery for industrial and military use and shipyards for marine equipment (Henriksson 1986: 180–1). In the 1890s, most of the growth was in machine building, metalworking, and light industries such as textiles and wood finishing. Lepse worked in Riga as a founder in one of the metalworks and Rudzutaks worked in a steel factory (Prokhorov 1969–78: 346; Granat 1989: 631). So unlike the Jewish artisan Piatnitsky in Vilna, who worked in the struggling trades, Rudzutaks and Lepse worked in the new and expanding heavy industries, giving their early radicalism as workers a different organizational base and commitment. Indeed, Lepse made his career organizing the Metalworkers Trade Unions in Riga, as well as conducting party work among metalworkers in Petrograd. In 1917, Lepse became a member of the Central Administration of Metalworkers Union and from 1918 Secretary of the Petrograd Committee of the Metalworkers Union (Prokhorov 1969–78: 346).

Moreover, Piatnitsky had joined the socialist Bund as a Jewish worker in small ateliers and workshops, but Rudzutaks and Lepse were active in large-scale all-Russian industrial strikes that had no distinctive Latvian dimension. Although they were part of the generation of politically active Riga urban factory workers around 1904–05, the first waves of labor radicalism had affected Riga and Libau in 1895, 1897, and 1898–99, with socialist literature

---

[14] More than 56% of Riga's Germans could read Russian. More than 46% of Riga's Jews and 48% of Latvians read Russian, on par with the nearly 50% of Russians who could read. More than 50% of Riga's Poles and 65% of its Ukrainians could also read Russian (Bauer et al. 1991: 421).

borrowed from Germany. Unlike Georgian or Armenian socialist movements, which initially developed outside their respective working classes, Latvian socialist radicalism from the start was led by, as much as it led, Riga labor unrest. Latvian workers led the 1905 events as socialists, and in the 1907 Duma elections the Latvian Social Democrats outpolled other parties in every Riga district except the conservative German city center (Henriksson 1986).

Fourth, after 1905, Riga's working-class radicalism was distinctive because it mobilized on a multiethnic basis. In 1897, 43.16 percent of Riga's Latvians were engaged in the manufacturing and industrial sector, compared to 32.18 percent of its Russians and 50 percent of Riga's Jews (Bauer et al. 1991: 446). Whereas in 1867 only 8 percent of Riga's inhabitants were from outside the Baltic provinces, by 1913 the figure rose to nearly 30 percent; Germans declined as a proportion of Riga's population as Latvians increased, but Russians, Poles, Jews, and Lithuanians also increased substantially (Henriksson 1986: 181). Most of these migrants found work in factories. This alone accounted for much of the activism of Russian, Bundist, SDKPiL, and Lithuanian SD parties in Riga. In the end it also accounted for much of the internationalism of Riga's multiethnic socialist mobilizations. After 1905, the city housed a great variety of radical, non-nationalist groupings: the Latvian SD Workers' Party, the Riga Bolshevik Committee of the RSDLP, the Riga Menshevik Committee of the RSDLP, the Latvian SRs, the Latvian Peasant Union branch, the Russian SRs, the Jewish Bund, the Polish-Lithuanian SDKPiL, and the Lithuanian SDs. In fact, during 1905 labor unrest, a federated Latvian-Russian-Jewish socialist committee functioned as an ad hoc city government and even formed a militia. Unsurprisingly, anti-Jewish pogroms, historically absent in the Baltics anyway but nevertheless a key feature of the 1905 Revolutions elsewhere in the empire, were nonexistent in Riga's politicization.

So Rudzutaks and Lepse were less part of an ethnically Latvian working class than they were part of an increasingly ethnically differentiated one. As we saw with Piatnitsky, Kapsukas, and Dzierżyński, Vilna's multiethnic, urban industrial workers in smaller shops and factories mainly segregated on an ethnic basis. This meant that activists' mobilizational strategies had to work to forge multiethnic organizations, both across ethnic groups and across factories. But because Riga's much larger industrial factories were much less ethnically segregated, class conflict was clearer and mobilization on a multiethnic basis was easier.

Rudzutaks's route through political radicalism in Riga went from involvement in Riga's network of legal workers' associations upon arrival (e.g., mutual aid societies and insurance fund groups) to political activism in factory worker circles and cells organized by the SDs. To some extent these two forms of association or organization were not incompatible, and I have suggested that part of the success of Latvian socialism owed something to its vibrant civil society and organizational life. Socialist organizations were grafted onto an already rich associational life; Riga not only had the greatest number and variety of radical groups in the empire, but it also had among the best organized (Raun 2006). Latvian workers and masters in the small factories and workshops had established mutual aid societies and secret strike funds; they administered schools, held evening lectures and discussions, and maintained libraries. Rudzutaks specifically recounts his activism in these various workers' groups, library societies, workers' associations, mutual aid societies, cultural-educational groups, and artisanal associations (Granat 1989: 632). But by 1905, when he began work in a steel factory, the labor struggle had itself radicalized and moved leftward. By his account, factory work made Rudzutaks "a true proletarian" and his political activism moved toward Riga's socialist underground mobilizational politics and to its industrial worker's circles (Granat 1989: 632). The overlap in these two spheres of association was likely considerable, as was their joint ability to organize and mobilize for specific economic or political demands (Henriksson 1986: 202). In short, Riga's social democratic radicalism was organizationally strong in part because it drew activism and commitment from a considerable and long-standing Baltic associational life.

By 1904, Rudzutaks was involved in illegal SD circles, and he began reading the progressive *Dienas Lapa*, taking part in demonstrations in 1905 in Riga, and circulating illegal literature (Granat 1989: 632). Working as a founder in a Riga factory in 1903, Lepse, too, had joined worker's radical circles, and official sources date his party membership to 1904 (Kopanev 1967: 37; Prokhorov 1969–78: 346). By this time Latvian socialism's base was workers, soldiers, students, teachers, and the rural landless. The Revolution of 1905 in Riga was characterized by considerable labor radicalism, and in this it led the rest of the empire: more than 80,000 people took part in a general eight-day strike in January, with the addition of numerous riots, demonstrations, and strikes throughout the year. Workers from the Russo-Baltic Wagon, the Aetna Wire Corporation, Provodnik, and other major factories led strikes in which Russian, Jewish, and Latvian socialists cooperated, and even demanded, in unison, an end to linguistic Russification. This was arguably the first instance of widespread working-class political radicalism: moving beyond the generally economic demands of 1899, they called for constitutional reforms, free speech, and other political reforms. The Riga labor movement only mildly abated after the Tsarist suppressions in 1905.

Lepse was a member of the RSDLP's Riga committee, and after the 1905 unrest, he led the Party's factory organization. In 1906, Rudzutaks joined the Riga committee of the RSDLP(b); he was arrested and spent more than a year in Riga and Moscow prisons (Granat 1989: 635). Official biographies date Rudzutaks's CP membership to 1905, or to roughly the time of its peak strike activity (Prokhorov 1969–78: 348–9). The *Granat* account suggests that the attraction of the SDs was that they addressed the nationality question and federalism through a strong cadre of Latvian organizers with materials in circulation in Latvian (Granat 1989: 633). In fact, the Bolshevik Latvian organization had split off into the first Latvian cadres at the beginning of 1905, the same year the first illegal Bolshevik press appeared in Latvian. Rudzutaks was dispatched into factories and workers' meetings in Riga and Mitau to distribute these Latvian-language brochures and leaflets among Latvian workers (Granat 1989: 633). In the end, the extent to which Rudzutaks's political radicalism identified with both Latvian and Russian as complementary identities is striking. His post-1917 roles in the Bolshevik government were Russian, not Latvian: he held positions in the All-Russian Central Council of the Union of Textile Workers, was a member of the Moscow City Soviet of Trade Unions, in 1920–21 was Chairman of the Turkestan Bureau of the RCP(b), and from 1922–24 was Chairman of the Middle Asian Bureau of the RCP(b) (Prokhorov 1969–78: 348–9). These assignments may have been a measure of Lenin's trust in Latvian loyalty, but at no time in his political career was Rudzutaks assigned to a Latvian post.

Thus urban working-class radicalism in Riga was distinctive in that it was multiethnic, socialist internationalist, and Russophilic or *rossiiskii* in character. Because of comparatively little ethnic tension, class conflict was more easily perceived and framed, and socialist mobilizations were less ethnically factionalized. Moreover, working- and lower-class political radicalism was built on an existing rich and dense rural and urban asssociational life, and by the last years of the empire it was largely Russian-oriented, not nationalist. Repressive policies politicized these socioethnic locations, to be sure, but they did so in a generally empire-friendly context.

Smilga: Rural Déclassé Gentry Radicalism

Usually considered an Old Bolshevik, and known as "the blonde intellectual," Smilga was the youngest in the Bolshevik elite, just twenty-five years old at the time of the Revolution, and a close confidant of Lenin's. His activism as a Latvian Bolshevik was decisive during revolutionary events in the Baltics. Between 1917 and 1920, he was elected to the Bolshevik CC, and Smilga's activities in Finland, in Petrograd, and with the Baltic Fleet made him a key organizer in military revolutionary work (Granat 1989: 676). The Bolsheviks propagandized most successfully among soldiers, particularly in the Baltic Fleet, in garrisons, among German soldiers on the eastern front, and among Russian and Latvian soldiers. Smilga was a key figure in the politicization of these military units.

He was born in 1892 in Lifland *guberniia* to a Latvian aristocratic, landed gentry family. His family was formally part of the wealthy and propertied rural elite – the so-called grey barons – though in practice they were upper intelligentsia. According to Smilga, his parents were radicals and intellectuals. His father admired Greek mythology and its ancient democracy, and Smilga considered him a "democratic educator" (Granat 1989: 675). He wrote that his revolutionary conscience developed in 1901 when the famous student Karpovich killed the Minister of Education. Smilga still considered himself devout despite his liberally inclined family, but by his account it was under the influence of radical social democratic students that he began to understand the implications of the assassination (Granat 1989: 676). He claimed that at age twelve he supported revolution, though he was not yet politically active. Although Latvian radicalism increased around him, post-1905 events in rural Livland affected the teenage Smilga. Much of the revolutionary violence was directed not at the Tsarist state, but at German privilege and landownership. In the rural areas, Latvian SDs successfully organized strikes of farmhands. About 300,000 people participated in the 1905 events in Livland and Courland. In Livland alone, some 183 German estates and 72 manors were torched, along with 229 estates and 442 manors in Courland, with rural destruction estimated at 8.8 million rubles in the two provinces combined (Zalevskii 1912: 90–100; Henriksson 1983: 110). In Kurland and rural Livland, or roughly the same regions that had experienced rapid economic development and the early mobilization of the SD movement, the violence was largely aimed at Baltic Germans, manor houses, and estates (Raun 2006: 48–50).

Smilga came to political activism, by his account, during the 1906–08 so-called punitive expeditions of the Tsarist armies following this social revolution in rural Livland. The Russian state's violent repression lasted nearly two years, and in the rural areas the infamous punitive expeditions of Russian army units were legendary, as were those of privately organized baronial German self-protection squads. Here Tsarist strategies of social control, police surveillance, and militarized punishments forcefully entwined with, and politicized, ethnic identities. Most viewed the reprisals as motivated not by a desire to restore order, but by revenge, as they moved across the countryside burning farms and hunting peasant activists and revolutionaries. Tsarist trials and summary executions ensued: by 1908, between 2,041 and 2,596 Latvian peasants and revolutionaries were executed, 724 tried by military tribunals and executed, 128 tried by civil courts and executed, 713 sentenced to hard labor, jail, or deportation, 2,652 were resettled and/or subjected to corporal punishment (among them 688 were members of Leftist groups, 80 percent of whom were SDs), and 1,817 were expelled from the Baltics; among these peasants and revolutionaries were also 600 Latvian rural schoolteachers and 5,000 political refugees who had fled either abroad or to the forests (Plakans 1995: 105).

Among those executed by the Tsarist army in these punitive expeditions was Smilga's father (Granat 1989: 676). His father was executed because he was a Leftist who he had been active both in local rural administration and in revolutionary politics. In Smilga's account, the brutality of this event formed in him a particular worldview, a set of political impressions that shaped his political radicalization in ways that made the influence of social democratic student circles more meaningful (Granat 1989: 676). Most striking in Smilga's later political radicalism was his combination of ruthless militarism and Leninist pragmatism, particularly as he organized desperate and disaffected soldiers. Never employed in any profession, Smilga became a quintessential professional revolutionary from a young age, with a proclivity for military solutions to political impasses. So his father's execution by the Tsarist state in these rural punitive expeditions no doubt goes some way to understanding these qualities in his political radicalism.

But Smilga's radicalization in this context was anyway quite common. The effects of the Tsarist-German punitive expeditions and the 1906–08 suppressions were firmly planted in the Latvian imagination more widely, and the trials and executions had a pronounced radicalizing effect on the Latvian intelligentsia more generally. Most importantly, it politicized them against the Tsarist state in ways that Russificatory policies had not, making revolutionary socialism comparatively more attractive (Raun 2006: 23). Smilga was fourteen years old at the time of his father's execution, and the following year he enrolled in a Riga *Realschule*, by which time he was amply receptive to the influence of revolutionary socialist politics (Granat 1989: 676). He joined the Latvian SDs in 1900, at a time when the party suffered most from Tsarist repression (Kalnins 1972: 144). He wrote that it was during his *Realschule* years that his "Marxist vision was completed" (Granat 1989: 676). In revolutionary socialism Smilga found an explanation for his experiences. It appealed not because of its scientific or materialist history or because of its accounts of class exploitation and capitalism – Smilga was himself of the "exploitive class" in rural Livland and showed little awareness of class conflict. Neither was he concerned with German influence. Rather, the elective affinity was in socialism's revolutionary and radical *political* potential for destroying the Tsarist order, something Smilga interpreted in very personal terms. The Russian state's imperial strategies of brutal suppression and social control had politicized, and antistate socialist radicalism held out a vision, for Russified Latvians like Smilga, of a better form of Tsarism – that is, a more universalist and tolerant, *rossiiskii* inclusiveness, a resonant political expression for those experiencing the heavy political costs of empire.

In 1907, Smilga was detained during the May Day demonstrations and arrested again in Moscow in student demonstrations, ending his *Realschule* studies and any subsequent education (Granat 1989: 676). In 1911, he was arrested for political party work, imprisoned, and exiled to Vologda. He was released in 1914 and began revolutionary work in St. Petersburg as a Bolshevik. Arrested again and exiled for three years to Enisei in Siberia, he was released with the February Revolution (Granat 1989: 676). Smilga therefore spent most of the war years in Siberia, far from German-occupied Latvia.

On his release, Smilga found that Bolshevik strength lay not only in Finland among Baltic sailors, in the Latvian countryside, and in Riga, but also among the eight Latvian *Strelnieki*, or the separate units of Latvian infantry within the Russian Army, in Petrograd, Helsinki, and Riga.[15] Though the evacuation

---

[15] The famous Latvian Battalions were formed in 1916 with 130,000 mostly volunteer soldiers who joined those Latvians conscripted into the Russian Army as a potential national army. There were only two other national forces in the Imperial Army: the Polish Legion and the Armenian Druzhinas. Highly politicized, these units suffered huge causalities. Some 5,000 Latvian Riflemen lost their lives, no doubt contributing to the formation of the radical Riflemen's Soviet of Deputies as "an organization of riflemen and officers from common Latvian goals" (Ezergailis 1974: 103, 174, and passim). Danishevskii was a key organizer of the Second Congress of the Riflemen's Soviet of Deputies as a representative of the Latvian SDs.

of Riga in 1915 weakened its SD organizations, the War had introduced the famous Latvian Rifles into the Latvian SD mobilization. Petrograd, Helsinki, and Riga formed the famed "rotten triangle," and here Smilga's revolutionary role in Petrograd was substantial. He was president of the Finnish Soviets and a Bolshevik party organizer in the important Baltic Fleet when it passed to Bolshevik control. With Lenin in Viipuri, Smilga was one of the key Bolsheviks in Finland, shoring up both Bolshevik military positions and the garrisons stationed in Finland (Upton 1980: 128).

But arguably Smilga's activities as a Bolshevik in the Baltic Revolutions invoked less an ethnic Latvian than a *rossiiskii* identity. We see this most clearly in connection with the Baltic Fleet. The Baltic Fleet was an integral part of Russian naval expansion before World War I, and during the war Helsingfors became its main base. But Baltic naval bases (in Revel, Kronstadt, Sveaborg, Libau, and Riga) were in close proximity to, and highly dependent on, the industrial bases. The radical underground organized by the Bolshevik Aleksandr Shliapnikov also used the routes through Finland and Norway, so the Baltic Fleet was "practically on top of the northern underground" (Saul 1978: 41; Allen 2005 on Shliapnikov's role). So Smilga organized radical cells among the Baltic Fleet sailors, who were no less affected by the growing disillusionment with the war and by industrial strikes in the port cities.

The Baltic Fleet had many loyal German and Finno-Swedish officers who often appeared German to Latvian, Estonian, and Russian sailors (Saul 1978: 13, 50). Nationalist sentiment increased as the war progressed, and the multiethnic composition of the Baltic Fleet became a source of disunity. Though instrumental in the Bolshevization of these military bases and their crews, it is unclear whether Smilga was sensitive to the national issue – and it is not clear that he needed to be. Smilga was a key member of the first Bolshevik committees in Kronstadt and Helsingfors, organizing May Day demonstrations of 1,000 Kronstadt sailors in Petrograd. But the Kronstadt soviet and the Helsingfors soviet represented ethnic Russians; the Revel soviet was predominantly ethnically Estonian and worker in composition; and there were Latvian party cells in Helsinki among radicalized Latvian diaspora refugees and servicemen. Revel, the most politically moderate of the bases, elected the most Bolsheviks to its soviet, and they tended to be ethnically Russian, not Estonian. Both the heavy losses sustained by the Latvian Rifles, and the perception of Russian military incompetence also served to radicalize the Latvian population, and Smilga articulated this (Raun 2000: 126). In short, his organizational work was geopolitically oriented and strategic, and largely indifferent to the ethnic dimensions of the social crisis.

Lenin had arranged for Smilga to join him in Helsinki. As head of the committee of the Helsingfors soviet, and as one of the few Bolsheviks in regular contact with Lenin during the latter's exile in Finland, Smilga was instrumental in Lenin's coming to the idea that they should capitalize on the Baltic sailors' radicalization. His loyalty to Lenin was also unconditional at the time of the debates on Brest-Litovsk, in part because his own assessments of circumstances were similar to Lenin's (Haupt 1969: 213), and in part because of his willingness to "lose Latvia" in favor of a reconstituted empire. As the empire lost Finland at Brest-Litovsk, Smilga, again like Lenin, read into the new socialist government of independent Finland confirmation that their position on national self-determination was correct: "fraternal, socialist Finland" now provided a basis for an internationalist federation. Smilga also wrote an article for *Izvestiia* as head of the Area Committee calling on all soldiers to fight the Finnish Whites in common struggle with the Finnish SDs and Red Guards, insisting that the Finnish Revolution – now usefully distinct from the Russian Revolution – was evidence of the spreading revolution across Europe (Upton 1980: 294–5). In Smilga's estimation, this committed the new Bolshevik government to full armed intervention in the Finnish Civil War. But the Russian rank and file did not share Smilga's, or indeed more generally the Bolsheviks', enthusiasm for the Finnish Revolution. And given the weakness of the Russian commitment on the ground, Smilga was forced to consider bringing in a disciplined Latvian regiment not only to deal with "anarchist sabotage," but also to fight on behalf of the Russians who would not fight on behalf of the Finns (on Smilga's role, see Upton 1980: 418–20). Smilga was thinking strategically, *rossiiskii*-oriented.

He had never been involved or implicated in Baltic society as a professional, as had Stuchka or Berzins, nor as a worker like Rudzutaks and Lepse. Smilga's radicalism, begun with his father's execution, made him a classic professional revolutionary from student demonstrations, through years of exile, and finally to the military seizure of power. As a professional, full-time revolutionary – one of the few among the non-Russian Bolsheviks – his activism was defined by pragmatism, militarism, and an imperial-minded, *rossiiskii* identity and political commitment. Saving the Russian Revolution was a way to render meaningful the price he had paid with his father's execution and his own years of exile and imprisonment. With a *rossiiskii*-minded inclusiveness, and as an ethnic Latvian, he was a key organizer of Russians, Estonians, Latvians, and Finns in pursuit of the Finnish and Russian Revolutions.

As a Leftist he opposed Trotsky, particularly for the latter's decision to appoint officers to the Red Army from the Imperial Army that he had hated since 1906. Smilga and Kaganovich were eventually dispatched to Ukraine, and he drew closer to Stalin. But because of subsequent tensions with Stalin, Smilga was not reelected to the CC after the 9th Congress and he was quietly moved into economic areas. He was again reelected at the Eleventh Congress, but in 1927 Smilga sided with the Left Opposition (Trotsky, Zinoviev, and Kamenev) (Haupt 1969: 214). Considered a threat by Stalin, he was sent to eastern Siberia in administrative exile, and in 1929 he joined the "conciliators," Radek and Evgenii Preobrazhenskii. He was readmitted into the Party in 1930. But in a final political *bouleversement*, in 1932 Smilga was condemned to five years in prison, disappeared in a concentration camp, and died in 1937 or 1938 (Haupt 1969: 214–15). With Smilga's death, not a single Latvian Bolshevik of the revolutionary elite survived Stalin. But more clearly than most non-Russian

Bolsheviks, Smilga's route to a Russian-inflected revolutionary socialism was closely bound up with the surveillance and social control regimes of the Tsarist empire, which by stigmatizing certain socioethnic groups (e.g., gentry or propertied Latvian rural elites) had inscribed new social identities and problematic relationships to the imperial state. Russian-inflected Bolshevism not only promised a new and better *rossiiskii* universalism, but also one that would protect minority elites' identities and positions.

Conclusion

The Latvian Bolsheviks were propertied, educated, rural elites and Russian-literate urban workers with rural roots, radicalized in multiethnic socialist organizations. Class was experienced – and socialism was organized – around ethnicity in multiethnic, imperial, and Russophilic contexts. In competition with Latvian nationalism, Bolshevik socialism became clearer about its ethnopolitical affinities, deepening its cross-class appeal and infusing its socialist critique with ethnic content. But Bolshevism was a very broad ideological tent: for the Germanized Stuchka it countered both Latvian nationalism and Russian centralism, whereas for the Russified Berzins and Smilga it offered an antistatist critique from within a Russified experience, appealing because of its antinationalism and *rossiiskii* politics.

Lenin famously had a particular fondness for Latvians, surrounding himself with Latvian servants, chauffeurs, Cheka guards, and kitchen maids. Berzins was one of Lenin's closest prewar confidants, and they hid together in a summerhouse in Finland in 1906; Smilga was a close contact in the revolutionary months in Finland; and Stuchka was Lenin's hunting companion and a pallbearer in 1924 (Ezergailis 1983: 178). More generally, there was a close affinity between Latvian socialism and Russian socialism. Russian socialism struck roots in certain Latvian cultural frameworks, particularly for those with relatively weak ethnic Latvian identifications.

Ezergailis (1974: 33) wrote that the Latvian party maintained strict internationalism "for good psychological and traditional reasons," and that this internationalism brought them closer to the Bolsheviks. There was something to this. Radek and Dzierżyński had become Bolshevik internationalists because of exclusion from ethnicizing socialist mobilizations. But the Latvian socialists embraced it through a combination of cultural identification with the imperial Russian (facilitated by their Russification) and because a Russian-inflected class universalism easily embedded within Riga's multiethnic working classes. For culturally sensitive elites, peripherality itself prompted an assimilatory attraction to a "great nation" culture, which had the added merit of overriding the historically dominant German. A Russia-inflected movement, therefore, also appealed to certain culturally marginal but Russified borderland elites.

So for many radicalized Latvians like Stuchka and Smilga, a Russian-inflected Bolshevism offered a universalist political expression in which the "good imperial ideal" was at the core of its mobilizational politics. Bolshevism as a political project in class-universalism would be a better version of Tsarism: a geopolitically stable empire that was orderly, modern, law respecting, ethnically tolerant, and nonarbitrary in its manner of rule. The appeal of this kind of imaginary – one in which the mobilization manifested a better version of certain qualities of the state – resonated most especially with those who had personally experienced the political costs of an imperial order that was violently and arbitrarily imposed.

Moreover, the relatively ethnically tolerant and politically liberal Baltics had created the basis of a vibrant civic and political associational life among Latvians – and the social resources, urban and rural, from which its nationalist and socialist revolutionary mobilizations would draw. Latvian Bolshevism politically mobilized around a rich rural ethnic associational life. This provided the organizational resources – the community-building, social trust, and indeed the social locations – from which Latvian socialists drew recruits and resources. These rural ethnic communities, then, provided a solid base and a certain mobilizational momentum from which Latvian socialism could then project and recruit among the multiethnic, urban working classes.

Finally, the socioethnic niches represented by the Latvian Bolsheviks were varied: the 1860s rural, Germanized milieu of liberal Baltic society; the Russified Lifland rural middle class of the 1880s and 1890s; Riga's multiethnic working class; and the rural gentry or upper intelligentsia of the years of Tsarist reaction. These socioethnic niches or locations were most affected by Tsarist policies of educational and assimilatory Russification, the repression of working-class radicalism, and the surveillance and policing of rural landed elites after 1905. Against a wider context of historic Latvian-German tensions, in combination these imperial strategies gave socialist radicalism its distinctive antistate but Russophilic imperial-minded quality. Russian imperial policies had shaped a political radicalism that was Russophilic and imperial-minded, but it had done so against a backdrop of severe repression and illiberalism, thereby funneling activism into leftist, but multiethnic, Russian-inflected mobilizations.

7

The South Caucasian Bolsheviks

There were nine Bolsheviks from the South Caucasus: four Armenians, four Georgians, and one Azerbaijani. Bolshevism was decidedly a minority political movement in the Caucasus. It was the weakest and least influential of the radical groupings because most Armenian activists were nationalist Dashnaks, most Georgians were Mensheviks, most Azerbaijanis were nationalist-socialist Müsavat, and most ethnic Russians in the cities of the South Caucasus joined the SRs. So it is important to emphasize that these nine Bolsheviks were politically marginal in their own social worlds, and an understanding of their routes to radicalism has to account for this. Although regional ethnopolitics contributed to political radicalism, as ethnic groups more generally, Georgians, Armenians, and Azerbaijanis were radicalized for slightly different reasons and in different relationships to the imperial state. The Armenian Bolsheviks were politicized for reasons that were fundamentally geopolitical; the Georgians because of imperial exclusions from political influence in the region; and the Azerbaijani because of colonialist, cultural, and religious exclusions. Despite different substantive motivations, however, their Russian-inflected socialist politics reflected preferences for federalist arrangements and shared political commitments to empire. And yet *rossiiskii* orientation in the South Caucasus did not produce real internationalists as it did in Latvia or Ukraine – something that also requires explanation.

Therefore, the substantive claim of this chapter is that the South Caucasian Bolsheviks were attracted to a Russian-inflected socialism as a political expression of a universalist, *rossiiskii* state: in the empire's southern borderland, this ideal was underpinned by commitments to the territorial integrity of the empire that derived from the geopolitical insecurities of vulnerable minorities along the empire's non-Christian border, and from a traditional dependence on the imperial state for a variety of status privileges and political protections – a ubiquitous motivation equally shared by the region's non-Bolshevik, nationalist and socialist parties.

Beyond this, the Georgian Bolsheviks were mostly déclassé, rural petty nobility, the Armenians were (lower) middle class, and the Azerbaijani was a member of the new Muslim intelligentsia. Each socioethnic group brought a distinctive set of social resources to Bolshevism. Like Bolshevism's organization in Latvia or Ukraine, South Caucasian Bolshevism politically mobilized these social resources and organizationally exploited its socioethnic diversity in order to widen its mobilizational base and undercut recruitment from competing nationalist movements. So because of particular class-ethnic alignments, they produced an effective, if numerically small, *rossiiskii* mobilization in the South Caucasus at a moment of potential geopolitical disintegration. But in contrast to the vertically ranked ethnicities in the western and Baltic provinces, South Caucasian ethnopolitics were horizontally segmented. This meant that while there was certainly competition among ethnicities, their class-ethnic stratifications were murkier, and class conflicts less well defined, than those in the vertically ranked, multiethnic regions of the empire. Ultimately this horizontal ethnic segmentation had important effects on the region's political radicalism because it had less need to ethnicize capitalist relations.

This chapter's substantive claim is therefore analytically framed against key imperial patterns of inclusion/exclusion. The Bolsheviks' biographies and routes to radicalism highlight most distinctly those imperial strategies and patterns of politicization that involved: (1) dissimilatory Russification or status-particularistic policies of ethnic or religious exclusion/inclusion that split emerging middle classes (notably through Russification in education) and similarly particularistic urban-rural policies that reversed groups' traditional political and commercial relationships with the imperial state; and (2) the incorporation of minority elites into the empire's bureaucracies or noble and commercial estates. Although applied inconsistently, these strategies intentionally and unintentionally impacted local ethnopolitics and fashioned different relationships between the various socioethnic groups and the Russian state. As a result, the South Caucasus produced an intricate variety of nationalist and socialist political groupings, and among them the comparatively weak Bolsheviks.

Imperial Strategies and Radicalism in the South Caucasus[1]

The South Caucasus was an exceedingly intricate mosaic of linguistic, religious, and ethnic populations.[2] This diversity persisted both because settled agriculturalists and nomads lived in interdependent socioethnic niches and because of the region's geostrategic positioning between contesting empires. In patterns similar to those of the Polish Partitions, boundary changes, wars, and administrative policies occasioned substantial population transfers and migrations: the famous 1828 Treaty of Turkmanchai permanently divided Azerbaijanis

---

[1] Except where otherwise noted, the following sections are drawn from Kazemzadeh 1951; Altstadt 1992; Suny 1993a, 1994; Mouradian 1995; Reisner 1995; Swietochowski 1995; Khodarkovsky 2002; Breyfogle 2003, 2005; Jones 2005; Mamedov 2008.

[2] Among other smaller groups there were Chechens, Ingush, Cherkassians, Ossetians, Avars, Mingrelians, Imeretians, Abkhazians, and Dagestanis.

and Armenians between the two empires, while Armenians migrated into the South Caucasus after the Russo-Turkish and Crimean Wars, the 1876–78 war, and the Kurdish massacre of Anatolian Armenians in the mid-1890s. With successive annexations, Tsarist reprisals, and military campaigns, Caucasian mountaineers and Azerbaijanis crossed the Araxes River for Persia and the Ottoman lands. Taken together, these migrations meant that the relative position of Armenians in the plateau of eastern Anatolia worsened as they became a small minority among Kurds and Turks. But their numbers were substantially increased in the South Caucasus – a permanent reality sanctioned in 1834 with the establishment of an Armenian district carved out of previous khanates. A similarly lasting effect was the attenuation of both khanate particularism and sectarian tensions between Sunni and Shi'a Azerbaijanis.

As with most imperial expansionism, eventually Tsarist elites no longer considered the Caucasus a forward border region, but a core and constituent part of the empire. The imperial state's political hold on the region was often fragile, though by the mid-nineteenth century they asserted control to a degree previously unseen. Because the region was difficult to govern bureaucratically, it was typically ruled either militarily or by neglect, and both were blended from a variety of motives: civilizing, Realpolitik, imperial expansionist, Great Power rivalry, and economic-colonialist. Very rarely was rule here based on a concern for fellow Christians under the threat of Ottoman rule.

Driven largely by the need to "pacify" the Muslim population, ethnic unrest was often conflated with geopolitical worries that instability might involve coethnics on the other side of the empire's border. In fact, the militarization of Russian rule distinguished the region for a time from other imperial borderlands. Tsarist use of military governors was common across the empire (Mosse 1968; Robbins 1987), but in the Caucasus there were as many military administrators as there were civil servants. Russians, Ukrainians, Germans, and Poles commonly received military training and administrative assignments in the Caucasus.[3] The arbitrariness of bureaucratized military rule, together with corruption and incompetence, caused great local opposition (Suny 1994a: 69; 1995: 65), as did the fact that ethnic Russians disproportionately comprised region's bureaucrats.[4] And although some administrators – especially Baltic Germans – never really developed local bonds, others "went native" (compare Hargrave 2004: 3 on Witte's family in Tiflis, with Mamedov 2008). But unlike the Russian state's securitization of Poles and Jews in the western borderlands, in the South Caucasus the state's response was a sustained effort to colonize rural and urban areas with Russian settlers and state peasants, often with the

---

[3] This classic imperialist policy of sending non-Russians to control the Caucasus was not lost on Lenin, who in 1922 sent the Pole Dzierżyński, the Lithuanian Kapsukas, and the Ukrainian Manuilsky to restore order in Georgia.

[4] Of the 84,406 imperial military posts in 1897, Russians held 36,222, Ukrainians 15,897, Poles 9,039, and Georgians 5,796. Of the 39,094 posts in local administration, Russian held 11,620, Azerbaijanis 7,933, Armenians 7,367, and Georgians 7,701. Figures based on mother tongue/ occupation (Bauer et al. 1991: 263–4).

support of the Georgian nobility (Breyfogle 2003: 147–8). While the state
had previously settled sectarians and other "unreliable peoples" for punitive
reasons (Mostashari 2003: 169–72; for similar dynamics in other areas, see
Geraci 2001b; Werth 2002), from 1881, Tsarist elites formally assisted landless
Russian Orthodox peasants in settling in the South Caucasus, a policy shift
premised on the belief that the presence of ethnic Russians intermarrying and
merging with the local population in the borderlands would both strengthen
the state's presence and create a new type of South Caucasian Russian. As a
form of Russification, however, this met with local resistance and the inevitable
politicization of Azerbaijani peasants as whole villages were often violently
exiled or resettled in order to accommodate Russian settlers (Mostashari 2003:
176–9).

Ethnic Exclusions/Inclusions and Assimilatory/Dissimilatory Russification

In their substance, then, the Russian Empire's strategies involved the co-optation
of Georgian and Azerbaijani nobles and Armenian capital via privileges and
status protections designed to create loyal elites. This combined with efforts to
increase the ethnic Russian presence in the border area and to Russify religious
and educational institutions. But as noted in Chapter 2, attempts at imperial
integration were often joined to policies of exclusion and inclusion targeted
at specific socioethnic groups, not at nationalities as such. This included contradictory policies toward religious and cultural elites, which impacted the
Azerbaijani secular and Muslim intelligentsias. Divide-and-rule policies similarly split commercial and educated elites and impacted the Armenian middle classes, and policies of inclusion and exclusion with clear urban-rural
dimensions impacted Georgian nobles and peasants. Taken together, these
status-particularist strategies exacerbated the region's already tense, horizontally segmented ethnopolitics and shaped the social and political dynamics that
variously funneled revolutionaries into nationalist and socialist mobilizations.

More specifically, South Caucasians historically experienced distinctive patterns of elite co-optation. Georgians' positions were ambiguous from their
early integration, although economic and (geo)political interests tied them to
those of the Russian Empire itself. But Georgian society was feudal-aristocratic
and hierarchical, with nobilities exercising complete power over the enserfed
peasantry. Towns were not self-governing, but rather the property of kings and
lords; they were comprised of serf craftsmen, serf merchants, and serf money-
lenders – all bound to king, noble, church, or monastery. Georgian society was
culturally recognizable to Russian administrators and settlers: the similarity of
Georgia's feudal structure, its noble culture, and its Christian religion to those
of Russian society facilitated its political integration. Following a series of
anti-Russian Georgian rebellions between 1802 and 1832, which called for the
restoration of former noble privileges without Russian tutelage, Tsarist elites
sought to fully integrate the South Caucasus into the empire. So in 1804, a Tiflis
noble school was opened (which the future Bolshevik Prokofii Dzhaparidze

would attend), and Georgians were encouraged into state service as their sons could then enroll in the Russian cadet corps. In 1808, the clergy was freed from serfdom and taxes; in 1827, Georgian nobles were given the same privileges and access as the Russian nobility, and noble and estate assemblies in Tiflis and Kutais were charged with overseeing the many petitions over claims to noble status – processes that took more than thirty years and sometimes challenged previous status security. But rural Georgia remained quite closed ethnically, and its nobility was the most privileged of the region's socioethnic strata.

Then in a series of regressive policies, Russian was introduced as the official language of state, local legal customs and laws were removed, and large numbers of Russian officials were assigned to the region's expanding bureaucracy. After 1841, however, Georgian nobles (and Azerbaijani aristocrats) were reincorporated, economic policies were liberalized, and an otherwise pragmatic and flexible rule took hold. Social relationships were changed when serf ownership was removed from the clergy, merchants, or other serfs, and nobles could no longer enserf free men (a historically common practice in Georgia). By mid-century there were few large, landed magnates; small landowners with fewer than twenty serfs comprised half the Georgian nobility in eastern Georgia. In light of the 1863 Polish rebellions, the Russian state was determined neither to create large numbers of landless peasants nor to render the Georgian nobility powerless. So the emancipation settlements required that the lands be divided between noble and peasant; the state controlled peasant migrations to maintain the landed elite's labor force and to firmly bind Georgian nobles to the state (Suny 1994: 83, 103–4). Although the middle-gentry in Tiflis province was sizable, and although it had benefitted from state service, most were driven into debt from a tendency to consume lavishly despite an income derived from peasant dues and state service. So as late as 1912, most Georgian peasants remained landlord serfs with temporary obligations (Reisner 1995), and Georgian dependency on the Russian state now also derived from economic insecurity (Suny 1994: 110–11).

Although Georgian nobles retained substantial status and privileges throughout, and although they became perhaps more dependent on the Russian state than other non-Russian nobilities, these policies affected social mobility and split the Georgian middle and noble strata: small and middling landholders (often outside state service) had felt the threats of emancipation the most and were the most vulnerable to impoverishment (Suny 1994: 98). So while greater nobles were highly supportive of Russian rule, middle and petty gentry were more ambivalent. These status-threatened sons of nobles would take part in socialist and nationalist mobilizations in large numbers – and indeed, three Bolsheviks had their origins in these social locations. This fact, combined with the absence of a substantial Georgian commercial middle class, meant that the role of the working class in Georgian socialism would be quite distinctive (on this latter point, see Jones 2005: 64–5).[5]

---

[5] Most urban craftsmen and merchants were Armenian: in Tiflis they comprised three-fourths of the urban population at the time of Georgia's annexation (Suny 1994: 88).

By contrast, imperial strategies toward Armenians were initially almost wholly preferential. Armenians had a large peasantry, an urbanized and differentiated commercial and educated class,[6] an influential clergy, and the notable absence of an aristocracy or nobility. The Armenian commercial middle classes were economically powerful, and as Christians in a largely Muslim world, Armenian merchants oriented toward Orthodox Russia. In the nineteenth century, Armenian capital supplied Russian arms during the Caucasian wars. It dominated the cotton, leather, and tobacco industries in Tiflis and the banking and oil industries in Baku. Historically resented by Georgian nobles, Armenians were supported by Georgian monarchs for their commercial activities, and on the belief that trade was civilizing, Armenian merchants flourished under the Russian state's protection (see Table 2.1, Chapter 2). Because Russophile Armenian elites were considered loyal and reliable, Muslim areas were often given over to them, causing resentment among Azerbaijanis. Moreover, from the post–Crimean War period, liberal Russophile sections of the Armenian intelligentsia firmly tied their geopolitical security to that of the Russian state. As one observer noted at the time, Caucasia was "Russified without Russification, and at the forefront of this natural Russianizing were ... the Armenians" (quoted in Suny 1993b: 41). Indeed, the period under Alexander II (1855–81) was notable for Armenian acculturation and Russification: the middle classes adopted Russian names or Russified their names, learned Russian, and viewed imperial culture as the gateway to European culture (Suny 1993b: 23).

Yet by the latter nineteenth century, Russian attitudes toward South Caucasia changed. It was increasingly seen less as a military outpost and more as a lucrative colony, or source of raw materials for Russian industry. So coupled with preferential policies toward Russian merchants and factory owners, Tsarist elites started to discourage Armenian industry because it would create more competition at the expense of Russian industry. A growing distrust of Armenian commerce started to drive policy by the last decades of the empire, but by then the congruence of interests between Armenians and the imperial state was also geopolitical.

The regions' "Tatars" were treated altogether differently. The Azerbaijani countryside remained traditionally agricultural, with comparatively little social stratification. Muslim bays and aghas owned small plots of land, barely distinguishable from peasant holdings. There was little class conflict, although the Azerbaijani rural aristocracy's political and religious influence was significant in village assemblies and courts. Azerbaijanis were of Irano-Turkish origin and spoke a mixture of the two languages, but their Shi'a sectarianism derived from a Persian cultural heritage with which many elites strongly identified. And yet the 1897 Census categorized them as Tatars, and therefore rendered them barely ascriptively different from other Muslim subjects of the empire. This complicated Azerbaijani positioning along cultural and linguistic fault lines consequentially shaped intelligentsia radicalism by the 1890s.

---

[6] This comprised small-scale artisans, petty merchants, journalists, teachers, a small yet wealthy commercial elite, and many in the liberal professions.

As noted in Chapter 2, Tsarist policies toward the empire's religious subjects were often class-contradictory, permissive of traditional religious elites but repressive of reformist elites. In the South Caucasus there were minimal attempts at religious conversion of Muslims, for instance, and the Il'minskii system of spreading Orthodoxy and Russification was never attempted. The Russian and Russo-Tataric schools in the region were designed to recruit bilingual civil servants – or sons of Azerbaijani aristocrats and commercial elites – into the empire's expanding bureaucracies. Despite relative impoverishment, in 1845, Azerbaijani elites' legal status rose in the empire to that of *dvorianstvo*. So again, in policies that had the effect of splitting the middle and noble strata, Muslim landed aristocrats were given full Russian noble rights, their sons were given access to imperial civil service careers, and a Muslim class of bilingual imperial bureaucrats was educated in the Russian-European curriculum of the Russo-Tatar schools. The Russian Empire had, in effect, created a new elite: a secular, progressive, semi-Russified Azerbaijani intelligentsia. But by subsequently excluding them from political society in a variety of administrative restrictions,[7] and through a series of cultural and religious repressions, the state's policies would also make them antistate.

Similarly, imperial strategies toward the Azerbaijani Islamic establishment both incorporated and weakened clerics. The Russian state created Sunni and Shi'a Ecclesiastical Boards and gave them judicial, administrative, and educational responsibilities in order to control and co-opt the ulema, which imperial elites considered most likely to lead opposition to Russian rule. They were given tax exemptions, rank and status privileges, and high wages (Altstadt 1992: 58–60). On the belief that the Muslim population would more likely follow clerical elites under Islam's lines of authority than they would Russian secular authority, the calculation was that the state would thereby also be in indirect control.[8] So the state's patronage of the Islamic establishment did not repress or ignore its Muslim subjects, as much as it assumed responsibility for policing them. As a result, the clerical establishment developed a dependence on the Russian state that they used when confronted with secular or

---

[7] For instance, *gubernii* reorganizations in 1867 included substantial non-Muslim minorities in Azerbaijani *gubernii*. So Muslim lower-level civil servants in the imperial bureaucracy were replaced with Russians and Armenians between 1881 and 1894 (Swietochowski 1995: 16). Similarly, Baku's 1874 municipal and city council reforms granted the vote based on wealth or religious qualification. Although Azerbaijanis were the majority property-holders and should have constituted more than 80% of the electorate, restrictions on non-Christians meant that they would only sit one-half of the council seats (Altstadt 1992: 25). The Reforms of 1892 were even more restrictive: they limited non-Christians to one-third of the seats, so Azerbaijanis only gained control of the city Duma after 1908.

[8] This is the only case I have found where the Russian state sought vertical associations between elites and peasantries, in contrast to its consistent policies of preventing any form of cross-class, intraethnic association. But Tsarist officials' role in adjudicating intracommunal disputes was nevertheless a way of extending state control over local life, and an official entrenchment of Islamic hierarchies (Crews 2003).

reformist ideologies (Crews 2003). Of course this caused widespread distrust and undermined much of the clerics' legitimacy in the eyes of the faithful (Altstadt 1992: 60–1). But significantly, it also made the possibility of social mobilization on a purely religious basis more remote because its potential leadership was undermined. And in fact, in a purely religious role, as we will see with the Bolshevik Nariman Narimanov, Islam played a minor role in Azerbaijani radicalization. By eliding Islam's political and religious lines of authority, then, Tsarist elites had misjudged the political effects of the co-optation of a religious elite in a context perceived as colonial, but they had equally underestimated a more generalized indifference to secular authority of any kind. So purely religious lines of authority continued despite the political impotence of the clergy, and with important effects on the political mobilization of the secular intelligentsia.

In addition to general imperial patterns of elite co-optation, Russian policies politically privileged very specific socioethnic strata, thereby contributing additional political insecurities and social envy to already existing economic tensions and anxieties. Armenian capitalists were in tense conflict with Azerbaijani peasant-workers, for instance, but these conflicts also arose out of historical differences manipulated over decades by Russian policies of social control (Altstadt 1992: 43 makes this argument); Tsarist policies politicized Georgian-Armenian socioeconomic resentments, which then crystallized into specific class resentments (Suny 1992: 231 makes this argument); the resentments of both impoverished Georgian nobles and peasants toward Armenian capitalists were refracted through the state's geopolitics (Kazemzadeh 1951: 12 and passim); and Armenian and Georgian religious authorities were granted censorship privileges over their own communities – privileges denied the Muslim ecclesiastical boards – and although this derived from the state's fear of pan-Turkic or pan-Islamic associations, and not from a desire to divide them from Armenians or Georgians, the experienced effects were the same. In short, political distinctiveness – favorable or otherwise – gave local ethnopolitics the distinct quality of social envy, often with effects similar to those resulting from Jewish restrictions in the western borderlands.

Patterns of Elite Incorporation into Imperial Bureaucracies and Estates
Beside specific ethnic exclusions/inclusions and Russification, imperial patterns of elite incorporation into civil and military bureaucracies, as outlined in Chapter 2, are also important for situating Bolshevism in the region's political mobilizations. While other minority elites across the empire sought positions in imperial-level service outside their provinces, Georgians, Azerbaijanis, and to a lesser extent Armenians, had higher rates of participation in local or provincial administrative posts than they did in imperial level posts (see figures in Bauer et al. 1991: 251–2, 263, 277–8, 329–30, 341). That is, if Poles and Jews were blocked locally, imperial venues remained open to them. The reverse was true for Georgians and Azerbaijanis, whose presence in provincial and local

administrative posts surpassed even their possibilities for imperial careers.[9] So Georgians served in large numbers in the empire's civil and military bureaucracies, but unlike the Poles, they did so in their native provinces.

The same was true of Azerbaijanis. As noted, Muslim elites were given access to imperial careers, awarded "personal noble" status (via Russian military or Russo-Tatar schools), and their sons entered the *dvorianstvo*. These educated elites also entered the local bureaucracy in large numbers. The Russian Empire's civil service posts were historically closed off to Muslims at the lowest bureaucratic levels, because they were given to Armenians and Georgians (Swietochowski 1995: 16), but with the municipal reforms in 1870, and especially after 1900, Azerbaijanis could legally engage in local politics, especially in the Baku City Council (Altstadt 1992: 62–3). So although ethnic Russians dominated provincial imperial administration, in proportional numbers Azerbaijanis held more posts than Armenians and Georgians (see Bauer et al. 1991: 315). Indeed, taking literacy levels into account (that is, availability for positions), Azerbaijani access to provincial imperial service was on par with that of other ethnic groups, and it was greater for local administration.

Of course Tsarist policies of placing minority elites in provincial civil bureaucracies had the effect of strengthening local identities, something also suggested by patterns of acculturation, Russification, and indeed radicalization. Consistent with educational access in the South Caucasus, 84.68 percent of Armenians, 80.23 percent of Georgians, and 96.72 percent of Azerbaijanis were illiterate; Georgians and Armenians also had similar levels of Russian language literacy, respectively 5.77 percent and 5.51 percent, while that for Azerbaijanis' was 0.55 percent (Bauer et al. 1991: 231–2, 241, for persons ten years and older). Urbanites who were literate in languages other than Russian reveal similar patterns: 22.34 percent of Armenian and 22.38 percent of Georgian urbanites could read Russian, and 6.63 percent of (empire-wide) "Tatars" could do so – below those of the empire's other minority urbanites (e.g., Jews, Latvians, Poles, Ukrainians, who all ranged between 25 percent and 50 percent [Bauer et al. 1991: 111–12]). These comparatively lower levels of linguistic Russification contributed to stronger local identities and a weaker internationalism in the political groupings. It also underscores how elite most of these Bolsheviks were.

Estate membership and ethnic stratification similarly reflected these patterns of Russification and elite co-optation. Employment in the free professions and administration in Tiflis and Baku reveal patterns similar to those of language acquisition. In 1897, ethnic Russians dominated Tiflis: one-half of those employed in the free professions and nearly 60 percent of those in administrative and civil service posts were ethnic Russians; Armenians and

---

[9] Of the more than 13,700 Georgians in combined administrative and military service, nearly 13,500, or 95%, were assigned to posts in the South Caucasus. By contrast, of the more than 187,000 Poles in similar posts, slightly more than 50% were assigned to (usually lower-level) posts in the Polish provinces, with the remainder assigned elsewhere in the empire (Bauer et al. 1991: 251–4).

Georgians each had one-fourth of the administrative or civil service posts, but educated Georgians (or sons of impoverished nobles) were underrepresented (in absolute and proportional terms) in the free professions (for figures, see Bauer et al. 1991: 437–8). Russians similarly dominated the Baku free professions and held more than 60 percent of the city's administrative posts, and in Baku proportionally twice as many Armenians found posts in the free professions and in administration than did Azerbaijanis. So ethnic Russians dominated both the free professions and the civil service in both cities. Given that these social locations (civil service and free professions) produced most of the radical intelligentsias of all three ethnic groups, these patterns of imperial inclusion and exclusion may have been just as important to the shape and content of their radical politics as their respective positions in the Baku oil industry, or in the economic relationship between Armenian capitalists and Georgian workers in Tiflis.

Estate memberships also revealed the region's horizontally segmented status relationships. Armenians occupied similar socioeconomic positions in Tiflis and Baku, but they were in ethnopolitical relationship with Georgians in Tiflis and Azerbaijanis in Baku. In absolute numbers, Azerbaijanis dominated the banking and commercial professions by more than two to one, but Armenians dominated as rentiers by the same margin (Bauer et al. 1991: 429, 440). Armenians had the fourth-greatest proportion of members in the distinguished citizens and merchant estates, surpassing Georgians, Azerbaijanis, and Russians, and the second-highest proportion of members in the urban merchant estate across the empire, after the Jews. Although few Georgians entered these two urban estates, they had the highest proportion of members in the hereditary noble, personal (service) noble, and clerical estates. This constituted an overproduction of nobles, with more hereditary nobles than Poles and Russians and more personal nobles than Russians (figures by nationality in Bauer et al. 1991: 197–8).

In short, Armenians dominated in the economic-status estates while Georgians dominated in the traditional-status estates; in Baku, Armenians dominated in one economic sphere while Azerbaijanis dominated in another. This pattern of horizontal ethnic segmentation is also consistent with the organization of capital in the oil industry. When oil lands were auctioned off, Armenians and Russians purchased them and rose as the financial elites of the oil industry. Although few Azerbaijanis succeeded in buying oil lands, Azerbaijanis were more numerous in small-scale extraction and refining. But the boom of the Baku oil industry also gave rise to a supporting financial and technical infrastructure, which included relatively well-developed banking and transportation systems. Azerbaijanis controlled the latter, and they owned one-half the ships, more than 40 percent of the Caspian's merchant fleet's carrying capacity, and more than half of the tankers – a dominance that was never relinquished (Altstadt 1992: 21, 23).

So although only one indicator among many, ethnic membership in the estates suggests that these nationalities were not vertically ranked like those

in Ukraine, Poland-Lithuania, or (with qualification) the Baltics. In the South
Caucasus, ethnic ranking was really limited to the working classes in the
industrial sectors, particularly in the newer oil industry. The region's ethnicities were organized horizontally or segmentally in complex, status-like
relationships. It also suggests that socioeconomic competition caused by
industrialization from the 1870s, even if exacerbated by inept Tsarist policies, may not have been the only basis of subsequent politicizations. Ethnic
conflict between Armenians and Georgians was only partly a result of changes
in economic stratification and competition. It was also a result of changes in
political power relations prompted by Russian imperial strategies. And I argue
that although both contributed, the latter was generally more important. This
is because while Armenian economic dominance was clear, it would have been
far more the concern of the new, small Georgian working class than of either
the impoverished Georgian nobility or the Georgian professional classes, for
whom the capitalist sphere held no interest anyway. And even here it is difficult to ascertain just how much of Georgian urban, working-class radicalism stemmed from Armenian control of capital and industry and how much
resulted from the more classical dislocating effects of large-scale industry on
traditional artisanal and craftwork production. Given the structure of Tiflis's
industry, the latter may have been more likely, although this is only a tentative
conclusion.[10]

Perhaps the impoverished Georgian noble and new professional classes
reacted less to Armenian economic power than to two entwined political exclusions: the Russianization of imperial military and civil bureaucracies, and the
fact that property and wealth, not birth and status, were increasingly the new
determinants of position in local government, thereby privileging Armenians.
Noble status was generally in decline, and more so in the economically colonial
conditions of the South Caucasus than in less dynamic parts of the empire.
This, in turn, privileged Armenian capital over the Georgian traditional nobility. Armenian economic dominance of Tiflis was hardly new, of course – it
had existed for centuries with Georgian nobles' assistance – and seigneurial
Georgia's anticapitalist ethos was pervasive and long-standing. But arguably
the impoverished Georgian aristocracy was politicized less by Armenian commercial ascendency per se than by Armenians' concomitant *political* ascendency, by the modern privileging of wealth and property over birth and status
that had previously underpinned and guaranteed Georgian positioning. So
political radicalism in the Southern Caucasus reflected – and reproduced –
these intricate ethnopolitical dynamics. Geostrategic realities on the southern

[10] The Georgian working class was small and limited largely to railroad workers and to a few
Tiflis industries, small-scale workshops, and craftsmen. Until 1900, manufacturing took place
either in the 4,000 artisanal workshops or in village households. In 1888, a single craftsman,
sometimes with one assistant, comprised 78% of workshops. But with Armenian capital and
Russian protective tariffs, the Tiflis economy shifted from transit trade and small handicraft to
larger-scale industrial production (Suny 1994: 117–18).

frontier, and the Russian state's colonial-bureaucratic political rule, meant that most political mobilizations were multiethnic and led by Russified elites who sought the empire's territorial integrity for geostrategic reasons, and signified an end to imperialist autocracy for reasons of social and political mobility. So I consider each socioethnic group in turn.

Narimanov and Azerbaijani Intelligentsia Politics

Narimanov (Nariman Kerbalai Nadzhaf-Ogly Narimanov) engaged in a range of cultural activities in addition to political activism; cultural and political activism worked in service of each other. But his route to radicalism was not typical of the Azerbaijani intelligentsia. One of only three Muslims in the entire Bolshevik elite, Narimanov was born in 1870 in Tiflis, the son of a petty Azerbaijani merchant. His family was not wealthy, but they were not impoverished either (compare Akhmedov 1988: 7, with Granat 1989: 559). They were of aristocratic rural origin, and a son in the liberal professions evidenced a certain status. Narimanov's father was a traveling musician who sang in Armenian, Azerbaijani, and Georgian and who had an interest in Georgian poetry.

Social Context, Education, and Assimilatory Russification

The family traced their descendents to the seventeenth-century rural hereditary nobility. Because at the time Azerbaijanis had few opportunities for advancement through the civil service (Altstadt 1992: 31), the increasingly impoverished rural nobility turned to commercial pursuits to compensate for absence of other venues of social mobility. But as noted, by 1900, Russified Azerbaijanis like Narimanov gained political and imperial access. In this Narimanov's socioethnic context was quite distinctive. First, as they were a comparatively small ethnoreligious minority in Tiflis and rural Georgia – the former characterized by Georgian, Armenian, and Russian influences, the latter dominated by the Georgian feudal nobility – for Azerbaijanis upward social mobility and urbanization necessarily entailed some form of assimilation. Georgian aristocratic culture was the most immediately accessible for Azerbaijani elites, because Armenian culture lacked an aristocratic tradition and Russian culture was not yet firmly planted. So identification with the hereditary Georgian nobility and the attractiveness of Georgian high culture on the father's part were plausible. Second, although Narimanov's brother studied at a madrassa, a broader secularization was necessarily part of assimilation and shaped the reformist politics of the Azerbaijani intelligentsia.

At age nine, Narimanov attended Muslim schools under the control of the Muslim ecclesiastical boards, and in turn subordinated to the Ministry of Internal Affairs – a line of authority that ensured that the schools taught Azeri, Persian, and Arabic languages, but most of the instruction was in Russian (on Narimanov, see Akhmedov 1988: 8–9; on the schools, see Altstadt 1992: 58–62). So Narimanov could already speak several languages by the time he was fifteen, and in 1885 he enrolled in the Gori Teacher's Seminary (Akhmedov 1988: 10; Granat 1989: 559).[11] The state designed this teachers' preparatory school to train bureaucrats for imperial service and to insulate them from religious influence. Yet the experience was more ambiguous: Narimanov correctly viewed it as connected with Tsarist Russification policies, but the instructors and the curriculum were quite progressive (Akhmedov 1988: 9). This discordant combination had the effect of radicalizing some students against the Russian state's colonialism-cum-Russification, but it did so while providing a progressive, European narrative through which to view both Russian and Azerbaijani cultures (on Narimanov's thinking along these lines, see Akhmedov 1988: 11; Granat 1989: 559).

Experiences in the empire's educational institutions and in middle-class, multiethnic Tiflis distinguished Narimanov from the majority of Azerbaijani reformers. This goes some way to understanding his attraction to a secular, class-universalist ideology as opposed to the more popular nationalism of the Müsavatists (the Muslim democratic party). Indeed, Narimanov's writings reflected an admiration for cosmopolitan Moscow – a city he thought belonged not to the Tsar or to the empire, but to the *narod* (Akhmedov 1988: 14–15). Narimanov also grasped in Russian poetry a struggle against despotism, backwardness, and ignorance; under the influence of Pisarev, Marx, and Pushkin, he developed an appreciation of a Marxist, "democratic world view" (Akhmedov 1988: 17). But caution is warranted in reading too much of what is known about his career as a Bolshevik into at least this stage of his early life. To the extent that Narimanov sought intellectual ideas to explain his social experiences, the critique that most resonated experientially likely concerned the political struggle against despotism, the Azerbaijani colonial experience in the Russian Empire, and a social world liminally situated culturally, religiously, and linguistically.

To put it another way, assimilation in an imperial-colonial context was at the core of his social experience, not socioeconomic injustice. In Tiflis, Narimanov was a privileged, acculturating Azerbaijani intellectual who lived as part of a tiny ethnic and religious minority – indeed he was one of only five Azerbaijanis at the Gori Teacher's Seminary (the figure is in Akhmedov 1988: 15, n. 1). Narimanov experienced the empire not socioeconomically, but culturally and religiously. His concerns were directed against political and cultural imperialism, and only derivatively against the socioeconomic injustices of Russian colonial rule. He was attracted to the culturally ecumenical empire of Peter the Great as the better imperial ideal, and he viewed the Protestant Reformation as a quasi-secular attack on religious hierarchy, absolute monarchy, and "backwardness" (Akhmedov 1988: 17–18). This was a critique of Azerbaijani culture vis-à-vis Russian imperial culture and its anti-ecumenical, colonial tendencies, as well as a critique of the "Catholicism" of the Muslim clerical establishment

---

[11] Granat says he entered the seminary at twelve, but it also has his birth as 1872, not 1870.

and its effects on "backwardness." It was pluralist and secularist, with room for his own cultural and religious and linguistic uniqueness.

Employment and Dissimilatory Russification

Narimanov's worldview was reinforced as a schoolteacher in the only Muslim school in a rural district in Tiflis *guberniia*, where he first experienced Tsarist repression and censorship (Akhmedov 1988: 21). Here he wrote dramatic works on peasant hardships and "cultural ignorance" (Granat 1989: 559). A year later he taught in a Russo-Tatar *gimnaziia* in Baku (Akhmedov 1988: 25–6), where he took part in theatrical productions, library associations, and literary groups – all on the belief that capitalism in the city threatened Azerbaijani culture (Akhmedov 1988: 27; Granat 1989: 559). Narimanov's cultural activism intensified from 1890, when Turkish-language newspapers were banned: so in 1894 he opened the first Azerbaijani public library and reading room with Azerbaijani-Turkish- and Turkish-language books (Prokhorov 1969–78: 251; Granat 1989: 559). In 1895, he published a second novel, but as a Muslim dramatist he was forced to submit it to the Caucasian Censure Committee. The same year he was allowed to publish another novel about the love between an Armenian and an Azerbaijani, where the twin enemies were capitalism and Tsarist autocracy (Akhmedov 1988: 29). He then taught at a Baku *Realschule* and published grammar and language books (Granat 1989: 560).

So an understanding of the distinctiveness of Narimanov's route to Bolshevik activism should be mindful of the ways in which imperial policies impacted these socioethnic locations. The earlier generation of Russified, secular Azerbaijani intelligentsia was the midcentury product of Russo-Tatar schools and military or civil service. Sons of Azerbaijani aristocrats studied in Russo-Tatar schools, *gimnazii*, *Realschulen*, and the empire's universities. They were a substantial social group by the 1870s, even though some linguistically and culturally identified with the Ottoman Empire (Georgeon 1996: 100; for a similar pattern among Kazan's Muslims, see Tuna 2011). But by the time Tsarist elites purged South Caucasia's civil bureaucracy of its "native" element, the Muslim intelligentsia was comprised almost solely of these Russified graduates of Russian universities and teachers' seminaries. In response, the second generation of Azerbaijani intelligentsia came of age espousing an Azerbaijani literary revival with a cultural affinity for Ottoman Turkey over Persia. Narimanov, then, was part of the third generation: an intelligentsia comprised of professionals, teachers, journalists, and writers, whose central dilemmas were now linguistic. And their politics reflected this: nation-building was sought through the dramatic arts and theater, as the Azerbaijani press tried to reduce clerical influence and heal sectarian divisions. The institutionalization of an Azerbaijani language was central to these efforts, and to this end, Narimanov helped set up reformist Azerbaijani schools (Georgeon 1996: 101).

But Russification among Azerbaijanis was rare and regarded as either retrograde or foreign: their Turkish Islamic inheritance was considered more distinguished than the imperial Russian that was on offer, so Russified political activists were criticized as assimilators and renegades (Altstadt 1992: 39; Swietochowski 1995: 25–6). Indeed, reformist elites' connections to wider Muslim reform projects in the Russian Empire were only tangential, because while the majority of the empire's Muslims were Sunni, 60 percent of Azerbaijanis were Shi'a. So large *jidadist* or reformist centers never developed in Azerbaijan as they had in Kazan, Ufa, or Orenburg. Therefore, in echoes of the Jewish intelligentsia's conflicts on the use of Russian or Yiddish, Azerbaijani debates over the linguistic base of reformist efforts were similarly divisive. Between 1879 and 1891, most of their writings reflected a linguistic Ottomanization, but there were calls for the use of the "popular dialect," or Azeri, to bring literature to the wider public – just as Yiddish-language proponents had done.

These internal debates, and Tsarist policies of religious elite co-optation, meant that this reformist Azerbaijani intelligentsia was strongly anticlerical and secular, effectively displacing the political influence of the Shi'a clergy (Georgeon 1996: 98). As with other minority and religious elites across the empire, imperial strategies had contributed to splitting the intelligentsia. Reformists turned away from a religious Shi'a Iranian identity and embraced their Turkish ethnolinguistic roots in their move toward a more secular nationalist politics (Swietochowski 1985, 1995; Georgeon 1996: 98, 102; see also Tuna 2011). Their political reformism sought to reconcile a Muslim identity (first Turkish, then Azerbaijani) within a modernizing Russia. And this, too, was at the core of Narimanov's political and cultural radicalism. Narimanov's reformism had been exclusively cultural and literary, and his experiences in the empire's "assimilationist" schools, which had sought to attract Azerbaijanis to Russian culture, had used Azerbaijani teachers such as Narimanov. But as of age thirty he had not participated in any political groups.

This changed when in 1902 he sat maturity certificate exams for *gimnaziia*, and with the financial assistance of wealthy benefactors, he studied medicine in Odessa and began his first direct political activity (Akhmedov 1988: 65; Granat 1989: 560). Odessa's university radicalism was associated with the city's wider revolutionary movement, and it was always premised on ethnic cooperation. While in medical school, Narimanov took part in multiethnic political circles and protests against the Russo-Japanese War and organized theatrical productions and political strikes that were politically oriented and in sympathy with multiethnic workers' movements (Akhmedov 1988: 65–9 on his strike participation; Granat 1989: 560). So Narimanov's distinctive route to radical politics reflected his Russified assimilation. He had drawn on both Russian and Azerbaijani culture, but his intellectual contacts were most often non-Azerbaijani. His generation struggled with the confluence of pan-Islam, pan-Turkism, Armenian-Azerbaijani tensions, and the arrival of socialism. And yet like the Lithuanian Kapsukas, while Narimanov's cultural abilities were notable as dramatist and writer, he was not among the most gifted of this cultural elite. It is easy to read back from his subsequent Soviet fame and ascribe to Narimanov a certain literary status, but judged from the literary perspective of the time he was a lesser, marginalized figure (Georgeon 1996: 103–5 lists key figures). More importantly, Narimanov's encounters with the Russian state were effectively limited to this cultural realm. Unlike other Bolsheviks' patterns of early and repeated arrest and exile because of political activism, for Narimanov, contact with Tsarist authorities involved cultural repression and literary controls, albeit within the context of a generally Russified experience. In fact, his work was again censored in 1904 when he staged a play for Muslim students, because Russian officials feared it could stoke social unrest. This suggests that his *rossiiskii* politics had a slightly different elective affinity than that of Dzierżyński or Smilga, for example.

Political Radicalism

Narimanov left for Baku where the working classes were highly politicized in 1905. Consistent with his commitment to an ecumenical empire, he joined the Muslim social democratic Hümmet (or Energy) as a publicist, and he translated the RSDLP program into Azeri while also a member of the RSDLP. Upper-class members of the secular intelligentsia, many of whom had studied in Russian secondary schools, had founded Hümmet in 1904 to organize Baku's Azerbaijani workers, but they used "Muslim" as a political designation in the official Tsarist sense, not in a religious sense (Altstadt 1992: 64). The Hümmet were typical of other radical groupings in multiethnic regions: though the rank and file was almost exclusively Azerbaijani, the leadership was ethnically mixed – hence the Georgian Bolshevik Dzhaparidze was one of its most influential leaders. Like groupings in the *kresy* or Ukraine, it similarly represented a range of views, entwining socialism, anticolonialism, and nationalism. Hümmet's Bolsheviks used the grouping as a vehicle to fight illiteracy and Azerbaijani workers' "religiosity," something Narimanov distinguished as politically compatible with an ecumenical empire but incompatible with autocracy (Akhmedov 1988: 15 and passim).

Narimanov became one of Hümmet's most important leaders just as the group's influence peaked in 1905. Ganja and Tiflis were important centers of Hümmet organization (Lazzarini 1976: 55), but while most Azerbaijani liberals aligned with the Kadets in 1905 to produce nearly all the Azerbaijani representation in the first two Dumas in 1906 and 1907, Narimanov and Baku's Azerbaijani socialist minority aligned with the RSDLP, in a more *rossiiskii*-minded alliance. Importantly, religious and ethnic affiliations converged in Hümmet's recruitment policies. Large numbers of Iranian immigrants in Baku became an important target of Hümmet recruitment, so in 1906 Narimanov created the first organization of Iranian workers, and it soon branched into Tabriz. He then founded a committee in Tiflis to supply Tabriz revolutionaries with contraband arms, munitions, and printed materials (Swietochowski 1995: 43–4).

Hümmet claimed, and Narimanov believed, that Baku's Muslim middle class sought to politically isolate Muslim workers from other nationalities because of its competition against the Russian, Armenian, and European middle classes – with the result that it contributed to a pan-Turkic and pan-Islamic nationalism (Akhmedov 1988: 79). And in fact Muslim middle-class civic associations organized the Muslim working classes in key cities on this basis. So Narimanov and other Azerbaijani SDs called for ethnic cooperation in the form of a working-class internationalist movement, and the Hümmet published leaflets (often in Russian) addressed to their "Muslim brothers," even dating them by the Islamic calendar (Altstadt 1992: 61). But the party's ideology may actually have been more liberal-nationalist than socialist, at least until 1917 (Lazzarini 1976: 56). Hümmet's members were not all Marxists, and although they opposed the traditional clergy, they were not anti-Islamic. By 1907, with Narimanov a key figure, a majority of the nationalist movement had folded into Hümmet's ranks. But it maintained close association with the RSDLP and the latter granted this mildly nationalist Muslim party autonomous status. Most leaders were arrested or fled to Persia in the post-1905 repressions, and by 1912 most Hümmetists joined the RSDLP.

Throughout his Hümmet activism, Narimanov completed his medical degree, continued cultural work, and in 1908 worked as a physician in Tiflis. In 1906, he attended the First Congress of Muslim Teachers in Baku as co-chairman of an educational committee composed of activists associated with the RSDLP or with the wider socialist movement; it had recommended a reformist, bicultural curriculum under an imperial umbrella to both protect Azerbaijani language and culture and to provide secular training for careers in imperial service (Altstadt 1992: 55–6). Then, in 1909, Narimanov was arrested and exiled to Astrakhan, where he wrote for Turkish journals and joined the new Astrakhan University before being elected to the Astrakhan city Duma (Prokhorov 1968–78: 251; Granat 1989: 650).

But on return from exile, Narimanov found a weakened socialist movement and a strengthening nationalist one. Former SDs and Hümmetists had founded the Azerbaijani nationalist Müsavat (Equality) party in 1911 in Baku, which he joined. Müsavat appealed to *umma* and pan-Islamic sentiment rather than to an ethnicized pan-Turkism, and it called for political reform regardless of sectarian affiliation. Although vague in direction, its following came loosely from the intelligentsia, and as it moved to the right it became the most important secular nationalist party of the Azerbaijani middle classes. But Azerbaijani nationalism's wider social base was in ethnically homogenous Ganja, not in multiethnic and socialist Baku. And for the urbane Narimanov, Tiflis's middle-class cosmopolitanism and Baku's multiethnic working classes were more comfortable than nationalist Ganja.

While anticolonial appeals worked for both the socialist Hümmet and nationalist Müsavat (Altstadt 1992: 69), religion played a relatively minor role in the politicization of Azerbaijani society because the secular intelligentsia was only secular up to a point: they advocated a reformed Islam, not a rejection of Islam. Narimanov's own politicization embodied this commitment, I think, just as it reflected the wider ambivalence of the secular Muslim intelligentsia. Religion was not integral to his own identity, and he regarded the clerical establishment as an impediment to social progress and to Azerbaijan's place in a modernizing

Russia. So he fought religious excess and backwardness. But he was in equal measure conciliatory to a more "Protestant" Islam and consistently supported religious education in school reforms, for instance. Because they had no real religious-secular schism, the successful politicization of "exploitation" did not reside in capitalism as much as it did in colonialism (Altstadt 1992: 64). The leaderships believed that most Azerbaijanis would remain Muslim, so the most successful mobilizational narrative would be predicated on anticolonialist sentiment. In fact, Narimanov later recalled how sensitive and flexible Muslim socialism was to religion (Altstadt 1992: 61).

Hümmet was subsequently excluded from the RSDLP because of its nationalist positions, so most socialist Hümmetists, Narimanov included, joined the RSDLP, while the remainder adopted a clearer Muslim identity (Swietochowski 1995: 63). Based in Baku, Narimanov joined the Bolsheviks while other Tiflis Hümmetists became Mensheviks, and Hümmet never regained its former strength against the Müsavat's powerful appeal. The Muslim community may have consolidated because, as Altstadt (1992: 43 and passim) argues, colonial Russian rule provided the focus or, as Swietochowski (1995: 42–3) argues, because tensions with Armenians caused Azerbaijanis to transcend sectarian loyalties. That is, nationalism could have been as much a response to sectarianism as it was to colonialism. But Azerbaijani attitudes toward the Russian Empire were more ambivalent than narrow anticolonialism implied (Swietochowski 1985: 192), often invoking three complex identities: pan-Islamic generally, ethnolinguistically Ottoman, and religiously Persian Shi'a. But this obscures from view the Muslim SDs who identified with the *rossiiskii* empire, particularly evident among Hümmetists and leftist Müsavatists like Narimanov.

This *rossiiskii*-mindedness was captured in the totality of Narimanov's biography: he was a secular Muslim, a Russified Tatar, culturally and linguistically Turkish, and ethnically Azerbaijani. This identity complexity was resolvable within a political commitment to an ecumenical, universalist empire. Indeed, Azerbaijani identification with Russian revolutionary socialists, democrats, and anarchists survived World War I's Turkish occupation (Pipes 1964: 205). Narimanov's subsequent nationality politics as a Bolshevik can only be understood against these identity complexities. He was deputy commissar to Stalin at Narkomnats, and when *korenizatsiia* was used to enforce central control, Narimanov worked for local interests, so he was discredited and removed from his post (Altstadt 1992: 123). One of his core beliefs was that socialism could liberate Azerbaijan from Russian cultural colonialism but still retain its position in an ecumenical imperial structure, something that presupposed an extension of native rule. So he was, in the end, a particular kind of nationalist. But his early politicization suggests, too, that he had always viewed his ethnic Azerbaijani identity in essentially cultural and political terms, because it was largely a product of imperial-minded struggles against cultural censorship. Narimanov fought cultural imperialism, not economic imperialism; his anticapitalism, though secondary, was more classically derivative of capitalism's encroachment into the cultural world of humanist elites. And he sought the ecumenical empire of Peter the Great at a time when the empire was Russianizing.

So a Russian-inflected, but ethnically tolerant, universalist ideology had a clear elective affinity. Narimanov's route to radicalism was predicated on a unique biography among Azerbaijanis: his semi-Russified assimilation in the empire's educational institutions permitted access to Russian-inflected socialist groups in addition to the more nationalist ones. But because of cultural repression as a Muslim intellectual, Narimanov's politics also sought a political expression of a better empire, one that was religiously tolerant and ecumenical. Like those of other non-Russian Bolsheviks, his ethnic identity was submerged within Bolshevism's universalism, but it did not disappear. The tensions of ethnic particularism that lay underneath eventually surfaced: in the 1930s, those who had associated with the Hümmet were considered nationalists. Indeed a common accusation was, "from what time did you begin your ties ... with the Narimanovshchina [the time of the influence of Narimanov]," by then considered by Soviet Bolshevism to be the incarnation of nationalism (quoted in Altstadt 1992: 144–5).

The Georgians and Petty Gentry Socialism

Georgian radicalism was premised on a different relationship to the Russian state. The first Georgian Marxist grouping appeared in 1892 in one of the least economically developed regions of the empire. But in contrast to Azerbaijani political mobilizations, in 1895, Marxism was the most powerful intellectual force among educated Georgians. By 1905 Georgian Menshevism was the most successful social democratic movement in the Russian Empire; by 1917, it was also a substantial, quasi-nationalist movement. Georgian Menshevism embraced the peasantry as a revolutionary force, while Bolshevism did better where industry was more developed (in Baku). Georgians' prominence in Bolshevism, and in the Revolution more widely, was of course most visible in the person of Stalin (Dzhugashvili). Yet in sociologically significant ways Stalin was neither representative of Georgian Bolshevism nor of Georgian socialism more generally: he was the son of a shoe cobbler, attended seminary, and received little education, whereas Dzhaparidze (Japaridze), Grigorii (Sergo) Ordzhonikidze (Orjonikidze), and Mamia Orakhelashvili were Russian-educated sons of impoverished rural gentry, and two of them were doctors. They were quite elite in terms of education, and they were employed in state-licensed professions.

The politicization of the three Georgians who came from the impoverished rural nobility raises the following question, however: given that Menshevism was so appealing to Georgian socialists, how can we situate the Georgian Bolsheviks' political radicalism at a time when the prospects for Bolshevism's success in the South Caucasus were so remote? Arguably they were distinguished less by ideology than by militancy and temperament (Jones 2005:

126). But Ordzhonikidze's subsequent brief rule in South Caucasia was notoriously brutal, Russificatory, and anti-Georgian, so it may be useful to examine
the degree to which Bolshevism's universalist ideological narrative was experienced as Russian-inflected or even Russified. Bolshevism was more centralized
and more closely identified with Russians, so the Georgian Bolsheviks were as
much part of an imperial-minded *rossiiskii* majority in the South Caucasus as
they were the minority of the Georgian minority (see Rieber 2005: 44 regarding Stalin).

Stalin's Distinctiveness
Stalin's biography is so well known that it does not need much sustained attention (for recent accounts, see Rieber 2001, 2005; Service 2005; Montefiore
2007; van Ree 2007).[12] However, certain dimensions of his early identity and
radicalism are worth highlighting, because while his class origins were unique
in the Georgian context, his general biography was actually emblematic of
many non-Russian Bolsheviks. His violent and alcoholic father was a cobbler
in Gori, and later in a shoe factory in multiethnic Tiflis, where he brought
the young Stalin on a regular basis (Service 2005: 19–23; Montefiore 2007:
27–34, 45). Stalin attended a Tiflis Orthodox seminary where he felt a strong
unease with humiliating Russian encroachments on Georgian language and
culture. His poems had "a nationalist edge" and notably extolled Georgian culture, nation, and nature, at a time when there was a good deal of antigovernment political activism (Jones 2005: 51–7; Rieber 2005: 20, 30; Service 2005:
36–9 on the Tiflis seminary; Montefiore 2007: 41). Stalin's published poems
were actually quite successful, but he preferred political activism to cultural
endeavors.

 Importantly, Stalin not only experienced ethnic tensions and nationalist
conflicts, but also became politically aware "at the margins of a nationalist
movement" (van Ree 2007: 62–3). Indeed, van Ree (2007) argues that Stalin's
Georgian background caused him to generalize the regional stereotyping of
nations as "heroes" (Georgians) and "merchants" (Armenians). So his politics
involved a hatred for Russian autocracy, even while he considered himself a
"russified Georgian": resentful of Russian rule, but admiring of Russian high
culture, he was never fully a Georgian nationalist (Rieber 2005: 18, 21, 43).

 And yet, Rieber (2001: 1652) writes, "Stalin could not escape his ethnic origins. His heavily accented Russian betrayed him as a man of the borderlands."
The frontier society that produced him, with its complex cultural and imperial imperatives, shaped Stalin's early politics (Rieber 2005; see also Service
2005: 30). Until age twenty-eight, Stalin wrote exclusively in Georgian. He

---

[12] Some biographical details and misconceptions are expertly dealt with in these recent accounts,
   including whether or not he was Ossetian, not Georgian (Service 2005: 18); whether or not he
   was a racist (van Ree 2007: 55–9); his first Marxist activity, and whether he left the seminary or
   was dismissed (Rieber 2005: 32–3, 36–7).

argued that the state's linguistic Russification policies had caused a political backlash among young Georgians like himself. Stalin described the evils of linguistic Russification under Tsarism in his early Georgian writings, and he had a strong sense that national sensitivities should be respected (Service 2005: 55, 57).[13] Although he was of peasant origin (his passport identified him as such until 1917), his self-presentation as a "proletarian served to mediate between his Georgian and Russian identities, firmly linking periphery to core" and bridging ethnicity and class (Rieber 2001: 1683, 1657–68). He wanted to appear proletarian, but he also considered himself an intellectual (Service 2005: 44). So the identity arc of his political journey went from being a Bolshevik in Georgia to being a Georgian in Russian Bolshevism (Rieber 2001: 1677). But most importantly, ethnic experiences in the empire's borderlands gave Stalin a geopolitical, territorial, rather than internationalist, understanding of socialist universalism (Rieber 2001; Shearer 2004: 841–2). This underscores the conservative dimension of Bolshevism and hints at the eventual triumph of the Russified, territorial socialist (Stalin) over the cosmopolitan, socialist internationalist (Trotsky).

SocioethnicLocation and Early Radicalism: Ordzhonikidze, Orakhelashvili, and Dzhaparidze

The other Georgian Bolsheviks were more sociologically representative of Georgian socialism. I highlight three essential features of their early radicalism and the social locations from which they came. Most immediately, their membership in the Russified Tiflis liberal professions – a would-be teacher, a medical assistant, and a doctor – draws attention to the fact that they were not implicated in capitalism, but in the empire's expanding bureaucracies and state-licensed professions. Secondly, their early radicalism was primarily among Armenian and Azerbaijani workers in Baku, or among Georgian and Azerbaijani rural peasants, but rarely among urban Georgian workers. They were more at home among the rural multiethnic working classes, and with Armenian and Muslim Bolsheviks, than they were among Georgian workers and socialists. Finally, all three were from the (relatively) impoverished rural nobility of Kutais *guberniia*, turning attention to the social and political context of this very particular social group. Kutais was a quintessential Christian border area, situated between threats of Muslim Caucasus highland invasions on one side and Turkish invasions on the other. Russian arms had historically protected western Georgia, where experiences of Turkish occupation were still fresh (Reisner 1995: 77). Less economically developed than eastern Georgia, it had mostly peasant seasonal labor and no industrial base. But it was linguistically diverse (with more than eleven Georgian language groups comprising 68.5 percent of the population), yet ethnically homogenous, and therefore a traditional center of Georgian cultural life (Jones 2005: 13–16, 26, 89, 134).

---

[13] Much of what we now know confirms Conquest's (1968: 116) early verdict that Stalin was anti-Semitic as a matter of policy, not dogma.

Ordzhonikidze was born in 1886 in Goresh to a rural, petty noble family (Ordzhonikidze 1986: 9; Granat 1989: 567). At the turn of the eighteenth century the family was solidly within the noble estates, but by the late nineteenth century they were emblematic of rural noble impoverishment. The serfs in the region had been emancipated in 1865, and the introduction of private property created a certain socioeconomic differentiation between petty and middle nobles (Suny 1994: 108; Reisner 1995: 76–7). Georgian peasants lost something economically in the emancipation, but they gained greater freedom and limited proprietorship, so that as urban workers they retained their ties to the countryside (Jones 2005: 82–3). The gradual nature of the emancipation and the police powers accorded to the nobility over the peasantry ensured the continuation of certain traditional political prerogatives. Yet Georgian nobles had failed to change agricultural techniques, and each year they extracted less from their holdings, especially in western Georgia. Indeed, Ordzhonikidze's family's level of impoverishment had declined to a point where his father worked transporting manganese extracted from the mines (Ordzhonikidze 1986: 9). So while they nominally retained their privileged noble status, in practice material circumstances were even more difficult than those of Dzierżyński's (comparatively less) impoverished Polish rural *szlachta* family. Yet for both the social effects were broadly the same: a generalized bitterness toward the Russian state and the flight of impoverished nobles' sons from the rural areas into the urban professions (on Georgia, see Jones 2005: 26). And as with the elite of the Polish socialist movements in the *kresy*, the sons of déclassé and petty Georgian nobles filled the ranks of the social democratic leaderships.

Shortly after Ordzhonikidze's birth, his mother died. He studied at a non-tuition parish school that included Russian-language courses and classical Georgian literature (Ordzhonikidze 1986: 9–10). His father died when Ordzhonikidze was ten, so a relative in Mingrelia raised him. He completed studies in 1898, and by 1901 he went to Europeanized Tiflis to enroll in its medical assistants' school (Khlevniuk 1995: 10). While there, at age seventeen, Ordzhonikidze became politically active and joined the RSDLP (Granat 1989: 567). Some accounts suggest that he immediately adhered to the party's Bolshevik Leninist wing (Ordzhonikidze 1986: 12–3; Granat 1986: 567), whereas another claims only that he joined the RSDLP (Khlevniuk 1995: 10). The latter is likely more accurate given the nature of the Russian groupings at the time. Actually Ordzhonikidze's studies in Tiflis coincided with the city's greatest revolutionary activity, especially among the social democratic groupings, and he joined a series of socialist student circles. The RSDLP had set up a small committee in Tiflis in 1901 with a Georgian-language paper, and the committee drew on anti-Tsarist student activism. But there was very little nationalist radicalism. As of 1902–03, social democracy in Tiflis had not yet split into its Bolshevik-Menshevik factions – a split that in any case would have very little practical organizational effect in the more pragmatic and isolated South Caucasus. Indeed, in a dynamic similar to that of Latvian socialism, in Georgia the organizational demarcation between Bolsheviks and Mensheviks did not really become fully clear until 1917 (Kazemzadeh 1951: 13; on Latvia, see Ezergailis 1974: ch. 10). Like Narimanov, Ordzhonikidze's radicalism also began with protests against the Russo-Japanese War, and he likely finally aligned with the Bolsheviks in 1905, when he undertook party work in Tiflis and in the surrounding areas (Ordzhonikidze 1986: 14).

Interestingly, then, Dzhaparidze, Orakhelashvili, Ordzhonikidze, and Stalin were active in multiethnic Baku or among rural Georgians – and in Dzhaparidze's case, among rural Azerbaijanis. None worked extensively among Tiflis's working classes. But Ordzhonikidze's rural radicalism among peasants, quite unique among Georgian socialists, deserves attention. The Tiflis working class was mostly ethnically Georgian and the middle-class was predominantly Armenian. Both were important factors in the success of Social Democracy in Georgia: a class war against the Armenian middle class and liberation from Russian and Armenian political rule made class and ethnic appeals virtually synonymous and, in effect, it fused the class with the national struggle (Kazemzadeh 1951: 12–13; Jones 1992: 248; Suny 1992: 252 and passim). But the social effects of rural Georgia's ethnic composition and its socioeconomic differentiation also impinged on socialist and nationalist politics.

So Ordzhonikidze's rural socialist activism was suggestive of important dynamics in the socialist politics of the impoverished Georgian rural gentry. Georgian SDs and the South Caucasian sections of the RSDLP had extended their influence into the countryside on the premise that poor and middle peasants and lower-class, non-proletarian groups were also "exploited working people" (Jones 1992: 248–50). Why not organize them on a nationalist basis, as Lithuanians, Latvians, Poles, or Ukrainians had done? Georgian socialists found a relatively homogenous rural population. Additionally, as a result of Tsarism's emancipation settlements and Georgia's low agricultural productivity, rural Georgian nobles and peasants had been economically converging for decades, so Georgian socialists also found relatively more socioeconomic sameness in the countryside. Rural Georgia did not have the socioeconomic differentiation of the Lithuanian and Latvian countryside, and with the exception of a small gentry, the majority of rural Georgians were by then impoverished nobles and small-propertied peasants.

Jones (1992: 250; 2005: 284) argues that this socioeconomic sameness contributed to a sense of solidarity between the impoverished gentry and peasants because of their embattled social statuses, and that this in turn muted the "working class versus intelligentsia" suspicions typical of other socialist parties. There may have been something of this, but I draw the opposite conclusion, for two related reasons. Socioeconomic sameness (read noble decline) had in fact contributed to the poorer gentry's radicalization in the first instance, while blocked mobility adversely affected the small-propertied peasant and the landless laborer. But these are two different social experiences, so the two social groups' respective elective affinities within socialism differed. Perhaps more importantly, though, the rural peasantry interpreted a noble-led nationalist politics as a restitution of the older feudal-seigneurial order, or as a variation of gentry nationalism. Reisner (1995: 76) observes that as much as they wanted social reform, Georgian peasants likely feared the restoration of the antecedent feudal order even more. This made mobilizing the peasantry on a socialist basis comparatively easier. Had socioeconomic sameness produced such a cross-class solidarity, it would have resulted in a purer nationalist politics. Instead socio-economic sameness politicized the group in decline, so the only successful basis for a nationalist mobilization of the peasantry was through the socialist revolutionary narrative. Suny (1994: 140) argues that the Georgia's traditional gentry nationalism was irrelevant to new Georgian working-class urbanites, but also consequential was the "absent" elective affinity: Georgian gentry nationalism was ideologically irrelevant to the Georgian rural peasantry.

The social context of Orakhelashvili's and Dzhaparidze's early radicalisms was similar to Ordzhonikidze's. According to Granat, Orakhelashvili was born in 1883 in the same region as Dzhaparidze, in Shoropani *uezd*, to a "poor peasant family" (Granat 1989: 567). Yet even the official Soviet biography claims that he was of *dvorianstvo* or gentry origin (Prokhorov 1969–78: 468). This is also suggested by the fact that his studies involved considerable financial resources on the part of the family. Like Ordzhonikidze, they were from the semi-impoverished rural aristocracy.

Orakhelashvili's experiences were across the Russian Empire: he studied at the Russified Kutais classical *gimnaziia* and then the Medical Faculty at the University of Kharkov; he subsequently joined the Military Medical Academy in St. Petersburg in 1902 and graduated in 1908 before working as a doctor in the South Caucasus (Prokhorov 1969–78: 468; Granat 1989: 567). Whether Orakhelashvili had been active in radical groupings while in *gimnaziia* or medical school is unclear, although if he had, it did not prevent him from completing his studies. The fact that he joined the empire's most important Military Medical Academy is testament both to his high level of identification with the Russian state and to the remaining possibilities for social mobility for young Georgians within the empire's bureaucracies. While in St. Petersburg, Orakhelashvili took part in the student unrest in 1905. In 1906, he left for Paris and Geneva, and on his return was imprisoned in Tiflis.

Dzhaparidze's youth was similarly privileged, although expulsion for radicalism meant that he was never professionally employed. He was born in 1880 in a village in Kutais *guberniia* to a landed family. Dzhaparidze's father died when he was young, leaving the family in difficult financial circumstances, but he nevertheless attended a Russified school for sons of the nobility and studied at the Aleksandrovskii Teacher's Institute in Tiflis until 1900 – the same multiethnic institute that Narimanov had attended (Prokhorov 1969–78: 193). So as all three Georgians made the transition from rural Kutais to multiethnic Tiflis and its Russified educational system, their educational and political paths crossed.

Routes to Political Radicalism
Russified backgrounds facilitated radical routes to multiethnic groupings for all three. In fact, two of them organized Muslim workers. While at the teachers'

institute in 1898, Dzhaparidze joined political circles, which soon dissolved into clearer nationalist, Marxist, and quasi-Marxist factions (Granat 1989: 407). Dzhaparidze joined the latter, as well as teachers' professional circles and associations. These were likely vague in orientation, but generally oppositional. Dzhaparidze also took part in the first strike of the Tiflis railroad workers in 1898. He joined the Imeretian-Mingrelian Committee of the RSDLP with Ordzhonikidze, where they worked almost exclusively among the peasantry. He was arrested in May Day demonstrations and spent eleven months in prison before returning to Kutais; he was expelled from the teacher's institute for radicalism and subsequently banned from residing in the three major cities of the South Caucasus. In 1901, he directed tobacco workers' strikes in Kutais, and by 1904 he began directing Armenian-Azerbaijani oil workers' strikes in Baku (all in Prokhorov 1969–78: 193; and Granat 1989: 407).

Ordzhonikidze, by contrast, graduated in 1905 and went to Batum to work as a medical assistant; however he continued to organize peasants – as well as his patients (Ordzhonikidze 1986: 19). To this point his activism among urban workers was limited. Ordzhonikidze's influence in the Batum RSDLP gradually increased, however, and he organized workers' strikes in Batum, Kutais, Gori, and other western Georgian cities. But he was arrested for transporting arms in Abkhazia in 1905 (Khlevniuk 1995: 10). This first arrest began a new phase of his revolutionary experience: Ordzhonikidze would spend at least eight of his fifteen years of prerevolutionary radicalism in prison, hard labor, or exile (also noted in Mikoyan 1988: 413). This was on par with Dzierżyński. Like Orakhelashvili, who had fled to Paris and Geneva during the post-1905 reprisals, in 1906, Ordzhonikidze left for Berlin, and six months later again returned to Baku to work as a medical assistant (Granat 1989: 567).

In these years the Baku working classes were among the most militant in the empire, and Ordzhonikidze's organizational skills brought him some prominence, even though as Georgians in an Armenian-Azerbaijani city, Ordzhonikidze and Dzhaparidze were clearly a minority. But the Baku Bolshevik committee attracted Georgian Bolsheviks largely because Mensheviks dominated the Tiflis party organization. As in Vilna and Kiev, the socialist parties' leaderships in Baku were more ethnically mixed in composition than the rank and file. Ordzhonikidze continued to work as a medical assistant despite activism among the Azerbaijani peasantry near Baku and in the Baku workers' barracks. He was arrested in May Day demonstrations with Dzhaparidze. From 1908, he was in administrative exile away from the Caucasus during the peak years of Tsarist reaction (Ordzhonikidze 1986: 32–4). While in prison and exile, he may have been sustained by Marxist ideas and literature, as his biography claims (Ordzhonikidze 1986: 36), although it is more likely that he was sustained by the politically active and diverse exile colony. Tsarist documents specifically make mention of his gentry status, which may explain the severity of the punishment despite his young age (nineteen). He spent almost two years in prisons and in exile in Enisei *guberniia* (Prokhorov 1969–78: 494–5; the arrest figure is in Ordzhonikidze 1986: 29; Granat 1989: 568).

In 1905, Dzhaparidze, too, remained distant from Georgian workers in Tiflis, but he organized strikes among Armenians and Azerbaijanis in Baku. According to his official biography, Dzhaparidze was a cofounder of the Muslim Azerbaijani SD Hümmet (Prokhorov 1969–78: 193). As a member of the RSDLP's Baku Committee, he maintained close relations with various Hümmetists, as apparently had Stalin who in 1906 unsuccessfully attempted a merger between the Hümmetists and the Caucasian Party Committee (Swietochowski 1985: 54). Dzhaparidze sought to present Russian socialism (Bolshevism) as the embodiment of Muslim working-class interests. That Ordzhonikidze and Dzhaparidze were more at home among Azerbaijani peasants than among the more nationalist and European-educated Georgian Mensheviks in Tiflis makes sense only in the context of their rural upbringing and subsequent Russified education. The relationship between the Georgian Bolsheviks and the Baku Muslim working class – or indeed the wider relationship between the leaderships of the radical groupings and the South Caucasian Muslim populations – was ambiguous, however. The Muslim working class was substantial and potentially determinative in the revolutionary movement, but Dzhaparidze's characterization of the problem was not that "political leadership had … ignored the Muslims – it was simply that they were culturally more backward than the rest of the population and revolutionary groups had no influence over them" (quoted in Swietochowski 1985: 103–4).

In the years of reaction, the RSDLP in fact had little impact, so Dzhaparidze organized non-Georgian oil workers in Rostov, Nakhichevan, and in the Kuban (Granat 1989: 407). After repeated arrests he was exiled to Rostov and forbidden from residing in the Caucasus for five years. While doing party work in Rostov, he was again arrested and exiled to Vologda for three years. On his return to Tiflis he attended university courses, was arrested during May Day demonstrations, and deported to Enisei. He escaped, joined the Red Cross, and conducted political work among soldiers of the imperial armies in Trebizond (Prokhorov 1969–78: 490; Granat 1989: 407). In other words, he worked as a semiprofessional revolutionary.

Similarly, Ordzhonikidze organized Muslim workers in Persia. In 1909, Ordzhonikidze escaped to Persia where he actively participated as a Bolshevik in Persia revolutionary activity (Ordzhonikidze 1986: 41–2; Granat 1989: 556). The Persian revolution began in 1905 after the first Russian Revolution and drew radical activists from the Russian Empire, in part because of the thinning of their ranks under Tsarist repression. In Tabriz, the Tsarist émigrés formed a distinctive colony – Russian, Azerbaijani, Armenian, and Georgian socialists and nationalist socialists. Once again Ordzhonikidze and Dzhaparidze worked with the multiethnic parties, not the ethnically Georgian parties, although much of the otherwise disparate politics of the various groups converged around anticolonialism. Ordzhonikidze's activities in Persian events involved work in the Baku committee and a position as a liaison between Persian radicals and the Bolshevik émigré group in Paris (Ordzhonikidze 1986: 41–2). In 1910,

Ordzhonikidze left for Paris and in 1911 he attended the famous Bolshevik party school in Longjumeau (Prokhorov 1969–78: 494–5; Granat 1989: 568). On his return to Russia he was arrested with Stalin and spent the next three years in the Schlüsselburg Prison, hard labor, and permanent residence in Iakutsk (Granat 1989: 568; Khlevniuk 1995: 11). While in Iakutsk, he worked as a medical assistant in a settlement colony with the Jewish and Ukrainian Bolsheviks Sverdlov, Yaroslavsky, and Petrovsky; they edited a Bolshevik paper to defend Bolshevik-Menshevik unity in the South Caucasus (Ordzhonikidze 1986: 61–2; Granat 1989: 568).

Georgians' Russified, Imperialized Bolshevism

Beyond this political activism, during the war and revolutionary years, Orakhelashvili, Dzhaparidze, Ordzhonikidze, and Stalin fought on the front lines of either the imperial or Bolshevik armies. Orakhelashvili served until 1917 near the front lines with an officer's rank, as a medical doctor in an imperial field army (Granat 1989: 567). In 1917–18, he became a member of the RSDLP Caucasian Regional Committee, but he was arrested by the Menshevik government and imprisoned for eighteen months. On release, he became chairman of the Georgian Bolshevik CC, and among other positions, he was on the editorial board of *Pravda*. With the Revolution, Dzhaparidze was elected to the RSDLP Baku Committee with Narimanov and the Armenian Stepan Shaumian (Shahumian). In 1918, he was on the Committee of Revolutionary Defense, which was responsible for the violent suppression of the nationalist Müsavat revolt. Similarly, Ordzhonikidze was on the CC of the Petrograd Soviet and worked in Ukraine and the Caucasus during the Civil War. In 1920–21, he was instrumental in securing Soviet power in Azerbaijan, Armenia, and Georgia; indeed, Ordzhonikidze and Stalin were famously responsible for the Soviet military offensive in Georgia. This was the beginning of his close ties with Stalin. In fact, Ordzhonikidze's Russification tactics were so vicious that Lenin condemned his policies and demanded his expulsion from the party (Haupt and Marie 1969: 172). Neither Ordzhonikidze nor Orakhelashvili survived Stalin's purges; they were either killed or committed suicide.

In sum, then, the three Georgian Bolsheviks were politicized in Tiflis as students and in the professions, and they were attracted to *rossiiskii* political mobilizations. But why did they not become Mensheviks? In social profile, Georgian Bolshevism and Georgian Menshevism were very similar, but a key difference was education. In response to the Russification of the Tiflis seminary, an anti-Tsarist response emerged in the Georgian seminaries. A substantial number of Georgian Mensheviks were Europeanized and cosmopolitan, and some of the key figures were educated in Warsaw and influenced by Polish nationalists and European socialists (Jones 2005: ch. 3). But Dzhaparidze, Orakhelashvili, and Ordzhonikidze attended the Russianized Kutais *gimnaziia* and *Realschulen*, Tiflis noble schools, feldsher's school,[14] the Russified Teachers'

---

[14] Feldshers were physicians' assistants, who usually provided medical services in the most rural areas.

Institute, and the Universities of Kharkov and St. Petersburg (Reisner 1995: 70 on the character of the schools). Their semi-Russified, assimilated education was in the more segregated Russian *gimnazii*, and their social and professional experiences were in multiethnic contexts. Unlike those Georgians who had studied in the nationalist-minded seminaries (of which Stalin was one), they were comfortable working among Russian, Azerbaijani, Muslim, and Armenian workers.

So the quality and character of Russification had subtle implications for elective affinities for either the national (Menshevik) or the class (Bolshevik) dimensions of Georgian socialism. Of course class and nation within Georgian socialism are notoriously difficult to disentangle. In Marxism Georgians had a non-nationalist political ideology to use against both the Armenian middle class and the Russian state, and from the 1890s, socialism resonated with ethnic Georgians as they were excluded from capitalism and increasingly from political power (Suny 1994: 140). Yet Georgian nationalists adopted a strong anticapitalist tone. Perhaps the most sophisticated Marxists in the empire, they had borrowed the imperative for ethnic cooperation of a multiethnic state from Austrian Marxists (Hosking 1997: 385–6; Jones 2005), and this may have been as much about redefining a political dependency on an increasingly exclusionary imperial state.

The socialist leadership of the 1880s and 1890s consisted mostly of intellectuals from the professional classes and the impoverished aristocracy, and most of them were European or Russian educated. The more impoverished nobility often entered the professions – as did these Bolsheviks. Yet they were not attracted to nationalism but to the RSDLP. Why did their anxiety on returning to find an autocratic colonial government and exclusion from municipal Dumas and civil service not make them nationalists? As noted, the political sociology at work was not tied to Armenian capitalist ascendancy per se, but rather to Armenians' newfound ability to translate economic power into political influence. The urban economic estates (merchants and distinguished citizens) were Armenian dominated, but imperial strategies moved them into positions of political influence once held by the status-based estates (the hereditary nobility and clergy) that had been Georgian dominated. Tsarist policies politically privileged one status (Armenian commerce) over another (Georgian nobility) – in electoral laws in the city dumas, in the liberal professions, and in access to the empire's civil bureaucracies. So there was a sense of exclusion from regional political influence among educated Georgians.

Despite the fact that political and civil society increasingly privileged Armenians and Russians, educated Georgians nevertheless continued to identify their security, position, and political status within the Russian Empire. This was true of Georgian Mensheviks and Bolsheviks. The series of status-particularistic policies identified in Chapter 2 had the effect of solidifying ethnopolitical tensions in the South Caucasus, and therefore opening up particular antistate but imperial-minded routes to radicalism for the sons of the declining Georgian nobility. They developed a nationalist-socialist identity not in confrontation with the Russian Empire, but rather in conjunction with it. But because of the social strength of Menshevism and Bolshevism's correspondingly weak ethnic social base, Georgian Bolshevism defined itself in Russian-centralist terms, in opposition to Menshevism's nationalist inflection and internationalism. By comparison, the extent to which Georgian elites were politically and economically dependent on, and incorporated into, the Russian state was matched – albeit for purer geopolitical reasons – by Armenian elites.

The Armenian Bolsheviks and Geopolitical Insecurity

Armenian socialists consistently pursued the good imperial ideal: a cosmopolitan, multiethnic, and liberal empire (Suny 1993b: 24–6). But as this possibility looked increasingly remote with greater repression and Russification, Armenian politics focused on a territorial homeland. Ethnic violence between Kurds and Armenians in Anatolia and Armenians and Azerbaijanis in the South Caucasus had cemented the impression that neither the Russian state nor the European powers would come to their rescue. So Armenian socialists' solutions lay in ethnic alliances. The reasons may be found in the sources of Armenian Russophilia, something at the core of Shaumian and Anastas Mikoian's early radicalism, and in a slightly different manner, that of Aleksandr Miasnikov (Miasnikian). Their biographies and radicalisms underline the influences of key imperial strategies of socioethnic exclusion that split middle-class minority elites: commercial elites were co-opted, while the intellectual and liberal professions were repressed, and dissimilatory Russification policies were pursued in Armenian seminaries and educational institutions. These policies produced both socialist and nationalist radicalism. But geopolitical realities also consistently gave their radicalism a *rossiiskii* inflection.

By the late nineteenth century, Tsarist elites came to view Armenians as disloyal radicals who drove social unrest and international conspiracies. So they responded repressively: in 1885, hundreds of Armenian parish schools with thousands of students and hundreds of – now unemployed – teachers were closed and replaced by Russian schools. Some were reopened in 1886, but under strict surveillance. Similarly, after the Hamidian massacres of Armenians in 1895–96, Tsarist elites did not respond with greater protection but with increased repression and restrictive censorship: in 1896, Armenian Church schools were again closed, as were charitable institutions and libraries, and in 1903, Church properties were seized. So the combination of Tsarist indifference to the anti-Armenian violence and a series of illiberal exclusions caused the Armenian upper and middle strata to stiffen into radical opposition not only to illiberalism, but increasingly also to Russification.

The loyalist Russophilic liberalism that had characterized the midcentury Armenian intelligentsia ceded to divided loyalties and to an increasingly anti-Russian stance. Russified middle-class Armenians de-Russianized their names (Suny 1993b: 81). But Armenian socialists found that because of their geographic dispersion and marginalization from the growing nationalist movement after 1903 and 1905, they could only be a viable political force in Tiflis or Baku through ethnic alliances with other South Caucasians. And this, too, would inform Shaumian and Mikoian's preoccupations with ethnic alliances. Moreover, socialist and nationalist battles with the Ottoman state on behalf of Anatolian Armenians similarly required ethnic alliances with Turkish, Azerbaijani, and Persian Muslim reformers – if only because politically mobilizing the numerically and economically weak Armenian peasants in the *vilayets* of Anatolia was a theory of revolution doomed to failure (Ter Minassian 1983: 183–4). So these were, in effect, *rossiiskii* and Ottomanist strategies deployed against both autocracies.

Put differently, the Armenian response to the Russian state's exclusions was rather diffuse for reasons of ethnic survival. Armenian radicalism was distinctive because of its persistent Russophilia, even when confronted with illiberalism, Russification, and political challenges to Armenian privileges. Many were certainly attracted to the empire's Russian language and culture, but at base it was largely geopolitical necessity. The nationalist radicalism of both socialist-cum-nationalist parties, the *Hnchak* (Bell) and the *Dashnaktsutiun* (or Dashnak), was motivated primarily by a fear of the disintegration of the region and of its probable fall to Turkish rule. This explains the Armenian Bolsheviks' unwavering support of Tsarist armies in the Russo-Turkish Wars and the large numbers of volunteers for the army, including the future Bolshevik Mikoian. Ethnopolitical struggles with Azerbaijanis (and to a lesser extent with Georgians) were of secondary concern. So was Russification. The response to anti-Armenian violence was either a territorial arrangement within the empire's geopolitical boundaries or nationalist separatism, but the latter depended on a level of Great Power assistance that did not materialize, and in the face of ethnic survival, Russification seemed the lesser infraction.

Shaumian

The Armenian Bolsheviks' political radicalizations reflected these tensions. Known as the Caucasian Lenin, Shaumian was the oldest and most influential of the Armenian Bolsheviks, although his early life is surprisingly rather sketchy (Shaumian 1978; Granat 1989: 762). He achieved heroic status in 1918 when, together with Dzhaparidze and twenty-four Bolshevik commissars, he was shot by the SRs in the Turkestan desert. Shaumian was born in 1878 in Tiflis, and this was where his radicalism began. Although Shaumian's official biography claims that his father was a commercial shop clerk, he was more likely a petty merchant, wealthy enough to send a son to a tuition-paying Tiflis *Realschule* and not to the seminaries, the most common destination of the Armenian lower classes (compare Prokhorov 1969–78: 299–300 with Granat 1989: 762 on his social origins). So the fact that he attended a multiethnic, Russified imperial secondary school testified both to the family's socioeconomic status and to their level of acculturation.

He joined the Marxist radical groupings, and at age sixteen organized student circles using illegal Russian radical literature (Shaumian 1978: 6).

He studied chemistry at Riga's Polytechnic Institute. He joined Riga's popular RSDLP movement and took part in all-Russian SD student congresses.
In fact, while Shaumian was active in Riga, the Jewish Bolshevik Kamenev,
who had attended the Tiflis *gimnaziia*, was politically active in Tiflis's multiethnic Georgian SD leadership (Granat 1989: 427; Jones 2005: 123). After three
years in Riga, Shaumian was expelled for political activities, so he began organizing the first Armenian national-social democratic circle in a village outside
Tiflis (Shaumian 1978: 6; Granat 1989: 762). This was among the first Marxist
circles in Armenia, most of which developed ties to the Georgian SDs on a multiethnic basis (Prokhorov 1969–78: 299–300; Ter Minassian 1983: 164).

Because many socialists blamed Armenian workers' organizational isolation on the nationalist movement, between 1896 and 1902, small groups
of Armenian, Russian, and Georgian SDs began to organize on an interethnic basis to broaden the socialist movement's base. Most of the leadership
had imperial educational experiences similar to Shaumian's: they had studied in the empire's universities in St. Petersburg, Moscow, Dorpat, and Riga.
Shaumian drew on this, and in 1902 he founded the Union of Armenian Social
Democrats, which affiliated with the Tiflis RSDLP and eventually merged with
the Caucasian Union. Shaumian published the group's first radical paper and
immediately drew Lenin's attention. Written before 1905's nationalist-tinged
rebellions, and fresh from three years in Riga's ethnically diverse radical circles,
Shaumian called for Armenian solidarity with the Russian labor struggle on
the grounds that the two proletariats' interests converged (Shaumian 1978:
29–33). He thought nationalist-socialist movements should become socialist
internationalist as he drew on his experiences with Riga's Russian, Polish, and
Jewish workers, and Tiflis's Georgian and Armenian workers. But Shaumian
also called for forms of political and cultural autonomy for the Caucasian
nationalities.

Then he entered the Philosophical Faculty of Berlin University, joined the
city's Russian radical groups, and participated in the German Social Democratic
labor movement, among other internationalist groupings (Prokhorov 1969–
78: 299–300; Shaumian 1978: 7; Granat 1989: 762). After three years of study
in Berlin,[15] in 1904 he returned to Tiflis and he was elected a member of the
Caucasian Union of the RSDLP. He then worked on the Bolshevik party committee in Baku with Dzhaparidze and Ordzhonikidze. This was now the center of working-class radicalism in the South Caucasus. Arrested and exiled in
Astrakhan in 1911, Shaumian returned in 1914 before another exile in Saratov
until the Revolution (Granat 1989: 762).

So Shaumian's radicalism was quite distinctive. For some Armenian radicals
the Austrian and Bundist models appealed because they emphasized federations
of autonomous national parties that could battle Russian centralism. Others

---

[15] It is unclear if he completed his studies. Official sources say he graduated (Prokhorov 1969–78:
299–300); Ter Minassian (1983: 17) writes that he dropped out; Granat 1989: 762 simply notes
that he attended.

argued that the Russian-internationalist model was more attractive because socialist goals countered "bourgeois separatism." But Shaumian's polemics against Dashnak nationalism maintained that national specificity such as that of the Jewish Bund would only lead to the disintegration of the empire (see Ter Minassian 1983: 168–71). The answer to the Armenian question, in other words, lay not only in destroying autocracy on a socialist basis and in cooperation with the Russian working class, but also in salvaging the territorial Russian Empire.

Without entering into the merits of his polemics, two substantive observations are worth making. First, Shaumian's desire for decentralized forms of national autonomy and his experiences to this point suggest the same imperative for ethnic cooperation that we saw in Dzierżyński's, Piatnitsky's, or Gusev's politics. But in Armenia the socialist response to nationalism was a "federative brotherhood" based on ethnic cooperation, not a purely socialist internationalism (Karinian 1928: 10). Borders mattered more for geopolitically fragile and insecure ethnicities. And yet, although the contexts differed, similar ethnopolitical dynamics prevailed. Specifically, Russification policies after 1903 and the ethnic violence of 1905 crystallized ethnic identities more coherently, and this was reflected in the various political mobilizations: the Armenian nationalist Dashnaks witnessed an influx of members between 1903 and 1905, with at least twenty-five new groups formed in Baku, Yerevan, and Alexandropol (Ter Minassian 1983: 167); the Mensheviks rapidly became a predominantly Georgian national party; and the Azerbaijani Müsavatists became increasingly influential among Muslim workers. The region's ethnopolitics prompted the radical parties to similarly balkanize.

Second, Shaumian subsequently also wrote on the Tatar-Armenian conflict of 1905 in which he polemicized against both Tatar and Armenian reactionaries: ethnic violence undermined the true revolutionary movement, even if it was itself underpinned by the "criminal Caucasian bureaucracy" – a commonly made contention (Shaumian 1978: 185–6). Moreover, Armenian-Azerbaijani violence in 1905 elicited a response by the nationalist Dashnaks similar to that of the Bund's response to anti-Jewish pogroms in the same year: they formed self-defense units to protect the Armenian community. But the Armenian Bolsheviks, and Shaumian most prominently among them, not only condemned the autocratic state and nationalist reactionaries on both sides; they also condemned the self-defense organizations and responded by organizing a Turkish-Armenian fraternal union through the Armenians sections of the Baku and Hümmet committees (Ter Minassian 1983: 177).

Shaumian revisited the need for national autonomy while working among Baku's multiethnic working classes in 1914 in a series of publications through the war years in which he canonically took Lenin's positions (Shaumian 1978: vol. 1, 418–19; vol. 2, 28–41). Yet Shaumian's writings on nationalism now differed from his earlier writings in at least one important respect: nationalism was no longer a theoretical question but a geopolitical issue threatening the imperial state. He viewed the nationality question as the Russian Empire's – not the Armenian peoples' – greatest concern. He continued to oppose Dashnak nationalism because it represented the interests of the Armenian middle classes, but he softened his position on the language issue. Not completely embracing the Austro-Marxists' positions, Shaumian, like Lenin, made accommodation for the nationalisms that the war had created, although by 1917 he argued that it was nationalist separatism in the South Caucasus that was causing a weakening of the front lines (see Karinian 1928: 11–13; Shaumian 1978: 28–41, 160–2, 418–19). Mindful of the political benefits of cultural recognitions, he called for three autonomous national regions in South Caucasia within a broader decentralized, federal structure. His proposals were rejected in favor of a more centralized model, but the change in his thinking was nevertheless significant. He had fought the bourgeois nationalism of the Dashnaks, as had other Armenian socialists, not because it undermined international working-class solidarity, but because it undermined the geopolitical position of Armenians within the Russian Empire.

Mikoian

Mikoian's revolutionary politics emerged from a slightly different context. He was elevated to national stature as part of the small group of Bolsheviks who took power in Baku in 1920. Arrested and jailed by the SRs, Mikoian was shot after the fall of the Baku Commune, but he was one of the few Old Bolsheviks to survive the purges, and he outlived Stalin to serve under Khrushchev and Brezhnev. And yet remarkably little is known about Mikoian's earliest political radicalism. His autobiography is silent on a ten-year period of early political activism, as is the Granat's account (see Mikoyan 1988; Granat 1989: 543). Some sources claim that he was active in the liberal Kadets before joining the Bolsheviks, while others note that he was involved in the Dashnaks (see Graziosi 1999: 26, n. 41). There may be some truth in these claims. In 1923, Mikoian accused Narimanov of nationalism, and the latter in turn accused Mikoian of carrying out "Dashnak work" in Azerbaijan; in fact, Narimanov recalled that his own 1890 novel on the love between an Armenian and an Azerbaijani was written "when Mikoian was still a Dashnak" (quoted and recounted in Altstadt 1992: 123–4).

Mikoian's early social world lends greater plausibility to the claim that he was a nationalist Dashnak before becoming a Bolshevik. He was born in a village near Tiflis in 1895, to illiterate parents (Mikoyan 1988: 7; Granat 1989: 543). On official documents his father was classified in the peasant estate, and his grandfather had been a serf. However, Mikoian's father was likely a laborer-carpenter (although this, too, is disputed), but he did spend six years as an apprentice to a master carpenter in Tiflis (Mikoyan 1988: 11, 14; Granat 1989: 543). His socioeconomic status was effectively lower-middle class, not strictly peasant, with important urban cultural influences despite surrounding illiteracy: the father's work brought him to cosmopolitan Tiflis on a daily basis where he acquired a simple, conversational knowledge of several languages in frequent contact with the city's multiethnic, urban lower classes. Indeed, he taught Mikoian to count to one hundred in Armenian, Russian, Georgian, Azeri, and Greek (Mikoyan 1988: 11). His father "looked like a Tiflis crafts-man" and he dressed neatly, with city shoes and a city hat, not the typical peas-ant Caucasian fur cap (Mikoyan 1988: 20).

Mikoian's father also worked as a carpenter in a French-owned copper mine, and his brother was a hammerman there. At one point the entire family lived in the factory barracks. Mikoian credited this experience as opening his eyes to factory working and living conditions: management was French and they lived luxuriously; Armenians, Russians, and others comprised the clerical staff; the miners were Greek; and the most menial jobs went to foreigners and "drifters, émigrés from northern Iran" (Mikoyan 1988: 26–7). In all, Mikoian considered his family to have experienced "prolonged oppression" by a "hostile regime" (Mikoyan 1988: 9–11). Some of this should be critically contextual-ized. European investments in Georgian mining in the rural areas were sub-stantial and locally resented, but the central feature of the ethnic composition of the miners was the competition between rural Armenians and Azerbaijanis for the same jobs, and the fact that most of the landlords were Azerbaijani, while peasants were Armenian and Azerbaijani.

In this socioethnic context, Mikoian's education began when an Armenian Narodnik, exiled to his village, taught the children to read. Then a bishop arranged for him to attend a seminary school in Tiflis. In 1906, at age ten, he left for an eleven-year course of study, and although initially the family paid for the schooling, Mikoian received further financial assistance from an Armenian charity (Mikoyan 1988: 13–14, 22–3). In the seminary he became the local atheist despite his family's devoutness, and he was given the nick-name, "Anastvats" (atheist) (Mikoyan 1988: 16–17). He was apparently also attracted to novels of Armenia's national struggles against foreign oppression and to a variety of literary works. Yet once he could read Russian, he became interested in science, Darwin, the French Revolution, and Russian literary works (Mikoyan 1988: 25–8). But he also witnessed waves of worker unrest in 1911–12, complemented by the circulation of Marxist revolutionary litera-ture. And after a few years of student radicalism, Tsarist authorities ransacked Mikoian's apartment for illegal literature (Mikoyan 1988: 32–3).

So Tsarist educational policies were felt in Armenian schooling of the lower classes also. Sons of the less well off, like Mikoian, typically attended semi-naries, because wealthier families could afford tuition-based *gimnazii* or com-mercial schools. Of course, the empire's *gimnazii* and *Realschulen* produced as many young radicals as did the less prestigious seminaries, but the differences lay in the direction and content of their politicizations: with some notable exceptions, seminaries mostly produced nationalists whereas *Realschulen* and *gimnazii* tended to produce socialists. Yet most of the seminary teachers had received their education and training in Germany, Switzerland, or France, so they tended to promote European liberal democratic views. Most of the sem-inary curriculum was not religious in content, but rather more general. While Tsarist language laws forbade the teaching of Armenian in secondary schools, religious seminaries were exempt from these restrictions, so they became religious in name but *gimnazii* in substance. If a student could not afford to study abroad, he would become a teacher in the Armenian schools (Mikoyan 1988: 44–5). Armenian nationalism was most commonly a product of these clerical institutions, importantly assisted by the fact that the Russian state's closure of so many Armenian schools had freed teachers for political activity. So through this conventional Armenian education, Mikoian formally learned German, Georgian, Russian, and Azeri (Ellman 2001: 141).

Mikoian volunteered to fight for the Imperial Army against the Turkish and German threats. This was quite typical of young, nationalist-minded, seminary-educated Armenians: in 1914, Armenian volunteer units were formed and sent to the Turkish front to support Russian forces' potential for liberating Armenians from Turkish rule. Mikoian joined these Armenian volunteer units and fought on the Turkish border – as an "opportunity to take part in [an Armenian] national liberation movement" (Mikoyan 1988: 33–4). Mikoian's account of fighting in support of Armenians is unique in Bolshevik memoirs because most were at pains to deplore the ethnic hatreds of World War I. But his response was typical for segments of the Armenian community. On the German declaration of war on Russia, the Armenian clerical establishment asked that Armenian *vilayets* in Anatolia be subsumed under a single Christian governor-general and that Armenians under Turkish rule be assisted (Kazemzadeh 1951: 24–5). Armenians were the only group, in fact, to engage in both diplomatic and quasi-independent military activities during the war; Georgians served in the Russian armies on the same basis as other nationalities with a somewhat lesser stake in events; and the Azerbaijanis were exempted from military service and generally remained inactive, despite perhaps hoping for a Russian defeat (Kazemzadeh 1951: 24–31).

Mikoian volunteered during the war because of his Armenian nationalist and anti-Turkish sentiments, something that likely also solidified his geopolitical imperial commitments. He viewed the Russian Empire as a guarantor of Armenian survival. Years later, he wrote that he had been overwhelmed by the news of the Armenian genocide in 1915, and that socialist class analysis and Bolshevism's class ideology resonated with him, so he joined the CP the same year (Mikoyan 1988: 37–8). Yet his commitment to imperial boundaries predated this, and it had more to do with ethnopolitical realities than with Lenin's class analysis. Mikoian's silence on the Armenian genocide at the time and his failure to write of any political affiliations suggest that he may have been most likely a Dashnak. Narimanov's assessment of Mikoian's nationalist politics was likely accurate: the antidote to Armenian problems lay more in socialism's political implications than in its class analysis.

After the war, Mikoian attended the Echmiadzin Theological Academy where he remained politically active and began to write for the SD press (Prokhorov 1969–78: 222). How, precisely, he came to Bolshevism is murky. He was active among soldiers, and by this time Bolshevism was no longer a part of the illegal underground. So in early 1917, he withdrew (or was expelled) from the academy and went to Tiflis to work on the Bolshevik committee (Granat 1989: 543). Friends tried to convince him to attend university, but he refused (Ellman 2001: 141). As we have seen, the leaderships of the Bolshevik Tiflis and Baku committees were multiethnic, yet Bolsheviks in Baku had few Armenian-speakers to compete with the Dashnaks, so Dzhaparidze recruited him as one of the few activists who could speak to Armenian oil field workers (Mikoyan 1988: 64, 73–4). So Mikoian headed the Baku Committee where worker-capitalist conflict was growing because of the increasingly important – and now internationalized – oil industry. Not only was there great diversity in the active political parties and a plethora of competing ethnic and class claims,[16] but multiethnic capital was also experiencing ethnic tensions. So Baku's Bolsheviks and Mensheviks remained organizationally unified, and Mikoian correctly noted that the key issue for the Bolsheviks in Baku was the ethnic one – both because it undermined class unity and because workers had difficulties clearly identifying the enemy (Mikoyan 1988: 73–4).

Mikoian was wounded in the repression of the Müsavatist nationalist uprising in 1918, but he continued organize Baku workers' "international friendship societies" for the various ethnic groups: he considered the need to attract Azerbaijanis to the Soviet cause particularly crucial because of the threat of a German-Turkish invasion of Baku (Mikoyan 1988: 110–11). Once again, the basis for ethnic cooperation remained geopolitical. In the same year he fought as a Brigade Commissar in the Caucasian Red Army against German-Turkish military offensives (Prokhorov 1969–78: 222; Mikoyan 1988: 124–33). So for a second time, when it mattered, his underlying commitment to the empire's geopolitical integrity was unqualified. His opposition to the SRs, Mensheviks, Dashnaks, and Müsavatists had less to do with ideological positions on class, the feasibility of social revolution in Russia, or nationalist-socialist disagreements. Rather, his opposition was rooted in a *rossiiskii* geopolitics: the nationalist-inflected parties were counterrevolutionary because they had closed ranks with the Entente powers, and this was treasonous to the new Soviet empire's integrity (see discussion in Mikoyan 1988: 167–8 and passim). Mikoian consistently supported Russian reoccupation, not Armenian independence.

Miasnikov

If Mikoian was a nationalist before becoming a Bolshevik partly because of his early experiences in seminary, for Miasnikov, Armenian-Azerbaijani ethnopolitics were at the core of his early experiences and first radicalization. He was born in 1886 in Nakhichevan in Yerevan *guberniia*. Historically a Safavid administrative center, it came under Russian rule with the Treaty of Turkmanchai. By 1897, slightly less than two-thirds of its inhabitants were Azerbaijani, and they held most of the local administrative posts (Altstadt

---

[16] Notably the Bolsheviks, Azerbaijani Hümmetists, Iranian immigrant SD Adaletists, Mensheviks, Azerbaijani nationalist Müsavatists, Armenian nationalist Dashnaks, and, the most numerous, SRs.

1992: 30–1, 92). The region was ethnopolitically complex: it was designated part of the Armenian Yerevan *guberniia* for Tsarist purposes, with the result that Russo-Armenian relations became critically important for the minority Armenians. So Miasnikov's family was part of a substantial ethnic minority in an otherwise Azerbaijani city. They came from a lower-middle-class family, but his father died when Miasnikov was young (Granat 1989: 558). Official sources claim his father had been a small merchant (Prokhorov 1969–78: 180), and although this occupational designation does not specify the type of activity or the level of the family's wealth, they would anyway have suffered a considerable reversal after the death of the breadwinner (see discussion in Granat 1989: 558).

Miasnikov attended four years at an Armenian parish school. As noted, parish schools were non-tuition-based and therefore permitted children of families with modest means to receive primary education. The curriculum was rigid, and the school disciplined, and Miasnikov wrote that he struggled with language studies because he only spoke a "Nakhichevan dialect," a mixture of Armenian, Russian, and Turkish (Granat 1989: 558). He then enrolled in the Nakhichevan Armenian Seminary, and by age thirteen he was living on his own. In 1901, at age fifteen, he joined radical student groups of "cultural and revolutionary character" (Prokhorov 1969–78: 180; Granat 1989: 558). These groupings were loosely associated with the nationalist Dashnaks, because social democracy had not yet penetrated the area, and they were Armenian and Azerbaijani in composition. In fact, as late as 1904–05, Miasnikov was "briefly under the influence of nationalist revolutionary trends" (see Granat 1989: 558, although not included in Prokhorov 1969–78). So in all likelihood, Miasnikov, like Mikoian, was involved in nationalist radical politics before becoming a Bolshevik.

Miasnikov only joined the CP in 1906, although he continued activism in other groupings while in *gimnaziia* in Moscow at the Lazarev Institute of Eastern Languages – a school that famously produced nationalist revolutionaries. The three key Armenian educational institutions were the Neresian Academy in Tiflis, the Academy in Etchmiadzin, and the Lazarev Academy for Oriental Languages in Moscow – though in practice the first two served as teacher-training schools and trained Armenian-language teachers, journalists, and writers in essentially nationalist subjects (Ter Minassian 1983: 147–8). Miasnikov wrote that he was gripped by revolutionary events in 1905 in Moscow, that they guided him to social democracy, and that he remained indifferent to the ethnic violence in Yerevan (Granat 1989: 558). So his earliest radicalism was in Armenian cities and effectively nationalist in content. Nationalist activism continued through his first years in a Moscow *gimnaziia*, after which he became involved in Russian social democratic politics in 1905. This sequence was similar to Mikoian's and suggests that Miasnikov experienced the 1905 revolution in the imperial center against a backdrop of Russian, urban worker radicalism, not in Yerevan amid the region's ethnopolitical violence.

Except for brief periods, then, from 1905 to 1917, Miasnikov's political life was largely outside Armenia and removed from South Caucasia's ethnopolitics. He was involved in workers' groups in Rostov in 1906, arrested in Moscow the same year, escaped, and fled to the South Caucasus where he joined both the leftist Dashnaks and the Baku Bolshevik underground at the same time. It was normal to be affiliated with more than one radical political mobilization simultaneously, even if they were ideologically incompatible – and one could still claim membership in the CP from 1906 (Prokhorov 1969–78: 180). In the years of Tsarist reaction, Miasnikov completed a degree in economics at the Moscow University's Law Faculty, despite extensive political activism (Prokhorov 1969–78: 180; Granat 1989: 558).

Between 1912 and 1914, he was employed as an assistant barrister and a freelance journalist. In 1914, he returned to the Caucasus and was drafted into the Russian army, where he served until the Revolution (Prokhorov 1969–78: 180; Granat 1989: 558). For the first two years of the Revolution, Miasnikov was active in Belarusia on the western front, editing the Bolshevik paper and preparing for the seizure of power in Minsk. Except for a brief period in Baku in 1906 following an arrest, his activity was largely in Moscow and Belarusia. As an Armenian loyal to the emerging Soviet empire in 1918, he was sent to the Volga front against the Czechoslovak Legion and later the Polish Front to "pacify" the multiethnic Belarusian territories (Granat 1989: 558–9). In fact, after Lenin had reprimanded the Caucasian Bolsheviks for their overly aggressive and violent tactics in the South Caucasus, he sent Miasnikov to head the Soviet Armenian government because of his more moderate party experiences in European Russia.

Armenians' Russified, Imperial-Minded Bolshevism
In summary, then, the political routes taken by the three Armenian Bolsheviks reflected the radicalizing effects of Tsarist exclusionary and dissimilatory Russification policies, particularly in its educational policies. They also suggest that while their common routes from a nationalist politics to a Russian-inflected socialism were no doubt a response to the homogenizing policies of the Russian state and local ethnopolitics, both in their socialist and nationalist commitments, they were underpinned by a geopolitical loyalty to the empire's territorial integrity. Radicalism used socialism as a defense against national oppression more than as a stage in economic development, but those (like Shaumian) who argued these positions through the prism of a Russified outlook usually joined the SDs or SRs (Ter Minassian 1983: 179).

For instance, it is impossible to understand Mikoian's political radicalism, first nationalist and then socialist, outside of the geopolitics of the region and outside of his fear of Turkish occupation. His politics was perhaps mostly driven by the geopolitical relationship between Armenians and the Russian state, almost consistently to the exclusion of both rural and urban class conflict, and largely to the exclusion of Armenian-Azerbaijani tensions, except as they affected the wider geostrategic relationship. Both class and ethnic conflict were read through a geopolitical prism whose key imperative was the preservation of imperial borders. It was for this commitment that Mikoian volunteered twice to fight to save the empire.

After 1905, Shaumian was almost exclusively in the South Caucasus where, like Stalin and Ordzhonikidze, he had become a typical revolutionary, organizer, and activist of the interior (Ter Minassian 1983: 171). Yet his writings and political radicalism reflected not so much the views of a radical of the interior as that of a middle-class Armenian whose activism was almost exclusively outside of Armenia. His political radicalism had already been formed in the empire's Russified schools, in Latvia, in Berlin, and in Tiflis. In establishing Soviet power, Shaumian assisted in the suppression of Dashnaks, of anti-Soviet Müsavatists, and rightist socialist parties by consistently supporting *rossiiskii* solutions in political arrangements. Shaumian, too, read South Caucasian politics through his imperial experiences.

In this respect, Miasnikov's commitment to the empire's territorial integrity differed from Mikoian's, but it was similar to Shaumian's: much of Miasnikov's Russification had taken place in the context of radical political activity in Moscow among students, initially Armenian and then Russian, while Mikoian's radicalism had been almost entirely in the South Caucasus. Like many young Jewish radicals, Armenian radicals also acculturated and Russified in the company of other acculturating and Russifying Armenians, where support for the empire's territorial integrity was not seen as disloyal to Armenian aspirations. Moreover, because Mikoian remained largely in the South Caucasus, his politics and wartime loyalties derived most directly from Armenians' geopolitical concerns. Most of Miasnikov's pre-1917 political activism was not only outside Armenia but also outside the Caucasus.

The South Caucasus balkanized into ethnopolitical groups: Georgian Mensheviks, Armenian Dashnaks, and Azerbaijani Müsavatists. As geopolitical events and imperial policies worked their way through local ethnopolitics, identities sharpened, and they viewed each other more distinctly. But commitments were not to a Russian or imperial culture; they were anyway not Russified or assimilated in the same way as Jews or Ukrainians. For the Armenians in particular, the commitment was to the geopolitical empire, not the cultural empire. By 1916, it was clear that Armenian fate would be tied to the Russian Empire's success in the war, and middle-class Armenians and Kadets became outspoken defenders of Russian expansionism, understood as the annexation of Turkish Armenia (Suny 1993b: 120–1).

Conclusion

The South Caucasus had complex ethnic and religious patterns of coexistence and Russian colonization, with intricate multiethnic stratifications of workers, peasants, craftsmen, industrial workers, intelligentsia, and impoverished nobilities and aristocracies, and with geopolitical insecurities and centuries of foreign conquest at the intersection of competing empires. The Bolsheviks' political radicalizations have to be understood within these borderland realities, where elites were Russified in imperial institutions with commitments to *rossiiskii* politics and empire, but where they were also resentful of autocracy and fearful of geopolitical instabilities and ethnic violence.

With the exception of Stalin, the Georgian Bolsheviks in this elite were characterized by experiences of relative rural poverty, linguistic Russification, a certain access to the professions, and activism in multiethnic mobilizations. And with the exception of Narimamov, South Caucasian Bolsheviks' attraction to a Russianized socialism reflected certain geostrategic realities. Bolshevism here did not produce any real internationalists. With few good geopolitical options, their commitments to a universalist political order were more purely territorial, not cultural or internationalist like those of the Ukrainian or Jewish Bolsheviks: they sought a stable and ecumenical empire – rooted in noncolonial imperial ideals – in the context of religious, ethnic, and geopolitical tensions and instabilities along the empire's Persian and Ottoman frontiers. As class, ethnic, and geopolitical grievances infused each other in complex ways, these borderland elites sought to redefine their positions and identities at the new imperial center of power. Bolshevism's class-universalism was in some sense less important in this context than its organizational or mobilizational ecumenicalism and ethnic tolerance. Here the elective affinity between Bolshevism's revolutionary narrative or ideology and the movement's social carriers resonated most in the ways in which the ideology actually organized materially: it politically embedded in those social locations where imperial, *rossiiskii*, or multiethnic social needs were often the most acute.

It is worth stressing again that Bolshevism was the region's least popular revolutionary option (though less so when organizationally integrated with Menshevism). But as in Ukraine, it was also the region's most socioethnically complex political movement. South Caucasian Bolshevism was the most *rossiiskii* or imperial-minded in leadership composition, even though it aimed much of its rank-and-file recruitment at ethnic Russian workers and settlers. Ethnic conflict in the South Caucasus presented any political movement with substantial political, organizational, and mobilizational problems if they were to expand their base, because socioethnic groups ranged from the tribal to the highly urbanized, with skilled Russian workers, unskilled Azerbaijanis and Georgians, and semi-skilled Armenians all combining crafts and newer industry as worker-craftsmen (see discussions in Jones 2005: 83–9, 96; Rieber 2005: 22–4). Most rural migrants to Baku or Tiflis organized around ethnic networks, and with very few large factories but lots of smaller shops, mobilizational strategies were similar to those of Lithuania: they sought to bring together workers, migrants, peasants, artisans, and traders of all ethnicities.

Most Georgians, moreover, thought of themselves as one of the many ethnic groups within the Georgian nation, so Georgian socialism had to develop a broader, but still coherent, Georgian nationalist narrative, while at the same time conceding that their geopolitical future was best protected within the territorial Russian Empire. This placed a premium on uniting the working classes without regard to ethnicity, and indeed their membership in the RSDLP embodied precisely this kind of imperial-minded commitment (see discussion in Service 2005: 46, 58). These structural realities were especially true of Georgian Menshevism: the Georgian rural intelligentsia generally accepted the empire's borders, even as they had few prospects for social mobility (Jones 2005: 2). Armenians were even less inclined to seek independence and even more fearful of geopolitical abandonment, while a segment of the Azerbaijani intelligentsia sought a noncolonial and multicultural political configuration in the South Caucasus. Rieber (2005) argues that Stalin's identity modularity or complexity was central to Bolshevism's political mobilization in South Caucasia. I think this was also perhaps true of the wider movement.

In short, ethnic-class positions, relationships to the imperial state and its institutions, and local ethnopolitics combined to define the particular social worlds of these Bolsheviks. The key substantive argument is that their commitments to a Russian-inflected and *rossiiskii* revolutionary ideology were products of very specific social locations – locations that facilitated the emergence of a multiethnic intelligentsia committed to saving the empire in the South Caucasus in a political movement of *rossiiskii*-oriented, but politically excluded, borderland elites who sought a place at the center of a newly reconstituted "class empire."

But their political radicalism also reflected key features of the imperial strategies outlined in Chapter 2. Because policies were status-particularistic and not applied to the South Caucasus's nationalities *as* nationalities, the shape and character of competing political radicalisms reflected not only complicated ethnopolitics, but also the socioethnic groups' varying relationships to the imperial state. Those inclusionary policies that incorporated certain minority elites into imperial bureaucracies (e.g., Georgian and Azerbaijani nobilities) worked in opposition to those dissimilatory or exclusionary policies of enforced cultural Russification (e.g., Armenian seminaries and Azerbaijani literary censorship) and those policies around religion directed at splitting traditional religious elites from reformist, modernizing elites. Notably, Mikoian, Miasnikov, and, to a lesser extent, Stalin were nationalists – and all three were products of the region's seminaries, not the empire's Russian schools. Tsarist policies differentially affected the experiences of class and ethnicity in ways that made them more receptive to either the class elements of nationalist politics (the Dashnaks) or to the nationalist elements of socialist politics (the Mensheviks). And these dynamics contingently affected Bolshevik routes to a Russian-inflected class-universalist movement.

8

The Russian Bolsheviks

Despite the predominance of ethnic minorities within Bolshevism, the Russians were the largest single contingent. Thirty-nine (or 42 percent) members of the Bolshevik elite were ethnic Russian. If the ethnic-minority Bolsheviks were overrepresented among the middling and upper classes, and if they were generally drawn from the elite strata of the empire's minorities, then by contrast, the basic class composition of the ethnic Russians closely mirrored that of Russians across the empire more generally. Of all the political parties and movements in revolutionary Russia, Bolshevism was among the most working-class in its leadership elite, and it had a very notable gentry element (Lane 1975). Most (twenty-three) were peasant-workers with a smaller number of educated middle-class members and service noble or "distinguished citizens." But for a better understanding of the social mechanisms of their political radicalization, and their place in the Bolshevik revolutionary movement, it is necessary to move beyond traditional accounts of class radicalism. The Bolshevik revolutionary movement did have a Russian inflection, but it was not Russified or Russianized and contained within it a great deal of ethnic, social, and political diversity. Much of this ethnic restraint, this chapter argues, was attributable to the identities and experiences of the ethnic Russians themselves. Put differently, the ways in which the ethnic Russians defined themselves was an important limiting condition to Bolshevism's core identity.

The scholarly literature on Russia's workers and intelligentsia is naturally enormous, and my analysis does not challenge the basic premises of standard interpretations: most peasants-turned-workers were radicalized because of economic exploitation and poor working conditions, wartime deprivations, the long-term effects of emancipation settlements, severe political repression of the right to organize, and general illiberal treatment by the Tsarist state. In short, they were drawn to Bolshevism's class politics as a result of class conflict, anticapitalism, political exclusion, or police repression (on this very large literature, see especially Haimson 1964, 1965; Koenker 1981; Bonnell 1983; Mandel 1983; Smith 1983; McDaniel 1988; Koenker and Rosenberg 1989; Steinberg 2002; Badcock 2007). And although the relative leadership roles of workers versus *intelligenty* are still contested, the consensus is nevertheless that it was broadly a two-class mobilization. Similarly, the Russian educated classes, intelligentsia, and nobility-service aristocracy have been the subject of substantial scholarly treatment, in particular regarding their political alienation from (or dependence on) the Russian state, their social weakness, their civic associationalism, the missing or weak middle class, their identification with (or rebellion from) autocracy and its geopolitical successes and failures, and their attraction to politics of both left and right (see, inter alia, Raeff 1984; Hosking 1997; Lieven 1989, 2000; Bradley 2002).

And yet until recently, a comparatively less analyzed aspect of their social worlds has been the extent to which *russkii* (ethnic Russian) and *rossiiskii* (imperial Russian) identities intersected with peasant, worker, *intelligent*, and noble identities (but see Lohr 2003; Sanborn 2003; and Smith 2008: 190, ch. 4, who argues that class and national identities were "mutually reinforcing and mutually counterposed"). So this chapter locates the politics of the Russian Bolsheviks along both class and ethnic axes. After outlining important contextual elements impinging on their identities and social worlds more generally, I separately consider those Russian Bolsheviks of peasant-worker origin and those from the intelligentsia and service-nobility.

In doing so, I make three substantive claims. First, the fact that tolerance (and, in many cases, acceptance) of diverse ethnic, cultural, and religious backgrounds was an integral part of the revolutionary movement's mobilizational identity was largely a result of the imperial-mindedness that characterized the ethnic Russians' identities and commitments. Put negatively, the ethnic Russian Bolsheviks were not nationalists. Second, although the interplay of class and ethnic origins was delicately calibrated across the Bolshevik elite as a whole, there was some truth to Slezkine's (1994: 434) claim that a "Russian could benefit from being a proletarian," whereas a "non-Russian could benefit from being a non-Russian." In fact, class tensions in Russian society in key social locations were important in inhibiting the successful mobilization of a cross-class Russian nationalism. And third, the relationship between the Russians and the ethnic minorities within Bolshevism was itself emblematic of the revolutionary movement's leadership dynamics: rank-and-file revolutionaries, the shock troops of the movement, were mostly ethnic Russian, and yet they willingly followed what was clearly and openly a predominantly non-Russian leadership. This imperial, *rossiiskii* quality – both within the leadership of the movement and between the movement's leadership and its followers – is suggestive not only of the weakness of Russian nationalism in 1917, but also of the appealing contrast between a tolerant *rossiiskii* orientation over a Russifying, nationalizing Tsarism. Bolshevism represented a better embodiment of some of the qualities of the imperial state, even for the ethnic Russians. In a mobilization committed to salvaging the empire's integrity, they fought the burdens of an illiberal empire, but did not seek its dissolution.

I contextualize these claims in three key imperial strategies outlined in Chapter 2, which I elaborate in the section that follows. The first involved the failure of the assimilatory Russification of the empire's titular nation. This contributed to a distinctive relationship between nation and empire in the imperial core. Depending on social location, it also contributed to rightist nationalist and leftist *rossiiskii*-minded routes to politics. The second related strategy involved the ways in which identity regimes and social ascriptions – as they affected ethnic Russians – were bound up with complicated and even fearful worries about the fragility of Russianness. This resulted in the ethnicization of imperial ascriptions and the detachment of ethnicity from *soslovie*. And third, the Russian peasantry was particularly affected by Tsarist policies toward its Orthodox subjects and by Orthodoxy's relationship to Russianness and to the empire. These broad imperial policy patterns gave shape, force, and direction to radical politics on the left and to reactionary or conservative political movements on the right. But the socioethnic locations than funneled revolutionaries into an antistate, yet *rossiiskii*, socialist movement sharply delimited those that inequitably sustained the burdens of empire from those that did not.

Imperial Strategies and Russian Radicalism

The first relevant set of imperial policies involved the relative failure of assimilatory Russification, or nation-building strategies, to the limited extent that they were attempted. Key to the ethnic Russians' involvement in a universalist political mobilization is a more general contextual framing of the relationship between the core nation and its diverse domains. Moving away from traditional explanations of autocracy and backwardness, the emergent scholarly consensus is that Russian nationhood was variously impeded, shaped, or inextricably bound by its imperial and colonial ambitions. Indeed, even Russian ethnographers at the time argued that the empire's diversity contributed to its lack of economic development (Clay 1995: 45–6). Hosking (1997: 478–81) argues that Russian nationhood was imperfectly or incompletely constructed because it was an empire. Viewed as a multiethnic service state, Russian nationalism was neither civic nor ethnic, because "nationhood had to be generated partly in opposition to the empire bearing its name...the effort required to mobilize revenues and raise armies for the needs of the empire entailed the subjection of virtually the whole population, but especially the Russians, to the demands of state service, and thus enfeebled the creation of the community associations which commonly provide the basis for the civic sense of nationhood" (Hosking 1998: xxiv). Suny (1995: 191), too, argues that in building an empire, Russia failed to create a nation. And Szporluk (1997: 65–6) notes that the Russian nation contributed to the fall of the empire because it had no identity distinct from empire and so it failed to solve the "Russian question." Russia's experience, in short, was one of incomplete nation-making. The implications of this fractured identity were also understood at the time. As Count Witte observed:"[T]he big mistake of our decades-long policy is that we still today do not understand that there hasn't been a Russia from the time of Peter the Great and Catherine the Great. There has been a Russian Empire" (quoted in Suny 2001: 55–6).

This said, however, certain features of Russian nationalism in the forms that it did take deserve highlighting. Most immediately, Russia was essentially a quasi-peasant nation in the fourth time zone, and Russian nationalism dates its political phase to the last decades of the nineteenth century, against an established political and geopolitical context of nearly 400 years of imperial consolidation. A national identity was only problematically fused into a long-standing imperial identity, so the imaginative geography, or mental maps, of Russian nationalism were conflated with empire. This meant that the constituent parts of the empire were appropriated in different ways: in the west it involved counting Ukrainians and Belarusians as Russians for census purposes; on the Volga, the fragmentation of minorities would solidify the dominant position of ethnic Russians; and Siberia's status would be changed from colony to homeland (Miller 2003: 21; 2004). In fact, Tsarist military elites latterly sought to transform the empire into a nation-state precisely because it would strengthen geopolitical power and autocracy (Sanborn 2003; Viterbo 2007). They considered this the key lesson of the nineteenth-century age of empire. And yet despite this late blooming nationalism-in-service-of-empire, the bureaucratic elite that had run the empire for 400 years was essentially an ethnically diverse *Staatsvolk*: the incorporation of non-Russian nobilities was so deeply insitutionalized that, despite its ethnic heterogeneity, it was nevertheless ideologically homogenous as it consistently identified with the imperial state.

Moreover, Russian nationalism was neither, to borrow Gellner's (1983) model, a high culture that was diffused or a low culture that was universalized. There were no coherent nation-making projects or clearly articulated Russification policies to nationalize non-Russians around the idea of the nation, as there had been in France. But neither was there such a nation-making program in Russia itself designed to make Russian peasants into Russians. This was especially notable in rural education. Serfdom and emancipation were much harsher in the Russian heartland than in the borderlands, leaving the Russian peasantry both non-Russianized and deeply suspicious of the Russian educated, propertied, and landed classes. Neither Populists, nor Tsars, nor Church effectively served as spokesmen for the Russian *narod*. Moreover, the Russian middle social strata were unable to articulate a national identity or speak for the nation, as had the French Third Estate, the towns, and the bourgeoisie (Hosking 1997: 319, 479, and ch. 5). More generally, of course, neither a state-directed "nationalism from above" on the Prussian model nor a social-movement "nationalism from below" could develop in a state that feared any societal association (the typology is Hall's 1993). Tsarist bureaucrats were even anxious about civil society's participation in the cause of Russification (Dolbilov 2004). In fact, Tsarist elites "looked upon every autonomous expression of nationalism with fear and suspicion," so Russian nationalism essentially became a problem of cultural identity for elites (Rogger 1962: 253, 256, 262). The existential fear of any form of societal mobilization – even a conservative *Russian* one – made it impossible to create civil institutions for either a civic or an ethnic nationalism. This inability or failure to pursue policies of assimilatory Russification among ethnic Russians themselves would be felt in the politics and social identities of the revolutionary years.

To be sure, in the last years of the empire, the monarchy did seek to appropriate the idea of the nation and identify itself with a Russian monarchical nationalism (Wortman 2000, 2003). Most rural and lower-class Russians identified with the monarchy, which did have a certain hold on the popular imagination (Lieven 1998: 256), and there were substantial efforts within the military to build a multiethnic nation using family, land, and fraternity as unifying identities (Sanborn 2003: chs. 2, 3). Yet there was a certain disconnect. Imperial Russian's high culture was European, cosmopolitan, and borrowed (Suny 1995; Hosking 1997), and of course this was precisely its potent assimilatory appeal among the empire's educated ethnic minorities. So the general social weakness of Russian nationalism, and the significant cultural gap between elites and peasantry, together with the sense of burden felt in the Russian core (Lieven 2000: 253–4, 384–6), meant that ethnic Russians across the empire generally had only a weak sense of Russianness, at every socioeconomic level. And indeed, the Russian Bolsheviks' biographies suggest very little sense of *russkii* self-ascription.

The second set of imperial policies involved identity regimes and social ascriptions, which implicated those Russians situated outside the empire's core as the social carriers of Russification. They often did have stronger and more distinctive ethnic or *russkii* identifications because of their more intimate experiences with the empire's diversity. The core constituents of conservative Russian nationalism were wealthy, landowning nobles of both country and St. Petersburg court. They were the mainstay of the conservative and rightist political parties (see Table 2.1, Chapter 2). They stressed that Russia's collective identity inhered in the peasantry, as they clung to their inherited noble status in the face of its inevitable erosion (Lieven 1998: 257–8). But as important, albeit less often noted, was (1) the distinctive ethnic Russianness that developed among Russian settlers and administrators in the western borderlands and in the Pale, and (2) the tolerance and willing assimilationism of Russian colonists in the Siberian, Volga-Ural, or Kazakh regions of the empire.

Imperial officials had long associated different ethnic groups with different levels of economic and agricultural development, regularly encouraging ethnic Russians to settle in the borderlands to increase agricultural production (Steinwedel 2001: 79; Sunderland 2004). So, for instance, whereas Stolypin's combination of authoritarian reform and pragmatic conservatism (e.g., liberal support for Jewish openings) championed a particular Russian nationalism in the western borderlands, in the east he had strongly supported the colonization of Siberia – the intention was less to repress minorities than it was to protect Russian interests and to preserve the empire, because the interests of the state were often identified with Russian colonists in the borderlands (Ascher 2001: 11–12, 320–67). Policies around the "Muslim question" were similarly more concerned with social stability than with cultural transformation (Campbell 2007). In this regard, it is often argued that Russian settlers and colonizers in the peripheries (in part because they included Cossacks and Old Sectarians) did not really develop a settler mentality or a distinctive cultural identity (Starr 1978; Rieber 1994: 85). And yet for a variety of related reasons – lack of cultural confidence, Russian settlers' low educational levels, an institutionally weak Russian presence in the borderlands, the rise of regional-national identities, Russians' assimilation into regional cultures, and the geopolitical securitization of borderland ethnicities – Russian settlers and imperial administrators did live in these cultural and imperial shatter zones in a kind of permanent insecurity and anxiety. While no systematic study on this exists, we know that they drove much of the social momentum for Russification (see, inter alia, Jersild 2002; Khodarkovsky 2002; Sunderland 2004; Breyfogle 2005). Indeed, Russianness itself was sometimes defined as a result of these encounters, especially in the Steppe and in the Muslim east; in the image of a "country colonizing itself," "wild fields" of nomadic inhabitants were transformed into "Russian spaces" of peasant farmers (Khodarkovsky 2002: ch. 3; Werth 2002; Sunderland 2004).

Often Russian administrators and elites who emigrated to the empire's peripheries, particularly the western borderlands and the Pale, strengthened their sense of ethnic Russianness and became the social carriers of forms of ethnic Russian nationalism and Russification: anti-Semitism, innovations in policies excluding Jews, Poles or Catholics, conservative rightism, Russificatory policies, various colonial policies (Werth 2002; Breyfogle 2003), illiberal economic practices and policies, and Great Russian nationalism itself – all originated *among ethnic Russians in the imperial peripheries*, not in the imperial center. Most of the empire's Russian nationalist administrators were not from St. Petersburg, Moscow, or the Central Russian provinces, but from the western borderlands (Vilna, Bessarabia, Volhynia, and Kiev). The Russian Nationalist Party received most of its support from the southwest, initially against Polish landed dominance and later against German landholding (Lohr 2003: 25–7). Particularly after 1905, the western borderlands became strongholds of nationalist and rightist parties, anti-Semitism, and Polonophobia (Rawson 1995; Weeks 1996). Russian landlords in the southwest were the core constituency of the Russian Nationalist Party and of rightists in the Third and Fourth Dumas. Innovations in Judeophobia (initially borrowed from Polish rule) came from Governor-Generals and other officials in the western provinces, not from St. Petersburg elites (Weeks 1996). Russification in the North Caucasus was a product of assertive, yet frightened, imperial administrators in the region (Jersild 2002). In the northwest provinces of Belarusia and Lithuania, the more local the decision making among Russian administrators regarding Russification policies, the more radical they became – and conversely, most liberalizing moves toward Jews came from St. Petersburg (Staliunas 2007). Demands for restrictions on non-Russian commerce and trade (toward Jews, Germans, and Armenians) came from Russian merchants and financiers in the borderlands.

Pogroms were primarily a southern Russian or Ukrainian phenomenon socially carried by migrant Russians from the inner provinces (Kuromiya 1998: 47), with Ukrainian workers, peasants, and agricultural colonists responding to calls from groups like the Black Hundreds who set out in reactionary defense of Fatherland and Tsar (Klier and Lambroza 1992). And the most influential proponents of official nationality in the early nineteenth century were most often *non-Russians*. In short, a very particular kind of ethnic Russian national identity did emerge from the empire's borderlands, and its impact was directly and often consequentially felt on both Tsarist nationalities policies and on political mobilizations of the left and right.

Moreover, a contributing lack of cultural confidence should also not be underestimated. Until the nineteenth century, with the development of a Russian belles lettres, most of the empire's high culture was western-derived or borrowed – as, of course, was much of its ruling elite (Hosking 1997). But the Russian population in general, not just educated society, also came to identify with this lack of cultural confidence. Popular literature depicted tales of losing one's Russianness: those ethnic Russians in the armies, or in the civil service, or settlers in the borderlands carried with them Orthodoxy and faith in the Tsar, but they were inevitably cut off and tempted into losing their nationality – either seduced by exotic delights or alienated by hardship and captivity (Brooks 1985: ch. 6; Slezkine 1997). As Brooks argues, under this conception of Russianness there could be no expatriates, only apostates. This was particularly true in the Muslin borderlands, because Muslim (often Tatar) culture was seen as the alternative to Russian culture, and worries intensified over Volga Tatars' influences over local non-Russian populations (Werth 2002; Campbell 2007). Popular literature emphasized the vulnerability of Russians far from their cultural homeland and, by extension, the fragility of their Russianness.

These cultural worries were lent further credence by demographic evidence. Russians "nativized" in the mixed settlements of the borderlands, in the Siberian North (and this pointedly even included Cossacks), in the northern Caucasus, and in the Volga-Ural region; on the Kazakh steppe, some even converted to Islam (see Jersild 2002; Werth 2002; Breyfogle 2005; Mamedov 2008). When ethnographers discovered that Russian settlers were assimilating into Siberian cultures, Russianness itself became problematized (Slezkine 1997). Colonized by ethnic Russians, and with long histories of cohabitation, the cultural boundaries between Russian and non-Russian, or conqueror and local, were blurred. Only the *soslovie* system seemed to have preserved the Russianness of the colonists: on census language questions, for example, Siberian communities often responded "peasant," but Russian colonists sometimes gave their estate membership to affirm their Russianness (Slezkine 1994; Cadiot 2005: 443).

In short, Russian settlers' assimilation or nativization was a blatant subversion of imperial rules of assimilation, and it threw into open question the weakness and fragility of Russian national identity (Sunderland 1996: 824–5). The first Russian settlers or colonists in Iakutsk *oblast*, for instance, were Cossacks, government officials, missionaries, peasants, tavern keepers, and petty traders, and their own weak identification with Russian nationalism facilitated their eventual assimilation (see Sunderland 1996: 822–3, but compare with Miller 2004b). In the South Caucasus, religious sectarians and colonizers played an important role in the Russian imperial agenda as exiles and sometimes empire-builders along the imperial margins (Breyfogle 2005); and the settlement laws of 1896–7 in the North Caucasus allowed only Orthodox settlers of ethnic Russian background to immigrate to ensure stable empire-building (Jersild 2002). In the Volga-Urals, by contrast, intermarriage and ethnic mixing were encouraged because they assisted in the assimilation of non-Russians into Russian culture (as they sometimes did in the Caucasus, Mostashari 2003); yet in the Siberian east it was discouraged because of fears that Russians would become Iakuts or Ostiaks, or otherwise lose their racial and cultural Russianness. In sum, Tsarism's complicated, fearful, and contradictory conception of Russianness implicated those Russians outside the empire's core and, in turn, the politics of nation and class that emerged.

The third related imperial strategy was the evolving relationship between Orthodoxy and the Russian nation, and indeed the Russian Empire's religious policies more broadly. Those who held modernist conceptions of Russianness generally stood against those who derived Russianness from Orthodoxy, but in the later years of the empire Orthodoxy became, for imperial elites, an important pillar of political legitimacy because of the erosion of the secular foundations of autocracy (e.g., the person of the ruler, the prosperity of the people, and international prestige). To take one example, the Church had only held four canonizations in 200 years, compared to six merely in the last two decades of the empire – with many more in preparation (Freeze 1996). The aim was to give both the regime and autocracy a new sense of legitimacy to distract from its domestic and foreign failures. But the state handled it so clumsily, and it so humiliated the Orthodox Church, that it alienated the clerical establishment and prompted the latter's own quiet revolution in 1912 (Freeze 1996). Tsarist elites' re-sacralization policy became inadvertently subversive. In important ways, then, Orthodoxy's legitimacy declined with that of the state (Lieven 1998: 257).

Yet Orthodoxy did have a hold among certain segments of the Russian peasant population, whose adherents were culturally self-assured and confident in terms of their superiority over other religions and cultures. This did not translate into either a strong identification with ethnic Russianness or with imperialness, however: the church played a weak role in fusing the political *rossiiskii* with the cultural *russkii*. While it did assist in creating a sense of national community, it was a culturally embedded *Russian* religion and lacked universalist appeal (Lieven 1998: 257; 2000: 275). So it was only very weakly able to offer a *rossiiskii* identification beyond its ethnic Russian base. Of course the degree to which Russianness derived from Orthodoxy posed a significant problem for assimilation. Certainly a non-Russian noble family would be culturally assimilated or Russianized if it had converted to Orthodoxy, thereby allowing intergenerational assimilation (Lieven 1989: 33–4). Yet this was limited to the upper classes: the Orthodox Church had never been a strong proselytizer, and reliance on the religiosity of Orthodox believers among the Russian lower classes was hardly a base from which to extend assimilation. So while Orthodoxy could – and did – fuse Russian and Ukrainian peasant populations to some extent, it increasingly lost its hold on the growing educated and secularizing middle classes.

Taken together, then, these imperial strategies shaped the social worlds of the empire's Russians. And they had important effects on revolutionary politics and mobilizations, especially for those sustaining the disproportionate economic and social burdens of maintaining the empire. They profoundly shaped ethnic Russian revolutionaries' attitudes to non-Russians in the political mobilizations of both left and right. The substantive argument is that together these policies defined the outer limits of Russianness by a remarkable tolerance of diversity and a commitment to the empire itself. The social carriers of these Russian- or *rossiiskii*-oriented identities bring us to the very core of the sociology of empire, to the ethnic Russians' views of non-Russians and of "their" empire, and so to the Russian Bolsheviks' understandings of a multiethnic political movement premised on a Russian-inflected imperial-minded ideology.

The Social Composition of the Russian Bolsheviks

In social origin the Russian Bolsheviks drew from two main classes, broadly defined: two-thirds came from the peasantry-working class and one-third came from the lower and upper intelligentsia (including the clergy and the military). They drew from very specific socioethnic locations outlined in Table 2.1, Chapter 2: rural and urban working classes (many of peasant origin) and educated middle classes. Lenin and Molotov were upper-to-middling class, whereas Kalinin was lower-to-middling class. And although they would anyway have fallen within the omnibus intelligentsia, finer distinctions highlight a more general claim: ethnic Russian ascriptions were weak at every socioeconomic level, but not at each level for the same reasons.

Of those of lower-class origins, some were from the very poor, rural peasantry (e.g., Timofei Sapronov, Ivan Smirnov, Alexsandr Smirnov, Nikolai Uglanov, and Aleksei Badaev), while others were from the small propertied peasantry, or small rural capitalists (Aleksei Rykov and Fedora Sergeev), judging from their sons' and daughters' secondary schooling and university studies. Similarly, those Bolsheviks whose fathers were workers represented both the highly skilled (e.g., Viktor Nogin, Leonid Serebriakov, Kliment Voroshilov, and Vasily Mikhailov) and the unskilled peasant-worker (e.g., Andrei Andreev, Ivan Kutuzov, and Mikhail Tomskii). There were also variations among those Bolsheviks from the intelligentsia, broadly conceived. Seven were from middle-class, professional families (Andrei Bubnov, Elena Stasova, and Georgi Piatakov) or lower-middle-class, educated families (Varvara Iakovleva, Sergei Kirov, Vladimir Miliutin, and Molotov); four were from the service gentry or formally the noble estate (Lenin, Valerian Osinskii, Georgii Lomov, and Nikolai

Bukharin); two had fathers who were Orthodox priests (Mikhail Vladimirskii and Evgenii Preobrazhenskii); and one was the son of a Cossack mother and a Tsarist army officer father (Valerian Kuibyshev).

Comparing their social origins with their occupations (Appendixes A and B) yields an approximate assessment of the possibilities for social mobility: nearly all of those of peasant-worker origin remained workers, and of those that were of lower or middle-intelligentsia origin, most either practiced a profession or became professional revolutionaries. This is underscored by educational opportunities and attainments: of those in the middle classes, ten attended secondary schools (seven *gimnaziia* and three *Realschule*); overall, fifteen Russian Bolsheviks attended some advanced education (technical institutes, universities, seminaries, or military cadet training); and the lower-class Russian Bolsheviks attended state primary, rural, parish, or *zemstvo* schools. Consistent with class backgrounds and occupations, then, educational backgrounds suggest that while there was indeed some degree of social mobility for those of peasant background into the urban working classes, those whose fathers were workers tended also to be workers, while those of service-gentry or gentry origin effectively dropped into the (upper) intelligentsia. In short, social mobility was mixed: positive mobility for some (peasant origins), class reproduction for others (worker origins), and slight downward mobility for others still (gentry origins). These patterns essentially mirrored the more general trends in social mobility among similarly located ethnic Russians across the empire.

The majority of the Russian Bolsheviks were from the North-Central and Volga-Ural industrial areas, or the historic "Russian" imperial core, although there was more geographic diversity among those of middle-class origin: eight were from Central and Northern Russia, four were from the Volga-Urals, and one each from the Ukraine and Western Siberia. Overall, then, all but two of the Russian Bolsheviks (Kuibyshev from Omsk and Piatakov from Kiev) were from regions incorporated into the empire between 1462 and 1584. These were long-standing "Russian" regions with lots of historic assimilation and extensive and institutionalized cultural contacts with non-Russians, distinguishing them from regions of the empire incorporated later (the western borderlands, parts of Ukraine, or the Caucasus).

Non-Bolshevik radicalism was generally a function of both age and access: the average age of first radicalization of the middle-class Bolsheviks was seventeen, and the average age of peasant-worker Bolshevik radicalism was eighteen. But the negligible difference in age masks the different social locations of their respective political radicalizations: in *gimnazii* for those with education and in factories for the workers. Most of the peasant-worker Bolsheviks had worked for several years in their early teens before they joined radical circles, however, and they also continued to work to support themselves; none of the working-class Bolsheviks became professional revolutionaries (whereas a number of middling-class Russians did), so they joined the movement leadership in their places of employment.

Their collective biographies suggest two additional patterns. First, eight of the Bolsheviks' fathers died young or left their families to search for work: Rykov, Serebriakov, I. Smirnov, A. Smirnov, Tomskii, Voroshilov, Osinskii, and Kirov (who was raised in an orphanage). This is important not only because it was extremely common in the rural areas, but also because they each made a point of including it in their autobiographies as testament to the hardships their families had endured.[1] Second, and as noted in Chapter 3 in connection with the Jewish Bolsheviks, at least one in five Bolsheviks married someone of another ethnicity or religion – a figure higher than that of the empire as a whole. This included both those of working-class background and those from the middle or higher classes. Conversion to Orthodoxy and intermarriage were traditionally measures of integration and assimilation (Lieven 1989: 33–4), and this commonly occurred among nobilities, but not at lower levels of the social strata. So high intermarriage rates in the Russian socialist groupings also offered a form of assimilation otherwise absent among the lower and middling classes of imperial society. Therefore, on the evidence – and paradoxically for a class-based movement – within the radical mobilizations there was actually greater social closure around class than there was around ethnicity.

The Peasant-Worker Bolsheviks

In 1917, Russia's industries had an estimated 15 million to 18 million workers or hired laborers (Rosenberg 2001: 152). Bolshevism formally represented only a very small fraction, but they were typical of a segment of the ethnic Russian "worker intelligentsia" of the central regions of the empire (see, for instance, the profiles in Steinberg 2002: appendix).[2] They were largely urbanized, moderately literate, highly mobile, and politically active; born in the years of rapid industrialization at a time of social and political turmoil, they came from the large cities and small provincial towns of central Russia, often from worker fathers who died young; and their work life was characterized by lots of mobility and instability, in constant search of semiskilled wage-labor work both because of labor volatility and as a result of strike activity and political repression (Steinberg 2002: 24–7). Two Bolsheviks, I. Smirnov and A. Smirnov, were also among the many Russian workers drafted into the wartime Tsarist army, whereas another, Voroshilov, enlisted voluntarily (Haupt and Marie 1969: 257; Granat 1989: 610, 680).

So I make two general but related claims. First, canonical scholarship on class conflict had this right: there was a deeply rooted social antagonism between the Russian working and peasant classes on the one hand and the Russian

---

[1] This was not limited to the Russian Bolsheviks; it was also the case for Radek, Smilga, and Ordzhonikidze. But it was more common among the lower classes as fathers left villages in search of work or died of disease or lack of medical treatment.

[2] Steinberg's sample of sixty-two individuals is similar in social profile to the peasant-worker Bolsheviks profiled here, and many of his workers were Bolsheviks.

propertied classes on the other (Haimson 1964, 1965, 1988; Lieven 2000: 236).
The revolutionary narrative's dichotomy captured this us-versus-them rubric:
landlords versus peasants, regime versus people, and upper versus lower classes. And it may be that this social imaginary made Russian workers receptive
to class politics, given that a nationalist politics was largely unavailable as a
basis for social mobilization (see Smith 2008: 166–7 for this argument). This
meant that Russian workers could see their interests in purer class terms than
Jewish, Latvian, Polish, or Armenian workers, whose ethnic exclusions, as we
have seen, intersected with class grievances. Class mattered more distinctly and
more consequentially in routes to radicalism because social inequality in central and northern Russia did not have the sting of a cultural marker, as it did,
for instance, in the Caucasus, Ukraine, the Baltics, or the Lithuanian *kresy*.

So the second claim is that ethnic Russianness, as a mobilizational identity,
was politically muted because it was not embedded in any real social conflict.
Indeed, to the degree that Russian nationhood was identified, it *reinforced* class
antagonisms rather than cross-cut them: newly urbanized peasant-workers
were suspicious of Russian nationalism because it was socially represented by
the very landed elites, nobility, and autocratic state they viewed as the source
of class oppression. While the class narrative framed a hatred of industrialists
or capitalists (McDaniel 1988), Great Russian nationalism and class oppression were seen as mutually constitutive because they were socially carried by
roughly the same set of elites. This would ultimately translate into a great deal
of ethnic tolerance on the part of the ethnic Russian working classes, particularly in the heartland industrial regions. So not only did this define the outer
limits of the Russianness of Bolshevism in the prerevolutionary years, but it
also distinguished it (and other center and leftist mobilizations) from rightist
political movements.

Socioethnic Locations

Three general categories of workers are usually identified among the Russian
working classes: skilled workers (metalworkers), unskilled workers (women
in textiles and peasants), and the so-called worker aristocracy (skilled printers). Classical scholarship on the Russian working classes has consistently
highlighted the role of skilled workers, especially metalworkers, printers, and
artisanal workers, as the organizational shock troops of radicalism, whether
in factory committees, trade unions, or other worker organizations (see, inter
alia, Koenker 1983: ch. 2; Mandel 1983; Smith 1983; Koenker and Rosenberg
1989; Steinberg 1992; Rosenberg 2001; Koenker 2005: ch. 1). This was particularly true of the Bolsheviks. Of the revolutionaries in this elite who were
workers (and for whom there is reliable evidence), at least nine were occupationally involved in metalworking (Andreev, Badaev, Mikhail Kalinin, Nikolai
Kolotilov, Nikolai Komarov, Semen Lobov, Nikolai Kubiak, Serebriakov, and
Tomskii). Several others were involved in the railroad industry (Badaev, Kubiak,
Lobov, and I. Smirnov) or in printing (Mikhail Chudov and Vasily Mikhailov)

and textiles (Kutuzov, A. Smirnov, and Konstantin Ukhanov).[3] The railroad and metal industries of course overlapped considerably because they connected the newly industrializing Donbas region in Ukraine with the capital's locomotive industries. So geographically, most worked in the main industrial areas: in the central industrial and textile region around Moscow (Tver, Ivanovo, Kostroma, and Kaluga) as well as the cities just southwest, Orel and Smolensk;[4] the northern metallurgical region in the Urals around Perm (Ekaterinburg and Ufa);[5] St. Petersburg/Petrograd, Riga, and Vyborg;[6] the southern metallurgical region around Ekaterinoslav (Kharkov and Lugansk);[7] and in the Volga-southern Ural region around Samara and Kazan.[8]

This means that metalworking and related industries in Russia's North-Central and Volga-Ural industrial regions are the occupational and geographical locations most important to understanding the character of their politics (see also Steinberg 2002: 25). This confirms Lane's (1975) finding on an earlier cohort of Bolsheviks (those in the party between 1898 and 1907), namely that they originated mostly from Central Russia and the Urals, while the Mensheviks drew from the southern regions and the Caucasus. But this also means that this later Bolshevik revolutionary cohort mobilized along already existing regional and occupational Bolshevik strongholds, and they politically organized along existing employment networks and communities of peasant-workers. In short, this generation of Bolshevik workers were socialized into an already established political culture paved by a previous generation of radicals. But while Lane (1975) found that the earlier generation of Bolshevik SDs tended to be more downwardly mobile than the Mensheviks, for this Bolshevik cohort I do not find downward mobility, but rather class reproduction because the vast majority came from families who were either peasants or unskilled workers. Indeed, two (Rykov and Sergeev) came from propertied peasant families and rose to attend universities.[9]

---

[3] Some are listed more than once because they worked in more than one industry.
[4] Lobov, Korotkov, Kolotilov, Chudov, Kalinin, Kubiak, Mikhailov, I. Smirnov, Nogin, Ivan Rumiantsev, Nikolai Uglanov, A. Smirnov, Sapronov, Badaev, Andreev, Kutuzov.
[5] Aleksandr Beloborodov.
[6] Tomskii, Komarov.
[7] Voroshilov was the one worker from this region, and his early work experiences from age seven in the Donbas mines and railroads (before Moscow metalworking) suggest that he experienced some tension between Ukrainian and Russian workers (Granat 1989: 735; Kuromiya 1998: 51–2).
[8] Serebriakov, Ukhanov.
[9] Rykov's social origins are murky. I classify him as peasant-worker origin, but he could also be considered lower-middle class. Official sources claim his family were peasants (Lazitch 1986:410) and Okhrana arrest records categorize him in the peasant *soslovie*, though it makes no distinction regarding property (HIAPO, HQ Circular, warning list no. 110, February 1, 1905, Box 164, Index XIIId (2), Processing Intelligence, Folder 35). However, Rykov's own account noted that although his father died young of cholera, he had been a peasant and then the owner of a small capitalist enterprise (Granat 1989: 636). Yet his family must have had some property for the son

In terms of educational backgrounds, nearly all of the peasant-worker Bolsheviks received some primary schooling in the 1880s and 1890s. For those for whom there is reliable data, nine attended rural primary schools, five attended city schools, three attended parish schools, and one attended a rural *zemstvo* school. Ukhanov attended a craftsman trade school in Kostroma, Uglanov briefly attended a seminary, and Sergeev attended a *Realschule* and a Moscow technical institute (Prokhorov 1969–78: 260; Granat 1989: 727, 735). Because schooling was not compulsory, those that did attend came from peasant, craft worker, migrant, or lower-class urbanite families who sought some form of social improvement for their children. And it came with some considerable sacrifice, because for those who helped their families on the land, they could only attend school in the winter months, depending on seasonal labor needs (e.g., Kutuzov only attended two full winters of parish school) (on the general phenomenon, see Brooks 1985: 44; on Kutuzov, see Granat 1989: 473). So most attended less than four years.

While the *zemstvo* schools were the best in terms of quality, by 1905 the church parish schools were boosted by state support. Religious education was considered an official foundation of primary education in both the state and church-run schools, and it became central to the school experience. Russian teachers created mutual aid societies, the only legal form of association permitted. And they regularly became vehicles for teachers' movements with strong antigovernment biases. Indeed, those conservative Ministry inspectors who suppressed teacher radicalism were often rewarded (Seregny 1999: 168, 173).[10] On the whole, however, these schools were not effective nation-builders. Assimilatory Russification strategies simply did not apply. They did not transform peasants into either Russian citizens or Russian-minded subjects: despite notable efforts at expanding the reach of popular schooling, the imperial state fundamentally lacked the capacity or ability to construct a Russian national identity through schooling (Seregny 1999).

Most children did learn basic reading, writing, and math skills, however, and the quality of the education was actually better than is usually thought (Eklof 2010). But in this regard, popular literature often had a greater influence as a source of information than the content of the schooling curriculum (Brooks 1985: 35, 54). The spread of commercially popular prints, or *lubki*, in the decades before 1917 was primarily aimed at those newly literate peasants, former peasants, and lower-class urbanites that could now read. This literature shaped the social imagination of the lower classes. They were most successful with peasant readers, whereas serials were more suited to urban lower-class audiences, and the mass circulation press was the key forum for

to attend *gimnaziia* and Kazan University to study law, the only university that would accept him because of a record of radicalism. So the slippage among the family's actual social situation, their official *soslovie* categorization, and their self-ascription is evident.

[10] *Zemstvo* schools were generally progressive: Voroshilov's *zemstvo* teachers were Trudoviki, for instance (Granat 1989: 393).

popular opinion or politics (McReynolds 1991). They testified to a Russian working class transitioning to modernity: the emphasis was on individual mobility and possibility, and shifts from rural life to urban prosperity; they showcased an increased ability to affect social mobility and to remake oneself based on greater confidence in one's new knowledge and abilities (Brooks 1985: xvii–xix; Steinberg 2002: 37–8).

So the importance of both primary schooling and this newly accessible literature to the social experiences of the Russian peasant-workers should not be underestimated. They were eager to improve themselves beyond the circumstances of their families: daily attendance in school was strikingly high, and schooling became, in effect, an instrument for social mobility (Eklof 2010: 17). Contemporary observers noted than those with even basic schooling were less willing to endure social deprivations than were their noneducated peers; exposure to new secular primers and readers resulted in a decline in the relative prestige of both traditional rural authorities and of the Church; and a 1909–10 study concluded that schooling increased interest in the world and reduced superstition and prejudice (Brooks 1985: 56–7). They absorbed radical, humanist, and universalist ideas beyond the popular literature also, because by their own accounts, many of the worker Bolsheviks were also able to read Gorky, Lermontov, and Tolstoy.[11] This was not at all unusual among educated workers. Steinberg (2002: 31–3) notes that literary encounters were crucially important in interpreting and explaining their social lives and often prompted their own writings. But if basic education tended to erode commitments to autocracy and Orthodoxy, it did not Russify – its assimilatory or Russificatory potential remained untapped.

Social Worlds of the Russian Workers

In addition to education, however, early work in factories also characterized the Bolsheviks' experiences and first radicalisms. After 1890, children under twelve were banned from industrial labor, but within this cohort there is reliable information on the following: Andreev began working at thirteen, Badaev "as a child," Beloborodov at age fourteen, Kalinin was at the famous Putilov Factory at age sixteen, I. Smirnov around age fourteen, A. Smirnov at age seven, Tomskii at age fourteen, Uglanov at age twelve, Ukhanov at age fifteen, and Voroshilov at age seven (Prokhorov 1969–78: 147, 207–8, 610; Granat 1989: 349, 359, 420, 680, 718, 727, 735). So whereas most of the Russian Bolshevik leadership was seventeen to eighteen years old when they were radicalized, the vast majority of those of peasant-worker origin were already seasoned factory workers by 1917. This is consistent with what we know more generally about Russia's revolutionary factory workers: the youth movement in the factories tended toward Bolshevism, with 19 percent of those in the Petrograd Bolshevik Party under age twenty-one (Smith 1983: 197).

---

[11] For instance, see Voroshilov (Granat 1989: 393), Tomskii's brother (Granat 1989: 717), Kalinin (Prokhorov 1969–78: 207–8; Granat 1989: 424), and Sapronov (Granat 1989: 649).

Within this Bolshevik elite, metalworkers were the largest contingent, followed by textile workers, railroad workers, and printers – a proportional representation that mirrored that of the labor movement leadership as a whole. For instance, Chudov came from the peasantry of Tver *guberniia* and became a printer and a member of the board of the Printers Union in St. Petersburg; Mikhailov, too, was a printer (like his father) and similarly served on the board of the Moscow Printers Union (Prokhorov 1969–78: 250, 345). The complexity of the work and the requisite high levels of skill and craftsmanship – usually acquired through apprenticeships – made printers the most highly paid workers after metalworkers (Koenker 2005: ch. 1). Known for their vanguard politics and craft orientation, and characterized by moderate politics, they were primarily Menshevik but became increasingly Bolshevik during the war (Smith 1981: 47–8; Steinberg 1992; Koenker 2005: ch. 1). Their skills contrasted with those of the less educated and less skilled rural workers (Kutuzov, A. Smirnov, and Ukhanov) of the Ivanovo mill villages and textile industries (Kutuzov, for instance, who worked from age fourteen in the textile industry, and eventually became chairman of the Moscow Textile Workers' Union, Granat 1989: 473).[12] The textile industry was notable for the high proportion of women, its low literacy rates, skills and wages, and workers' ties to the land from adjacent districts. These features contributed to a distinctive homogeneity and a sharply perceived class contrast between capital and labor.

So organizationally the labor movement was stratified, although there is still debate about whether skilled metalworkers – long held to be at the vanguard of workers' radical politics – were in fact the most frequent strikers, or whether they were actually co-opted into political activism with the socialist parties (see Koenker and Rosenberg 1989). The Petrograd working class in 1917, for example, was comprised mainly of proletarianized, skilled male workers and the newer, younger peasant and female workers who maintained ties to the land (Bonnell 1983: 31–2; Smith 1983: ch. 8). The former had a greater capacity to lead a social movement because of better organizational resources and experiences, and they show up in key leadership roles in Bolshevism: Tomskii, Komarov, and Badaev, for instance, were metalworkers in the St. Petersburg-Vyborg factories in the crucial years between 1907 and 1914 (Prokhorov 1969–78: 489, 515), and Kalinin was a metalworker in the famous Putilov factory (Granat 1989: 425). Vyborg's metalworkers were famously known as the most militant and the region was highly Bolshevized: Badaev became a Bolshevik deputy to the Duma; Komarov was on the Vyborg Regional Committee of the RSDLP in 1911 and later in Petrograd organizing committees (Prokhorov 1969–78: 489); Tomskii was first involved in factory work and radical activism in St. Petersburg, and then in the Moscow area, and in 1905 he organized wage demonstrations for the Revel Professional

---

[12] Kiselev, the Belarusian Bolshevik, also worked from age fourteen as an apprentice metalworker in Ivanovo-Vosnesensk and became an SD in 1898 (Prokhorov 1969–78: 194; Granat 1989: 442).

Metalworkers Soviet before being arrested and imprisoned (Granat 1989: 718–19); and in 1906, Kalinin was a member of the Putilov Factory's union regional committee, which he considered to be one of the most technologically advanced and revolutionary factories (Granat 1989: 425).

When Tomskii and Komarov were active in St. Petersburg in 1909, the overwhelming majority of Bolsheviks were workers (Smith 1999: 186–8). But interestingly, in 1908–09, the Bolsheviks also had proportionally more high-level Okhrana spies than any other political grouping: four of the five members of the Bolshevik St. Petersburg CC were Okhrana agents (Leggett 1981: ch. 1). These workers lived in the same industrial suburbs where they worked, famously creating a distinctive and relatively concentrated urban workforce subculture (Hogan 1993: 8, 26). Occupational location mattered to politics: the "hot" shops, or the foundries where the work was extremely heavy, were dominated by recently arrived peasant-workers who retained ties to the countryside, and they became the recruiting ground for the anti-Semitic Black Hundreds and Russian nationalist mobilizations; in contrast, the "cold" shops, with the more skilled and literate de-ruralized workers, had the most SD activists (Smith 1981: 36; Bonnell 1983: 61–2). The Bolsheviks did not direct or organize these committees, but often committee members became Bolsheviks and the Bolshevik leadership used them to further their own mobilizational aims (Rosenberg 2001: 153).

Most of the metalworker Bolsheviks, however, worked in Moscow and in the central industrial region, which were ethnically homogenous. Moscow's working conditions were poor and wages were lower than in St. Petersburg. Two-thirds of workers were in textile, metalworking, and food industries (see figures in Bonnell 1983: 33–5). On the whole it was less socially polarized than St. Petersburg, perhaps because its workforce was more diversified among factory, artisanal, and migrant labor (Koenker 1987). In 1914, Moscow's metalworking industry was enormous, and like that of St. Petersburg's Putilov factory, Moscow Metalworks employed more than half of its 3,000 workers in its "hot" departments, where the Bolsheviks and the SRs competed for influence. The SDs generally drew from the most skilled, the Bolsheviks from the depressed textile industry, and the SRs from the less skilled (Lane 1975: 117). Most industries were Russian-owned and Moscow was less "proletarian" than St. Petersburg: half of all Moscow workers were not factory workers but artisans, employees in the service or transport sectors, domestic servants, cooks, and so forth (Bonnell 1983: 35; Koenker 1987: 83). Similarly, Ivanovo-Voznesensk, where Kolotilov, Ukhanov, Rumiantsev, and I. Smirnov worked, was the oldest and most ethnically Russian industrial region in Russia.

In short, an alignment of interests developed between Bolshevik politics and those of certain segments of the ethnically homogenous working classes in North-Central Russia. A politics that cleanly captured socioeconomic antagonisms was an important Bolshevik appeal. There was a tendency to identify with particular factories, communities, crafts, and shared village backgrounds (Hogan 1993: 37–8; Rosenberg 2001: 157). Many viewed themselves in

occupationally sectarian ways even within factories (e.g., as Putilov iron workers or *Putilovtsy*, or in *tsekhovshchina*, or shop orientation and craft consciousness). This derived from differing wages and factory conditions, as well as rural
community origins (Smith 1981: 36; Koenker 2005: 21–6). What is striking in
a number of the Bolsheviks' autobiographies is the emphasis they placed not
on being workers, but on pride in their particular skills, craftsmanship, or the
quality of their work.[13] This is consistent with the general literature: the skilled
craftsmen, or *masterovye*, particularly in metalworking, worked independently
from technical drawings and used sophisticated instruments, and so they were
respected by other workers and by management (Smith 1981: 42–3; Bonnell
1983: 47–52; Koenker 2005: 21–6 on printers). This gave them confidence as
shop committee leaders – and as political organizers. In turn, metalworkers'
radicalization increased Bolshevik influence, and with growing confidence in
their ability to shape events, they extended greater demands (Haimson 1964,
1965; see discussion in Suny 1987: 4–5; Mandel 1992).

But worker particularism should not be overdrawn. With the exception of
the highly skilled, most workers actually drifted from a variety of semiskilled
jobs: leather, tobacco, mines, railroads, stevedore, bricklaying, and so on. This
was true of the Bolsheviks.[14] As Steinberg (2002: 26–7) points out, because of
their great occupational and residential instability and mobility, workplaces
should not be reified into identities. Even though many were active in political groups, strikes, and organized protests, itinerant workers' activism tended
to be outside the formal trade unions because their work life spanned several trades. So organizing workers across factories, trades, and industries was
challenging.

But a class mobilization did emerge, held together by state repression at
one end and by the network of socialist mobilizations at the other. Russian
workers' growing weariness with wartime, factory, and other political and
economic burdens, exclusions, and sacrifices continued unabated. And this
political reality meant that whatever particularistic ascriptions they had, more
universalist ones would eventually come to dominate as they began to identify
with wider senses of repression or exploitation. Factory committees and shared
village backgrounds or craft/skill identities found common cause with those
from different factories, villages, and skill levels. Shared political repression
and incoherent governance ensured that particularistic social ascriptions fused
into wider working-class ascriptions. As Koenker (1987: 91) put it, "the important thing is that in 1917, class analysis worked." Existing social relations of

---

[13] Kalinin (Granat 1989: 425) wrote with pride, for example, of his skills and his consistent
   employment opportunities as a lathe operator in various metalworks.
[14] For example, Sapronov worked as a janitor, carpenter, and factory pieceworker (Prokhorov
   1969–78: 260); Beloborodov worked as a mechanic and an electrician in small guilds and large
   factories as he moved from town to town (Granat 1989: 360); Andreev was a shepherd/farm-
   worker, a dishwasher, an unskilled railway worker, and an apprentice in a metalworks (Granat
   1989: 349); Tomskii worked in a basket factory, a metal factory, and as an apprentice craftsman
   in a lithograph factory (Granat 1989: 718).

the old order mapped perfectly onto the struggles in the factories – and the Bolsheviks' social and political imaginary was in part attractive because it, too, suggested that bringing one down meant bringing down the other. This lay on top of relatively recent memories of serfdom, the bedrock of the antagonism between Russian elites and the peasant classes (Lieven 2000: 236). In short, autocratic repression and the state's hundreds of interventions in labor unrest attenuated intra-worker conflicts and particularism, and they strengthened a broader class-based mobilization (McDaniel 1988; Mann 1993: 660–6). Tsarist repression not only politicized, but especially after 1905 and the Lena killings,[15] it also shaped the direction of the movement and the identities of its participants.

Just as importantly, however, the peasant-worker Bolsheviks from rural villages also brought with them a distinctive set of *rural* social resources, often missed if we focus solely on factory or work lives. We know, for instance, that village life in the Central Russian regions needs redefinition: it was not simply "backward," institutionally weak, or socially inert. Rather, the Tsarist state did succeed in institutionally penetrating peasant administrative structures in important ways, often through peasant intermediaries: village assemblies used these structures, for example, in a plethora of court proceedings to resolve civil disputes around land use or tenure rights – key issues facing rural migrants experiencing lots of geographic mobility. This amounted to a vibrant village politics that sought to make use of Tsarist institutions (Gaudin 2007). This was even more evident during the war: villages actively sought information about the war as anxieties intruded into nearly every aspect of rural life – not least because almost one-half of all men of working age were taken from their villages by wartime mobilizations (Gaudin 2008: 394). Peasant soldiers expressed their demands and fears over conscription rules, requisitions, taxes, and exactions: "[R]esentments over the unequal distribution of the burdens of war extended not only to sons of the privileged who found protected jobs in the rear but to neighbors exempted on health or family grounds" (Gaudin 2008: 400). In short, if wartime ethnic dilemmas were muted here because there were no Russian Germans or Jews, local village disputes were anyway linked to both larger and local loyalties. So migrant peasant workers' ties to the countryside were very real and institutionally buttressed. They often sought to reclaim allotments and maintain property rights in formal bureaucratic claims, petitions, disputes, and grievances. And we know, too, that this rested on top of widespread rural litigation in civil matters in local townships in the Moscow countryside, from where so many Bolsheviks came. There were numerous lawsuits over family properties, small crimes, labor and land disputes, inheritance claims, and so on. Indeed, rural village courts in the region witnessed a 78 percent increase in disputes between 1905 and 1914 (Burbank 2004). In short, the peasantry of the central Russian provinces, from where the Russian Bolsheviks came, was rather litigious.

---

[15] On April 4, 1912, government troops opened fire on striking Lena miners, killing 500 of them.

In its totality, then, all of this suggests that rural life was in important respects associationally and institutionally quite vibrant. So the peasants of the rural provinces who migrated to find work in the cities and towns – as did the Bolsheviks – often not only maintained institutional ties to the country-side, but also brought to their political radicalism important social experiences and organizational resources learned in an active village associational life. Put differently, unskilled workers were not merely passive followers in political mobilizations or socialist groupings; they contributed certain social resources and distinctive ways of mobilizing or interacting with the state and its institutional structures.

Nation, Empire, and Working-Class Russian Bolsheviks

And yet if they were not implicated in the empire's multiethnicity, what were the Russian working-class Bolsheviks' relationships to, and understandings of, Russianness and the Russian nation? What specific ethnic identities did they carry into the Bolshevik movement? For the Bolsheviks of peasant-worker origin, weak *russkii* identities are largely explained by the fact that there had been no formal nationalizing project to "make them into Russians," despite the fact they drew primarily from a Russian heartland characterized by Orthodoxy's cultural homogeneity. As noted earlier, they were not educated that way in rural schools (Seregny 1999, 2000). Russianness was experienced ambiguously and inchoately, though there was often a certain pride in Russian culture (Steinberg 2002: 28–9; Smith 2008: 168). Joseph Roth (1975–76: 355) famously claimed that the Russian peasant is "peasant first and Russian second," whereas for the Jewish peasant it is the other way around. There is something to this. The scholarly consensus has been that Russian peasants were too rooted in particularistic interests, values, and local identities to have a broader sense of national identity (Haimson 1988: 15–19; Moon 1996). Recent work is revisiting this, particularly in wartime patriotic mobilizations (von Hagen 1998; Seregny 2000a, 2000b; Smith 2000, 2008: ch. 4; Sanborn 2000a, 2000b, 2005; Gaudin 2008), And although much turns on definitions of patriotism, citizenship, and nationalism (all variously used), my interpretation of the Bolsheviks' autobiographical accounts takes this into consideration and suggests (1) that they conceived of "patriotic" Russia in *rossiiskii* terms (especially those in the imperial army) so their Russianness was not ethnicized, and their mobilizational identities fell within a conception of a '*rossiiskii* nation'; and (2) that they proudly embraced self-ascribed peasant identities, something that may have been related to what we now know to be a greater vibrancy of rural associational life.

In contrast to the non-Russian Bolsheviks, many of the Russians did not write their autobiographies (in the 1920s) with a view to erasing peasant backgrounds. Indeed quite the reverse. One need only compare the Russians' accounts embracing peasant origins, even over proletarian credentials, such as those of Sapronov, Kalinin, or Kirov (Granat 1989: 424, 440, 649), with the ferocity with which the Jewish peasant Kaganovich (Kaganovich 1996: 26, 41, 61; Davies et al. 2003: 22, 34, 36) or the Georgian peasant Stalin defensively asserted their "proletarian" credentials to discredit peasant origins

(Rieber 2001). In Bolshevik socialist morality, being a Russian peasant implied something different than being a Jewish or Georgian peasant. While highlighting Bolshevism's intolerance of suspect class ascriptions, this underscores the sensitivity of ethnic over class identifications among the minorities – and the reverse for the Russians.

But it also suggests that *russkii* identities were often compensated with stronger peasant and *rossiiskii* or imperialized ascriptions. Bolshevik peasant-workers mostly had *rossiiskii*, not *russkii*, identities, although there were various idioms through which they imagined themselves part of a wider, even ethnically constituted community, especially in terms of history, territory, and empire (Gaudin 2008; Smith 2008: 155–6 on the latter point). While we know far too little about popular, lower-class conceptions of Russianness and ethnic self-ascriptions, certain key identities – local, religious, estate, occupational, regional, imperial-*rossiiskii*, and even class – did seem to be more important than an ethnic Russian identity, even during wartime patriotic mobilizations. Ethnicity and class intersected, and particularism overrode nationalism, yet state repression eventually constructed a coherent collective identity in a class-universalist narrative.

But even revolutionary political terminology was largely foreign to peasants and uneducated workers. The better educated and those living close to towns, where there were networks of peasant and party organizations (e.g., the north, mid-Volga, or western Siberia), had access to political discourse: in Perm, Vladimir, Saratov, and Viatka, the *zemstva* paid local intelligentsia to explain the main issues of the day to the peasants (Figes 2001: 76, 81). The most common mobilizational narrative was that of family and kinship. The use of familial language or imagery, and the metaphoric kin, was so locally pervasive that military elites concerned with the army's social cohesion and mobilizational capacity became, in effect, "civic" nationalists. To unite ethnically diverse and socially disparate men without a wider sense of national community, the Ministry of War used the language of kinship to build affective bonds between soldiers, based on their putative membership in the wider "Russian family" (Sanborn 2001, 2003: chs. 2, 3).Moreover, until the late nineteenth century, *lubok* tales conceived of Russianness as embodied in the Church and the Tsar. To be sure, the social imagination of the lower classes nevertheless became unanchored because of the breakdown of village insularity, greater geographic mobility, wars and conscription, the diffusion of literacy and schooling, the empire's incorporation of new and ethnically diverse territories, and especially the surprisingly rapid discrediting of both the Russian state and the Orthodox Church (Brooks 1985; Suny 2001). And yet organizers of lectures for workers, for instance at the St. Petersburg Tailoring Union, found that workers were particularly animated in discussions of religious themes – something no doubt connected to their parish schooling and to the fact that they regularly attended Sunday services (Bonnell 1983: 70). The writings and poetry of the scarcely literate "writer workers," as Steinberg (2002) has nicely demonstrated, suggest that a sense of the sacred was essential to their understandings of themselves, of their work, and indeed of modernity itself. Although not

religious, their writings often used religious idioms, imaginaries, and narratives
(see also Hernandez 2001). In fact, urban religious movements after the 1890s
in St. Petersburg and Moscow were especially popular with artisans, workers
in shops and factories, domestic servants, sales clerks, and the unemployed
(Steinberg 1994: 217–18). It constituted, in effect, a (re)definition of what it
meant to be ethnically Russian in a multiethnic empire led by ethnic Russians.
Nation and empire crashed together in political and social imaginaries of the
peasant-worker's social world.

But the most tangible and immediate sense of the diversity of "their" empire
was gained through their exceptional geographic mobility. Because of the need
to search for work, because they were sent by party committees, and because of
imprisonment, exile, and escape from authorities, they were constantly on the
move.[16] Experiences with occupational and residential mobility were indeed very
common (see Steinberg 2002: 25–6; 1992 on the printing industry). In this the
Russian Bolsheviks were not exceptional: children often began wandering through
the towns of the countryside in search of work and adventure, particularly those
whose fathers had died and left families in difficult financial conditions.

An awareness of the empire's diversity also permeated wider social worlds.
Popular cultural frameworks portrayed the multiethnic empire in parades,
pageantry, and coronations that represented the empire's nationalities in full
cultural dress and regalia; the monarchy intended it to create a love between
Tsar and people, combining references to "all the Russias" with the diffusion
of family imageries (Wortman 2000: 29–35; Sanborn 2001). The extent to
which these were successful in reinforcing or consolidating Russianness with
Orthodoxy is unclear, but popular culture did take up these issues and portrayed the multiethnicity of the empire positively (Wortman 2000: 29–35).
The commercial press promoted renditions of Russianness that went beyond
Orthodoxy for peasants who increasingly read newspapers and became politically aware (Smith 2008: 157–8). Russian popular literature was notably moving in a more tolerant, cosmopolitan, less exclusive, and xenophobic direction
(Brooks 1985: ch. 6; McReynolds 1993). In prerevolutionary fiction the empire
was seen as interesting and diverse to appeal to lower-class readers' new geographic mobility – the young Bolsheviks who traveled a great deal. *Lubok* sto-
ries, newspaper serials, and women's novels were not "about becoming Russian,
but about what it means to be Great Russian among the various peoples of the
empire" (Brooks 1985: ch. 6, 216). These new imaginaries filtered into popular

---

[16] For instance, between early radicalization, factory work, party work, and political exile, Nogin
moved from Tver to Rostov and Nicoleav in the south, to Moscow, to Saratov on the Volga;
Rumiantsev from Iaroslav to Orel, Perm, Moscow, and Ufa; Sapronov from Tula, to Saratov,
Moscow, Nizny Novgorod, and St. Petersburg; Serebriakov from Samara, to Ufa, Vologda, and
Narym in Siberia, the Volga region, and Lugansk; Sergeev from Kursk to Moscow, Siberian
exile, Perm, Ekaterinoslav, and Kharkov; Ukhanov from Kazan to Nizhny-Novgorod, Voronezh,
Kostroma, St. Petersburg, and Moscow; Kolotilov from Vladimir to Ivanovo, Briansk, and Perm;
and Kalinin from Tver to St. Petersburg for work, exile in the Caucasus and Tomsk (Siberia),
Tiflis for railroad work, and Moscow.

milieux and helped define the limits of their social worlds. The extremely popular St. Petersburg newspaper, the *Gazeta kopeika*, actively promoted attempts to fight anti-Semitism: it called for compassion against Jewish exclusions and promoted visions of political equality, racial solidarity or harmony, and a multiethnic empire based on racial democracy (McReynolds 1993: 163, 169).

Not coincidentally, the Bolsheviks' autobiographical accounts contain explicit references to ethnic cooperation, a denunciation of Russian nationalism, pro-Jewish anti-pogrom defense, and a heightened sensitivity to the diversity of "their" empire (see the accounts by Andreev [Prokhorov 1969–78: 16; Granat 1989: 349], Voroshilov [Granat 1989: 393], Tomskii [Granat 1989: 717], Kutuzov [Granat 1989: 473], and Kalinin [Granat 1989: 424]). The geographic imagination of popular fiction and other simple readers shifted attention from central Russia to the diversity of landscapes and peoples in the newer border regions and in Siberia. If "Russia as Orthodox" distanced the ethnic Russians from others, then "Russia as empire" opened up all sorts of interesting possibilities. A very important theme embedded in this framing was that non-Russians could become acceptably Russian – something that was absorbed into the socialist movements more broadly and contributed to a distinctive ethnic tolerance. Russians were almost always portrayed as superior to the minority peoples of the empire, but the relative ease with which the latter could gain acceptance and status in Russian society indicated a diffused measure of cultural tolerance, or indeed a pluralism predicated on certain terms of entry (Brooks 1985: 227).

So the Bolshevik peasant-workers had *rossiiskii* and imperialized, not *russkii*, identities and cultural frameworks, and they carried these into socialist mobilization, with important effect on the political movements' ethnic tolerance. Within the socialist movements this paved the way for a less rigid social closure around ethnicity and a more solid social boundary around class, prefiguring the Soviet problematic of the early 1920s. Combined, then, imperial strategies outlined in Chapter 2 resulted in (1) political radicalisms predicated on purer class exclusions; (2) an experience of the imperial state not so much as Russian but as deeply illiberal and as disproportionately and unjustly burdensome; (3) imperial, *rossiiskii* ascriptions over *russkii* ones; and (4) a weak identification with Orthodoxy, either as social ascription or as social glue.

The Service-Gentry and Middle-Class Russian Bolsheviks

The smaller, middle-class cohort of Bolsheviks comprised six from the intelligentsia/middling classes (Vladimir Miliutin, Viacheslav Molotov, Sergei Kirov, Andrei Bubnov, Piatakov, Iakovleva, and Stasova),[17] four loosely from

---

[17] Stasova's positioning is ambiguous, and my categorization somewhat arbitrary. Her father was a lawyer/jurist, so some sources indicate she was a noblewoman (service gentry), whereas others simply designated her as upper-middle class. This is because her father was a trained jurist with a senatorial career, but political activism was followed by arrests and a series of demotions (Granat 1989: 701).

the (upper) middle-class intelligentsia sons of the service nobility (Lenin, Bukharin, Lomov, and Osinskii), and three sons of priests or army officers (Preobrazhenskii, Vladimirskii, and Kuibyshev). Occupationally, more than half became "professional revolutionaries" (Bukharin, Piatakov, Preobrazhenskii, Kuibyshev, Bubnov, and Molotov), while the others joined the liberal professions (Lenin and Lomov were lawyers, Vladimirskii was a doctor, Kirov was a *zemstvo* draftsman, Iakovleva a teacher, Stasova a Red Cross worker and women's charitable activist, and Miliutin and Osinskii were economists). Educational patterns also reflected social origins and occupations: Iakovleva studied at the Moscow Mathematics Faculty after *gimnaziia*; Kirov at Kazan's Mechanical and Technical School; Lenin at Kazan's Law Faculty; Lomov at the St. Petersburg Law Faculty (which was the main source of recruits to the higher civil service, and most students were, like Lomov, from noble families); Miliutin, Stasova, and Piatakov studied at St. Petersburg University; Molotov studied at a St. Petersburg Polytechnic; Kuibyshev at an officer cadet school; Bubnov at an agricultural institute; Bukharin and Osinskii at Moscow University; Preobrazhenskii at a *gimnaziia*; and Vladimirskii at Kazan, Moscow, and Berlin Universities.

A central claim of this book is that social locations and varying relationships to the imperial state often accounted for divergent politics. And a key argument of this chapter is that educated Russians who became leftist radicals tended to come from different social locations than those that produced state-supporting Russian nationalists. Russian conservatives, monarchists, and nationalists drew from the propertied nobility, the upper levels of the imperial bureaucracy, landed country gentry, commercial-industrial and capitalist elites, and economic nationalists (particularly from Moscow and in the cities of the western borderlands). The Octobrists were essentially a moderate Great Russian nationalist party, whereas the Black Hundreds were monarchists, anti-Semitic, and more reactionary. By contrast, by 1900, the liberal opposition and the Kadets drew from the service gentry, *zemstva*, the intelligentsia (or the intellectual liberal aristocracy and liberal, and professional middle class such as doctors, lawyers, and academics), and some small landowners and clergy. The socialist movements – only slightly different from the Kadets – drew from the same milieux, albeit with more students, younger educated Russians in the universities, and fewer intellectuals and cultural elites (see Table 2.2, Chapter 2).

But geography mattered, too, and so did regional ethnopolitics. Russian nationalist mobilizations drew from the central provinces and borderlands, with some Baltic Germans, Moscow merchants and bankers, Russian settlers, migrants, and local officials in the borderlands, Russian railway workers and peasants in south-southwestern provinces, and generally from Astrakhan, Bessarabia, Vitebsk, Kiev, Mogilev, and Podolsk *gubernii*; the liberals and Kadets drew Muslim and Polish support, and in the Russian areas they attracted non-Russian (especially Jewish) support; Menshevism was strongest east of the Astrakan-St. Petersburg line – Minsk, Kharkov, Odessa, and the Caucasus –

with lots of Georgians, while Bolshevism drew from west of the line, or the Moscow, central industrial, and Volga-Urals regions.

Socioethnic Location, Nation, and Empire

We saw that the Bolshevik peasant-workers were primarily from the Moscow-St. Petersburg central industrial regions. Based on this cohort of educated, middling-class Bolsheviks, two overlapping social locations tended to funnel activists into Bolshevik mobilization: in terms of social class, the Russian upper-intelligentsia service gentry, which in practice blurred into the educated, middle-class professions (and it included women); and geographically and ethnopolitically, the Volga-Urals region. Clearly not everyone in these locations became Bolsheviks (or even SDs), but a sufficient proportion of Bolsheviks came from these locations that their social worlds are worth exploring. In important respects, the experiences of the Russian middle classes in the Volga-Urals were also emblematic of the social world that produced educated Russians in the other leftist political mobilizations more generally, especially the SRs. So this is also, in its outline, an argument about leftist radical groupings more generally.

Formal and practical distinctions between the upper intelligentsia and the lower civil service gentry were ambiguous and in constant flux. And so were the distinctions between the middling intelligentsia and those in the *meshchanstvo*, merchant, and even upper peasant estates (see Appendix B for an extended outline of these distinctions). The Table of Ranks (1772) criteria for promotion of education, achievement, and experience had permitted the ennoblement of commoners, particularly with the penetration of *gimnazii* and university education into the middle social orders. The hereditary and personal nobilities comprised landowning and non-landowning nobility, higher officials in the imperial civil and military bureaucracies, most of the free professions – doctors, lawyers, and educated careerists – and much of the intelligentsia. Lomov and Osinskii's fathers, for instance, were members of the traditional *dvorianstvo*. Lomov was raised in the intelligentsia milieu of the Saratov lower nobility, became a Menshevik, and graduated with a law degree from St. Petersburg University (Prokhorov 1969–78: 7–8; Granat 1989: 515); Osinskii's father (a political radical himself) was a veterinarian-aristocrat who wrote specialist books on veterinary medicine, and Osinskii attended *gimnaziia* and graduated from Moscow University with a degree in economics (Prokhorov 1969–78: 558; Granat 1989: 569). Lenin and Bukharin's fathers, by contrast, had formally risen into the noble estates: Lenin's father made his way through the empire's civil bureaucracy to achieve Rank Four, or hereditary nobility; Bukharin's father had been a mathematician school teacher with a university education, who later became a tax inspector in Bessarabia and eventually received an official title of provincial councilor, or Rank Seven of the fourteen-rank civil service (Cohen 1971: 6–7). By the late nineteenth century, then, educational levels were the formal barriers to entry to top administrative posts, not social origin (Lieven 1984: 202–4; 1989: 28), so this is what permitted their civil service careers.

Together with petty nobles, they constituted a social class whose traditional ethos was based on state service. Most were not independently wealthy and had to serve the imperial state to supplement incomes and social status. In practice they (and their sons and daughters) were more accurately second- or third-generation professionals in the (upper) intelligentsia. After midcentury, the composition of the intelligentsia had shifted from nobility to commoners, from an upper intelligentsia of well-established academics and government officials to a lower intelligentsia of university-educated teachers, scientists, and civil servants. But by 1900, the sons were in turn replaced by the grandsons – or the Bolsheviks: a modern, professional middle class, many of whom came to view liberalism as a class movement of the (declining) nobility (see extended discussion in Fischer 1958: ch. 2).

Molotov's (born Scryabin) family, for instance, was typically lower-middle class. Distantly related to the pianist composer Scriabin (Molotov played the violin), his father was a *prikazchik*, a lower-middle-class salesman whom Molotov described as a clerk with a salary equal to that of a teacher but less than a *zemstvo* doctor; his mother was from a wealthy merchant family (Granat 1989: 553; Watson 2005: 4). One brother became a doctor, another a painter, and another a composer – and all three were also political radicals in Kazan (Granat 1989: 553). After expulsion for radical activities as an SR from a Kazan *Realschule*, Molotov took exams as a external candidate in Vologda and then enrolled in the St. Petersburg Polytechnic (Prokhorov 1969–78: 484–5; Granat 1989: 554; Watson 2005: 8, 10–11). But he was politically active among students, not workers, although he lived in the very radicalized, Bolshevized workers' Vyborg district of St. Petersburg (Watson 2005: 12–13).

Similarly, Miliutin was from Kursk *guberniia*, where his father was a rural schoolteacher (Prokhorov 1969–78: 267). He studied at St. Petersburg University, became an economist, and 1903 sided with the Mensheviks. Kirov, too, came from a lower-middle-class family in rural Viatsk *guberniia*. After attending a local city school, he studied at the Kazan Mechanical and Technical School on a *zemstvo* bursary while he was politically active in the city's radical movements. Kirov then worked as a draftsman for a *zemstvo* in Tomsk and organized an underground printing press (Prokhorov 1969–78: 183–4; Granat 1989: 440, although Molotov claimed that Kirov was a journalist for a provincial newspaper; see Chuev 1991: 178). Like most *zemstva* middling and low-level employees of the 1880s and 1890s, he was a politically minded reformer who gravitated toward liberal-socialist, not nationalist, movements.

There were also two sons of priests in this elite. Vladimirskii was the son of an Orthodox priest in Nizhny Novgorod *guberniia* (Prokhorov 1969–78: 148). He studied medicine at Moscow and Kazan Universities, and at Berlin University he became a doctor (Granat 1989: 388). His first political activism was as a medical student in the 1890s, so official records date his membership in the CP to 1895 (Prokhorov 1969–78: 148). He was abroad from 1905 to 1917, where the Okhrana followed his political activities as a Bolshevik – including surveillance of his Paris apartment.[18] Preobrazhenskii, one of the Bolsheviks' leading economists, was also the son of an Orthodox priest from Orel *guberniia* (Haupt and Marie 1969: 189–90; Granat 1989: 584). He joined radical groups while in *gimnaziia*, and although he was torn between the SRs and SDs, during revolutionary events in 1905 he nevertheless fought organizers of anti-Jewish pogroms (Granat 1989: 586–7).

Finally, Bubnov and Piatakov were also from Russian middle-class families. Bubnov attended *Realschule* in Ivanovo-Voznesensk before he was expelled for revolutionary activity from the Moscow Agricultural Institute; most of his political activity was in this northern industrial area, and he became a Bolshevik in 1903 (Granat 1989: 370–1). Bubnov's prerevolutionary career was made in prisons: each time he was arrested he was promoted within the Bolshevik committee structure. Piatakov was a Ukrainian-born Russian from a wealthy middle-class family: his father was an engineer and director of a sugar refinery (Granat 1989: 591). After previous expulsions in 1905 and 1907, Piatakov was expelled from St. Petersburg University in 1910 when he joined the RSDLP. He had attended a *Realschule*, joined the Anarchists in 1906, and in 1907 a terrorist group, with whom he was involved in the attempted assassination of the governor-general of Kiev (Lazitch 1986: 361; Granat 1989: 591). Anarcho-terrorist or anarcho-communist radicalism was historically typical of the sons of the wealthy and privileged. Kiev's Russian migrant labor force, its Polish cultural influences, and its Jewish middle classes all contributed to the city's radical politics, but ethnic Russians typically joined either Russian nationalist movements or leftist internationalist ones – opposing responses to the same socioethnic tensions, as we saw in Chapter 5. Theorizing the ethnopolitical world of Kiev – and in reaction to the political strength of Ukrainian nationalism – Piatakov became such a strong opponent of Ukrainian nationalism that Lenin accused him of arriving full circle at Great Russian chauvinism (Haupt and Marie 1969: 178–9).

But Piatakov's politics were atypical, most likely influenced by ethnopolitics in a combustible multiethnic borderland. More commonly, none of the Bolsheviks' revolutionary activism had any real Russian nationalism within it. None were involved in Russian nationalist or proto-nationalist groupings (including Piatakov), despite considerable non-Bolshevik activism: as noted, Preobrazhenskii was torn between the SRs and the SDs, Molotov was an SR in Kazan, Piatakov an Anarchist, and Lomov and Miliutin were Mensheviks. Even their non-Bolshevik radicalism, in other words, was still broadly in *rossiiskii* mobilizations. Moreover, like those of a significant segment of these new, professional middling classes deriving from the noble-service gentry, they carried moral codes that were neither anti-Semitic nor nationalist. Lenin and Molotov fundamentally viewed non-Russian nationalisms as responses to Russification.

[18] HIAPO, Index No. XIIIb(1), Box 123, Folder 1G, Outgoing Dispatch No. 1331 Paris October 19 – November 1, 1912.

Indeed, they both attributed the high numbers of Jewish revolutionaries to state repression and to the exclusion of Jews. Lenin was certainly not anti-Semitic – he considered the Jews a particularly "gifted race"– and his Judeophilia was commonly accepted, as was the rumor of his Jewish background (Service 2000: 28); Preobrazhenskii fought against pogroms in Orel in 1905 and wrote about it with pride (Granat 1989: 587); Molotov was ethnically tolerant – he married a Jewess, Polina Semenovna Zhemchuzhina – but he was not "unaware": of the Jewish Bolshevik Kamenev, Molotov said, "he had quite Russian handwriting. He didn't even look like a Jew except when you were looking into his eyes" (Chuev 1991: 198–9).[19]

On the whole, then, their cultural frames were benignly imperialist: paternalism toward the non-Russians, an aversion to Great Russian chauvinism, an atheistic rejection of Orthodoxy, weak *russkii* identities, and an identification with the humanism of Russian literature. These qualities also gave Bolshevism an especially ethnically tolerant culture, in part because it had proportionally more members of noble/aristocratic origin than other groups. The politics of this social world, in other words, offered a sharp contrast to the xenophobic, conservative Russian nationalism of the landowning gentry that had aligned itself with Tsarism.

And yet nationalist, ethnic, and gender identity ascriptions and politics did impinge on these worlds in more subtle ways. The emergence a Russian middle class, drawing socioeconomically from above and from below, did bring with it a certain kind of Russian nationalism located within the professions and among those social groups that were most fearful or resentful of minority (often Jewish) competition. Indeed, estate identities were generally weak among the Russian-educated urban classes, but so were ethnic (*russkii*) identities, and Russian worries of Jewish competition in the liberal professions, particularly in the *advokatura*, were conservative, vocal, and influential (Baberowski 1995). But on the whole, Russian professionals and intellectuals were resistant to fully developed race thinking (Weitz 2002: 19). Like the peasant-worker Bolsheviks, particularistic identity ascriptions were more common than ethnicized Russian ascriptions. For instance, slavophilism combined with nationalism in fears of competition among Moscow's commercial classes, and these fears were folded into their Octobrist politics; but these came from a different source than the official nationalism of the bureaucracy, or the frustrations of landowners of the western provinces (Pinchuk 1974: 13–14; Lieven 1989: 28). The Moscow Society of Jurisprudence mirrored Moscow's gentry and moderate, upper intelligentsia, for instance, whereas the St. Petersburg Economic Society (among whom were leading liberals and moderate socialists) typified the greater role of the St. Petersburg professions and the radical, lower intelligentsia (Fischer 1958: 56–8).

---

[19] In the early 1940s, Stalin insisted that Molotov divorce his wife. She was then arrested and exiled.

Describing themselves as Muscovites – and notably not as Russians – Bukharin and Osinskii, for example, had an especially close friendship because of shared social experiences in Moscow: they both came from intellectual-aristocratic families, both attended Moscow *gimnazii*, they attended Moscow University together in 1909 where they continued political activism in university socialist groups, and they were in prison together in 1910 (Haupt and Marie 1969: 33–5; Prokhorov 1969–78: 559; Cohen 1971: 6–7 on Bukharin; Schapiro 1977: 108 on Osinskii; Lazitch 1986: 347; Granat 1989: 372–4, 569–70).

The three women in the Bolshevik elite explicitly identified with women's causes. Two were Russian from the service intelligentsia, part of a cohort of SD women of an earlier, pre-1905 generation (see Fiesler 1989: 199–202).[20] Women comprised roughly 15 percent of the RSDLP membership in 1905 (and fewer later), and nearly all drew from the (upper) intelligentsia – a higher percentage than any other European socialist party at the time, though roughly the same as that of the SRs (Perrie 1972; Fiesler 1989). But women were generally underrepresented in the leaderships of the SD or SR parties, and working-class women were not at all represented among the leadership ranks. Those in leadership positions tended to be of Russian or Jewish background and in the medical or teaching professions (Fiesler 1989: 210).

For instance, Iakovleva was born in 1884 to a Russian (upper) middle-class family in Moscow. She attended *gimnaziia*, graduated with a degree in Physics and Math from Moscow University, and secured employment as a teacher (Prokhorov 1969–78: 487; Granat 1989: 783–4). She was politically active in women's groups and in various Moscow SD organizations, and most of her friends were Mensheviks (Granat 1989: 784). She was under police surveillance (even abroad), with a series of arrests and then exile in Astrakhan.[21] Similarly, Stasova was born in 1873 to a demoted noble family of the humanist intelligentsia of St. Petersburg. After attending a private *gimnaziia*, she worked for the Red Cross and women's and charitable organizations, and she joined the RSDLP in 1898 – indeed, these were the same groups to which her parents had belonged (Granat 1989: 701). She also taught evening classes for women in textile factories. So while (semi)skilled male workers rose into leadership positions, the generally unskilled women did not; the RSDLP did offer some gender equality, but it had a very strong class bias toward educated, privileged, and professional women, distinguishing them somewhat from most of their male Russian counterparts (Fiesler 1989). Importantly, however, in their activism they tended to identify *as* women in feminist organizations.

So it may be that as educated service nobilities became the intelligentsia, their views of the Russian nation changed: the intelligentsia was excluded

---

[20] Alexandra Kollontai could also be included. She was Ukrainian-Finnish from an aristocratic family, educated as a teacher, multilingual, and a socialist feminist (Clements 1979; Farnsworth 1980).

[21] HIAPO, Outgoing dispatch, Index No. XIIIb(1), Box 124, Folder 1H, No. 1550, Paris October 3/16, 1913.

from modern constructions of the Russian nation because of its opposition
to the illiberal state, its generalized political exclusion, and the social fact of
its ambiguous suspension between the traditional estates. Importantly, however, they were subject to both upward and downward mobility: their children
could, and did, move in either direction, thereby making them more receptive
to socialist political mobilizations. But their identity ascriptions were generally
particularist or *rossiiskii*, not nationalist.

Political Radicalism in the Volga-Urals

The character of politics in the Volga-Urals is also a key to understanding
this Bolshevik cohort. Apart from Piatakov, who was radicalized in Kiev, and
Kuibyshev, who was from Omsk in Western Siberia,[22] several of the Bolsheviks'
political radicalism was from around Saratov-Kazan, and more broadly the
Volga-Urals.[23] Two characteristics of the Volga-Urals are important for contextualizing the Bolsheviks' identities and radicalizations. First, the region
was fused into the imperial imagination as *Russian* territory – predicated on a
demographic reality that was the result of centuries of colonization, and very
much unlike the empire's still fragile hold on the Caucasus or Central Asia
(Khodarkovsky 2002: chs. 2, 3). The intricately multiethnic, multiconfessional
region and the cities along the Volga (Kazan, Simbirsk, Samara, and Saratov)
were incorporated, as noted, into the empire between 1505 and 1584. So they
were no longer borderlands per se, but settled Russian areas bordering the less
politically incorporated lands to the east. In 1897, the largest non-Russian
population was the Tatars, followed by the indigenous non-Muslim Mordvins,
Chuvash, Votiaks (or Udmurts), and Cheremises (or Maris); and although
these groups comprised 35 percent of the population, and Kazan was the least
Russian of the region's provinces, ethnic Russians stabilized as the dominant
majority at 65 percent with the end of large-scale Russian migration (Geraci
2001a: 31–2 for figures and discussion).

As Russian administrators and elites transferred their conceptions of
Russianness onto the region's peoples, and in turn, as the latter affected conceptions of Russianness, Kazan became a two-way window to the east (Geraci
2001a). It was an important trading city, with the largest Muslim population
of the empire. Over time, ethnic Russian migrations were "diluted" by high

---

[22] Omsk was two-thirds Kirghiz and one-third Russian/Ukrainian.
[23] Kirov graduated from the Kazan Mechanical and Technical School and worked in Kazan
(Prokhorov 1969–78: 183–4); Lenin was famously from Simbirsk and attended Kazan
University; Molotov began his political activism as a *Realschule* student in Kazan (Prokhorov
1969–78: 484–5); Vladimirskii attended Kazan University from 1903 (Granat 1989: 388);
Lomov was from Saratov, as noted earlier, and joined SD groupings in Saratov and the RSDLP
in 1903 (Granat 1989: 515; Prokhorov 1969–78: 7–8); and in 1908, Preobrazhenskii was active
in the Urals (Granat 1989: 588). Among the peasant-workers discussed earlier, Rykov was an
SR and a member of the *Narodnaia Volia* in Saratov; Serebriakov was active in Samara and Ufa;
Ukhanov worked in a manufacturing plant in Kazan before working in the Dinamo Plant in
Moscow; and Beloborodov was a factory worker in Perm (Granat 1989: 636, 665, 735).

intermarriage rates, which were generally encouraged by the state as an additional instrument of nation building. Ethnic mixing and linguistic and religious assimilation were facilitated by the fact that most of the Volga populations did not have modernized elites that could threaten either Russian culture or imperial stability: the Chuvash intelligentsia was generally antistate or oppositional, but they were not anti-Russian because most were confessionally Orthodox; and there was a general openness among Russian elites to the Finno-Ugric culture of the Cheremises, Udmurts, and Mordvins (Miller 2004b: 19–20). In this way, the regions' non-Russians – especially Kazan's Tatars – entered into the Russian imperial imaginary. In fact, between 1740 and 1760, hundreds of thousands Tatars and indigenous non-Muslims had converted to Orthodoxy. Tatar society was in many ways culturally recognizable to Russians: it was socially stratified, urban, literate, and commercial. A Tatar nobility was created and fully incorporated into the *dvorianstvo*, with lots of assimilation as many entered state service. Indeed, Volga Tatar merchants were not only encouraged by the state, but they were even used as intermediaries by Russians in their dealings with Central Asian Kazakhs (Geraci 2001a: ch. 1; Werth 2002: 179). So assimilation was typically limited to elites and left peasant or nomadic populations with tribal, ethnic, or religious identities largely intact (Suny 2001: 41). Despite – or because of – Russian conquest, then, the Volga-Urals was historically characterized by socially deep and normalized assimilation, or by hybridized and *rossiiskii* identity ascriptions.

But by the late nineteenth century, large-scale apostasy worried Russian elites, particularly since the non-Tatar Chuvash began to Islamicize. With worries of Islam's assimilatory appeal to non-Muslim and non-Russian indigenous peoples, and with the Orthodox Church on the defensive because of its weakened local influence, imperial elites increasingly viewed the region as an area of struggle between two high cultures (Werth 2002: 187–98). These worries were compounded by the growing number of Muslim-Tatar schools, to which the famous Il'minskii model of missionary education (discussed in the next section) was a localized, semi-enlightened, but ultimately Russificatory response. In short, by the latter decades of the empire, Muslim Tatars were becoming the Poles of the Volga-Urals (Miller 2004b: 20).

Kazan's Muslim community, for instance, began to reform madrasas based on Ottoman models, but they still worked within a broadly Russian imperial framework and in the process started to secularize (Tuna 2011). And yet for Tsarist elites, Islam came to be seen as a cultural obstacle as growing Russian nationalism crashed headlong into the empire's diversity. An already ethnically intricate region in terms of identities, it was further politicized as the imperial state experimented with discordant policies of Russianization, cultural integration, and instruments of social control over what was anyway considered part of the empire's heartland (Geraci 2001b; Campbell 2007). Educational missionary efforts, combined with the state's drift rightward toward more nationalist, dissimilationist minority policies, resulted in the creation of small, native intelligentsias that were increasingly (1) semi-Russified *and* resistant to Russification, (2) mobilized into political groupings after 1905, and (3) ascriptively strengthening "Muslim ethnic" layers of identity (Noack 1999; Geraci 2001a: chs. 7, 8; Werth 2002: ch. 9).

The second important characteristic of the Volga-Urals region is that it was a fertile area of political activity, with lots of revolutionaries and radicalized workers mostly among the ethnic Russians, as a kind of ethnic tolerance was absorbed by many in this social world. It formed the base from which Bolshevism projected power outward; the Urals especially were a bastion of left communist exiles and revolutionaries in the years just before and after 1917. Saratov had received mass influxes of Russian and Ukrainian peasants and migrants, and the region was characterized by long-standing, state-supported gentry predominance over serfs. This left a strong social imprint that eventually resulted in both a restive peasantry open to socialist political mobilizations and a provincial landed gentry open to conservative, nationalist political mobilizations (see Tables 2.1 and 2.2, Chapter 2).

So in 1902, Saratov was the center of the Russian SDs and SRs with a large number of political organizations, among which (and at various times) Rykov, Lomov, Preobrazhenskii, and Lenin took part (see also discussion in Kanatchikov 1986: 302–12). It had been an SR and populist stronghold in the 1890s because it drew from the surrounding peasantry. SDs came relatively late and eventually gained traction, but even as late as 1905, the SDs and SRs were organizationally joint mobilizations, as they were in other provinces of Central Russia (Melancon 1989: 112).[24] *Zemstva* also played a crucial role in the province's social mobilization, because it had the highest number of radical *zemstvo* employees in the empire (Seregny and Wade 1989: 6–7). So the city's political culture developed as a popular place of political exile, and leftist radical traditions were passed on to the Bolsheviks' generation.

Importantly, however, Saratov was also a key location of nationalist gentry reaction after 1905. So SRs and the SDs locally mobilized not against the nationalisms of local ethnic minorities – as we have seen in the multiethnic western or southern parts of the empire – but rather against Russian nationalist and provincial conservatism. This gave socialist mobilizations a slightly weaker universalist narrative than they had in other multiethnic regions of the empire because they did not have to recruit local ethnic minorities into the movement. Here universalist politics had comparatively weak nationalisms against which to define itself. This meant that they were more attuned to the purer class dimensions of the socialist revolutionary narrative because cultural markers were absent.

More specifically, ethnic Russians dominated political and administrative life of Kazan *guberniia*, so the non-assimilated members of the non-Russian groups were excluded not only from formal power structures, but also from

---

[24] From his years at Kazan University, Rykov (the worker Bolshevik) was a leading figure in Saratov's SR and SD revolutionary politics, most of which involved cooperative SR-SD efforts (Granat 1989: 636; Melancon 1989: 82–6).

urban culture (Badcock 2007). The region's minorities were geographically dispersed in socioeconomic niches, so political mobilizations took place along the web of ethnic networks. And Kazan's political culture had a cosmopolitan dimension too: after 1905, Muslim students in Kazan's reformist schools fraternized with Russian students as they read the socialist revolutionary literature and organized politically (Tuna 2011: 559). Kazan was also regularly used as a place of administrative and political exile, and Kazan University was one of the oldest and most radicalized universities in the empire, with a politically active student population, which included Kirov, Lenin, Vladimirskii, Rykov, and Molotov. Kazan's political groupings were numerous, varied, and active. Okhrana records show, for instance, that Molotov was ranked second in importance by police in a small Kazan radical student group that had SRs, SDs, and Anarchists (Watson 2005: 6–8). Official sources claim he became a Bolshevik in 1906, though his biographer dates it to 1908–09 (compare Prokhorov 1969–78: 484–5 with Watson 2005: 7). And Lenin – whose political activism famously began after his brother was executed for revolutionary activities by Tsarist authorities – had spent summers in the Kazan and Samara countryside in the People's Will and in the SDs in Samara itself.

Of course we now know of Lenin's Jewish-German-Tatar (or Chuvash or Mordvin) roots, and of his Jewish, apostate maternal grandfather, just as we know of his noble origins (Service 2000: 17–18; Petrovsky-Shtern 2010).[25] But in this Lenin was not altogether singular among the Volga's ethnic Russians. His sensibilities also characterized those of many in the area. Lenin thought of himself as Russian, albeit with strong Lutheran German influences from his mother (Service 2000: 29). He had a certain detachment on nationalism in general and a strong aversion to Great Russian nationalism, in part because of his respect for the ethnic sensitivities of the Volga region in which he was socialized, and in part because of his father's work in Chuvash education and language instruction among the Volga's non-Russians (Kreindler 1977; Service 2000: 29, 386, 469). Lenin was of course well aware of the potency of ethnic sensitivities in a diverse empire: he refused to appoint Jews to Ukrainian administrative posts so as not to anger Ukrainians, and he famously lamented those non-Russian Bolsheviks who compensated for their origins by becoming too Russian.

In an early work, Kreindler (1977) made a plausible case that at least some of Lenin's thinking on ethnic minorities was formed in Kazan and Simbirsk through his father, and especially through the family's friendship with the inspector of Chuvash schools and follower of Il'minskii. The Il'minskii system (after Nicholas Ivanovich Il'minskii [1822–91]) taught Orthodoxy to the

---

[25] Petrovsky-Shtern (2010: ch. 1) shows that Lenin's great-grandfather, Moshko Blank, regularly denounced Jews to Russian authorities as he tried to assume a Russian imperial identity, while converting his sons to Orthodoxy. He argues that Lenin approached Jews pragmatically and did not "see" nationality. This is perhaps true with regard to Jewishness.

Volga-Urals' indigenous peoples in their own languages (using the Cyrillic alphabet). Its proponents sought to foster religious adherence by teaching it in native languages, while instilling a Russian nationalism that identified with Orthodoxy (Dowler 1995; Geraci 2001a: ch. 2; Werth 2002: ch. 9). Lenin's father was a state director of schools in Simbirsk, charged with spreading literacy among the Chuvash. He enthusiastically promoted the Il'minskii schools in 1870 and even worked closely with Il'minskii himself (Kreindler: 1977: 90). These influences were confirmed by Nadezhda Krupskaia, Lenin's wife, who later recounted the atmosphere Lenin's father had created in the home regarding the Volga region's minorities, and commented on Lenin's tutoring of a Chuvash student for Kazan University's entrance exams (cited in Kreindler 1977: 91). The claim is that Lenin's very intimate familiarity with Chuvash culture allowed him to see the political benefits of cultural recognition. In sync with Il'minskii's reasoning, Lenin also opposed linguistic Russification. Noting the political costs of Russian nationalism's "residue of national mistrust" among minorities, he believed that minorities would naturally assimilate "in the course of social life" and that "artificial" measures to speed this up were counterproductive (see discussion in Kreindler 1977: 93–9). Importantly, Il'minskii and his followers viewed local nationalisms as responses to Russification – something that Lenin, too, would later argue.

In sum, then, the Russian intelligentsia Bolsheviks came from those middle class/service gentry that were oppositional in their politics: class tensions were clear and unambiguous between peasant and landowner, and worker and capitalist, so socialist political mobilizations found their elective affinities. Social inequalities here did not have the stark cultural markers or politically problematic ethnic rankings that they did in other parts of the empire. These middling-class social locations did not produce Russian nationalist politics, though the region's provincial landed gentry did. With the exception of Piatakov in Ukrainian Kiev and Kuibyshev in Omsk, their contact with the empire and its diversity was limited to regions in which non-Russian minorities – Tatars and indigenous non-Muslims – had experienced centuries of socially normalized assimilation, historic tolerance of religious difference, and a comparatively conflict-free coexistence. This was especially true when compared with the fractious ethnopolitics of the western, southwestern, and Caucasian borderlands. Experienced through the prism of the Volga-Urals, Russianness had relatively softly delineated boundaries. *Russkii* and *rossiiskii* blurred into each other, although this began to change in the latter Russianizing years in part because Russianness here did not politically develop in stark opposition to non-Russianness. In fact, the Russian nationalism of the provincial landed gentry was so closely aligned with Tsarism that there was hardly a distinction made between opposition to the state and opposition to the nationalizing state. All of this with the consequence that those middle-class Russians from the Volga-Urals brought a comparatively tolerant and non-nationalist imperial imaginary into multiethnic Bolshevism.

Conclusion

As the burdens of empire affected Russia's political culture in the decades before the Revolution, two nationalizing tendencies became mutually reinforcing: while imperial elites began finding their ethnic Russian identity – in the service of maintaining the empire – the empire's middle classes, and certain of the educated estates and professions, nationalized as well. Caught within these tensions were the educated and professional ethnic minorities, and with them the ethnic minority Bolsheviks. But at the center of this tension, and crucial to defining the ethnic tolerance of Bolshevism, were ethnic Russians. Three key imperial strategies contributed to the identities of the Russian Bolsheviks: the absence or weakness of assimilatory Russification, in education especially; the fragility of Russian as a social ascription as it was bound up with wider patterns of inclusion and repression; and the fractured relationships among Orthodoxy, nation, and empire.

Under the rubric of official nationality, Russians and non-Russians were accustomed to rule by a multiethnic, culturally westernized governing elite, albeit latterly a Russianized one. The ethnicization or Russianization of the monarchy began from 1881 with Alexander III's explicit attempt to identify with pre-Petrine Russia's historic Muscovite roots in an effort to distance the monarchy from the tensions of Moscow's factories, intelligentsia, and divided nobility (Wortman 2000; 2003: 59). But the Bolshevik revolutionary narrative rejected this ethnic narrowing and social deepening of what it meant to be Russian in favor of something loosely resembling the old model of a multiethnic elite of Petrine Russia. Where the intelligentsia or educated society was previously excluded from nationalist-imperialist narratives, Bolshevism placed it center stage in a key nation-building moment. And where Tsarist elites were Russifying and Russianizing, Bolshevism was purposely and openly multiethnic and *rossiiskii*.

As we saw in Table 2.2, Chapter 2, overall the socialist (and liberal) movements were highly multiethnic political mobilizations, in contrast to those on the political right. Even in St. Petersburg, which was overwhelmingly ethnically Russian, the SD Petrograd Committee had fifty-eight Russians and forty-two non-Russians in 1917 (Smith 1999: 190). To the extent that some ethnic minority Bolsheviks were chosen for leadership positions for strategic reasons, so too were certain Russian peasant-workers. It fact, arguably it was the Russian worker Bolsheviks who might have been strategically recruited for ideological and "narrative" purposes, in a search for actual workers as the public face of the revolutionary movement. The scarcely educated and semiskilled worker Badaev, for instance, was sent to the Duma as a Bolshevik. He had minimal education in a rural primary school and struggled with the theoretical aspects of socialist ideology. But the Bolsheviks needed a worker to represent them, and as Molotov later recounted, "they began to look for the least offensive man, someone who had participated only slightly in revolutionary actions… he turned out to be an honest man, tough, poorly educated and not very active" (Chuev 1991: 178). There were certainly well-documented class tensions between the workers and the intelligentsia leadership of the movement (see Kanatchikov 1986; Hogan 1993: ch. 2). And as Smith (1999: 190) briefly suggests, the fact that the leadership was largely ethnic minority while the rank and file was largely ethnically Russian may also have contributed a certain social distance to the movement's class tensions. The rank and file understood that many of the non-Russian leadership were Jewish or Latvian because most of the latter spoke in accented Russian, including, famously, Trotsky. Low marriage rates between workers and intelligentsia among the revolutionaries might also have been a measure of the social distance between them.

And yet on the broader evidence, ethnic intermarriage was quite common within the leftist mobilizations – more common actually than marriages between workers and intelligentsia. Given, too, that the women in positions of leadership within the socialist movements were from the (upper) middle classes, with virtually no working-class women, the problematic social boundary in the revolutionary years was more likely class, not ethnicity.[26] Within the political culture of the socialist mobilizations, in fact, class boundaries were perhaps harder to cross than ethnic ones in terms of the ultimate indicator of social assimilation: marriage. But in terms of self-ascriptions, the line between worker and intelligentsia grew increasingly blurred as educated skilled workers began to consider themselves *intelligenty* (see Zelnick on Kanatchikov; Hogan 1993: 38–42), as the activists among them moved into positions of political leadership (Allen 2005 on Shliapnikov), and as the intelligentsia leadership gradually sought to proletarianize their social identities to align them more closely with the ideological framing of the mobilization (for instance, van Ree 2007 on Stalin). The socialist revolutionary mobilizations, in short, offered opportunities for class and ethnic boundary crossing at a time when these social ascriptions were politically problematized in imperial society. Ethnic opening and class closure were reversed within the revolutionary narrative.

And yet the contrast between the multiethnic revolutionary leadership and the ethnic Russian shock troops of the Revolution (workers, soldiers, and conscripts) is even more significant when considered against three years of a war that was to have deepened Russian patriotic sentiments, clarified national identities, and increased populist anti-Semitism. The government sought to make the imperial state more "national" in order to rally support for the war, and wartime mobilizations sought to transcend ethnic differences among conscripts (Sanborn 2003). Though hardly a success in its intended aim, it did have the unintended effect of radicalizing minorities (Lohr 2003; Sanborn 2003). Peasant responses to wartime mobilization have been empirically understudied,

[26] There were exceptions: the relationship between the Bolsheviks Shliapnikov, a worker-trade union leader and devout Old Believer, and Kollontai, the upper-middle-class daughter of a Ukrainian father and Finnish mother, crossed both religious/ethnic and class boundaries (see discussion in Clements 1979: 86–7).

although there is emerging evidence that they experienced a greater connection with the wider identifications of citizenship, patria, and community (Gaudin 2008). On the one hand, wartime *zemstvo* adult education and literacy campaigns were popular for those wishing to better understand wartime events in which their families were directly implicated in peasant conscription (Seregny 2000a, 2000b). But even liberal attempts to foster a growing sense of patriotic awareness in the pages of Petrograd's most read paper, *Gazeta kopeika*, failed to forge a sense of nationalism or common vision of patria in the face of growing identification as workers in lower-class bonds of solidarity (McReynolds 1993).

Despite these efforts, even deep into the war, peasants, former peasants, and lower-class urbanites were still less likely to identify as Russians than they were either particularistically (by locality, city, or community), as part of a wider *rossiiskii*, multiethnic empire or, increasingly, as workers, peasants, and conscripts in terms of their most immediate and pressing political and economic social realities. Narrow ethnic or *russkii* ascriptions were rare among the lower classes, particularly in the most ethnically homogenous regions of the empire. Most were accustomed to seeing non-Russian Tsarist elites as a constitutive feature of "their" empire, just as Russian peasants especially distrusted the Russian landed classes.

All of this underscores the political weakness of Russian nationalism in a key moment of geopolitical collapse. Deep into World War I, most Russian workers in the capital cities – and most of the ethnic Russian revolutionary leadership – had not yet expressed the need to be ruled by coethnics – a defining criterion of an articulated nationalism. But by 1916, ethnic and class ascriptions diverged as workers increasingly viewed the privileged classes as insufficiently bearing the costs of war. The Bolsheviks' politics of linking war and capitalism was persuasive, just as their "toilers" versus "gentlemen" narrative resonated (playing on *narod* both as "nation" and as "common people") and fused a workers' language of class with that of nation (Smith 2008: 170–9). All of this unambiguously advertised who was bearing the burdens of empire and strengthened the class narrative as the best explanation of their experiences. Therefore, their socialist universalism contained a certain tension: it was radical in its class attack on Tsarist autocracy but conservative in its desire to preserve the empire.

So the ethnic Russian Bolsheviks carried the distinctive imperial-mindedness of social worlds characterized by culturally weak *russkii* identities into the Bolshevik movement. Lower-class Russians suffered imperial exclusions: historically the Russian peasantry and working class paid most of the economic costs of maintaining the empire in dues, taxes, and conscription, and they were repressed as urban workers. Class alienation was clearer and ethnic exclusions almost nonexistent, but the Russian Bolsheviks were characterized by social worlds of *rossiiskii*, imperial inclusiveness, in vivid contrast to a Russianizing Tsarism. The Russian Bolsheviks' social experiences complemented those of the ethnic minorities and mirrored the latter's commitments to a universalist

political vision. The ethnic tolerance they brought into Bolshevism was abso-
lutely critical in defining Bolshevism's universalist inclusiveness. As Smith
(1999: 201) argued, the political movement "inculcated members of different
backgrounds with its distinctive norms and values which served to mitigate the
influence of wider social divisions." Thus Shliapnikov, a practicing Old Believer,
could fiercely defend his religious identity unproblematically inside Bolshevism
at the height of the Revolution (Allen 2005). At every socioeconomic level,
for these Bolsheviks Russianness had a tentative and fragile quality that lent
itself to political universalism. State repression made this kind of culturally and
economically pluralist mobilization easier: the more the state repressed, the less
cultural and class differences mattered, and the more the state *Russianized*, the
more ethnically tolerant the movement and its members actually became.

Conclusion

In a now famous article, the historian Yuri Slezkine pointed out that scholars have tended not to notice the "chronic ethnophilia" of the early Soviet regime, the fact that the "dictatorship of the proletariat was a Tower of Babel" (Slezkine 1994: 414–15, 420, 439). In fact, socioethnic particularism did conspicuously underlay the unity of class-universalism. Arguably some of this is traceable to the ways in which the early Soviet elite was a product of – and indeed responded to – the political exclusions and marginalizing experiences of an industrializing and Russianizing multiethnic empire. The biographical chapters illustrated how Bolshevik radicalism appealed most to those who valued a secular, universalist, ecumenical, or ethnically neutral, *rossiiskii*-oriented, or imperial-minded politics, particularly in those social locations across the empire where ethnic violence, religious sectarianism, Russification, imperial imaginaries, or geopolitics were most threatening to belonging, identity, or position. Class-universalism was a product of specific socioethnic conditions. Socioethnic locations in the multiethnic borderlands or in the Russian heartland, multiethnic urbanism, rural ethnic conflict, and incomplete or problematic assimilationism were all shared dimensions of experience that funneled young radicals into a Russian-inflected, class-universalist radicalism; class communities were often experienced through – and constructed around – ethnic, religious, or cultural solidarities; and political radicalism often resulted from the entwining of socioethnic position, assimilation, relationship to the Tsarist state, and regional ethnopolitics.

But as political repression suppressed ethnic divisions and reinforced class-based mobilizational identities, it firmly embedded socioethnic marginality into the Bolshevism's core identity. So Bolshevism offered a resonant political expression and social experience of belonging for those most marginalized by disproportionately paying the political costs (middle-class minority elites) and economic burdens (lower-class ethnic Russians) of maintaining the Russian Empire in the half-century before the Revolution.

The strategies of empire outlined in Chapter 2 and woven through the empirical chapters shaped experiences of marginality and created a radicalized, but *rossiiskii*-oriented, multiethnic intelligentsia. In this, the emergence and composition of socialist class-universalism was as intimately related to the burdens of empire as it was to industrialization. I highlighted four broad imperial dynamics that helped produce and funnel Bolshevik radicalism, as well as other leftist and rightist mobilizations: (1) incorporation or exclusion from the empire's civil and military bureaucracies and political hierarchies; (2) assimilatory Russification of, or access to, and exclusion from, educational institutions; (3) ethnicized ascriptive identities created by the empire's systems of social surveillance, policing, measurement, or control; and (4) a variety of policies around dissimilatory Russification, which differentially affected social mobility and ethnic inclusion/exclusion depending on the imperial region's ethnopolitical context and relationship to the state.

Together these strategies of empire broadly shaped the social locations and experiential contexts that produced political radicalism in late Imperial Russia. As they organize the biographical material, these imperial dynamics suggest five broad, but closely related observations. *First*, while most sociological scholarship has paid almost exclusive attention to class identities and to the class narrative of Russia's revolutionary movements and to its political ideology, in revolutionary imperial society ethnicity was often a slightly more salient dimension to social experiences – and therefore to social identities and political radicalism – than was class. Bolshevisms' revolutionary ideology framed the struggle in a class narrative that did not entirely reflect some of the most important underlying social and experiential forces that gave the movement much of its social force and ideological potency. So the disconnect between the revolutionary narrative and the substantive experiences and radicalizations of the movement's social carriers in particular ethnic, social, and political worlds requires a more considered analysis of the precise elective affinities at work.

Writing on the relationship between nation and class in nationalist mobilizations, Gellner (1996) argued that it was the conflation of class with cultural difference that gave rise to revolutionary potential: while national movements were effective if they were sustained by class rivalry, class conflict by itself could not engender revolution. Neither class nor nation, Gellner (1996: 143) wrote, can mobilize to revolutionary levels on its own, but they become most politically consequential when they converge. In his work on ethnic cleansing, one of Mann's (2005: 5) key claims is that "ethnonationalism is strongest where it can capture other senses of exploitation," when ethnic groups believe that they are being materially exploited, and class or ethnicity capture or channel one another. Suny (1993a: 29, 77) argued more specifically that social conflict in the Russian Empire's peripheries was made all the more turbulent because of the intersection of culture with other social cleavages. And as John A. Hall (inter alia, 2003: 22; 2010: ch. 10) has written, there is greater social bite when inequalities are marked by cultural differences, but the political context matters very much. More generally, then, most politically consequential movements occur when social conflict is politicized through cultural differences, or when cultural differences are reinforced and politicized by social inequality, because a politics that addresses these confluences can more effectively articulate more than one dimension of identity, and more than one dimension of exclusion, alienation, or marginality.

This is generally right, and broadly applicable to the Bolsheviks, so I have repeatedly stressed their socioethnic exclusions and marginalities. However, at the core of understanding Bolshevism's socioethnic complexity is the issue of apportioning, to the extent possible, the relative weight to be given to class versus ethnicity in their social experiences and radicalizations – or, to put it another way, how much class and ethnicity intersected, overlapped, or diverged as dimensions of social experience. Did their radicalism reflect the effects of class structures on ethnic experiences, or did they reflect the class or economic effects of the empire's ethnic ranking? And what role did Tsarist policies play in this? The biographical accounts provide an empirical basis for claiming that identities and radicalism were indeed shaped by certain socioeconomic factors, classical blocked social mobility, or some form of class decline or alienation. This dimension of radicalization in its purer form was particularly important for the ethnic Russians, as well as for some of the Ukrainian peasant-workers. Traditional class-based sources of identity and radicalism mattered.

Overall, however, social class was a dimension of only varying significance for this leadership elite, and my findings indicate not the most experientially important one. The biographical reconstructions of the Bolsheviks' social worlds suggest that for most of them, ethnopolitical and cultural exclusions were perhaps the most salient dimension of their social experiences because of the way in which social identities were affected by imperial strategies – or, more precisely, because of the experiential intersection of identity formation and political marginality in the Russian Empire. As we saw in the biographical chapters, their experiences of wrestling with marginality, belonging, and exclusion were significant. It was reflected repeatedly in their experiences in nationalist or *rossiiskii* groups, in "imperial" experiences in the empire's educational institutions and bureaucracies, in the ambiguities in attempts at assimilation, and in a political search for community in difficult regional ethnopolitics. Of course ethnocultural exclusions are often anyway experienced most acutely at the middle and top of the social ladder, where social identities are most strongly in need of articulation and protection. And it was in these social locations that imperial policies, both conciliatory and exclusionary, affected specific socioethnic niches across the empire's ethnicities, Russian and non-Russian, urban and rural.

But, for instance, whether an ethnic quota restricting middle-class Jewish access to universities, or to the *advokatura*, is categorized as class-alienating, ethnic-exclusionary, or some combination of both is, in important respects, irrelevant in terms of understanding its individual and social effect: the aspiring and assimilating Jewish youth *experiences* it at the level of identity most intimately and most directly as a Jew, and only vaguely as a member of the intelligentsia, because it differentially affects that dimension of his or her social identity which is experienced or felt most personally or most intimately. Jewishness is

ascriptively forced on them, and they are acutely conscious that they would not have been distinguished had they not been Jewish. In a Russianizing empire, marginality was often experienced as unrequited assimilation or lack of access, not as a purely class exclusion.

And yet middle-class membership did make ethnic slights sting even more. As was the case with so many non-Russian Bolsheviks, the desire to assimilate, or to find a place in a community, was often felt acutely – hence their activism in multiple groups because of underlying shifts in ethnopolitics as the groupings ethnicized. Significantly, imperial policies that increasingly made ethnicity the most salient political and official ascription gave rise to anxieties around particular social identities. Especially in middle-class contexts, which were becoming more multiethnic, and in which status ambiguities were most pronounced, socioethnic exclusions were typically experienced most intimately in ethnocultural terms, and only secondarily as class-inflected illiberalisms. When social mobility was predicated on an assimilated (Russified) belonging in the middling classes – which in late imperial society were also increasingly characterized by expectations of meritocracy – even minor ethnic indignities and distinguishing discriminations meant shame and humiliation. And this gave radicalism much of its experiential potency. In these contexts, a political ideology that problematized class-ascriptions opened up much needed social space and submerged personal ethnic humiliations. In effect, a *rossiiskii* grouping guaranteed belonging both at the level of a political narrative that neutrally problematized class and, as we have seen, at the level of social relationships within the radical movement. Bolshevism' socialist narrative problematized class ascriptions, not ethnonational identities, and in doing so it corrected a key source of political exclusion, marginality, and social conflict in Imperial Russian society. But the underlying ethnic dynamics were powerful enough to become embedded into the movement's core identity.

This leads to a *second* observation. The account I offer shifts the focus away from the narrative's content or revolutionary discourse, toward a greater emphasis on actual social relations and social locations, and to the ways in which revolutionary narratives are embedded in experiences and social relationships. Methodologically, this meant exploring the locations or specific social coordinates that produced socialist radicalism and Bolshevik revolutionaries, and in particular their social relationships, communities, workplaces, neighborhoods, and ethnopolitics realities. The most important substantive finding on the social embeddedness of the revolutionary discourse validates an emerging consensus that revolutionary actors are mobilized or "recruited through pre-existing networks of residence, occupation, community, and friendship" (Goldstone 2001: 153). My general findings support Gould's (1995: esp. ch. 6) findings on the 1870s radical mobilizations in France, where class identities were rooted in preexisting urban communities, neighborhoods, and social relationships. In a multiethnic empire, these were usually ethnically, culturally, or religiously constituted. The Bolsheviks' biographies suggest that to the extent that class or socioeconomic position was felt or experienced, it was generally mediated through rural cultural communities, ethnic neighborhoods, Russified schools, and ethnic occupational networks. Of course socioeconomic dimensions were purer for the ethnic Russians given their comparatively more homogeneous contexts, but as we saw in Chapter 8, these were defined in imperial *rossiiskii* terms, not in ethnic *russkii* terms. In short, in the late Russian Empire, social class was mostly experienced through ethnocultural location.

A substantial portion of the Bolshevik leadership was assimilated, and assimilating, cultural outsiders. For the non-Russians, Russification, assimilation, and promises of social mobility created discordant experiences and identities when combined with illiberal ethnic exclusions. But the combination of cultural Russification and political marginalization facilitated the emergence of an intelligentsia committed to reconstructing the empire – that is, to a universalist, socialist, *rossiiskii*-oriented political imaginary. Most were first- or second-generation ethnic minorities seeking Russified assimilation, so most were only quasi-assimilated and straddled ethnocultural boundaries. But cultural assimilation itself created blurred ethnic and social boundaries while redrawing new status markers. Russification meant higher educational levels, literacy rates, and increased social mobility, which paradoxically meant not integration into Russian society, but rather increased cultural difference from the surrounding populations (Nathans 1996). In multiethnic contexts, Russification or assimilation actually increased social marginality, as quasi-assimilated individuals felt culturally suspended between cultural groups. Against this, the ethnic Russian Bolsheviks' imperial-minded or *rossiiskii*-oriented identities significantly shaped the ethnic tolerance of the movement as a whole, most influentially in the figure of Lenin.

For all its moral collectivism, then, Bolshevism actually provided crucial neutral social space – absent in wider imperial society – within which problematic and marginal ethnic and socioethnic identities could be cultivated and ambiguous assimilation could be validated with few identity costs. That is, in creating a strong mobilizational collective identity, Bolshevism paradoxically individualized identities in at least one key sense: it accepted individuals as revolutionaries first and as ethnics second. So if the marginality of an elite can be critical to the social power of its "transformative" ideology (Goldstone 1991: 424–5 and passim; Skocpol 1994: 14–15), a Russified, ethnocultural marginality had become embedded in this revolutionary movement's core identity. Bolshevik revolutionary politics was (at least temporarily) able to render experiences of ethnocultural or socioethnic particularism into a commitment to universalist revolutionary politics. It became a mobilizational product of ethnopolitical marginality and organizational isolation.

This had another important dimension. As we saw in Chapters 3 and 8, respectively on the Jews and the Russians, there was a stronger social closure around class within the leftist revolutionary mobilizations, including Bolshevism, than there was around ethnicity. There were higher levels of ethnic intermarriage than cross-class marriages: there were, for instance, more Russian-Jewish marriages within Bolshevism than there were working-class/

middle-class marriages. On the evidence, the more problematic social boundary within the culture of the leftist mobilizations was class, not ethnicity. In the Russian Empire more generally, marriage was typically a form of social assimilation usually reserved for the upper classes and nobilities. But despite the mobilization's class-universalism, within the Bolshevik leadership there was greater individual ethnic boundary crossing than class boundary crossing (for a general sociological discussion of this dynamic, see Loveman 1999; Wimmer 2008).

The *third* conclusion concerns Bolshevism's multiethnic mobilizational effect, or the revolutionary movement's extensive cross-class and cross-ethnic alliances. In part because their numbers were small compared to other socialist parties, the Bolsheviks accepted anyone, of any social origin, of any ethnicity, religion, and level of assimilation, regardless of previous involvement in nationalist groupings – hence the many Bolsheviks who came to the movement after activism in cultural, religious, and nationalist groupings. As Molotov claimed in 1917, the new revolutionary elite desperately needed educated and articulate men: "[Lenin] knew how to make use of everyone – Bolsheviks, half-Bolsheviks, and quarter Bolsheviks alike, but only literate ones" (quoted in Chuev 1991: 178). This not only brought a great deal of ideological and political diversity into Bolshevik radicalism, but also served to widen and deepen its mobilizational base. A movement organizationally predicated on cross-class and interethnic membership alliances could effectively expand the revolutionary situation as it fused social movement resources with political party politics. It is tempting to read the Russianness of Bolshevism from 1917 back into the preceding revolutionary decades. But Bolshevism's revolutionary politics organizationally depended on – and indeed exploited – ethnic diversity and political marginality.

So if Bolshevism's substantial socioethnic and ideological heterogeneity and its distinctive class-ethnic alignments gave the movement a socially wide and diverse mobilizational base under revolutionary conditions, part of its organizational strength derived from its ability to culturally homogenize both vertically (in cross-class coalitions) and horizontally (in ethnocultural networks) within the same movement.[1] Although nominally a socialist (two-class) horizontal mobilization, it could organizationally compete with vertical (multi-class) nationalist movements because its multiethnic and dual identity leadership could effectively pull in a diversity of cross-class ethnic networks and social resources, urban and rural. This was especially evident, as we saw in Chapters 5 and 7, respectively in Ukraine and the South Caucasus.

More specifically, we know that under certain conditions, ethnic and religious communities can facilitate class mobilizations because they can provide the social trust and shared values necessary to overcome certain collective action problems; when the costs of action are potentially high, ethnic communities' shared norms and social trust can provide mobilizational momentum

---

[1] The same could be said for the Mensheviks and the SRs.

(cf. Katznelson 1981: 21–2; Mann 1993: ch. 7). For those in certain socioethnic locations in revolutionary Russia, ethnic communities and organizations served this integrative and facilitative function, even though they could also pull in the other direction: where capitalists were of a different social group (e.g., in the western borderlands), capitalism as the class enemy could be distinguished from the (Russian) state. But once the state intensified its repression, ethnic divisions across working classes were more easily overcome, confronted by common repression.

So while part of Bolshevism's organizational strength did classically derive from its centralized, disciplined, and ideologically cohesive elite, as important was its ability to culturally homogenize the resources of a socioethnically complex elite into what functionally resembled a nationalist movement. It was able to translate a variety of socioethnic exclusions into a commitment to a new social category – class – and in so doing it changed the nature of the political conversation. It not only created a new mobilizational identity, but a new social identity as well. Its mobilizational politics created a homogenous, Russian-inflected, universalist revolutionary elite out of ethnically diverse segments of the empire's minority middling classes and lower-class Russians in a key state-building moment. And this functional requirement of the revolutionary mobilization would also be a functional requirement of nation-state building out of a disintegrating multiethnic empire.

Fourth, the difference between the socioethnic composition of the Bolshevik leadership and that of the movement's followers deserves attention. The contrast in ethnic composition between the Bolshevik leadership and the movements' largely Russian rank and file, as well as that between the Bolshevik leadership and the wider population, implies something about the ethnic and imperial dynamics inside the revolutionary movement. If Bolshevism was highly cosmopolitan and complex in socioethnic composition, its ethnocultural diversity was not problematic in the early revolutionary years, both because it emerged out of the interstices of the multiethnic empire and because there was little to distinguish Bolshevism's non-Russianness from that of the imperial ruling Romanovs that they replaced. The Bolshevik elite's ethnic diversity was not regarded as problematic – except by the rightist, nationalist parties who famously thought it full of Jewish conspirators and cosmopolitans. But the contrast between the multiethnic revolutionary leadership and the ethnic Russian shock troops of the Revolution (workers, soldiers, and conscripts) is even more significant considered against three years of a war that was to have deepened Russian patriotic sentiments, clarified national identities, and increased populist anti-Semitism. To be sure, military conscription was used by Russian elites as an instrument of nation-building (Sanborn 2003; Petrovsky-Shtern 2009b), and Russian elites attempted to "nationalize" the land and to mobilize a certain economic nationalism against foreign and ethnic minority commercial diasporas. But these efforts did not have the desired effects, and in fact they undermined social order, exacerbated ethnic conflicts, and radicalized minorities even further (Lohr 2003: 171–3). On the whole, most Russians were accustomed to seeing non-Russian Tsarist elites as a constitutive feature of "their" empire. Russian peasants especially distrusted the Russian landed classes, and most had little, if any, personal contact or experience with the empire's minority subjects, although they absorbed knowledge of the empire's diversity through its representations in wider popular culture and sometimes through their own geographical mobility. But this underscores the political weakness of Russian nationalism in a key moment of geopolitical collapse.

This early continuity in terms of the ethnic composition of the ruling elite with the Tsarist regime stood in contrast to the composition of the Soviet leadership from the late 1920s onward. If the CCs of the early revolutionary years were notable for their ethnic and class diversity, Stalin's subsequent consolidation of power witnessed the concomitant Russianization and proletarianization of the CCs. This contrast marked off the heterogeneity of the Bolshevik elite that was a product of the collapsing empire, from the more homogenous Soviet elite of the late 1920s and 1930s that was a product of the Revolution.

By the 1930s, the Soviet "affirmative action" empire and the Bolsheviks' early ethnophilic strategies – including gerrymandering the state along ethnic principles more than economic ones – ceded to more racialist ascriptions and exclusionary policies of ethnic deportations (Martin 1998, 2001: ch. 8; Hirsch 2002, 2005: 159; Weitz 2002). Whether these repressive ethnic exclusions were a result of Soviet xenophobia and the securitization of ethnicity (Martin 1998) or whether they were inevitable processes in nation-building (Brown 2004; Hirsch 2005), ethnic enemies were added to class enemies. And the cultural technologies of social control used to count and assess these ethnic threats were similar to those used by the Tsarist state: the census and the passport (Torpey 1997; Holquist 2001). So while language and *soslovie* questions on the 1897 Census had provided administrators with some assessment of the *success* of Tsarist Russification (Cadiot 2005), by the first Bolshevik census the combination of language and nationality questions was seen as indicative of which groups had been the *victims* of Tsarist Russification (Hirsch 2005: 126). Eventually ethnicity became firmly linked to economic development and Tsarism's earlier ethnographic criteria would be discounted.

To put this another way, the move from a class-heterogeneous and ethnically diverse revolutionary leadership that was a product of the multiethnic empire to a class-homogenous and Russianized leadership that was the product of the Revolution mapped onto two distinct nation-building moments: in the first, a Russian-inflected, class-universalist movement mobilized ethnically diverse, minority middle classes and lower-class Russians in a way that functionally resembled a nationalist mobilization, and it held together and geopolitically steered a crumbling multiethnic empire. So in the early revolutionary years, the ideological problems were strategic. The Bolsheviks were inescapably a product of the empire's ruins, so mobilizational identities were constructed with a view to strategic appeal – hence the probable recruitment of certain minorities (Caucasians or Ukrainians) into the leadership ranks. But once the state was consolidated, there arose the problem of ideological legitimation. This second nation-building moment prompted a conscious – and often vicious – effort to purify class- and ethnically based identities in order to both legitimate the elite and to align it with the content of the ruling ideology's narrative – hence the systematic recruitment of ethnic Russians of "proletarian" origin into the CCs and the ethnic cleansing of the party ranks.

The *fifth* key finding more concretely concerns the elective affinity between the revolutionary ideology and its social carriers, and the way in which it offered a resonant account of social experiences and marginalizations. Revolutionary ideologies are effective when they strike roots in certain cultural contexts or frameworks (Goldstone 2001:155), and commitments to a Russian-inflected revolutionary politics were very context dependent. Social location mattered – as did assimilation, ethnic politics, socioethnic positioning, and the group's relationship to the Russian state. So at least four closely related dimensions of Bolshevism's radical politics were entwined with the social locations and ethnocultural biographies of its social carriers. They *experientially* addressed certain imperial, class, or colonial grievances while also protecting – and indeed elevating – the positions of key politically marginalized groups. Most immediately, we know that in general a protest group gains commitment by manifesting the same qualities that are expected from the state (cf. Goldstone 2001: 154). So, as was evident in a number of the biographies, for many, Bolshevism represented a better version of "the good *rossiiskii* ideal" where Tsarism was losing ground.[2] That is, they sought a *Rossiia* that was universalist and socialist, rather than nationalizing and autocratic, but one that was nevertheless Russian-inflected because of their various identifications with the *rossiiskii* empire. A *rossiiskii*-minded intelligentsia emerged committed to a political vision of a secular, non-nationalist, ecumenical, geopolitically stable, and non-colonial multiethnic state, partly as an ideological antidote to a morally faltering, intolerant, geopolitically insecure, and Russianizing Tsarism.

But if Bolshevism was to manifest the qualities expected from the imperial state, as such it was less radical a revolutionary ideology than may first appear. This leads to a second dimension of the elective affinity between the ideological narrative and its social carriers. I have argued that Russian Bolshevism experientially offered certain marginalized, yet assimilating, elites in the empire's multiethnic borderlands an ideology that would sustain certain imperial structures, protect identity and position, and provide the experiences of community for those who were most ethnoculturally and politically marginalized. Paradoxically, Bolshevism was a modernization ideology of the Left, but when considered together with the social composition of its ideological carriers, the functionally conservative tensions within it become clear: it provided its social carriers an ideological underwriting of the sociopolitical organization of the empire, which was being threatened not only by rapid social change, but also by a nationalizing Russian state and by empire-subverting, exclusionary nationalisms. Referring to an altogether different kind of historical transition,

---

[2] I thank Michael Mann for this framing.

Gellner (1988: 92) wrote that in moments of profound social transformation, "to a considerable extent the social base and need for some communal religion remains effective: hence a form of ritual which underwrites and reinforces social organization, rather than one which replaces it and consoles for its absence, also continues to be in demand." Bolshevism served precisely this "conservative," "empire-saving" function.

Thirdly and relatedly, this underscores what Rieber (2000) has called the "borderland factor" in the emergence of an ideology and its social carriers (Gerasimov et al. 2005; Brown 2004; Rieber 2004; Hirsch 2005: ch. 4). A particular kind of leadership can emerge from the debris of empire – one that is intensely suspicious of nationalism because in illiberal or imperial contexts, nationalism was nearly always conceived in ethnically exclusionary terms. Borderland and regional ethnic elites in empires have often sought to reconstruct new social orders, placing themselves at the political (and geographic) center of power (Rieber 2001: 1645). Bolshevism's borderland marginality was crucial to its antinationalist appeal and to its Russified mobilizational class politics.

Finally, and most importantly, the Bolsheviks' socioethnic marginalizations suggest a new interpretation of routes to radicalization in revolutionary Russia more generally (combining Tables 2.1 and 2.2 in Chapter 2). The Russian higher classes, alienated after 1861, closed ranks after the 1905 revolutions in nationalist defense of a Russified autocracy. Conservative, anti-Semitic Russian nationalism was most popular among Russian settlers in the borderlands and among propertied elites inside the imperial state, both to quell social revolution and to maintain *Staatsvolk* unity against minority unrest. This explained their notable presence in rightist, conservative movements. Most of the lower classes (especially the peasantries) of the empire's ethnic minorities had largely been ignored by the Russian state. Non-Russified and non-politicized until World War I, they were subsequently courted in later nationalist mobilizations.

But lower-class Russians and (upper) middle-class ethnic minorities were the two social categories that disproportionately sustained the heaviest burdens of maintaining the Russian Empire in the half-century before the Revolution: ethnic minority elites disproportionately paid much of the political and geopolitical costs of imperial cohesion, while Russian peasants in the empire's core disproportionately paid its economic costs in dues, taxes, and conscription. So these two socioethnic groups show up in disproportionate numbers not only in Bolshevism, but also in roughly the same proportions in other center-left radical movements in revolutionary Russia – the Mensheviks, the SRs, and the Kadets. The emergence of this *rossiiskii*-oriented elite should occasion a rethinking of the roles of ethnicity, class, and imperial rule in both revolutionary and reactionary politics in the last years of the Russian Empire.

If Bolshevism's class-universalist politics was a response to those most affected by the dilemmas of imperial exclusions and marginalizations, it effectively mapped the revolutionary transition from a multiethnic empire problematized by ethnicity to a multiethnic Soviet state problematized by class. Universalist ideologies emerge from specific social and political conditions – and Bolshevism embodied a distinctive ethnopolitical marginality that defined the last years of the Russian Empire. Bolshevism reflected the political costs of empire; social dislocations and political exclusions created quasi-assimilated social worlds that generated distinctive kinds of marginalities and enabled reinventions. In this way, socialist class-universalism was as much a product of imperial particularism and socioethnic marginality as it was constituted by it.

Appendix A

In addition to autobiographies, biographies, and memoir accounts pertaining to individual Bolsheviks, the following general sources have been used to compile the biographical data contained in this appendix: Kaznelson and Günzberg (1912–14); Drizulis (1957); Kopanev (1967); Prokhorov (1969–78); Zaionchkovskii (1976); *Granat* (1989); Izdatel'stvo Tsentral'nogo Komiteta KPSS (1989a, 1989b, 1990); Vilenskii-Sibiriakov and Kon ([1927–33] 1997); HIAPO; and the Boris I. Nicolaevsky Collection at the Hoover Institution of Stanford University.

TABLE A1: *Social Origins (Father's Class or Estate) of the Bolsheviks, by Nationality/Ethnicity*

	Rus.	Jew.	Ukr.	Pol./Lith.	Lat.	Cauc.	Other[1]	Total
Class								
Peasant	14	2	1		2			19
Worker:								
Skilled[2]	4					1[3]	1	6
Unskilled	4		1	2	2		1	10
Artisan/small manufacturer	1	3	1					5
Professional/educated bourgeoisie:[4]								
Low level	4	1[5]	2				1	8
Professional	2	2	1					5
Commercial bourgeoisie:[6]								
Petty merchant[7]		2				2		4
Middling merchant		2				2		4
Haute bourgeoisie[8]		1		1	1			3
Military	1		1				2	4
Clergy	2		1					3
Noble/gentry:[9]								
Landed noble				1	1	3[10]		5
Service/personal	4		1					5
Estate								
No recognized estate	1	1	1					3
Hereditary noble	3			1		3		7
Personal noble	2		1					3
Clergy	2		1					3
Distinguished citizen	1	2	2[11]				2	7
Merchant		3	1			2		6
Meshchanstvo	13	5		2	2	2	1	25
Peasant	14	2	1	1[12]	4[13]	2[14]	2	26
Cossack								
Inorodtsy								

Note: N = 81 for classes, 80 for estates, omitting unreliable data that was either Sovietized, uncorroborated, or conflicting. Empty rows are included to preserve the full list of classes and official tsarist categories from the imperial census.

[1] Includes Kazakhs, Germans, and others.

[2] Workers in middling to large manufacturers and factories.

[3] Mikoyan's father's skill level is unclear.

[4] *Bildungsbürgertum*, low level (petty bureaucrats/civil servants, elementary teachers, clerks, etc.) or professionals (doctors, barristers, engineers, agronomists, university/gimnaziia professors). A number of these positions were in the employ of the local or imperial government.

[5] Iaroslavskii's father was a furrier, but his mother, a schoolteacher, is not counted here; Kuibyshev's (Russian) schoolteacher mother is also not counted. Radek is included here.

[6] Includes middling commerciants/merchants and capitalists, as well as landowners and commercial property elites and small property owners of non-noble status.

[7] "Merchant" could refer both to wealthy commercial entrepreneurs and to petty traders, usually very poor.

[8] Includes wealthy merchants and capitalists, well-off landowners of non-noble status only.

[9] These groups may overlap. Each can include hereditary nobles.

[10] Dzhaparidze's family were landowners, but their noble status in unclear; Ordzhonikidze's family were nobles, but their landowning status is uncertain.

[11] Skrypnyk's and Tsiurupa's fathers, a petty railroad official and a municipal civil servant, were both at the lower end of the distinguished citizens estate.

[12] Kapsukas's family were prosperous landowners but still considered in the small Lithuanian rural bourgeoisie to be in the peasant estate because they held no noble titles.

[13] Smilga's and Stuchka's families were prosperous non-noble landowners, and like Kapsukas's were at the higher end of the peasant estate.

[14] Dzhaparidze's family were wealthy landowners at the higher end; Ryskulov's father was a nomadic stock raiser whose wealth is unclear.

TABLE A2: *Occupation (Class or Estate) of the Bolsheviks, by Nationality/Ethnicity*

	Rus.	Jew.	Ukr.	Pol./Lith.	Lat.	Cauc.	Other	Total
Class								
Peasant								
Worker:								
Skilled	5	1			3	1	2	12
Unskilled	16	1	3			1		21
Artisan/small manufacturer	1	2						3
Professional/educated bourgeoisie:								
Low level	3	2	2		1	3	1	12
Professional	6	5	3		1	4	1	20
Commercial bourgeoisie:								
Petty merchant								
Middling merchant								
Haute bourgeoisie								
Military								
Clergy								
Noble/gentry:								
Landed noble								
Service/personal								
Professional revolutionary[1]	6	4		1	2	1	2	16
Estate								
No recognized estate[2]	7	7[3]	4		1	7		26
Hereditary noble								
Personal noble								
Clergy								
Distinguished citizen	2		1		1		1	5
Merchant								
Meshchanstvo	7[4]	4	3	3			3	20
Peasant	15[4]				2			17
Cossack								
Inorodtsy								

Note: N = 84 for classes, 68 for estates, omitting unreliable data that was either Sovietized, uncorroborated, or conflicting. Empty rows are included to facilitate comparison with Table A1.

[1] Professional revolutionary was the only occupation of these Bolsheviks; they had no other practicing occupation or qualification.
[2] This category included humanists/writers, lawyers, economists, teachers, draftsmen, doctors, pharmacists, (nonradical) journalists, agronomists, statisticians, and chemists.
[3] Sokolnikov was both a trained economist and a lawyer.
[4] These categories blend into one another for the Russians.

Appendix B

Merging Class and Estate

The *clerical estate* comprised mostly Russian Orthodox clergy, with significant numbers of Georgians and Armenians, but almost entirely excluded Jewish, (Catholic) Polish, and (Buddhist) Kalmyk clergy.

The *noble estates* included the hereditary nobility, the personal nobility, the urban and rural gentry, and the aristocracy, in practice comprising a diverse set of social positions and occupations, both urban and rural, including the following: the 150 aristocratic families that ruled Russia, landowning and non-landowning nobility higher bureaucratic officials (armed forces and civil bureaucracy), a considerable portion of the free professionals and service elite (overlapping with the intelligentsia and *raznochintsy* [people of various ranks]), higher government service, and certain educated careerists. With the promotion of commoners, the sons of landed elites and déclassé nobilities became part of the new urban upper middle classes. Georgian, Polish, Lithuanian, Tatar, and German nobilities were, in proportional terms, more significant than the Russian nobility.

The *merchant* and *distinguished citizen* estates blurred into the noble estate. They were primarily nonofficial urban upper and middle classes, comprising non-noble, nonofficial elites, both urban and rural, elements of the educated bourgeoisie, and the "great" bourgeoisie or wealthy merchants. Occupationally, these estates included professionals and rentiers, bureaucrats and civil servants, a segment of the business elite in banking and commerce, and some of the free professions. The merchant estate, or much of the commercial bourgeoisie, could include some the above, the middling-level business and banking classes, as well as members of the *gildii* (guilds), incorporated artisans with rules for apprenticeship (*tsekhi*), and small agricultural entrepreneurs. The presence of ethnic minorities in these estates was hugely significant. Significantly, the intelligentsia and *raznochintsy* (mostly composed of professionals employed by the state, provincial municipalities, *zemstva* courts, and universities) and those associated with the *zemstva* fell between official classifications. They drew from the cultural and intellectual elites, but also from the commercial bourgeoisie, bureaucrats, careerists, and segments of the petty bourgeoisie. Subject to upward and downward mobility, they were usually defined by exclusion – non-noble, non-peasant, non-merchant, nonregistered urbanites. The largest ethnic intelligentsias were Russian, Polish, Jewish, and Armenian.

The *meshchanstvo estate* (small burghers and townsmen) was roughly equivalent to the petty bourgeoisie and skilled and unskilled workers, comprising mostly urban, noncorporative, nonregistered guild artisans, small shopkeepers, white-collar employees, owners of small family businesses, petty capitalists, and a large floating population of the urban poor. Jews were the most prominent ethnic group in this estate; slightly more than 94 percent of the empire's Jews were classified as townsmen or urban and rural petty capitalists. Together the *meshchanstvo* and distinguished citizens included a very heterogeneous educated bourgeoisie of government officials in local administrations, judicial officials, the gendarmerie and the police, army officers, professionals (teachers, journalists, writers, intellectuals, doctors, etc.), and *zemstvo* officials/ clerks (some quite well off and others very poorly paid). The lower strata of the *meshchanstvo* and large portions of the peasant estate covered the whole of the working classes, especially those in factories, mining, and transport and the unskilled and unemployed urban poor. As late as 1895, the imperial state regarded workers as a subgroup of the peasantry.

The *peasant estate* in practice blurred with the *meshchanstvo*, comprising rural peasants without property or land, the largest proportion of the urban unskilled working class and manual labor, an unskilled, (un)employed urban poor, and a small rural bourgeoisie, or prosperous farmers.

The *inorodtsy* designated alien ethnic minorities, including Jews and unassimilable ethnics. The remaining estates were the *Cossack* and *military* estates.

Bibliography

Akhmedov, Teimur. 1988. *Nariman Narimanov*. Baku: Iazychy.

Allen, Barbara. 2005. "Alexandr Shliapnikov and the Origins of the Workers' Opposition, March 1919–April 1920." *Jarhbücher für Geschichte Osteuropas* 53: 1–24.

Altstadt, Audrey. 1992. *The Azerbaijani Turks: Power and Identity under Russian Rule*. Stanford, CA: Stanford University Press.

Alston, Patrick. 1969. *Education and the State in Tsarist Russia*. Stanford, CA: Stanford University Press.

Aminzade, Ronald, Jack A. Goldstone, and Elizabeth Perry. 2001. "Leadership Dynamics and Dynamics of Contention." Pp. 126–54 in *Silence and Voice in the Study of Contentious Politics*, by Ronald Aminzade et al. Cambridge: Cambridge University Press.

Anfimov, Andrei and Avenir Korelin, eds. 1995. *Rossiia 1913 god: statistiko-documental'nyi spravochnik*. St. Petersburg: BLITS.

Ascher, Abraham. 2001. *P.A. Stolypin: The Search for Stability in Late Imperial Russia*. Stanford, CA: Stanford University Press.

Avrutin, Eugene M. 2007. "Racial Categories and the Politics of (Jewish) Difference in Late Imperial Russia." *Kritika* 8(1): 13–40.

Avrutin, Eugene. 2010. *Jews and the Imperial State: Identification Politics in Tsarist Russia*. Ithaca, NY: Cornell University Press.

Baberowski, Jörg. 1995. "Juden und Antisemiten in der russischen Rechtanwaltschaft." *Jahrbücher für Geschichte Osteuropas* 43: 498–99.

Badcock, Sarah. 2007. *Politics and the People in Revolutionary Russia*. Cambridge: Cambridge University Press.

Balkelis, Tomas. 2005. "Provincials in the Empire: The Making of the Lithuanian National Elite, 1883–1905." In "Nation and Empire," special issue, *Studies in Ethnicity and Nationalism* 5: 4–23.

Baron, Nick and Peter Gatrell, eds. 2004. *Homelands: War, Population and Statehood in Eastern Europe and Russia, 1918–1924*. London: Anthem.

Bauer, Henning, Andreas Kappeler, and Brigitte Roth, eds. 1991. *Die Nationalitäten des Russischen Reiches in der Volkszählung von 1897*, vols. 1 and 2. Stuttgart: Franz Steiner Verlag.

Beauvois, Daniel. 1993. *La bataille de la terre en Ukraine: Les polonais et les conflits socio-ethniques*. Lille: Presses Universitaires de Lille.

Beria, Sergo. 2001. *Beria, My Father: Inside Stalin's Kremlin*. London: Duckworth.

Bilinsky, Yaroslav. 1978. "Mykola Skrypnyk and Petro Shelest: An Essay on the Persistence and Limits of Ukrainian National Communism." Pp. 105–43 in *Soviet Nationality Policies and Practices*, edited by Jeremy Azrael. New York: Praeger.

Birth, Ernst. 1974. *Die Oktobristen (1905–1913): Zielvorstellungen und Struktur*. Stuttgart: Ernst Klett.

Blobaum, Robert. 1984. *Feliks Dzierżyński and the SDKPiL: A Study of the Origins of Polish Communism*. Boulder, CO: East European Monographs.

1995. *Rewolucja: Russian Poland, 1904–1907*. Ithaca, NY: Cornell University Press.

Bonnell, Victoria. 1983. *The Roots of Rebellion: Worker's Politics and Organization in St. Petersburg and Moscow, 1900–1917*. Berkeley and Los Angeles: University of California Press.

Bradley, Joseph. 2002. "Subjects into Citizens: Societies, Civil Society, and Autonomy in Tsarist Russia." *American Historical Review* 107: 1094–123.

Breyfogle, Nicholas. 2003. "Colonization by Contract: Russian Settlers, South Caucasian Elites, and the Dynamics of Nineteenth-Century Tsarist Imperialism." Pp. 143–81 in *Extending the Borders of Russian History: Essays in Honor of Alfred J. Rieber*, edited by Marsha Siefert. Budapest: Central European University Press.

2005. *Heretics and Colonizers. Forging Russia's Empire in the South Caucasus*. Ithaca, NY: Cornell University Press.

Brooks, Jeffrey. 1985. *When Russia Learned to Read: Literacy and Popular Fiction, 1816–1917*. Princeton, NJ: Princeton University Press.

Brower, Daniel and Edward Lazzarini, eds. 1997. *Russia's Orient: Imperial Borderlands and Peoples, 1700–1917*. Bloomington: Indiana University Press.

Brown, Kate. 2004. *A Biography of No Place. From Ethnic Borderland to Soviet Heartland*. Cambridge, MA: Harvard University Press.

Brubaker, Rogers. 1996. *Nationalism Reframed: Nationhood and the National Question in the New Europe*. Cambridge: Cambridge University Press.

Brym, Robert. 1978. *The Jewish Intelligentsia and Russian Marxism: A Sociological Study of Intellectual Radicalism and Ideological Divergence*. London: Macmillan.

Brym, Robert and Rozalina Ryvkina. 1994. *The Jews of Moscow, Kiev, and Minsk: Identity, Antisemitism, Emigration*, edited by Howard Spear. London: Houndsmill, Macmillan.

Burbank, Jane. 2004. *Russian Peasants Go to Court: Legal Culture in the Countryside, 1905–1917*. Blooington: Indiana University Press.

2006. "An Imperial Rights Regime: Law and Citizenship in the Russian Empire." *Kritika: Explorations in Russian and Eurasian History* 7 (3): 397–431.

Cadiot, Juliette. 2004. "Le recensement de 1897: Les limites du contrôle imperial et la representation des nationalités." *Cahiers du monde russe* 45 (3–4): 441–64.

2005. "Searching for Nationality Statistics and National Categories at the End of the Russian Empire (1897–1917)." *Russian Review* 64: 440–55.

2007. *Le laboratoire impérial: Russie-URSS, 1870–1940*. Paris: Éditions du CNRS.

Calhoun, Craig. 2003. "'Belonging' in the cosmopolitan imaginary." *Ethnicities* 3 (4): 531–68.

Campbell, Elena. 2007. "The Muslim Question in Late Imperial Russia." Pp. 320–47 in *The Russian Empire. Space, People, Power, 1700–1930*, edited by Jane Burbank, Mark von Hagen, and Anatoly Remnev. Bloomington: Indiana University Press.

Carr, E.H. 1951. "Radek's Political Salon in Berlin in 1919." *Soviet Studies* 3(4): 411–30.

Chuev, Feliks. 1991. *Sto sorok besed s Molotovym*. Moscow: Terra.

Clay, Catherine B. 1995. "Russian Ethnographers in the Service of Empire, 1856–1862." *Slavic Review* 54(1): 45–61.

Clemens, Elisabeth. 2007. "Toward a Historicized Sociology: Theorizing Events, Processes, and Emergence." *Annual Review of Sociology* 33: 24.1–24.23.

Clements, Barbara Evans. 1979. *Bolshevik Feminist: The Life of Alexandra Kollontai*. Bloomington: Indiana University Press.

Cohen, Stephen. 1971. *Bukharin and the Bolshevik Revolution, 1888–1938*. Oxford: Oxford University Press.

Conquest, Robert. 1968. *The Great Terror. Stalin's Purges of the Thirties*. Houndmills: Macmillan.

Corrsin, Stephen. 1982. "The Changing Composition of the City of Riga, 1867–1913." *Journal of Baltic Studies* 13(1): 19–39.

Crews, Robert. 2003. "Empire and the Confessional State: Islam and Religious Politics in Nineteenth-Century Russia." *American Historical Review* 108 (1): 50–83.

Darrow, David. 2002. "Census as a Technology of Empire." *Ab Imperio* 4: 145–77.

Davies, R.W., Oleg V. Khlevniuk, E. A. Rees, Liudmila P. Kosheleva, and Larisa A. Rogovaya. 2003. "Lazar Kaganovich: The Career of a Stalinist Commissar." Pp. 21–36 in *The Stalin-Kaganovich Correspondence 1931–36*, edited by R.W. Davies et al. New Haven, CT: Yale University Press.

Deutscher, Isaac. 1954. *The Prophet Armed: Trotsky, 1879–1921*. Oxford: Oxford University Press.

  ed. 1968. *The Non-Jewish Jew and Other Essays*. Oxford: Oxford University Press.

Dolbilov, Mikhail. 2004. "Russification and the Bureaucratic Mind in the Russian Empire's Northwestern Region in the 1860s." *Kritika* 5(2): 245–71.

Donkov, I. P. 1990. "Lev Borisovich Kamenev." *Voprosy istorii KPSS* 4: 90–105.

Dowler, Wayne. 1995. "The Politics of Language in the Non-Russian Elementary Schools in the Eastern Empire, 1865–1914." *Russian Review* 54(4): 516–38.

Drizulis, A.A., ed. 1957. *Oktiabr'skai revoliutsiia v Latvii, dokumenty i materialy, 1917–1957*. Riga: Izdatel'stvo Akademii nauk Latviiskoi SSR.

Dubnow, Simon, Judah L. Kazenelson, and Baron Günzburg, eds. 1912–14. *Evreiskaia entsiklopediia: svod znanii o evreistve i ego kul'ture v proshlom i nastoiashchem*. Vols. 3, 4, 6, 10. St. Petersburg: Izdatel'stvo Brockhaus-Efron.

Duval, Charles. 1971. "The Forgotten Bolshevik: Jacob Mikhailovich Sverdlov, 1885–1917." PhD dissertation, University of Texas at Austin.

Dzerzhinskii, Felix. 1977 [1897]. *Izbrannie proizvedeniia v dvukh tomakh*, vol. 1. Moscow: Izdatel'stvo politicheskoi literatury.

  1984 [1902]. *Dnevnik zakliuchennogo: pis'ma*. Moscow: Molodaia Gvardiia.

  2002. *Prison Diary and Letters*. Honolulu, HI: University Press of the Pacific.

Eklof, Ben. 2010. "*Laska i Poriadok*: The Daily Life of the Rural School in Late Imperial Russia." *The Russian Review* 69: 7–29.

Eley, Geoff. 1988. "Remapping the Nation: War, Revolutionary Upheaval and State Formation in Eastern Europe, 1914–1923." Pp. 205–46 in *Ukrainian-Jewish Relations in Historical Perspective*, edited by Peter Potichnyj and Howard Aster. Edmonton: Canadian Institute of Ukrainian Studies.

Ellman, Michael. 2001. "The Road from Il'ich to Il'ich: The Life and Times of Anastas Ivanovich Mikoian." *Slavic Review* 60(1): 140–50.

Elyashevich, Dmitry A. 1999. *Pravitel'stvennaia politika i evreiskaia pechat' v Rossii, 1797–1917: Ocherki istorii tsenzury.* St. Petersburg/Jerusalem: Mosty Cultury/Gesharim.

Eriksen, T.H. 1993. *Ethnicity and Nationalism.* London: Pluto Press.

Evreiskoe naselenie Rossii po dannym perepisi 1897 g i po noveishim istochnikam. 1970. Tel Aviv: Aticot.

Ezergailis, Andrew. 1974. *The 1917 Revolution in Latvia.* New York: Columbia University Press.

   1983. *The Latvian Impact on the Bolshevik Revolution. The First Phase September 1917 to April 1918.* Boulder, CO: East European Monographs.

Farnsworth, B. 1980. *Alexandra Kollontai: Socialism, Feminism and the Bolshevik Revolution.* Stanford, CA: Stanford University Press.

Fiesler, Beate. 1989. "The Making of Russian Female Social Democrats, 1890–1917." *International Review of Social History* 34: 193–226.

Figes, Orlando. 2001. "The Russian Revolution of 1917 and its Language in the Village." Pp. 75–103 in *The Russian Revolution: the Essential Readings*, edited by Martin Miller. London: Blackwell.

Fischer, George. 1958. *Russian Liberalism: From Gentry to Intelligentsia.* Cambridge, MA: Harvard University Press.

Fitzpatrick, Sheila. 1993. "Ascribing Class: The Construction of Social Identity in Soviet Russia." *Journal of Modern History* 65: 745–70.

Frankel, Jonathan. 1981. *Prophecy and Politics: Socialism, Nationalism, and the Russian Jews, 1862–1917.* Cambridge: Cambridge University Press.

Frankel, Jonathan and Stephen Zipperstein, eds. 1992. *Assimilation and Community: The Jews in Nineteenth Century Europe.* Cambridge: Cambridge University Press.

Freeze, Gregory. 1986. "The *Soslovie* (Estate) Paradigm and Russian Social History." *American Historical Review* 91: 11–36.

   1996. "Subversive Piety: Religion and the Political Crisis in Late Imperial Russia." *The Journal of Modern History* 68(2): 308–50.

Gassenschmidt, Christoph. 1995. *Jewish Liberal Politics in Tsarist Russia, 1900–14: The Modernization of Russian Jewry.* Houndsmill: Macmillan.

Gatrell, Peter. 1999. *A Whole Empire Walking: Refugees in Russia during WWI.* Bloomington: Indiana University Press.

Gaudin, Corinne. 2007. *Ruling Peasants. Village and State in Late Imperial Russia.* DeKalb: Northern Illinois University Press.

   2008. "Rural Echoes of World War I: War Talk in the Russian Village." *Jahrbücher für Geschichte Osteuropas* 56(3): 391–414.

Gellner, Ernest. 1983. *Nations and Nationalism.* Ithaca, NY: Cornell University Press.

   1988. *Plough, Sword and Book.* Chicago: University of Chicago Press.

   1994. *Conditions of Liberty.* London: Penguin.

   1996. "The Coming of Nationalism and Its Interpretation: The Myths of Nation and Class." Pp. 98–145 in *Mapping the Nation*, edited by Gopal Balakrishnan. London: Verso.

   1997. *Nationalism.* New York: New York University Press.

   1998. *Language and Solitude: Wittgenstein, Malinowski and the Habsburg Dilemma.* Cambridge: Cambridge University Press.

Georgeon, François. 1996. "Note sur le modernisme en Azerbaijan au tournant du siècle." *Cahiers du Monde Russe* 37(1/2): 97–106.

Geraci, Robert. 2001a. *Window on the East: National and Imperial Identities in Late Tsarist Russia*. Ithaca, NY: Cornell University Press.

2001b. "Going Abroad or Going to Russia? Orthodox Missionaries in the Kazakh Steppe, 1881–1917." Pp. 274–310 in *Of Religion and Empire: Missions, Conversion, and Tolerance in Tsarist Russia*, edited by Robert Geraci and Mikhail Khodarkovsky. Ithaca, NY: Cornell University Press.

Gerasimov, Ilya, Serguie Glebov, Alexandr Kaplunovski, Marina Mogilner, and Aleksandr Semyonov. 2005. "In Search of a New Imperial History." *Ab Imperio* 1: 33–55.

Goldstone, Jack. 1991. *Revolution and Rebellion in the Early Modern World*. Berkeley and Los Angeles: University of California Press.

2001. "Toward a Fourth Generation of Revolutionary Theory." *Annual Review of Political Science* 4: 139–87.

ed. 2003. *States, Parties, and Social Movements*. Cambridge: Cambridge University Press.

Gould, Roger. 1995. *Insurgent Identities. Class, Community, and Protest in Paris from 1848 to the Commune*. Chicago: University of Chicago Press.

2003. *Collision of Wills: How Ambiguity about Social Rank Breeds Conflict*. Chicago: Chicago University Press.

Granat. 1989. *Deiateli SSSR i revoliutsionnogo dvizheniia Rossiia: entsiklopedicheskii slovar' Granat*. Moscow: Sovetskaia Entsiklopediia.

Graziosi, Andrea. 1999. "The New Soviet Archival Sources. Hypotheses for a Critical Assessment." *Cahiers du Monde Russe* 4(1–2): 13–64.

Haberer, Eric. 1992. "Cosmopolitanism, Anti-Semitism, and Populism: a Reappraisal of Russian and Jewish Response to the Pogroms of 1881–1882." Pp. 98–134 in *Pogroms: Anti-Jewish Violence in Modern Russian History*, edited by John Klier and Shlomo Lambroza. Cambridge: Cambridge University Press.

1995. *Jews and Revolution in Nineteenth Century Russia*. Cambridge: Cambridge University Press.

Hacohen, Malachai Haim. 1999. "Dilemmas of Cosmopolitanism: Karl Popper, Jewish Identity, and Central European Culture." *Journal of Modern History* 71: 105–49.

2000. *Karl Popper, the Formative Years, 1902–1945: Politics and Philosophy in Interwar Vienna*. New York: Cambridge University Press.

Hagen, Manfred. 1978. "Russification via 'Democratization'? Civil Service in the Baltic after 1906." *Journal of Baltic Studies* 9 (1): 56–65.

Hagen, William. 1996. "Before the Final Solution: Toward a Comparative Analysis of Political Anti-Semitism in Interwar Germany and Poland." *Journal of Modern History* 68(2): 351–86.

Haimson, Leopold. 1955. *The Russian Marxists and the Origins of Bolshevism*. Cambridge, MA: Harvard University Press.

1964. "The Problem of Social Stability in Urban Russia, 1905–1917 (Part One)." *Slavic Review* 23 (4): 619–42.

1965. "The Problem of Social Stability in Urban Russia, 1905–1917 (Part Two)." *Slavic Review* 24 (1): 1–22.

1988. "The Problem of Social Identities in Early 20th Century Russia." *Slavic Review* 47: 1–20.

Haimson, Leopold and Charles Tilly, eds. 1989. *States, Wars, and Revolutions in an International Perspective*. Cambridge: Cambridge University Press.

Halevy, Zvi. 1976. *Jewish University Students and Professionals in Tsarist and Soviet Russia*. Tel Aviv: Diaspora Research Institute.

Hall, John A. 1993. "Nationalisms: Classified and Explained." *Daedalus* 122(3): 1–28.
    1995. "In Search of Civil Society." Pp. 1–31 in *Civil Society: Theory, History, Comparison*, edited by John A. Hall. Oxford: Polity.
    2003. "Conditions for National Homogenizers." Pp. 15–31 in *Nationalism and Its Futures*, edited by Umut Özkirimli. Houndsmill: Palgrave Macmillan.
    2010. *Ernest Gellner. An Intellectual Biography*. London: Verso.
Hargrave, Signey. 2004. *Count Sergei Witte and the Twilight of Imperial Russia, A Biography*. New York: M.E. Sharpe.
Haupt, Georges and Jean-Jacque Marie. 1969. *Les Bolchéviks par eux-memes*. Paris: F. Maspero.
Hausmann, Guido. 1993. "Der Numerus clausus für jüdische Studenten im Zarenreich." *Jahrbücher für Geschichte Osteuropas* 41: 509–31.
Hechter, Michael. 2000. *Containing Nationalism*. Oxford: Oxford University Press.
Henriksson, Anders. 1983. *The Tsar's Loyal Germans. The Riga German Community: Social Change and the Nationality Question, 1855–1905*. Boulder, CO: East European Monographs.
    1986. "Riga: Growth, Conflict, and the Limitations on Good Government, 1850–1914." Pp. 209–48 in *The City in Late Imperial Russia*, edited by Michael Hamm. Bloomington: Indiana University Press.
Hernandez, Richard. 2001. "The Confessions of Semen Kanatchikov: A Bolshevik Memoir as Spiritual Autobiography." *Russian Review* 60 (1): 13–35.
Hildermeier, Manfred. 1978. *Die Sozialrevolutionäre Partei Russlands. Agrosozialismus und Modernisierung im Zarenreich (1900–1917)*. Cologne: Böhlau Verlag.
Hillmann, Henning and Brandy L. Aven. 2011. "Fragmented Networks and Entrepreneurship in Late Imperial Russia." *American Journal of Sociology* 117 (2): 484–538
Hirsch, Francine. 2002. "Race without the Practice of Racial Politics." *Slavic Review* 60 (1): 30–43.
    2005. *Empire of Nations: Ethnographic Knowledge and the Making of the Soviet Union*. Ithaca, NY: Cornell University Press. Edin : 2nd DK 33 H r
Hogan, Heather. 1993. *Forging Revolution: Metalworkers, Managers, and the State in St. Petersburg, 1890–1914*. Bloomington: Indiana University Press.
Holquist, Peter. 2001. "To Count, to Extract, to Exterminate: Population Statistics and Population Politics in Late Imperial and Soviet Russia." Pp. 111–44 in *A State of Nations, Empire and Nation-Making in the Age of Lenin and Stalin*, edited by Terry Martin and Ronald Grigor Suny. Oxford: Oxford University Press.
Hosking, Geoffrey. 1997. *Russia: People and Empire, 1552–1917*. London: Fontana.
Hundley, H.A. 2010. "Defending the Periphery: Tsarist Management of Buriat Buddhism." *The Russian Review* 69: 231–50.
Iaroslavskii, Emilian. 1925. *Na antireligioznom fronte. Sbornik statei, dokladov, lektsii i tsirkuliarov za shest' let 1919–1925*. Moscow: Gosizdat.
Ioffe, Nadezhda. 1997. *Moi otets. Adolf Abramovich Ioffe*. Moscow: Vozvrashchenie.
Iukhneva, N.V. 1984. *Etnicheskii sostav i etnosotsial'naia struktura naseleniia Peterburga. Vtoraia polovina XIX – nachalo XX veka. Statisticheskii analiz*. Lenningrad: Nauka.
    1987. "Materialy k etnicheskomu raionirovaniiu gorodskogo naseleniia evropeiskoi Rossii (po dannym perepisi 1897 g.)." Pp. 112–26 in *Gruppy v gorodakh evropeiskoi chasti SSSR: formirovanie, rasselenie, dinamika kul'tury*, edited by Evgenii M. Pospelov. Moscow: Akademiia nauk SSSR.

Iuzhalov, S.N. 1904. "Rossia." In *Bolshaia entsiklopediia*, vol. 16, St. Petersburg: Prosvieshchenie.

Izdatel'stvo Tsentral'nogo Komiteta KPSS. 1989a. "O partiinosti lits, prokhodivshikh po delu tak nazyvaemogo 'antisovetskogo pravotrotskistogo bloka.'" *Izvestiia Tsentral'nogo Komiteta (ITsK) KPSS* 5: 69–92.

1989b. "O sud'be chlenov i kandidatov v chleny TsK VKP (b) izbrannogo XVIIs s"ezdom partii." 1989. *Izvestiia Tsentral'nogo Komiteta (ITsK) KPSS* 12: 82–113.

1990. "Sostav rukovodiashchikh organov Tsentral'nogo Komiteta partii – Politbiuro (Prezidiuma), Orgbiuro, Sekretariata TsK (1919–1990 gg)." *Izvestiia Tsentral'nogo Komiteta (ITsK) KPSS* 7: 69–136.

Janos, Andrew. 1991. "Social science, communism, and the dynamics of political change." *World Politics* 44: 81–112.

Jersild, Austin. 2002. *Orientalism and Empire: North Caucasus Mountain Peoples and the Georgian Frontier, 1845–1917.* Montréal: McGill-Queens University Press.

Joffe, Nadezhda A. 1995. *Back in Time. My Life, My Fate, My Epoch: The Memoires of Nadezhda A. Joffe*, translated by F. S. Choate. Oak Park, MI: Labor Publications.

Johnson, Robert E. 1982. "Liberal Professionals and Professional Liberals: The Zemstvo Statisticians and Their Work." Pp. 343–63 in *The Zemstvo in Russia: An Experiment in Local Self-Government*, edited by Terrence Emmons and Wayne Vucinich. Cambridge: Cambridge University Press.

Jones, Stephen. 1992. "Georgian Social Democracy in 1917." Pp. 247–73 in *Revolution in Russia: Reassessments of 1917*, edited by Edith Rogovin Frankel, Jonathan Frankel, and Baruch Knei-Paz. Cambridge: Cambridge University Press.

2005. *Socialism in Georgian Colors. The European Road to Social Democracy 1883–1917.* Cambridge: Cambridge University Press.

Jowitt, Kenneth. 1983. "Soviet Neotraditionalism: The Political Consequences of a Leninist Regime." *Soviet Studies* 35(3): 275–97.

1992. *New World Disorder: The Leninist Extinction.* Berkeley and Los Angeles: University of California Press.

Kaganovich, Lazar Moiseevich. 1996. *Pamiatnye zapiski rabochego, kommunista-bol'shevika, profsoiuznogo partiinogo i sovetsko-gosudarstvennogo rabotnika.* Moscow: Vagrius.

Kalnins, Bruno. 1972. "The Social Democratic Movement in Latvia." Pp. 134–56 in *Revolution and Politics in Russia*, edited by Alexander Rabinowitch and Janet Rabinowitch, with Ladis Kristof. Bloomington: Indiana University Press.

Kanatchikov, Semen. 1986. *A Radical Worker in Tsarist Russia. The Autobiography of Semen Ivanovich Kanatchikov*, translated by Reginald Zelnick. Stanford, CA: Stanford University Press.

Kappeler, Andreas. 1979. "Zür Characteristik russischer Terroristen (1878–1887)." *Jahrbücher für Geschichte Osteuropas* 27: 520–47.

1982. "Historische Voraussetzungen des Nationalitätenproblems im russisches Vielvölkerreich." *Geschichte und Gesellschaft* 8(2): 59–83.

1992. *Russland als Vielvölkerriech: Entstehung, Geschichte, Zerfall.* München: Beck.

1993. "Aspekte des Ukrainischen Nationalbewegung im 19. und fruhen 20. Jahrhundert." Pp. 70–81 in *Ukraine: Gegenwart und Geschichte eines neuen Staates*, edited by Guido Hausmann and Andreas Kappeler. Baden-Baden: Nomos Verlagsgesellschaft.

Karinian, A. 1928. *Shaumian i natsionalisticheskie techeniia na Kavkaze.* Baku: Tipografiia 3-i internatsional.

Katz, Martin. 1966. *Mikhail Katkov: A Political Biography, 1818–1887.* The Hague: Mouton.

Katznelson, Ira. 1981. *City Trenches. Urban Politics and the Patterning of Class in the United States.* Chicago: University of Chicago.

Kazemzadeh, Firuz. 1951. *The Struggle for Transcaucasia.* New York: Philosophical Library.

Kaznelson, Judah L. and Baron D. Günzburg. 1912–14. *Evreiskaia entsiklopediia. Svod znanii o evreistve i ego kul'ture v proshlom i nastoiashchem,* vols. 3, 4, 6, 10. St. Petersburg: Izdatel'stvo Brockhaus-Efron.

Khlevniuk, Oleg. 1995. *In Stalin's Shadow: The Career of 'Sergo' Ordzhonikidze,* edited by Donald J. Raleigh. London and Armonk, NJ: M.E. Sharpe.

Khlevniuk, Oleg V., R.W. Davies, E.A. Rees, Liudmila P. Kosheleva, and Larisa A. Rogovaya, eds. 2001. *Stalin i Kaganovich perepiska. 1931–1936 gg.* Moscow: ROSSPEN.

Khodarkovsky, Mikhail. 2002. *Russia's Steppe Frontier. The Making of a Colonial Empire, 1500–1800.* Bloomington: Indiana University Press.

Klier, John. 1995. *Imperial Russia's Jewish Question, 1855–1881.* Cambridge: Cambridge University Press.

2003. "Why Were the Jews Not *Kaisertreu?*" *Ab Imperio* 4: 41–58.

Klier, John and Shlomo Lambroza. 1992. *Pogroms: Anti-Jewish Violence in Modern Russian History.* Cambridge: Cambridge University Press.

Koenker, Diane. 1981. *Moscow Workers and the 1917 Revolution.* Princeton, NJ: Princeton University Press.

1987. "Moscow in 1917: The View from Below." Pp. 81–97 in *The Workers' Revolution in Russia 1917. The View from Below,* edited by Daniel H. Kaiser. Cambridge: Cambridge University Press.

2005. *Republic of Labor: Russian Printers and Soviet Socialism, 1918–1930.* Ithaca, NY: Cornell University Press.

Koenker, Diane and William Rosenberg. 1989. *Strikes and Revolution in Russia 1917.* Princeton, NJ: Princeton University Press.

Kohut, Zenon. 1988. *Russian Centralism and Ukrainian Autonomy: Imperial Absorption of the Hetmanate 1760s–1830s.* Cambridge, MA: Harvard University Press.

Kopanev, Grigorii, ed., 1967. *Geroi Oktiabria. Biografii aktivnykh uchastnikov podgotovki i provedeniia Oktiabrskogo voorushennogo vosstaniia v Petrograde.* 2 vols. Leningrad: Lenizdat.

Kotsonis, Yanni. 2004. "'Face-to-Face': The State, the Individual, and the Citizen in Russian Taxation, 1863–1917." *Slavic Review* 63 (2): 221–46.

Kreindler, Isabelle. 1970. "Educational Policies Toward the Eastern Nationalities in Tsarist Russia: A Study of Il'minstkii System." PhD dissertation, Columbia University.

1977. "A Neglected Source of Lenin's Nationality Policy." *Slavic Review* 36 (1): 86–100.

Kucherov, Samuel. 1966. "Jews in the Russian Bar." Pp. 219–52 in *Russian Jewry 1860–1917,* edited by Jacob Frumkin, Gregor Aronson, and Alexis Goldenweiser. Translated by M. Ginsburg. New York: T. Yoseloff.

Kuromiya, Hiroaki. 1998. *Freedom and Terror in the Donbas: A Ukrainian-Russian Borderland, 1870s–1990s.* Cambridge: Cambridge University Press.

Kymlicka, Will. 2004. "Justice and Security in the Accommodation of Minority Nationalisms." Pp. 144–75 in *Ethnicity, Nationalism, and Minority Rights*, edited by Stephen May, Tariq Modood, and Judith Squires Cambridge: Cambridge University Press.

Lane, David. 1975. *The Roots of Russian Communism: A Social and Historical Study of Russian Social Democracy, 1898–1907*. London: Martin Robertson.

Lazitch, Branko, ed. 1986. *Biographical Dictionary of the Comintern*, rev. ed. Stanford, CA: Hoover Institution Press.

Lazzarini, Edward. 1976. "Himmät." Pp. 55–57 in *Modern Encyclopedia of Russian and Soviet History*, Vol. 14, edited by Joseph L. Wieczynski. Ann Arbor, MI: Academic International Press.

Lederhendler, Eli. 2008. "Classless: On the Social Status of Jews in Russia and Eastern Europe in the Late 19th Century." *Comparative Studies in Society and History* 50: 209–34.

Leggett, George. 1981. *The Cheka: Lenin's Political Police*. New York: Oxford University Press.

Lerner, Warren. 1970. *Karl Radek: The Last Internationalist*. Stanford, CA: Stanford University Press.

Leslie, Robert. 1963. *Reform and Insurrection in Poland, 1856–1865*. London: Althone.

Levin, Alfred. 1973. *The Third Duma, Election and Profile*. Hamden, CT: Archon.

Lieven, Dominic. 1984. "Russian Senior Officialdom under Nicholas II, Careers and Mentalities." *Jahrbücher für Geschichte Osteuropas* 32(2): 199–223.

   1989. *Russia's Rulers under the Old Regime*. New Haven, CT: Yale University Press.

   1998. "Russian, Imperial and Soviet Identities." *Transactions of the Royal Historical Society* 8: 253–69.

   1999. "Dilemmas of Empire, 1850–1918. Power, Territory, Identity." *Journal of Contemporary History* 32(2): 163–200.

   2000. *Empire: The Russian Empire and Its Rivals*. London: John Murray.

Lohr, Eric. 2003. *Nationalizing the Russian Empire. The Campaign Against Enemy Aliens During World War I*. Cambridge, MA: Harvard University Press.

Loveman, Mara. 1999. "Is 'Race' Essential?" *American Sociological Review* 64 (6): 891–98.

Löwe, Heinz-Dietrich. 1993. *The Tsars and the Jews: Reform, Reaction, and Anti-Semitism in Imperial Russia, 1792–1917*. Basel: Harwood Academic.

Luckyj, George. 1956. *Literary Politics in the Soviet Ukraine, 1917–1934*. New York: Columbia University Press.

McAdam, Doug, Sidney Tarrow, and Charles Tilly. 2001. *Dynamics of Contention*. Cambridge: Cambridge University Press.

McCaffray, Susan. 1996. *The Politics of Industrialization in Tsarist Russia: the Association of Southern Steel and Coal Producers, 1874–1917*. Dekalb: Northern Illinois University Press.

Mamedov, Mikail. 2008. "'Going Native' in the Caucasus: Problems of Russian Identity, 1801–64." *The Russian Review* 67: 275–95.

Mandel, David. 1983. *The Petrograd Workers and the Fall of the Old Regime*. London: Macmillan.

1992. "October in the Ivanovo-Kineshma Industrial Region." Pp. 157–87 in *Revolution in Russia: Reassessments of 1917*, edited by E. G. Frankel, J. Frankel, and B. Knei-Paz. Cambridge: Cambridge University Press.

Mann, Michael. 1993. *The Sources of Social Power*, vol. 2. Cambridge: Cambridge University Press.

1994. "In Praise of Macro-Sociology: A Reply to Goldthorpe." *British Journal of Sociology* 45 (1): 37–54.

2004. *Fascists*. Cambridge: Cambridge University Press.

2005. *The Dark Side of Democracy. Explaining Ethnic Cleansing*. Cambridge: Cambridge University Press.

Manning, Roberta. 1982. "The Zemstvo and Politics, 1864–1914." Pp. 133–75 in *The Zemstvo in Russia: An Experiment in Local Self-Government*, edited by Terence Emmons and Wayne Vucinich. Cambridge: Cambridge University Press.

Marcucci, Loris. 1997. *Il commissario di ferro di Stalin. Biografia politica di Lazar' M. Kaganovic*. Turin: Einaudi.

Martin, Terry. 1998. "The Origins of Soviet Ethnic Cleansing." *Journal of Modern History* 70: 813–61.

2001. *The Affirmative Action Empire: Nations and Nationalism in the Soviet Union, 1923–1939*. Ithaca, NY: Cornell University Press.

Martov, L., P. Maslov, and A. Potresov. 1912. *Obshchestvennoe dvizhenie v Rossii v nachale XX-go veka*, vol. 4. St. Petersburg: Tipografiia Tovarishchestva "Obshchestvennaia pol'za."

Mawdsley, Evan. 1995. "Makers of the Soviet Union Revisited: The Bolshevik Central Committee Elite in the Revolutionary Period." *Revolutionary Russia* 8(2): 195–211.

McCagg, William. 1989. *A History of the Habsburg Jews, 1670–1918*. Bloomington: Indiana University Press.

McDaniel, Tim. 1988. *Autocracy, Capitalism, and Revolution in Russia*. Berkeley and Los Angeles: University of California Press.

McReynolds, Louise. 1991. *The News under the Old Regime: The Development of a Mass Circulation Press*. Princeton, NJ: Princeton University Press.

1993. "Mobilizing Petrograd's Lower Classes to Fight the Great War; Patriotism as Counterweight to Working-Class Consciousness in *Gazeta Kopeika*." *Radical History Review* 57: 160–80.

Melancon, Michael. 1989. "Athens or Babylon? The Birth of the Socialist Revolutionary and Social Democratic Parties in Saratov, 1890–1905." Pp. 73–112 in *Politics and Society in Provincial Russia: Saratov, 1590–1917*, edited by Rex A. Wade and Scott Seregny. Columbus: Ohio State University Press.

Medvedev, Roy. 1983. *All Stalin's Men*, translated by Harold Shukman. Oxford: Blackwell.

Meir, Natan. 2003. "Varieties of Jewish Philanthropy among Kiev Jewry, 1859–1914." *Ab Imperio* 4: 185–206.

2006. "Jews, Ukrainians, and Russians in Kiev: Intergroup Relations in Late Imperial Associational Life." *Slavic Review* 65 (3): 475–501.

Mendelsohn, Ezra. 1969. "Jewish Assimilation in L'viv: The Case of Wilhelm Feldman." *Slavic Review* 28 (4): 577–90.

1971. "From Assimilation to Zionism in Lvov: The Case of Alfred Nossig." *Slavonic and East European Review* 49: 521–34.

Mikoyan, Anastas. 1988. *Memoirs of Anastas Mikoyan, 1895–1978: The Path of Struggle*, vol. 1, edited by Sergo Mikoyan, translated by Katherine T. O'Connor and Diane L. Burgin. Madison, CT: Sphinx Press.

Miller, Alexei. 2002. "Russifikatsiia: klassifitsirovat' i poniat'." *Ab Imperio* 2: 133–48.

2003. *The Ukrainian Question: The Russian Empire and Nationalism in the 19th Century*. Budapest: Central European University Press.

2004a. "Between Local and Inter-imperial: Russian Imperial History in Search of Scope and Paradigm." *Kritika* 1: 7–26.

2004b. "The Empire and the Nation in the Imagination of Russian Nationalism." Pp. 9–26 in *Imperial Rule*, edited by Alexei Miller and Alfred Rieber. Budapest: Central European University.

Miller, Alexei and Alfred Rieber, eds. 2004. *Imperial Rule*. Budapest: Central European University Press.

Mishkinsky, Moshe. 1992. "'Black Repartition' and the Pogroms of 1881–1882." Pp. 62–75 in *Pogroms: Anti-Jewish Violence in Modern Russian History*, edited by John Klier and Shlomo Lambroza. Cambridge: Cambridge University Press.

1997. "Regional Factors in the Formation of the Jewish Labor Movement in Czarist Russia". Pp. 62–97 in *Essential Papers on Jews and the Left*, edited by Ezra Mendelsohn. New York: New York University Press.

Möller, Dietrich. 1976. *Revolutionër, Intriguant, Diplomat. Karl Radek in Deutschland*. Köln: Wissenschaft and Politik.

Montefiore, Simon Sebag. 2007. *Young Stalin*. London: Phoenix.

Moon, David. 1996. "Peasants into Russian Citizens? A Comparative Perspective." *Revolutionary Russia* 9(1): 43–81.

Moore, Barrington. 1966. *The Social Origins of Democracy and Dictatorship*. Boston: Beacon.

Mosse, Werner. 1968. "Makers of the Soviet Union." *Slavonic and East European Review* 46: 141–54.

Mostashari, Firouzeh. 2003. "Russian Colonization of Caucasian Azerbaijan, 1830–1905." Pp. 167–81 in *Extending the Borders of Russian History: Essays in Honor of Alfred Rieber*, edited by Marsha Siefert. Budapest: Central European University.

Mouradian, Claire. 1995. "Die armenische Nationalbewegung im Osmenischen und Russischen Reich bis zum Ersten Weltkrieg." Pp. 80–93, in *Krisenherd Kaukasus*, edited by Uwe Halbach and Andreas Kappeler. Baden-Baden: Nomos Verglagsgesellschaft.

Nathans, Benjamin. 1996. "Conflict, Community, and the Jews of Late Nineteenth-Century St. Petersburg." *Jahrbücher für Geschichte Osteuropas* 44: 178–216.

2002. *Beyond the Pale: The Jewish Encounter with Late Imperial Russia*. Berkeley and Los Angeles: University of California Press.

Noack, Christian. 1999. "Russischen politik und muslimische identität: Das Wolga-Ural-Gebiet im 19 Jahrhündert." *Jarhbücher für Geschichte Osteuropas* 47: 525–37.

Nodgot, D.N. 1990. "Avtobiografiia G. E. Zinovieva (Iz arkhivnikh fondov TsGSoR SSSR)." Pub. I. *Voprosy Istorii KPSS* 7.

Ordzhonikidze, G.K. 1986. *Grigorii Konstantinovich Ordzhonikidze: Biografiia*. Moscow: Izdatel'stvo Politicheskoi Literatury.

Page, Stanley. 1959. *The Formation of the Baltic States: A Study of the Effects of Great Power Politics Upon the Emergence of Lithuania, Latvia, and Estonia*. Cambridge: Cambridge University Press.

Penati, Beatrice. 2011. "Beyond Technicalities: Land Assessment and Land-Tax in Russian Turkestan (ca. 1880–1917)." *Jahrbücher für Geschichte Osteuropas* 59: 1–27.

Perrie, Maureen. 1972. "The Social Composition and Structure of the Socialist Revolutionary Party before 1917." *Soviet Studies* 24 (2): 223–50.

Petrovsky-Shtern, Yohanan. 2002. "The 'Jewish Policy' of the Late Imperial War Ministry: The Impact of the Russian Right." *Kritika* 3 (2): 217–54.

2009a. *The Anti-Imperial Choice: The Making of the Ukrainian Jew*. New Haven, CT: Yale University Press.

2009b. *Jews in the Russian Army, 1827–1917: Drafted into Modernity*. New York: Cambridge University Press.

2010. *Lenin's Jewish Question*. New Haven, CT: Yale University Press.

Piatnitskaia, Iulia. 1993. *Po materialam arkhivno-sledstvennogo dela No. 603 na Sokolovu-Piatnitskuiu Iu. I*. St. Petersburg: "Palitra."

Piatnitskii, Osip. 1933. *Memoirs of a Bolshevik*. New York: International Publishers.

Pinchuk, Ben-Cion. 1974. *The Octobrists in the Third Duma, 1907–1912*. Seattle: University of Washington Press.

Pinter, William and D.K. Rowney, eds. 1980. *Russian Officialdom: The Bureaucratization of Russian Society from the Seventeenth to the Twentieth Century*. London: Macmillan.

Pipes, Richard. 1964. *The Formation of the Soviet Union: Communism and Nationalism, 1917–1923*. Cambridge, MA: Harvard University Press.

1990. *The Russian Revolution 1899–1919*. London: Fontana.

2000. "Solzhenitsyn and the Jews Revisited." *New Republic*, November 25.

Plakans, Andrejs. 1981. "Latvia before the 1880s." Pp. 207–226 in *Russification in the Baltic Provinces and Finland, 1855–1914*, edited by Edward C. Thaden. Princeton, NJ: Princeton University Press.

1995. *The Latvians*. Stanford, CA: Hoover Institution Press.

Plassarand, Yves and Henri Minczeles. 1996. *Lituanie Juive, 1918–1940: Message d'un Monde Englouti*. Paris: Editions Autrement, Collection Memoires, No. 44.

Plotnikov, Iuri Pavlovich. 1976. *Ia. M. Sverdlov v turukhanskoi ssylke*. Krasnoiarsk: Krasnoiarskoe knizhnoe izdatel'stvo.

Pomeranz, William. 1999. "'Profession or Estate'? The Case of the Russian Pre-Revolutionary *Advokatura*." *Slavonic and East European Review* 77 (2): 240–68.

Porter, Brian. 2000. *When Nationalism Began to Hate: Imagining Modern Politics in Nineteenth Century Poland*. Oxford: Oxford University Press.

Potichnyji, Peter and Howard Aster, eds. 1988. *Ukrainian-Jewish Relations in Historical Perspective*. Edmonton: Canadian Institute of Ukrainian Studies.

Priedite, Aija. 2004. "Latvian Refugees and the Latvian Nation State during and after World War I." Pp. 35–52 in *Homelands: War, Population and Statehood in Eastern Europe and Russia, 1918–1924*, edited by Nick Baron and Peter Gatrell. London: Anthem.

Prokhorov, Aleksandr M., ed. 1968–78. *Bol'shaia sovetskaia entsiklopediia*, 30 vols., 3d ed. Moscow: sovetskaia entsiklopediia.

Radek, Karl. 1935. *Portraits and Pamphlets*. London: Wishart Books Ltd.

2000. *Karl Radek in der 'Russischen Korrespondenz': politische Zeitschrift aus Sowjetrussland (1921–22)*. Cologne: Neuer ISP Verlag.

Raeff, Marc. 1971. "Patterns of Russian Imperial Policy toward the Nationalities." Pp. 22–42 in *Soviet Nationality Problems*, edited by Edward Allworth. New York: Columbia University Press.

1984. *Understanding Imperial Russia: State and Society under the Old Regime*, translated by A. Goldhammer. New York: Columbia University Press.

Raun, Toivo. 2000. "The Nationalities Question in the Baltic Provinces, 1905–17." Pp. 121–30 in *Ethnic and National Issues in Russian and East European History*, edited by John Morison. New York: Basingstoke.

2006. "Violence and Activism in the Baltic Provinces during the Revolution of 1905." *Acta Historica Tallinnensia* 10: 48–59.

Rawson, Don. 1995. *Russian Rightists and the Revolution of 1905*. Cambridge: Cambridge University Press.

Reisner, Oliver. 1995. "Die Entstehungs- und Entwicklungsbedingungen der nationalen Bewegung in Georgien bis 1921." Pp. 63–79 in *Krisenherd Kaukasus*, edited by Uwe Halbach and Andreas Kappeler. Baden-Baden: Nomos Verlagsgesellschaft.

1999."Zwischen Zarentreue und ethnischen Selbstbewusststein – der 'Fall' Dimit'ri Qipiani und die Georgier (1885–1887)." *Jahrbücher für Geschichte Osteuropas* 47: 512–24.

Reshetar, John. 1952. *The Ukrainian Revolution, 1917–1920: A Study of Nationalism*. Princeton, NJ: Princeton University Press.

Rieber, Alfred. 1994. "Struggle over the Borderlands." Pp. 61–90 in *The Legacy of History in Russia and the New States of Eurasia*, edited by S. Frederick Starr. Armonk, NJ: M.E. Sharpe.

2000. "The Marginality of Totalitarianism." Pp. 265–84 in *The Paradoxes of Unintended Consequences*, edited by Ralf Dahrendorf and George Soros. Budapest: Central European University Press.

2001. "Stalin: Man of the Borderlands." *American Historical Review* 106 (9): 1651–91.

2004. "The Comparative Ecology of Complex Frontiers." Pp. 177–207 in *Imperial Rule*, edited by Alexei Miller and Alfred Rieber. Budapest: Central European University Press.

2005. "Stalin as Georgian: The Formative Years." Pp. 18–44 in *Stalin: A New History*, edited by Sarah Davies and James Harris. Cambridge: Cambridge University Press.

2006. "The Problem of Social Cohesion." *Kritika* 7(3): 599–608.

Rigby, T.H. 1968. *Communist Party Membership in the USSR, 1917–1967*. Princeton, NJ: Princeton University Press.

Robbins, Richard G. 1987. *The Tsar's Viceroys: Russian Provincial Governors in the Last Years of the Empire*. Ithaca, NY: Cornell University Press.

Rodkiewicz, Witold. 1998. *Russian Nationality Policy in the Western Provinces of the Empire (1863–1905)*. Lublin: Scientific Society of Lublin.

Rogger, Hans. 1962. "Nationalism and the State: A Russian Dilemma." *Comparative Studies in Society and History* 4(3): 253–64.

1986. *Jewish Policies and Right-Wing Politics in Imperial Russia*. Berkeley: University of California Press.

1992. "Conclusion and Overview." Pp. 314–72 in *Pogroms: Anti-Jewish Violence in Modern Russian History*, edited by John D. Klier and Shlomo Lambroza. Cambridge: Cambridge University Press.

Rosenberg, William. 1974. *Liberals in the Russian Revolution: The Constitutional Democratic Party 1917–1921*. Princeton, NJ: Princeton University Press.

———. 2001. "Russian Labor and Bolshevik Power: Social Dimensions of Protest after October." Pp.149–79 in *The Russian Revolution: The Essential Readings*, edited by Martin A. Miller. Malden, MA: Blackwell Publishers.

Roth, Joseph. 1975–76. "Juden auf Wanderschaft." Pp. 295–357 in *Werke*. Vol. 4, edited by Christian Büttrich. Köln: Kiepenheuer & Witsch.

Rubenstein, Joshua and Vladimir Naumov, eds. 2001. *Stalin's Secret Pogrom. The Postwar Inquisition of the Jewish Anti-Fascist Committee*, translated by L. Wolfson. New Haven, CT: Yale University Press.

Sabaliunas, Leonas. 1990. *Lithuanian Social Democracy in Perspective, 1893–1914*. Durham, NC: Duke University Press.

Sanborn, Joshua. 2000a. "The Mobilization of 1914 and the Question of the Russian Nation: A Reexamination." *Slavic Review* 59(2): 266–89.

———. 2000b. "More Than Imagined: A Few Notes on Modern Identities." *Slavic Review* 59(2): 300–05.

———. 2001. "Family, Fraternity, and Nation-Building in Russia, 1905–1925." Pp. 93–109 in *A State of Nations: Empire and Nation-Making in the Age of Lenin and Stalin*, edited by Ronald Grigor Suny and Terry Martin. Oxford: Oxford University Press.

———. 2003. *Drafting the Russian Nation: Military Conscription, Total War, and Mass Politics, 1905–1925*. Dekalb: Northern Illinois University Press.

———. 2005. "Unsettling the Empire: Violent Migrations and Social Disaster in Russia during World War I." *Journal of Modern History* 77: 290–324.

Saul, Norman E. 1978. *Sailors in Revolt: The Russian Baltic Fleet in 1917*. Lawrence: Regents Press of Kansas.

Saunders, David. 1995. "Russia's Ukrainian Policy (1847–1905): A Demographic Approach." *European History Quarterly* 25: 181–208.

Schapiro, Leonard. 1960. *The Communist Party of the Soviet Union*. New York: Random House.

———. 1977. *The Origins of Communist Autocracy: Political Opposition in the Soviet State, First Phase, 1917–1922*. Cambridge, MA: Harvard University Press.

———. 1986. "The Role of Jews in the Russian Revolutionary Movement." Pp. 266–89 in *Russian Studies*, edited by Ellen Darendorf. London: Collins Harvill.

Seregny, Scott. 1999. "Power and Discourse in Russian Elementary Education." *Jahrbücher für Geschichte Osteuropas* 47(2): 161–86.

———. 2000a. "Zemstvos, Peasants, and Citizenship: the Russian Adult Education Movement in World War I." *Slavic Review* 59 (2): 290–315.

———. 2000b. "Peasants, Nation, and Local Government in Wartime Russia." *Slavic Review* 59 (2): 336–42.

Seregny, Scott and Rex Wade. 1989. "Saratov as Russian History." Pp. 1–9 in *Politics and Society in Provincial Russia: Saratov, 1590–1917*, edited by Rex Wade and Scott Seregny. Columbus: Ohio State University Press.

Service, Robert. 2000. *Lenin: A Biography*. London: Macmillan.

———. 2005. *Stalin: A Biography*. London: Macmillan.

Seton-Watson, Hugh. 1967. *The Russian Empire, 1801–1917*. Oxford: Clarendon.

Shaumian, S.G. 1978. *Izbrannyie proizvedeniia*, vols. 1, *1902–1914*, and vol. 2, *1915–1918*. Moskva: Izdatel'stvo Politicheskoi Literatury.

Shearer, David. 2004. "Elements Near and Alien: Passportization, Policing, and Identity in the Stalinist State, 1932–1952." *Journal of Modern History* 76: 835–81.

Skocpol, Theda. 1979. *States and Social Revolutions*. Cambridge: Cambridge University Press.

1994. *Revolutions in the Modern World*. Cambridge: Cambridge University Press.

Slezkine, Yuri. 1994a. "The USSR as a Communal Apartment, or How a Socialist State Promoted Ethnic Particularism." *Slavic Review* 53 (2): 414–52.

1994b. *Arctic Mirrors: Russia and the Small Peoples of the North*. Ithaca, NY: Cornell University Press.

1997. "Nationalists versus Nations: Eighteenth-Century Russian Scholars Confront Ethnic Diversity." Pp. 27–57 in *Russia's Orient: Imperial Borderlands and Peoples, 1700–1917*, edited by Daniel R. Brower and Edward J. Lazzarini. Bloomington: Indiana University Press.

2004. *The Jewish Century*. Princeton, NJ: Princeton University Press.

Slocum, John. 1993. "The Boundaries of National Identity: Religion, Language, and Nationality Politics in Late Imperial Russia." PhD dissertation, University of Chicago.

1998. "Who, and When, Were the *Inorodtsy*? The Evolution of the Category of 'Aliens' in Imperial Russia." *Russian Review* 57: 137–90.

Smith, Steve. 1981. "Craft Consciousness, Class Consciousness: Petrograd 1917." *History Workshop Journal* 11: 33–58.

1983. *Red Petrograd: Revolution in the Factories, 1917–1918*. Cambridge: Cambridge University Press.

1999. "Workers, the Intelligentsia, and Social Democracy in St. Petersburg, 1895–1917." Pp. 186–205 in *Workers and Intelligentsia in Late Imperial Russia: Realities, Representations, Reflections*, edited by Reginald E. Zelnik. Berkeley: Institute and Area Studies, University of California.

2000. "Citizenship and the Russian Nation during World War I: A Comment." *Slavic Review* 59 (2): 316–29.

Smith, S.A. 2008. *Revolution and the People in Russia and China: A Comparative History*. Cambridge: Cambridge University Press.

Snyder, Timothy. 1997. *Nationalism, Marxism, and Modern Central Europe: A Biography of Kazimierz Kelles-Krauz, 1872–1905*. Cambridge, MA: Harvard University Press.

2003. *The Reconstruction of Nations: Poland, Ukraine, Lithuania, Belarus, 1569–1999*. New Haven, CT: Yale University Press.

Sokolov, Boris. 2005. *Molotov: ten' vozhdia*. Moscow: AST-PRESS KNIGA.

Solzhenitsyn, Aleksandr. 2006. *Dvesti let vmeste*. Moskva: Vagrius.

Spiridovich, Aleksandr. 1918. *Revoliutsionnoe dvizhenie v Rossii v period imperii*. vol. 2, 2d ed. Petrograd: Voennaia Tipografiia.

Staliunas, Darius. 2004. "Did the Government Seek to Russify Lithuanians and Poles in the Northwest Region after the Uprising of 1863–64?" *Kritika* 5 (2): 273–89.

2007. *Making Russians: Meaning and Practice of Russification in Lithuania and Belarus after 1863*. Amsterdam: Editions Rodopi.

Stanislawski, Michael. 2001. *Zionism in the Fin de Siècle: Cosmopolitanism and Nationalism from Nordau to Jabotinsky*. Berkeley: University of California Press.

Starr, Frederick. 1978. "Tsarist Government: The Imperial Dimension." Pp. 3–37 in *Soviet Nationality Policies and Practices*, edited by Jeremy Azrael. New York: Praeger.

1992. *Decentralization and Self-Government in Russia, 1830–1870*. Princeton, NJ: Princeton University Press.

Steffen, Jochen and Adalbert Wiemers. 1977. *Auf dem letzten Verhör. Erkenntnisse des verantwortlichen Hofnarren der Revolution Karl Radek.* Munich: C. Bertelsmann.

Steinberg, Mark. 1992. *Moral Communities: The Culture of Class Relations in the Printing Industry, 1867–1907.* Berkeley and Los Angeles: University of California Press.

    1994. "Workers on the Cross: Russian Imagination in the Writings of Russian Workers, 1910–24." *Russian Review* 53: 213–39.

    2002. *Proletarian Imagination.* Ithaca, NY: Cornell University Press.

Steinwedel, Charles. 2001. "Making Social Groups, One Person at a Time: The Identification of Individuals by Estate, Religious Confession, and Ethnicity in Late Imperial Russia." Pp. 67–82 in *Documenting Individual Identity: The Development of State Practices in the Modern World*, edited by Jane Caplan and John Torpey. Princeton, NJ: Princeton University Press.

Strazas, A.S. 1996a. "From *Auszra* to the Great War: The Emergence of the Lithuanian Nation." *Lituanas* 42 (4): 34–73.

    1996b. "Lithuania 1863–1893: Tsarist Russification and the Beginnings of the Modern Lithuanian National Movement." *Lituanas* 42 (3): 36–75.

Strobel, Georg. 1974. *Die Partei Rosa Luxemburgs, Lenin und die SPD. Der polnische "europäische" Internationalismus in der russischen Sozialdemokratie.* Wiesbaden: Franz Steiner Verlag.

Subtelny, Orest. 1994. *Ukraine: A History*, 2d ed. Toronto: University of Toronto Press.

Suhr, Gerald. 2003. "Ekaterinoslav City in 1905: Workers, Jews, and Violence." *International Labor and Working-Class History* 64: 139–66.

Suiarko, L.O. 1979. *Dmitro Zacharovich Manuil'skii.* Kiev: Naukova dumka.

Sunderland, Willard. 1996. "Russians into Iakuts? 'Going Native' and Problems of Russian National Identity in the Siberian North, 1870s–1914." *Slavic Review* 55 (4): 806–25.

    2004. *Taming the Wild Field: Colonization and Empire on the Russian Steppe.* Ithaca, NY: Cornell University Press.

Suny, Ronald Grigor. 1972. *The Baku Commune 1917–1918: Class and Nationality in the Russian Revolution.* Princeton, NJ: Princeton University Press.

    1983. "Toward a Social History of the October Revolution." *American Historical Review* 88 (1): 31–52.

    1987. "Revising the Old Story." Pp. 1–19 in *The Workers, Revolution in Russia, 1917: The View from Below*, edited by Daniel H. Kaiser. Cambridge: Cambridge University Press.

    1992. "Nationalism and Class in the Russian Revolution: A Comparative Discussion." Pp. 219–46 in *Revolution in Russia: Reassessments of 1917*, edited by Edith R. Frankel, Jonathan Frankel, and Baruch Knei-Paz. Cambridge: Cambridge University Press.

    1993a. *The Revenge of the Past: Nationalism, Revolution and the Collapse of the Soviet Union.* Stanford, CA: Stanford University Press.

    1993b. *Looking Toward Ararat: Armenia in Modern History.* Bloomington: Indiana University Press.

    1994a. *The Making of the Georgian Nation.* Bloomington: Indiana University Press.

    1994b. "Revision and Retreat in the Historiography of 1917: Social History and Its Critics." *Russian Review* 53 (2): 162–82.

    1995. "Ambiguous Categories: States, Empires, and Nations." *Post-Soviet Affairs* 11(2): 185–96.

2000. "Nationalities and the Russian Empire." *The Russian Review* 59: 487–92.

Suny, Ronald Grigor and Terry Martin, eds. 2001. *A State of Nations: Empire and Nation-making in the Age of Lenin and Stalin*. Oxford: Oxford University Press.

Suziedelis, Simas, ed. 1970–78. *Encyclopedia Lituanica*. Boston, MA: Judzas Kapocius.

Swietochowski, Tadeusz. 1985. *Russian Azerbaijan, 1905–1920: The Shaping of a National Identity in a Muslim Community*. Cambridge: Cambridge University Press.

1995. *Russia and a Divided Azerbaijan: A Borderland in Transition*. New York: Columbia University Press.

Szporluk, Roman. 1997. "The Fall of the Tsarist Empire and the USSR: The Russian Question and Imperial Overextension." Pp. 65–93 in *The End of Empire*, edited by Karen Dawisha and Bruce Parrot. New York: M.E. Sharpe.

Ter Minassian, Anahide. 1983. "Nationalism and Socialism in the Armenian Revolutionary Movement, 1887–1912." Pp. 141–84 in *Transcaucasia, Nationalism, and Social Change. Essays in the History of Armenia, Azerbaijan, and Georgia*, edited by Ronald Grigor Suny. Ann Arbor: University of Michigan Press.

Thaden, Edward. 1981. *Russification in the Baltic Provinces and Finland, 1855–1914*. Princeton, NJ: Princeton University Press.

1984. *Russia's Western Borderlands, 1710–1870*. Princeton, NJ: Princeton University Press.

Thompson, E.P. 1963. *The Making of the English Working Class*. London: Gollancz.

Tilly, Charles and Sidney Tarrow. 2007. *Contentious Politics*. Boulder, CO: Paradigm Publishers.

Tobias, Henry. 1972. *The Jewish Bund in Russia, from Its Origins to 1905*. Stanford, CA: Stanford University Press.

Tocqueville, Alexis de. (1856) 1955. *The Old Regime and the French Revolution*, translated by S. Gilbert. New York: Doubleday.

Torpey, John. 1997. "Revolutions and Freedom of Movement: An Analysis of Passport Controls in the French, Russian and Chinese Revolutions." *Theory and Society* 26: 837–68.

Trotsky, Leon. (1970 [1930]). *My Life: An Attempt at an Autobiography*. New York: Pathfinder.

Tuck, Jim. 1988. *Engine of Mischief. A Analytical Biography of Karl Radek*. New York: Greenwood Press.

Tuna, Mustafa. 2011. "Madrasa Reform as Secularizing Process: A View from the Late Russian Empire." *Comparative Studies in Society and History* 43 (3): 540–70.

Tyszkiewicz, Antoni. 1895. *Russko-Pol'skiia Otnosheniia*, Ocherk napisal Graf Leliva [pseud.] Leipzig: E.L. Kasprovich'.

Upton, A.F. 1980. *The Finnish Revolution, 1917–1920*. Minneapolis: University of Minnesota Press.

van Ree, Erik. 2007. "Heroes and Merchants. Stalin's Understanding of National Character." *Kritika* 8 (1): 41–65.

Velychenko, Stephen. 1995. "Identities, Loyalties, and Service in Imperial Russia: Who Administered the Borderlands?" *Russian Review* 2: 188–208.

1997. "Empire Loyalism and Minority Nationalism in Great Britain and Imperial Russia, 1707–1914: Institutions, Law, and Nationality in Scotland and Ukraine." *Comparative Studies in Society and History* 39 (3): 413–41.

2000. "Local Officialdom and National Movements in Imperial Russia." Pp. 74–87 in *Ethnic and National Issues in Russian and East European History*, edited by John Morison. New York: St. Martin's Press.

2001. "The Size of the Imperial Russian Bureaucracy and Army in Comparative Perspective." *Jahrbücher für Geschichte Osteuropas* 3: 346–62.

Vilenskii-Sibiriakov, Vladimir, and Feliks Kon, eds. (1927–1933) 1997. *Deiateli revoliutsionnogo dvizheniia v Rossii: bio-bibliograficheskii slovar, ot predshestvennikov dekabristov do padeniia tsarizma*, vols. 1–5. Leipzig: Zentralantiquariat der Deutschen Demokratischen Republik.

Viterbo, Gregory. 2007. "Nationality Policy and the Russian Imperial Officers Corps, 1905–1914." *Slavic Review* 66 (4): 682–701.

von Hagen, Mark. 1998. "The Great War and the Mobilization of Ethnicity in the Russian Empire." Pp. 34–97 in *Post-Soviet Political Order: Conflict and State-building*, edited by Barnett Rubin and Jack Snyder. New York: Routledge.

von Pistholkors, Gert. 1992. *Baltischer Länder*. Vol. 2 of *Deutsche Geschichte im Osten Europas*, edited by Boockmann von Hartmut. Berlin: Siedler Verlag.

Voroshilov, Kliment. 1968. *Rasskazy o zhizni: vospominaniia*. Moskva: Politizdat.

Wandruszka, Adam and Peter Urbanitsch, eds. 1980. *Die Habsburgermonrachie 1848–1919 Band III, 2 Teilband*. Wein. Österreichischen Akademie der Wissenschaften.

Watson, Derek. 2005. *Molotov: A Biography*. Houndmills: Palgrave/Macmillan.

Weber, Max. 1989 [1905–1912]. "Zur Lage de burgerlichen Demokratie in Russland" and "Russlands Übergang zum Scheinkonstitutionalismus." Pp. 129–52 in *Max Weber. Zur Russischen Revolution von 1905: Scriften und Reden, 1905–1912*, edited by Wolfgang J. Mommsen. Tübingen: JBC Mohr.

1968. "Ethnic Groups." Pp. 385–95 in *Economy and Society*, vol. 1, edited by Gunter Roth and Claus Wittich. Berkeley and Los Angeles: University of California Press.

Weeks, Theodore. 1994. "Defining 'Us' and 'Them': Poles and Russians in the Western Provinces, 1863–1914." *Slavic Review* 53 (1): 26–40.

1996. *Nation and State in Late Imperial Russia: Nationalism and Russification on the Western Frontier, 1863–1914*. Dekalb: Northern Illinois University Press.

2001. "Russification and the Lithuanians, 1863–1905." *Slavic Review* 60 (1): 96–114.

Weinberg, Robert. 1992. "The Pogrom of 1905 in Odessa: A Case Study." Pp. 248–90 in *Pogroms: Anti-Jewish Violence in Modern Russian History*, edited by John D. Klier and Shlomo Lambroza. Cambridge: Cambridge University Press.

Weinerman, Eli. 1994. "Racism, Racial Prejudice and Jews in Late Imperial Russia." *Ethnic and Racial Studies* 17(3): 442–95.

Weissman G. and D. Williams, eds. 1982. *The Balkan Wars, 1912–1913: The War Correspondence of Leon Trotsky*, translated by B. Pearce. New York: Monad Press.

Weitz, Eric. 2002. "Racial Politics without the Concept of Race: Reevaluating Soviet Ethnic and National Purges." *Slavic Review* 61 (1): 1–29.

Werth, Paul. 2000. "The Limits of Religious Ascription: Baptized Tatars and the Revision of 'Apostasy', 1840s–1905." *Russian Review* 59: 493–511.

2002. *At the Margins of Orthodoxy: Mission, Governance, and Confessional Politics in Russia's Volga-Kama Region, 1827–1905*. Ithaca, NY: Cornell University Press.

2004. "Schism Once Removed: Sects, State Authority, and Meanings of Religious Toleration in Imperial Russia." Pp. 83–105 in *Imperial Rule*, edited by Alexei Miller and Alfred Rieber. Budapest: Central European University Press.

White, Elizabeth. 2007. "The Socialist Revolutionary Party, Ukraine, and Russian National Identity in the 1920s." *The Russian Review* 66: 549–67.

White, James. 1975. "Scottish Lithuanians and the Russian Revolution." *Journal of Baltic Studies* 6 (1): 1–8.

1990. "Latvian and Lithuanian Sections of the Bolshevik Party on the Eve of the February Revolution." *Revolutionary Russia* 3 (1): 90–106.

1994. "National Communism and the World Revolution: The Political Consequences of German Military Withdrawal from the Baltic Area, 1918–1919." *Europe-Asia Studies* 46 (8): 1349–69.

Wimmer, Andreas. 2008. "The Making and Unmaking of Ethnic Boundaries: A Multilevel Process Theory." *American Journal of Sociology* 113 (4): 970–1022.

Wirtschafter, Elise Kimerling. 1992. "Problematics of status definition in Imperial Russia: The *Raznocincy*." *Jahrbücher für Geschichte Osteuropas* 40: 319–39.

1997. *Social Identity in Imperial Russia*. Dekalb: Northern Illinois University Press.

Wistrich, Robert. 1976. *Revolutionary Jews from Marx to Trotsky*. London: Harrap.

1979. *Trotsky: The Fate of a Revolutionary*. London: Robson Books.

1982. *Socialism and the Jews: The Dilemmas of Assimilation in Germany and Austria-Hungary*. London: Associated University Press.

Witte, Sergei. 1921. *The Memoirs of Count Witte*, A. Yarmolinsky Trans. London: William Heinemann.

Wittram, Reinhard. 1973. *Baltische Geschichte: Die Ostseelande Livland, Estland, Kurland, 1180–1918*. Darmstadt: Wissenschaftlische Buchgesellschaft.

Wortman, Richard. 2000. *Scenarios of Power*, vol. 2. Princeton, NJ: Princeton University Press.

2003. "National Narratives in the Representation of Nineteenth-Century Russian Monarchy." Pp. 51–64 in *Extending the Borders of Russian History: Essays in Honor of Alfred Rieber*, edited by Marsha Siefert. Budapest: Central European University Press.

Wynn, Charters. 1992. *Workers, Strikes, and Pogroms: The Donbass-Dnepr Bend in Late Imperial Russian, 1870–1905*. Princeton, NJ: Princeton University Press.

Zaionchkovskii, P.A., ed. 1976. *Istoriia dorevolutsionnoi Rossii v dnevnikakh i vospominaniakh. Annotirovannyi ukazatel knig i publikatsii v zhurnalakh. Nauchnoe rukovodstvo*. Moscow: Kniga.

Zalevskii, K. 1912. "Natsional'nyie dvizheniia." Pp. 151–243 in *Obshchestvennoe dvizhenie v Rossii v nachale XX-go veka*, vol. 4., edited by L. Martov, P. Maslov, and A. Potresov. St. Peterburg: Tipografiia Tovarishchestva "Obshchestvennaia pol'za."

Zhao, Dingxin. 1998. "Ecologies of Social Movements: Student Mobilization during the 1989 Prodemocracy Movement in Beijing." *American Journal of Sociology* 103(6): 1493–529.

2001. *The Power of Tiananmen. State and Society Relations in the 1989 Beijing Student Movement*. Chicago: University of Chicago Press.

Zimmerman, Joshua. 2004. *Poles, Jews, and the Politics of Nationality: The Bund and the Polish Socialist Party in Late Imperial Russia, 1892–1914*. Madison: University of Wisconsin Press.

Zuckerman, Fredric. 1996. *The Tsarist Secret Police in Russian Society, 1880–1919*. New York: New York University Press.

Index of Names

Note – Bolsheviks appear with ethnicity/nationality in parentheses. No specific mentions are made of Grigorii Evdokimov (Russian), Georgi Safarov (Jewish/Armenian), I. A. Tuntul (Chuvash/Mordvinan), Daniil Sulimov (Russian), Abdullo Rakhimbaev (Tadjik), Mikhail Frunze (Rumanian/Moldovian), Timofie Krivov (Chuvash/Russian), Vasilii Schmidt (German) and Petre Zalutskii (Polish).

Andreev, Andrei (Russian), 235, 238, 239, 241, 244, 249
Antonov-Ovseenko, Vladimir, 151

Badaev, Alexei (Russian), 235, 238, 239, 241, 242, 261
Beloborodov, Aleksandr (Russian), 239, 241, 244, 256
Berzins, Jan (Latvian), 161, 162, 163, 168–74, 183–4
Bosh, Evgeniia, 124
Brooks, Jeffrey, 233
Bubnov, Andrei (Russian), 235, 249, 250, 253
Bukharin, Nikolai (Russian), 236, 250, 251, 255

Chubar', Vlas (Ukrainian), 131, 134–41, 150
Chudov, Mikhail (Russian), 238, 239, 242
Conquest, Robert, 206
Cummings, A.J., 112

Danishevskii, Karl (Latvian), 168–74, 181
Deutscher, Isaac, 76, 77–8, 112–3
Dmowski, Roman, 108–9
Dzhaparidze, Prokofii (Georgian), 189–90, 201, 204–12, 215, 216, 221, 278
Dzierżyński, Feliks (Polish), 3, 88–9, 90, 91, 92, 93, 95, 96, 98, 99, 100, 102–12, 114–5, 116–7, 118, 119, 120, 121–2, 143, 146, 147, 150, 151

Ezergailis, Andrew, 166, 184

Gellner, Ernest, 24–5, 27, 230, 266, 273–4
Goldstone, Jack, 7, 51
Gould, Roger, 8, 268
Gusev, Sergei (Jewish), 60, 69, 79–84, 87, 88

Haimson, Leopold, 52
Hall, John A., 40, 266

Iakovleva, Varvara (Russian), 235, 249, 250, 255
Ioffe, Adolf (Jewish), 60, 72, 74–6, 78, 87

Jogiches, Leo, 118
Jones, Stephen, 208

Kaganovich, Lazar (Jewish), 60, 70–9, 82, 87, 88, 145
Kalinin, Mikhail (Russian), 235, 238, 239, 241, 242, 243, 244, 246, 248, 249
Kamenev, Lev (Jewish), 60, 79–84, 87, 88, 89
Kapsukas, Vintsas (Lithuanian), 90, 91, 92, 93, 95, 96–102, 104, 105, 106, 120–1, 122, 143, 146, 147, 278
Kautsky, Karl, 143
Kirov, Sergei (Russian), 235, 237, 246, 249, 250, 252, 256, 259
Kiselev, Aleksandr (Belarusian), 90, 92, 242
Koenker, Diane, 244

Kollontai, Aleksandra (Ukrainian/Finnish), 124, 255, 262
Kolotilov, Nikolai (Russian), 238, 239, 243, 248
Komarov, Nikolai (Russian), 238, 239, 242, 243
Korotkov, Ivan (Russian), 239
Kosior, Stanislav (Polish), 90, 92, 134, 145
Kreindler, Isabelle, 259
Krestinsky, Nikolai (Ukrainian), 124, 130, 140, 144, 146–52, 153
Kubiak, Nikolai (Russian), 238, 239
Kuibyshev, Valerian (Russian), 236, 250, 256, 260, 278
Kutuzov, Ivan (Russian), 235, 239, 240, 242, 249
Kviring, Emmanuil (German), 124, 145

Lane, David, 15, 239
Lashevich, Mikhail (Jewish), 60
Lebed', Dmitri (Ukrainian), 131, 134–41, 150, 153
Lenin, Vladimir (Russian), 3, 9, 11, 14, 59, 68, 75, 76, 81, 84, 88, 89, 108, 110, 111, 119, 120, 133, 142, 150, 151–2, 155, 166, 167, 179–80, 182–3, 184, 188, 212, 216, 217–8, 220, 223, 235, 250, 251, 253–4, 256, 258, 259–60, 269, 270
Lepse, Ivan (Latvian), 155, 158, 174–9, 183
Lobov, Semen (Russian), 238, 239
Lomov, Georgii (Russian), 235, 250, 251, 253, 256, 258
Luxemburg, Rosa, 108, 110, 117, 118, 119

MacDaniel, Tim, 5
Mann, Michael, 7, 9, 13, 15, 266, 273
Manuilsky, Dmitri (Ukrainian), 124, 130, 140, 142, 146–52, 153
Martov, Iulii, 79
Mawdsley, Evan, 9, 15, 17
Miasnikov, Aleksandr (Armenian), 221–2, 226
Mikhailov, Vasili (Russian), 235, 238, 242
Mikoian, Anastas (Armenian), 214, 215, 218–21, 222, 223–4, 278
Miliutin, Vladimir (Russian), 235, 249, 250, 252, 253
Molotov, Viacheslav (Russian), 64, 89, 146–7, 235, 249, 250, 252, 253–4, 256, 259, 261
Morozov, Lev (Jewish), 60
Mosse, Werner, 15
Muranov, Matvei (Ukrainian), 124, 136

Narimanov, Nariman (Azerbaijani Turk), 193, 197–204, 208, 209, 212, 218, 220

Nathans, Benjamin, 79, 88
Nogin, Viktor (Russian), 235, 239, 248

Orakhelashvili, Ivan (Georgian), 204, 206–12
Ordzhonikidze, Grigorii (Georgian), 204–5, 206–12, 216, 224, 237, 278
Osinskii, Valerian (Russian), 235, 237, 250, 251, 255

Petrovsky, Grigori (Ukrainian), 131, 134–41, 150, 153
Petrovsky-Shtern, Yohanan, 259
Piatakov, Georgi (Ukrainian), 124, 145, 235, 236, 249, 250, 253, 256, 260
Piatnitsky, Iosip (Jewish), 60, 66–70, 73, 81, 83, 87, 88, 89, 92, 105–6, 147
Piłsudski, Józef, 68, 103, 109
Pipes, Richard, 15, 64
Popper, Karl, 78
Preobrazhenskii, Evgenii (Russian), 236, 250, 253, 254, 256, 258

Radek, Karl (Jewish), 90–1, 102–3, 105, 111, 112–20, 121–2, 237, 278
Rakovskii, Khristian (Rumanian), 151–2
Reisner, Oliver, 209
Rieber, Alfred, 205, 226, 274
Rigby, T.H., 15
Roth, Joseph, 246
Rudzutaks, Jan (Latvian), 155, 158, 174–9, 183
Rumiantsev, Ivan (Russian), 239, 243, 248
Rykov, Alexei (Russian), 235, 237, 239, 256, 258, 259
Ryskulov, Turar (Kazakh), 278

Sapronov, Timofei (Russian), 235, 239, 241, 244, 246, 248
Schapiro, Leonard, 15
Serebriakov, Leonid (Russian), 235, 237, 238, 248, 256
Sergeev, Fedora (Russian), 124, 235, 239, 240, 248
Service, Robert, 59
Shaumian, Stepan (Armenian), 166, 212, 214–5, 215–8, 223–4
Shliapnikov, Aleksandr (Russian/Old Believer), 3, 262, 264
Skocpol, Theda, 5
Skrypnyk, Nikolai (Ukrainian), 124, 127, 130, 131, 140–6, 151–2, 278
Slezkine, Yuri, 53, 59, 65, 228, 265
Smilga, Ivar (Latvian), 155, 158, 162, 163, 179–84, 237, 278

Smirnov, Aleksandr (Russian), 235, 237, 239, 241, 242

Smirnov, Ivan (Russian), 235, 237, 238, 239, 241, 243

Smith, Steve, 262

Sokolnikov, Grigorii (Jewish), 60, 79–84, 87, 279

Solzhenitsyn, Alexsandr, 59, 63–4

Stalin, Iosef (Georgian), 3, 9, 14, 70, 72, 82, 90, 112, 120, 134, 146, 169, 183, 203, 204, 205–6, 208, 211, 212–3, 218, 224, 225, 226, 246, 254, 262, 272

Stasova, Elena (Russian), 235, 249, 250, 255

Steinberg, Mark, 237, 244, 247

Stuchka, Petr (Latvian), 144, 155, 158, 162–8, 169, 170, 172, 173, 174, 183, 184, 278

Suny, Ronald Grigor, 229, 266

Sverdlov, Iakov (Jewish), 60, 79–4, 87, 88, 89

Szporluk, Roman, 229

Thompson, E.P., 5

de Tocqueville, Alexis, 26, 35, 40, 62

Tomskii, Mikhail (Russian), 235, 237, 238, 239, 241, 242, 243, 244, 249

Trotsky, Lev (Jewish), 60, 70–1, 72, 73, 74–9, 82, 84, 86–7, 89, 120, 150

Tsiurupa, Alexandr (Ukrainian), 130, 131–3, 134, 278

Uglanov, Nikolai (Russian), 235, 239, 240, 241

Ukhanov, Konstantin (Russian), 239, 240, 241, 242, 243, 248, 256

Uritsky, Mikhail (Jewish), 60, 70–4, 76, 78, 87, 144

van Ree, Erik, 205

Vladimirskii, Mikhail (Russian), 236, 250, 252, 256, 259

Voroshilov, Klimenti (Russian), 137, 235, 237, 239, 240, 241, 249

Weber, Max, 11, 143

Wistrich, Robert, 59

Witte, Sergei, 64–5, 88, 229

Yaroslavsky, Emilian (Jewish), 60, 79, 81–4, 278

Zelensky, Isaak (Jewish), 60, 79, 81–2, 84

Zinoviev, Grigorii (Jewish), 60, 72, 74–8, 89, 120

Subject Index

Anarchists, 134, 139, 141, 150, 203, 253, 259
Armenians. *See* Caucasian Bolsheviks
Assimilation: and Bolshevism/universalism appeal, 18, 22–3, 58–9, 85–6, 87, 88–9, 121–2, 123–4, 133, 138, 141, 153–4, 197, 200, 204, 267, 269–70, 273; experiences of, 8, 19–20, 27, 55–6, 58–9, 62, 66, 70–9, 86–7, 90, 112–20, 121–2, 123–4, 128–9, 198, 200, 231–5, 256–7, 260, 265, 267–8; measurement of, 13, 26–8, 32, 38, 47; and social mobility/integration, 35, 37, 45, 61–2, 84, 88–9, 113–4, 123–4, 127–9, 133, 197, 237, 257, 262, 270; *See also* education; imperial strategies; Russification
Austrian Socialist Party (SPÖ), 78
Azerbaijani Turks. *See* Caucasian Bolsheviks

Black Hundreds (URP), 49–50, 81, 140, 143, 149, 233, 243, 250
Bolshevism: and class conflict, 4–5, 52, 120, 137, 140, 152–3, 179, 187, 224, 237–8, 245, 260; as conservative/status protecting ideology, 22–3, 52–3, 56–7, 91, 103, 112, 156, 186, 206, 225–6, 263, 273–4; ethnic/class composition of, 4–5, 9–10, 15–18, 24, 271–3, 278–9; geopolitical appeal of, 4, 16, 20, 22–3, 56, 91, 125, 172, 184–5, 186, 196–7, 206, 214–5, 221, 223–4, 225, 265, 273; as "good imperial ideal," 22–3, 56, 156, 181, 184–5, 198, 214, 225, 228, 263, 273; and marginality, 8, 19–23, 31–2, 35, 51–4, 55, 56, 58–9, 66, 86, 89, 96, 103, 112, 114–5, 121–2, 124–5, 146, 154, 155–6, 184, 265–6, 267–8, 269, 270, 273–5; Russified/Russian-inflected composition of, 3–4, 63–4, 89, 90, 105, 119–20, 122, 124–5, 134–41, 143, 148, 150, 153–4, 168–72,

173, 184–5, 203–4, 205–6, 212–4, 223–4, 227; and socioethnic exclusions, 4–5, 14, 19, 20–1, 22–3, 28, 48–9, 53–4, 55, 56, 58, 101, 107, 124–5, 153, 187, 225, 235, 253, 265, 267–8, 269–7, 271; as socioethnically organized, 3–4, 7–8, 20, 22, 50, 52–4, 265, 269, 270–2; universalist/rossiiskii appeal of, 4–5, 7, 8, 14, 19–23, 24, 31, 52, 55, 56, 57, 58–60, 78, 85–9, 90–2, 96, 103, 106, 112, 121–2, 125, 153–4, 156, 181, 184–5, 186, 198, 203–4, 205, 206, 225, 226, 229, 258, 263–4, 265–6, 269–70, 271, 272, 273, 274–5; *See also* individual ethnic/nationality groups
Bremen Left Radicals, 118–9
Bund, 47, 64, 66–7, 79, 81, 82–4, 88–9, 98, 99, 100, 105, 107, 108–9, 111, 139, 155, 166, 176–7, 216–7

Capitalism/capitalists, 5, 8, 10–11, 17, 26, 41–5, 50–2, 60–1, 63, 65–6, 69, 71–2, 78, 80, 131, 133–40, 181, 187, 189, 191, 193, 195–6, 199, 203, 206, 213, 221, 227, 235, 238, 242, 250, 263, 271; *See also* class
Caucasian Bolsheviks: Armenian assimilation/Russification, 191, 214–5, 217, 223–4; Armenian middle classes, 219, 221–2; bureaucratic inclusion/exclusion of, 186, 187, 189–90, 193–7, 214, 225, 226; capitalist relations, 193, 195–6; colonialist exclusions, 186, 226; dissimilatory Russification of, 187, 188–9, 190–3, 215, 219–20, 222–3, 223–4, 226; divide and rule, 193, 213; Dzhaparidze's petty gentry origins, 209; Dzhaparidze's russified education, 209, 212–3; Dzhapraidze's russified radicalism, 209–10, 211; ethnopolitical radicalization

of, 186, 187, 189, 193, 196–7, 214–5,
217, 222, 223–4, 226; and geopolitical
empire, 187–8, 191, 214–5, 224, 225, 226;
Georgian gentry socialism, 186, 190, 204–5,
207; Georgian social structure, 206; and
imperial strategies, 187, 189–93, 193–7,
199–200, 213–4, 223–4, 226; marginality/
composition of Bolshevism, 186–7, 225–6;
Menshevism vs. Bolshevism, 204–5, 207,
212–4, 226; Miasnikov's education, 222;
Miasnikov's imperial army, 223; Miasnikov's
nationalist radicalism, 221, 222, 226;
Miasnikov's non-Caucasian radicalism,
223, 224; Miasnikov's socioethnic origins,
221–2; Mikoian and imperial army, 215,
220, 221, 224; Mikoian's education,
219–20, 220–1; Mikoian's multiethnic
alliances, 215, 221, 223; Mikoian's
nationalist (Dashnak) activism, 218, 220,
226; Mikoian's rossiiskii empire, 220–1,
223–4; Mikoian's socioethnic origins,
218–9; Muslim reformism, 199–200, 202;
Narimanov and Russification, 198, 199–201,
204; Narimanov's cultural radicalization,
199–200, 202–3, 204; Narimanov's rossiiskii
socialism, 198, 200–1, 203–4; Narimanov's
socioethnic origins/education, 197–8; and
nationalist-socialist politics, 186, 201–4,
208–9, 212–3, 214–5, 216, 219–20, 222,
223–4, 225–6; Orakhelashvili's petty gentry
origins, 209; Orakhelashvili's imperial
experiences, 212; Ordzhonikidze's imperial
experiences, 212; Ordzhonikidze's russified
education, 207, 212–13; Ordzhonikidze's
russified radicalism, 207–8, 210, 211–23;
Ordzhonikidze's petty gentry origins, 206,
207; radicalization of Muslim intelligentsia,
192–3, 198–9, 199–200; religious policies,
188, 189, 191–3, 194, 199–200; Shaumian's
early radicalism, 215–6; Shaumian's
geopolitical empire, 217–8, 224; Shaumian's
multiethnic alliances, 215, 216–8;
Shaumian's Russified education, 215, 216,
224; Stalin's nationalism, 205, 226; Stalin's
Russification, 205–6; Stalin's socioethnic
origins, 205–6; Stalin's understanding of
empire, 212; and universalist/rossiiskii
politics, 186, 197, 213–4, 214–5, 223–4,
225–6
Class: and class conflict, 4, 7, 19, 24,
51–2, 116, 120, 137, 140, 158, 177,
179, 181, 187, 191–3, 224, 237–8, 245,
260, 266; definitions/measurements of,
10–12, 278–9, 280–1; *See also* Bolshevism;

estates/*sosloviia*; capitalism; imperial
strategies; *meshchanstvo*; middle classes/
intelligentsia; nobility/*dvorianstvo*;
peasantry; working classes

Dashnaktsutiun (Dashnaks), 69, 186, 215,
216–8, 220–1, 222–3, 224, 226

Education: and cultural assimilation, 18–9, 26,
28, 32–5, 47, 56, 58, 62, 94, 148, 156, 159,
161–3, 169–71, 185, 187, 194, 197–9, 204,
209, 212–3, 214, 216, 257–9, 266, 267,
269; primary/parish/seminary, 19, 33–4,
97, 104, 134, 143, 159, 163, 174–5, 197,
205, 207, 214, 219–20, 221–2, 236, 240–1,
247, 261; and radicalization, 8, 20, 63–5,
66, 89, 103, 174, 222–3, 236; and Russian
nation-building, 230, 240–1, 261; secondary
(gimnazii/Realschulen), 11, 18–9, 25–6,
32–3, 34–5, 61, 62, 63, 68, 72–3, 75, 76,
77, 79, 80, 82, 83, 84, 93, 94, 97, 103–5,
114–6, 134, 143, 145, 146–7, 148, 161,
163, 170, 181, 199, 200–1, 209, 212–3,
215–6, 219–20, 222, 235–6, 240, 250, 251,
252, 253, 255, 256; and social mobility, 26,
31, 39, 58, 62, 79, 84, 159–60, 163, 251–2;
university, 18–19, 25–6, 32–3, 35, 62–4, 73,
75, 79, 80, 83, 84, 88, 93, 94, 97, 103, 113–
4, 147, 148, 149, 158, 163–4, 169–70, 199,
200, 202, 209, 211, 212–3, 216, 221, 223,
235–6, 239–40, 250, 251–2, 253, 255, 256,
258, 259, 260, 267–8; *See also* assimilation;
imperial strategies; Russification
Elective affinity, 106, 115, 121, 146, 155–6,
181, 201, 204, 208–9, 213, 225, 260, 266,
273–4
Ethnicity: and Census, 12–13, 36–7; as identity
marker, 3–4, 14, 37–8; *See* ethnopolitics;
imperial strategies; *inorodtsy*
Ethnopolitics, 20, 21, 22, 25, 26, 35, 43, 46,
48, 55, 58, 65–6, 85–6, 88, 89, 90, 96,
102–3, 106–7, 108–9, 112, 116, 117, 119,
120, 123–4, 126, 138, 140, 148, 150–4,
159, 162, 184, 186–7, 189, 193, 195–6,
213–5, 217, 222, 223–4, 226, 250, 251,
260, 266–8
Estates/*sosloviia*, 6, 8, 10–13, 15, 16–7,
18, 20, 25, 27–8, 29, 31–2, 35–9, 41,
42, 44–5, 46, 47–8, 53, 57, 60, 72, 128,
131, 147, 157–8, 165, 187, 190, 193–7,
213, 233, 235–6, 239–40, 247, 251, 254,
255–6, 261, 272, 278–9, 280–1, 299;
See also class; *inorodtsy*; *meshchanstvo*;
nobility/*dvorianstvo*; peasantry

Geopolitics. *See* Bolshevism; imperial strategies; Russian Empire
Georgians. *See* Caucasian Bolsheviks
German Social Democratic Party (SPD), 70, 75, 78, 105, 118, 143

Hnchak (Armenian socialist/nationalist party), 216
Hümmet (Muslim Social Democrats), 201–4, 211, 217, 221

Imperial strategies: 28–48, 55–7, 60–6, 92–6, 125–31, 156–62, 187–97, 229–35; as assimilatory/homogenizing, 28, 32–5, 39, 41, 53, 56, 93, 95, 97, 126–7, 200; and bureaucratic incorporation, 26, 28–9, 29–32, 39, 41, 44–6, 49, 51, 53–4, 56, 58, 87, 92–3, 94–5, 103, 123–4, 125–8, 129–30, 133, 148, 153, 160, 162, 187, 188, 190, 193, 194–7, 198, 199, 206, 213, 226, 230, 250, 251, 266–7; as divide and rule, 28, 39–40, 44–6, 56, 91, 93–6, 126–7, 129–31, 187, 189–90, 192, 193, 213; and education, 28, 32–5, 39, 56, 79, 84, 92–4, 97, 161–2, 174, 185, 187, 189, 192, 219; as exclusionary/dissimilatory: see Russification; as nationalities policies, 6, 12, 25, 28–9, 35, 38, 42, 44–5, 47, 48, 93, 95, 233; and geopolitics, 5–6, 39–40, 43, 52, 63, 95–6, 187–9, 230, 232, 263, 272; and identity regimes/social control, 14, 28, 32, 33, 35–9, 40, 42–3, 46, 55–6, 66, 84, 86, 87, 89, 91–2, 95–6, 121, 156, 162, 180–1, 183–4, 193, 229, 231–4, 266, 272; and marginalized middle classes/ intelligentsias, 21, 24, 28, 30–2, 34–5, 39, 40, 41, 44–6, 102, 265–6, 267–8, 269, 274; and religion, 13, 30–1, 32, 34, 35, 37, 38–9, 40, 41, 46–8, 53, 57, 62–3, 74, 95–7, 126–7, 161, 186–7, 189, 192–3, 200, 219–20, 226, 234, 240–1, 259–60, 261, 268; and routes to radicalism, 20, 24, 39, 41, 48–52, 55–7, 59, 121–2, 124, 141–2, 150, 165, 174, 186, 187, 213–4, 223–4, 226, 228–9, 274–5; and social mobility, 10, 13, 15, 17–21, 25–8, 32, 35, 37–40, 42–3, 45–6, 48–52, 55–6, 58, 61–4, 66, 74, 86, 90–1, 92, 102–4, 125, 129, 132, 159–60, 163, 169–70, 179–80, 190, 196–7, 208–9, 226, 236, 237, 239, 240–1, 255–6, 266–8, 269; and socioethnic exclusions, 28–48, 50, 58, 86, 89, 91–2, 93, 102, 103, 121, 124, 125–6, 153, 179, 183–4, 185, 187, 189, 193, 199, 214, 226, 265, 274–5; as status particularistic, 28, 37, 40–3, 56–7, 91–6, 97, 124, 129–31, 153,

187, 189, 190–3, 213, 226; urban-rural dimensions, 25, 26, 34, 40, 41, 43–4, 45, 50, 103, 148, 158, 185, 187, 188–9, 207, 223–4, 267; *See also* assimilation; class; education; individual ethnic/nationality groups; Russification
Inorodtsy, 13, 38, 48, 58, 86, 278–9, 280–1; *See also* ethnicity; estates/*sosloviia*

Jews/Jewish Bolsheviks: and anti-Semitism, 3, 5, 7, 30, 31, 43, 50, 58–9, 60, 61, 62–3, 65, 66–7, 69, 70, 71–2, 74, 77, 78, 79–81, 82, 86–7, 88–9, 105, 113, 114, 115, 116, 117, 118, 120, 121, 123, 126, 135, 138–9, 140, 141, 148, 149, 152–3, 175, 206, 232, 243, 249, 250, 253–4, 262, 271, 274; and assimilation/Russification, 58–60, 62, 63–5, 65–6, 66–7, 69, 70, 72–3, 78–9, 84, 85, 86–8, 89; and Bolshevism's appeal, 59, 70, 71, 74, 86, 88–9; and education, 58, 61, 62, 64; ethnic exclusions/ethnopolitics of, 50, 58–60, 61, 65–6, 69, 71, 73, 79, 80, 86, 87–8, 89, 267–8; Gusev's early radicalism, 80–1, 217; Gusev's Jewishness, 79–81, 84, 87, 88; Gusev's middle class exclusions, 80; Gusev's socioethnic origins, 80–1; and identity regimes/social control, 58, 84, 87, 89; and imperial strategies, 42–3, 60–6, 74, 79, 84, 85, 86–7, 89; Ioffe's radicalism, 75–6; Ioffe's Jewishness, 75–6, 78, 87; Ioffe's socioethnic origins, 74–5; Kaganovich's anti-nationalism, 71; Kaganovich's Jewishness/ assimilation, 77, 78, 87, 88; Kaganovich's radicalism, 71–2; Kaganovich's socioethnic origins, 70–1; Kamenev's Bundist radicalism, 83; Kamenev's experiences of exclusion, 84; Kamenev's Jewishness, 83, 84, 88; Kamenev's socioethnic origins, 81, 82; liberal politics of, 60, 85–6; and Lithuanian Jewish radicalism, 66–70; marginality of, 58–9, 64, 66, 68, 78–9, 86; and nationalist/ socialist mobilizations, 68–70, 73–4, 85; and numerous clausus, 62–3, 76, 80; and Pale of Settlement, 25, 31, 46, 56, 59, 65, 66–7, 75, 79, 82, 123, 126, 129, 139, 146, 158–9, 231, 232; Piatnitsky and multiethnicity, 67, 69–70, 217; Piatnitsky's Bundist radicalism, 67–70; Piatnitsky's Jewishness, 69–70, 87, 88, 89; Piatnitsky's socioethnic origins, 66–7; and pogroms, 50, 60, 64, 65, 69, 71, 72, 80–1, 85, 86–7, 138, 139–40, 141, 153, 233, 249, 253, 254; and Russian Jewish radicalism, 79–84; social mobility of, 61–3; social origins/class structure, of 60–1, 65; Sokolnikov's early radicalism, 79; Sokolnikov's Jewishness, 79, 84, 87; Sokolnikov's socioethnic origins, 79; Sverdlov's Russification/Jewishness, 82, 84, 87, 88, 89; Sverdlov's socioethnic origins, 81; Sverdlov's SR radicalism, 82; Trotsky's Jewishness/assimilation, 76–9, 87, 89; Trotsky's radicalism, 75, 78–9; Trotsky's socioethnic origins, 74–5, 76, 78; and Ukrainian Jewish radicalism, 70–9; universalist/rossiiskii politics of, 58–60, 66, 70, 71, 78, 86, 88–9; Uritsky's Jewishness, 72, 78, 87; Uritsky's middle class exclusions, 72–3, 74; Uritsky's radicalism in Kiev, 72–3; Uritsky's socioethnic origins, 72; Yaroslavsky's experiences of exclusion, 81–2; Yaroslavsky's Jewishness/Russification, 83, 84; Yaroslavsky's non-Bolshevik radicalism, 82–3, 84; Yaroslavsky's socieoethnic origins, 81, 82; Zelensky's radicalism, 81–2; Zelensky's socioethnic origins, 81; Zinoviev's radicalism, 75, 78–9; Zinoviev's Jewishness, 78, 89; Zinoviev's socioethnic origins, 74–5

Kadets (Constitutional Democrats), 10, 21, 45, 49, 50, 143–4, 149, 201, 218, 224, 250, 274

Latvian social democracy, 163–4, 168, 177
Latvian Social Democratic Workers' Party (LADWP, Bolsheviks), 165–6, 169
Latvians/Latvian Bolsheviks: and assimilation/Russification, 156, 161–2, 171, 185; and attraction of Russian culture, 155–6, 159–60, 174, 179, 184–5; Baltic German dominance of, 158–60, 163, 164–5, 168, 184; Berzins and rural middle class, 168–70; Berzins as russified teacher, 170–1; Berzins's internationalism, 172–4; Berzins's Russification/radicalism, 162–3, 164, 169–70; and civic associationalism, 157, 160–1, 162, 179, 185; Danishevskii's internationalism, 172–4; Danisheviskii's middle class context, 168–70; and imperial strategies, 156–62, 171; Lepse's working class radicalism, 174–5, 177–9; and multiethnic mobilizations, 156, 175–7; and nationalist/socialist mobilizations, 159–60, 161, 165; and repression/social control of, 156, 162, 180–1, 185; Rudzutaks's working class radicalism, 174–5, 177–9; Smilga and Tsarist repression, 180–1; Smilga's geopolitical vision, 182–4, 183; Smilga's radicalism, 181–4; Smilga's

socioethnic context, 179–80; and socioethnic context, 155, 156, 184, 185; Stuchka's geopolitical commitments, 167–8; Stuchka's 1860s radicalism, 163–4; Stuchka's socialist radicalism, 165–7; Stuchka's socioethnic context/education, 163–4; and universalist/imperial ideal, 156–6, 179, 183–4, 184–5
Lithuanian Social Democratic Party (LSDP), 69, 98–100, 143
Lithuanians/Lithuanian Bolsheviks: and appeal of universalist/rossiiskii politics, 90–1, 102, 121, 122; assimilation/Russification of, 93–6, 97; and dissimilatory Russification, 91, 92, 97, 121; education of, 96–7; and ethnic exclusions/ethnopolitics, 90, 91, 93–4, 102; and imperial strategies, 92–6, 121–2; Kapsukas's cultural marginality, 96, 101–2, 120–1, 122, 146; Kapsukas's exclusion from LSDP, 99–101; Kapsukas's internationalism, 101–2; Kapsukas's LSDP radicalism, 98–9, 122; Kapsukas's nationalist radicalism, 90, 96, 97–9, 120–1, 122; Kapsukas's religious education, 96–7, 121; Kapsukas's Russian socialism, 100–2, 122, 146; Kapsukas's socioethnic origins, 93, 96–7; and marginality, 92, 96, 102, 121; and nationalist/socialist mobilizations, 90, 91, 94, 96, 97, 101–2, 122; and Polonization, 93–4, 97; religious exclusions of, 94, 95, 97; social origins/class structure of, 92–4, 97; *See also* imperial strategies; Russian state/Empire

Mensheviks, 10, 15, 21, 49, 50, 60, 64, 69, 74, 76, 81, 83, 109, 136, 139, 144–5, 150, 155, 166, 169, 177, 186, 203, 204, 207, 210, 211, 212–4, 217, 221, 224, 225, 226, 250, 251, 252, 253, 255, 270, 274
Meshchanstvo, 10–11, 15, 17, 31, 44, 60, 81, 251, 278–9, 281; *See also* class; middle classes/intelligentsia; working class
Mezhraionka, 151
Middle classes/intelligentsia, 4, 5, 10–11, 17, 20, 21–2, 24, 26–7, 30–2, 34, 35, 40, 44–5, 48–9, 50, 52, 58, 63, 64–5, 67, 71, 74, 76, 85–6, 97–8, 100, 103, 105, 106, 107, 112, 113, 123, 125, 128, 138, 148, 151, 153, 155, 164, 168–74, 185, 187, 189, 191–3, 195, 197, 199–200, 201, 202, 208, 214, 224, 226, 227–8, 235–6, 237, 247, 249–56, 257, 260, 261–2, 266, 269, 273, 278–9, 280–1; *See also* class; imperial strategies; *meshchanstvo*

Müsavat (Muslim Democratic Party), 198, 202, 217

Narodnaia volia (Peoples' Will), 19, 80, 256
Nationalist movements/mobilizations, 21, 34, 35, 39, 43–4, 45, 48, 51, 52–3, 59, 67–9, 71, 85, 90–1, 95–6, 97–8, 101–2, 104, 106–7, 109, 114, 116, 117, 122, 123–5, 128–9, 130, 141, 144, 148–9, 153, 156, 158, 159–61, 162, 164, 166, 167–8, 173–4, 186, 187, 190, 198, 202, 204, 205, 209, 212, 216, 217, 220, 225–6, 238, 243, 250, 253, 258, 260, 266–7, 270–1, 274
Nationalist/socialist movements' competition, 39, 44, 50, 68, 69, 73, 91, 96, 97–8, 99–100, 102, 103, 105–7, 108–9, 111–2, 114, 115–6, 117–8, 120, 122, 123–4, 126, 128–9, 141, 143–4, 145, 148, 149–50, 153, 156, 158–61, 164–6, 167–8, 173–4, 179, 186–7, 202, 208–9, 211, 212, 214–5, 216, 221, 226, 252, 258, 266–7; *See also* individual ethnic/nationality groups
New Current (*Jaunā strāva*), 164
Nobility/*dvorianstvo*, 11, 17–8, 26, 28, 29–32, 38, 41, 42, 43–6, 60, 88, 92–6, 103, 106, 125, 127–8, 129–30, 132, 138–9, 148, 153, 157, 187, 189–93, 194, 195, 196, 207–9, 227–8, 231, 234–5, 235–6, 251–2, 257, 278–9, 280–1; *See also* class; estates/*sosloviia*

Octobrists, 49–50, 250–4
Okhrana, 11, 14, 19, 27, 35, 36–7, 72, 73, 74, 109, 118, 142, 143, 170, 171, 172, 239

Peasantry, 10, 28, 34–5, 39–40, 41, 42, 43–4, 61–2, 94–5, 96, 100, 115–6, 125, 126–7, 128, 129–30, 133, 138, 150, 156–7, 161, 189, 191, 192, 204, 207, 208–9, 229, 230–1, 235, 245, 258, 263, 274, 278–9, 280–1; *See also* class; estates/*sosloviia*
Poale Zionism, 81
Poles/ Polish Bolsheviks: and assimilation/Russification, 90, 93–6, 106, 120; and Austrian Empire's Polish strategies, 113–4; and dissimilatory Russification, 91, 92, 112, 121; Dzierżyński and repression, 102–4; Dzierżyński's assimilation/Russification, 90, 105, 106, 111–12; Dzierżyński's attraction to Bolshevism, 111–12, 121; Dzierżyński's education, 104–5, 116; Dzierżyński's ethnopolitical marginality, 106–7, 115–6, 121, 184; Dzierżyński's imprisonment/exile, 107, 109, 111; Dzierżyński's

internationalism, 104, 107, 108–10, 111–12, 121; Dzierżyński's Jewish influences, 105–6, 107, 108; Dzierżyński's nationalist radicalism, 90, 104, 106, 111–12, 115, 120, 121; Dzierżyński's social origins, 93, 103–4, 112, 115–6; Dzierżyński's socialist/nationalist radicalism, 104, 105–6, 108–12, 217; and education, 92–3; and elective affinities with socialism, 115–6, 121–2; and ethnic exclusions/ethnopolitics, 90, 91, 93–4, 103–4, 112, 115–6, 120; geopolitical concerns of, 95–6, 112; identity regimes/control of, 91–2, 121; imperial strategies toward, 92–6, 103–4, 121–2; and internationalism, 91, 96; and nationalist/socialist mobilizations, 90, 91, 94, 96, 105–6, 108–12, 114–6; and Polonization, 45, 93, 94, 97–8, 102, 105, 106, 109–10, 113–6, 120; Radek and Bolshevik universalism, 119–20, 121; Radek's assimilationism, 113–6, 121–2; Radek's education, 114, 115, 116; Radek's ethnopolitical exclusion, 115–6, 117–8, 119, 121, 184; Radek's experiences of anti-Semitism, 116, 117, 118, 120, 121; Radek's Galician socioethnic origins, 113, 115–6; Radek's German socialist activism, 117–20; Radek's Germanization, 113–4; Radek's internationalism, 112–3, 116–20, 121; Radek's Jewishness, 112–3; Radek's nationalist radicalism, 90, 113–6, 120, 121; Radek's nationalist/socialist radicalism, 115, 116; Radek's Polonization, 90, 112, 113–4; and religious exclusions, 94, 95; social mobility of, 90–1, 92, 120–1; social origins/class structure of, 92–4; and universalist/rossiiskii politics, 90–1, 106, 108, 109, 110, 112, 121; *See also* imperial strategies; Russian state/Empire; *szlachta*
Polish National Democratic Party (*Endecja*), 108, 149
Polish Peasant Party (in Austria), 114
Polish Social Democratic Party (PPSD in Austria), 115
Polish Socialist Party (PPS), 68, 73–4, 99
Polonization. *See* Poles/Polish Bolsheviks; Lithuanians/Lithuanian Bolsheviks

Radical Democratic Party (Ukrainian), 149
Religion: and Muslims/Islam, 2, 6, 12–3, 28, 30–1, 34, 36, 38, 46–8, 50, 187, 188, 191–2, 193–4, 197–204, 206, 209, 211, 213, 215, 217, 231–3, 250, 256–60; and non-Christian minorities, 34, 36–7, 38–9, 46–8, 200, 256–60; and Old Believers/

Sectarians, 2, 232, 234, 235, 262, 264; and Orthodoxy, 6, 12–3, 25, 36–7, 41, 42, 46–8, 57, 128, 148, 189, 191, 192, 229, 233–5, 237, 241, 246–9, 254, 257, 259–60, 261; *See also* imperial strategies; Jews/Jewish Bolsheviks; Russian state/Empire; Russians/ Russian Bolsheviks

Ritterschaften, 30, 157, 160, 171

Russian Social Democratic Labor Party (RSDLP), 15, 68, 74, 75, 81, 83, 99, 101, 108, 110, 117, 129, 132, 139, 141, 143, 144, 149, 155, 166, 171, 172, 173, 177, 178, 201, 202, 203, 207, 208, 210, 211, 212, 213, 216, 226, 242, 253, 255, 256

Russian socialism/social democracy, 19, 45, 49, 50, 69, 73, 75, 81, 83–4, 88, 91, 100, 108, 111, 117, 119, 123, 134, 136, 137, 138, 139, 140, 141, 143, 144, 145, 147, 148, 149, 150, 151, 153–4, 156, 168, 173, 184, 202, 208, 211, 216, 220, 222, 223, 239, 242, 243, 251, 253, 255, 256, 258, 259, 261

Russian state/empire: costs/burdens of maintaining, 20–1, 22–3, 24, 39, 43, 48–52, 59, 112, 121, 181, 185, 263–4, 265, 274–5; geopolitics of, 5–6, 16, 39, 91, 127, 153, 167–8, 186–7, 191, 193, 214–5, 217–8, 225–6, 228, 230; diversity/ composition of, 5–8, 12–13, 25, 26–7, 156, 158, 161, 224–5, 280–1; as industrializing/modernizing, 4, 5, 7, 10–1, 20, 25–6, 28, 51–3, 63, 138, 139, 140–1, 153, 158, 196, 200, 202–3, 237, 238–9, 241, 265–6; and nation-building/ Russianness, 6–7, 12–3, 20, 21–2, 24–7, 29–30, 32, 35, 38–9, 43, 47, 52–3, 57, 93, 95–6, 154, 158, 229–35, 238, 240, 247–9, 256–8, 261–3, 272–4; and socioethnic exclusions, 8, 12–3, 24–5, 32, 39, 50–1, 52–5, 66, 123–4, 129, 131, 141, 148, 187, 190, 197, 229, 267–8; as traditional/ status particularistic, 24, 25–7, 38–40, 213, 265, 280–1; *See also* Bolshevism; imperial strategies

Russians/Russian Bolsheviks: and assimilation/ Russification, 229–31, 240–1, 261; Bukharin, 251–2; Bubnov, 253; and burdens of empire, 229, 235, 261; class radicalism/ exclusions of, 227–8, 241–5, 263–4; education of, 236, 240–1, 250, 251–2, 257–8, 261; ethnic tolerance of, 227, 228, 235, 238, 259–60, 261, 264; and fragility of Russianness, 229, 231–4, 235, 246–7, 256, 261, 264; and gentry/nobility, 249–60; Iakovleva, 255; and identity regimes/

ascriptions, 231–4; and imperial strategies, 228, 229–35, 257–8; and intelligentsia radicalism, 228, 249–60; and interethnic marriages, 237, 249, 256–62, 269–70; and Kazan Tatars (Muslims), 256–7, 258–9, 260; Lenin, 252–2, 258, 259–60; Lomov, 251, 258; Miliutin, 252, 253; Molotov, 252, 253–4; and nation-building/nationalism, 228, 229–31, 232–4, 238, 246–7, 261, 263; non-Russian leadership of, 228, 261–2, 262–3; and non-Russian minorities, 231–2, 233, 256–7, 258–9, 260; and Orthodoxy, 229, 234–5, 241, 248–9, 254, 257, 261; Osinskii, 251; and peasantry, 229, 237–41, 245–6, 258; Piatakov, 253–4, 256; Preobrazhenskii, 252–3; russkie/rossiiskii identities of, 228, 231, 234, 246–9, 254–5, 260, 263–4; Rykov, 239–40, 258; socioethnic origins/ composition of, 227, 235–7, 238–9, 249–50, 251; Stasova, 249, 255; and views of imperial diversity, 235, 247–9; and Volga-Urals radicalism, 234, 236, 239, 250–1, 256–60; Vladimirskii, 252–3; and working class radicalism, 238–9, 241–6

Russification: as assimilation, 13, 16, 18–9, 32, 61–2, 67, 72–4, 78–9, 79–84, 87, 121, 124–5, 127–90, 137–8, 146–7, 153–4, 156, 161–2, 173, 184–5, 205–6, 209, 211, 212–4, 214–5, 223–4, 269; as assimilatory/ homogenizing strategy, 4, 18–9, 28–9, 30–1, 32–5, 39, 42–3, 52, 56, 94–5, 104, 169, 171, 174, 189–97, 197–9, 226, 240–1, 257–8, 261, 266, 272; as dissimilatory/exclusionary strategy, 28–9, 30, 39–48, 55–8, 64, 65–6, 89, 91–2, 92–3, 95–6, 97, 103–4, 112, 121–2, 124–5, 126–7, 153–4, 161–2, 187, 189–97, 199–201, 214–5, 266; and radicalization, 20, 26, 34–5, 47, 51–2, 57, 59, 63–6, 90, 92–3, 96, 103–4, 105–6, 112, 115–6, 121–2, 124–5, 140–1, 145–6, 153–4, 170, 181, 184–5, 197–9, 205–6, 217, 253–4, 257–8, 260, 269; *See also* assimilation; education; imperial strategies

Social Democracy of the Latvian Krai (SDLK), 166, 171

Social Democratic Party of the Kingdom of Poland and Lithuania (SDKPiL), 99, 100, 108, 109, 110, 111, 114, 116–9, 166, 177

Socialist Revolutionaries (SRs), 10, 19, 21, 49, 50, 69, 72, 79, 80, 81, 82, 83, 129, 135, 138, 141, 143–4, 145, 150, 151, 154, 177, 186, 215, 218, 221, 223, 243, 251, 252, 253, 255, 256, 258, 259

Spilka (Ukrainian Socialist Democratic Union), 73, 76, 144–5, 149
Szlachta, 43–4, 46, 74, 93–4, 96–7, 102–3, 104, 125, 126, 127, 207

Tatars, 13, 28, 29, 32, 34, 38–9, 41, 42, 44–5, 46, 47, 127, 131, 135, 191–2, 194, 199, 203, 217, 233–4, 256–8, 259–60, 280

Ukrainian Peoples' Party, 145, 149
Ukrainian Revolutionary Party (RUP), 144–5, 149
Ukrainian Socialist Party, 73–4, 144
Ukrainians/Ukrainian Bolsheviks: and anti-Semitism, 138–40, 141, 149, 153; Chubar' and Jews, 134, 135, 138, 140; Chubar' and socialism's class appeal, 134, 136, 140; Chubar's imperial army service, 141; Chubar's left-bank context, 136–7; Chubar's russified worker radicalism, 134, 135–6, 139, 140; Chubar's socioethnic origins, 135; Chubar's Ukrainian nationalism, 134; class radicalization of, 131, 152–4; and dissimilatory Russification, 123, 124, 153; education of, 131, 148; and ethnopolitics in Ukraine, 123–4, 129, 138–9, 148, 150, 152–3; imperial/ bureaucratic incorporation of, 123, 125–6, 127–8, 129–30, 147–8, 150, 153, 154; and imperial strategies, 123–4, 125–31, 148, 150, 153; Krestinsky's employment as lawyer, 147; Krestinsky's internationalism, 146; Krestinsky's Russification and Bolshevism, 140, 146–7, 150; Krestinsky's socioethnic origins/education, 146–7; Lebed' and socialism's class appeal, 134, 136, 137, 140; Lebed's anti-Jewish activity, 134–5, 140; Lebed's imperial army service, 141; Lebed's left-bank context, 134, 136–7; Lebed's radicalism as russified worker, 134–5, 135–6, 139–40, 141, 150; and left-bank radicalism, 125–6, 130–1, 134–41, 140, 141–6; Manuilsky and internationalism/ rossiiskii, 140, 146, 148, 150, 151–2; Manuilsky's education/early radicalism, 148, 149; Manuilsky's emigration, 149, 150; Manuilsky's right-bank socioethnic origins, 147; Manuilsky's Russification, 147–8; and multiethnic mobilizations, 124–5, 137, 138–9, 143, 144, 147, 153; and nationalist-socialist-internationalist mobilizations, 123–4, 128–9, 131, 137, 141–2, 143–4, 149–50, 152–3, 153; and peasantry, 130–1; Petrovsky and pogroms, 140; Petrovsky and socialism's class appeal, 134, 136, 137, 140; Petrovsky's imperial army service, 139, 141; Petrovsky's left-bank context, 136–7; Petrovsky's russified worker radicalism, 134, 135–6, 139–40, 141, 150; and right-bank radicalism, 125, 126, 129, 130–1, 146–52; and Russian centralism, 124, 129, 142, 144, 152, 154; and Russian socialism's class appeal, 137, 139–40; Russification/ assimilation of, 123, 125, 128, 129, 130, 141, 150, 153–4; Skrypnyk's education, 143, 144; Skrypnyk's left-bank origins, 142–3, 146; Skrypnyk's opposition to Russian centralism, 142, 145, 146; Skrypnyk's Russification and socialism/internationalism, 140, 141, 145, 146; Skrypnyk's socialist-nationalist radicalism, 143–4, 144–5; Skrypnyk's Ukrainian nationalism, 142; Skrypnyk's Ukrainianization efforts, 142, 146; social origins/class structure of, 129, 130–1, 136–7, 148; and split middle classes, 126, 129–31, 153; Tsiurupa's early radicalism, 131; Tsiurupa's imprisonment/arrests, 123–3; Tsiurupa's socioethnic origins/education, 131; Tsiurupa's statistician/zemstvo radicalism, 131–3; and universalist/rossiiskii politics, 124–5, 129, 138, 141, 150, 153–4
Union of the Struggle for the Emancipation of the Working Class, 134, 137

Working classes, 5, 7, 10–12, 15, 26, 29, 50, 51–2, 56, 65, 66, 67–8, 72, 88, 100, 107, 110, 117, 125, 141, 150, 153, 156, 157–8, 160–1, 175–9, 184–5, 190, 195–6, 201–2, 206–9, 210–11, 216–8, 226, 235–8, 241, 242, 243–6, 255, 263, 269–70, 271, 278–9, 280–1; multiethnic character of, 67–8, 72, 107, 110, 156–8, 175, 177, 179, 185, 196, 202, 206, 217; *See also* class; *meshchanstvo*

Zemlia i Volia, 84
Zemstvo, 19, 30–1, 34, 61, 85, 94, 125, 129, 131–3, 134, 135, 143, 148, 151, 153, 160, 162, 236, 240, 247, 250, 252, 258, 263, 280, 281
Zionism, 47, 68, 69, 86